The Ottoman "Wild Wes

C000186889

In the late fifteenth century, the northeastern Balkans were under-populated and under-institutionalized. Yet, by the end of the following century, the regions of Deliorman and Gerlovo were home to one of the largest Muslim populations in southeast Europe. Nikolay Antov sheds fresh light on the mechanics of Islamization along the Ottoman frontier, and presents an instructive case study of the "indigenization" of Islam – the process through which Islam, in its diverse doctrinal and socio-cultural manifestations, became part of a distinct regional landscape. Simultaneously, Antov uses a wide array of administrative, narrative-literary, and legal sources, exploring the perspectives of both the imperial center and regional actors in urban, rural, and nomadic settings, to trace the transformation of the Ottoman polity from a frontier principality into a centralized empire. Contributing to the further understanding of Balkan Islam, state formation and empire building, this unique text will appeal to those studying Ottoman, Balkan, and Islamic world history.

Nikolay Antov is an Assistant Professor of History at the University of Arkansas. He holds a Ph.D. in Middle East and Islamic history from the University of Chicago.

The Ottoman "Wild West"

The Balkan Frontier in the Fifteenth and Sixteenth Centuries

Nikolay Antov

University of Arkansas

CAMBRIDGE
UNIVERSITY PRESS

CAMBRIDGE
UNIVERSITY PRESS

University Printing House, Cambridge CB2 8BS, United Kingdom

One Liberty Plaza, 20th Floor, New York, NY 10006, USA

477 Williamstown Road, Port Melbourne, VIC 3207, Australia

314-321, 3rd Floor, Plot 3, Splendor Forum, Jasola District Centre, New Delhi - 110025, India

79 Anson Road, #06-04/06, Singapore 079906

Cambridge University Press is part of the University of Cambridge.

It furthers the University's mission by disseminating knowledge in the pursuit of education, learning and research at the highest international levels of excellence.

www.cambridge.org
Information on this title: www.cambridge.org/9781316633748
DOI: 10.1017/9781316863084

© Nikolay Antov 2017

First published 2017
First paperback edition 2020

A catalogue record for this publication is available from the British Library

Library of Congress Cataloging in Publication data
Names: Antov, Nikolay, author.
Title: The Ottoman "wild west" : the Balkan frontier in the fifteenth and sixteenth centuries / Nikolay Antov.
Description: First edition. | New York : Cambridge University Press, 2017. | Includes bibliographical references and index.
Identifiers: LCCN 2017011179 | ISBN 9781107182639 (hardback : alk. paper)
Subjects: LCSH: Balkan Peninsula – History – To 1500. | Balkan Peninsula – History – 16th century. | Turkey – History – 1453– 1683. | Muslims – Balkan Peninsula – History – To 1500. | Muslims – Balkan Peninsula – History – 16th century. | Ludogorie (Bulgaria) – History – To 1500. | Ludogorie (Bulgaria) – History – 16th century. | Gerlovo Region (Bulgaria) – History – To 1500. | Gerlovo Region (Bulgaria) – History – 16th century.
Classification: LCC DR39 .A57 2017 | DDC 949.6/ 031– dc23
LC record available at https:// lccn.loc.gov/ 2017011179

ISBN 978-1-107-18263-9 Hardback
ISBN 978-1-316-63374-8 Paperback

To my parents

Contents

Conclusion   282

Figures

Maps

Tables

Acknowledgments

This book is the product of a long journey that started during my undergraduate studies at the American University in Bulgaria. I wish to thank Frederick Anscombe, then a freshly minted Princeton Ph.D. (and now department head at Birkbeck College, the University of London) for sparking my interest in Ottoman history. It was upon his encouragement that I undertook to pursue a master's degree in Ottoman studies at Bilkent University in Ankara.

The years I spent at Bilkent proved to be truly formative in my shaping as an Ottomanist. There I had the opportunity to receive training that followed a comprehensive and systematic curriculum which provided me with a thorough grounding in the study of things Ottoman. I am particularly indebted to the late Professor Halil İnalcık for generously sharing with me (as well as with his other students) his immense expertise and erudition and for providing much inspiration to my scholarly pursuits. At Bilkent I also greatly benefited from the guidance and support of Oktay Özel, Eugenia Kermeli, and Slobodan Ilić.

The present book grew out of a dissertation that I completed at the University of Chicago. I would like to express my gratitude to my mentor Professor Cornell H. Fleischer. It has been a true privilege to be his student and I thank him wholeheartedly for his understanding and his confidence in me and for serving as an inspirational role model as a scholar of Ottoman studies. His unfailing support has extended well beyond the completion of my doctoral studies, indeed, till the very moment I am writing these lines.

At Chicago I also benefitted much from the guidance of Holly Shissler, Michael Khodarkovsky, Fred Donner, John Woods, and Constantin Fasolt, who helped me to situate and reconceptualize my research interests in and understanding of Ottoman history in the broader Islamic world, Eurasian, and early modern contexts.

This project would not have been completed without the friendship, support, and advice of Rita Koryan and Kaya Şahin, Mariya Kiprovska, and Grigor Boykov, as well as York Norman. I have also enjoyed the friendship and scholarly advice of a number of friends and colleagues at various locations to which my scholarly pursuits brought me, whether Chicago, Istanbul, Ankara, Sofia, or Razgrad. I would like to thank Mehmetcan Akpınar, Veysal Ali, Toygun Altıntaş, Abdurrahman Atçıl, Orit Bashkin, Snjezana Buzov, Tolga Cora, Ferenc Csirkes, Géza David, Side Emre, Tolga Esmer, Simeon Evstatiev, Julia Fein, Vural Genç, Rossitsa Gradeva, Nevena Gramatikova, Mayte Green, Carlos Grenier, Machiel Kiel, Tijana Krstić, Emin Lelić, Christopher Markiewicz, Milena Methodieva, Michael Połczyński, Evgeni Radushev, Tunç Şen, and Nükhet Varlık.

At the University of Arkansas I have especially enjoyed the friendship and support of Joel Gordon, Elizabeth Markham, Rembrandt Wolpert, Sarwar Alam, Kaveh Bassiri, and Raja Swamy.

I thank the Social Science Research Council, the National Endowment of the Humanities, and the American Research Institute in Turkey for providing me with additional funding for my research at both the dissertation and post-doctoral level. I would also like to thank the staff members of the Prime Ministry Ottoman Archive and Topkapı Palace Archive and Library in Istanbul, the Archive of Land Deeds and Cadastre in Ankara, and the Ottoman Archive at the Oriental Department of the National Library "Saints Cyril and Methodius" in Sofia, as well as the staff members of The Joseph Regenstein Library at the University of Chicago, the University of Arkansas Libraries, and the American Research Institute in Turkey, Koç University's Research Center for Anatolian Civilizations, and İSAM libraries in Istanbul.

I am very much indebted to Maria Marsh, my editor at Cambridge University Press, for her guidance and support at the various stages of the realization of this project. James Gregory greatly facilitated the production process and kindly answered every question. I also thank the three anonymous readers at Cambridge University Press for their valuable suggestions as well as York Norman, Lynda Coon, and Sarwar Alam who also read the manuscript in full or in part and provided much-needed feedback. Thanks also go to Jason McCollum who prepared the maps.

I thank Central European University Press for allowing me to use, in a slightly abridged and revised form, aspects of a chapter published in an edited volume collection.

Last, but not least, I would like to express my gratitude to my parents – Radka Antova and the late Atanas Antov – for their unconditional support and affection throughout my life. It is to them that I dedicate this work.

Abbreviations, Transliteration, Dates, and Pronunciation

The following abbreviations are used throughout the book:

Archives

BOA	Başbakanlık Osmanlı Arşivi
	KK – Kamil Kepeci tasnifi
	MAD – Maliyeden Müdevver
	MD – Mühimme Defterleri
	TD – Tapu Tahrir Defterleri
NBKM	Natsionalna Biblioteka "Sv. Sv. Kiril i Metodii"
TKG KK TTd	Tapu ve Kadastro Genel Müdürlüğü, Kuyûd-ı Kadîme, Tapu Tahrir Defterleri
TSMA	Topkapı Sarayı Müzesi Arşivi
TSMK	Topkapı Sarayı Müzesi Kütüphanesi

Printed materials

BSOAS	*Bulletin of the School of Oriental and African Studies*
DBV	*Demir Baba Velâyetnâmesi*
EI1	*Encyclopaedia of Islam*, 1st edition
EI2	*Encyclopaedia of Islam*, 2nd edition
İA	*İslam Ansiklopedisi*
IAI	*Izvestiia na Arkheologichekiia Institut*
IBID	*Izvestiia na Bâlgarskoto Istorichesko Druzhestvo*
IČ	*Istorijski Časopis*
IJTS	*International Journal of Turkish Studies*
IP	*Istorichecki Pregled*
İÜİFM	*İstanbul Üniversitesi İktisat Fakültesi Mecmuası*
JESHO	*Journal of the Economic and Social History of the Orient*
OA	*Osmanlı Araştırmaları/The Journal of Ottoman Studies*
OBV	*Otman Baba Velâyetnâmesi*
POF	*Prilozi za Orijentalnu Fililogiju*
TD	*Tarih Dergisi*
TDVİA	*Türkiye Diyanet Vakfı İslâm Ansiklopedisi*

TIBI	Turski izvori za bâlgarskata istoriia/Fontes Turcici Historiae Bulgaricae
TKHBVAD	*Türk Kültürü ve Hacı Bektaş Veli Araştırma Dergisi*
TM	*Türkiyat Mecmuası*
VD	*Vakıflar Dergisi*
VSAS	*Velâyetnâme-i Seyyid Ali Sultan*
ZDMG	*Zeitschrift der Deutchen Morgenländischen Gesellschaft*

A considerable number of Arabic, Persian, Ottoman Turkish, and Slavic names, titles, and concepts have been used throughout the present study. For Arabic, Persian, and Ottoman Turkish titles, names, and technical terms I have generally followed the transliteration system used by the *International Journal of Middle East Studies*. For Ottoman Turkish, I have generally used modern Turkish orthography in the main text (with the exception of keeping the '*ayn*s), in the footnotes I have used Ottoman Turkish transliteration, especially in quotations from primary sources. In certain cases I have used the Arabic transliteration of a term when discussing it in the context of wider Islamic history and the Turkish transliteration in a strictly Ottoman context. Similarly, in some cases I have given the Turkish transliteration side by side with the Arabic or Persian transliteration – e.g. *vakıf* (Ar. *waqf*), *fetva* (Ar. *fatwa*).

In the case of Slavic names, titles, and terms I am using a modified version of the Library of Congress transliteration system. In Bulgarian I use "â" instead of "û."

For all foreign names, titles, and terms that are familiar to the English speaker, I have generally preferred to use the respective anglicized forms.

Although the original dates in the Ottoman sources used here use the *Hijri* lunar calendar (AH), which begins at CE/AD 622 (the year of the Prophet Muhammad's exodus from Mecca to Medina), dates are generally given in the Common/Anno Domini calendar, unless otherwise specified – in the cases in which the *Hijri* calendar is used, this is done in conjunction with the respective Anno Domini era dates (e.g. "AH/AD").

The following is a list of Turkish letters that are either not found in modern English or represent sounds often different from the sounds represented by the same letters in English:

a – as in **father**

c – as in **j**am or **J**ohn

ç – as in **ch**est or **ch**in

e – as in b**e**d

ğ – a soft "g" – lengthens previous vowel only. For example, "ağaç" is pronounced "aa-ach."

i – as in b**i**t

ı – a soft "i" – as in tens**io**n or curta**i**n

o – as in **T**o**m** or **no**t

ö – as in German

ş – as in **sh**ip or Turki**sh**

u – as in b**oo**k

ü – as in German

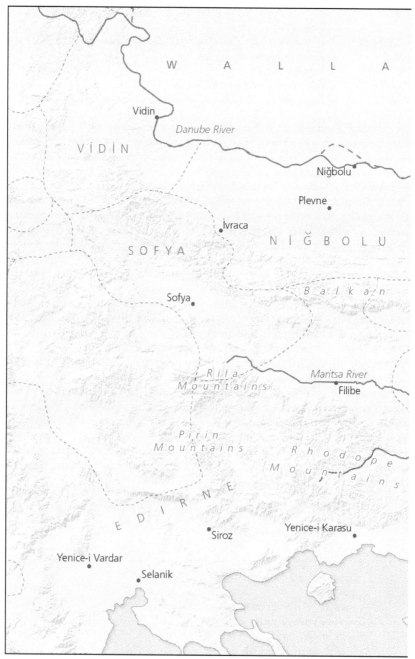

Map 1 The wider eastern Balkans c. 1570, including the focus area of the present study (shaded) as a part of the province of Niğbolu. Ottoman provincial boundaries adapted from "East Central Europe, ca. 1570," in Paul R. Magosci, *Historical Atlas of East Central Europe* (Seattle: University of Washington Press, 1993), 14. Map by Jason McCollum.

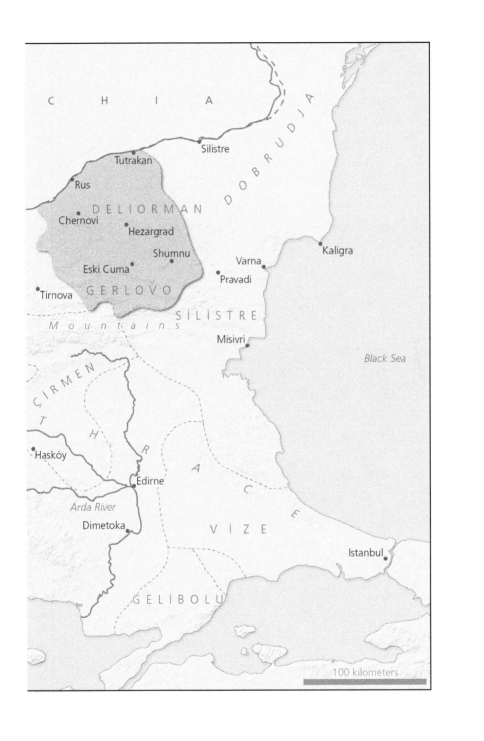

C H I A

Silistre

Tutrakan

Rus

D E L I O R M A N

Chernovi

Hezargrad

Shumnu

Eski Cuma

Tirnova

G E R L O V O

M o u n t a i n s

Ç I R M E N

T

H

Hasköy

R

Edirne

A

Arda River

Dimetoka

D O B R U D J A

Kaligra

Varna

Pravadi

S I L I S T R E

Misivri

V I Z E

C

E

Istanbul

G E L I B O L U

Black Sea

100 kilometers

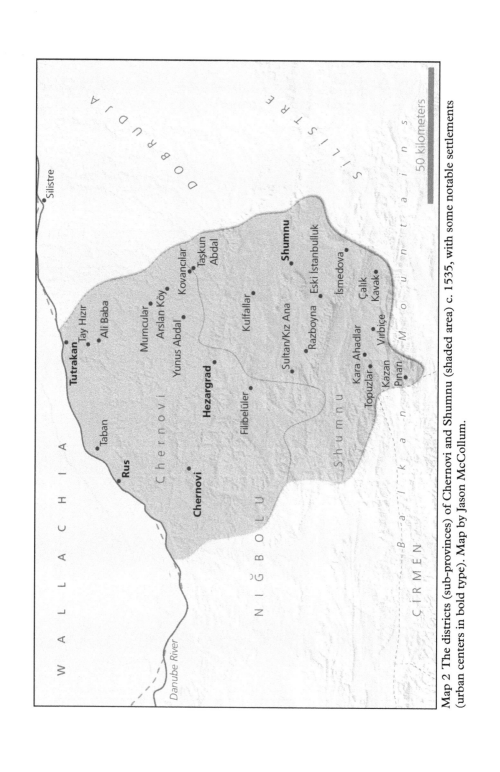

Map 2 The districts (sub-provinces) of Chernovi and Shumnu (shaded area) c. 1535, with some notable settlements (urban centers in bold type). Map by Jason McCollum.

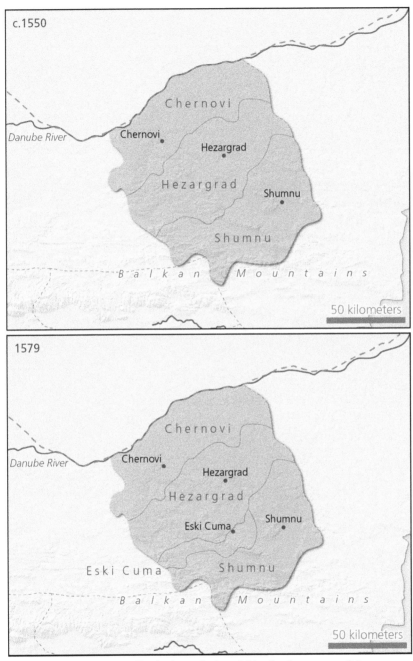

Map 3 The evolution of district boundaries within the focus area of the present study in the second half of the sixteenth century. Map by Jason McCollum.

Introduction

The present study explores the formation of the Muslim community in the regions of Deliorman and Gerlovo (and adjacent areas) in the north-eastern Balkans (modern northeastern Bulgaria) from the late fifteenth through the sixteenth centuries. In the late fifteenth century, Gerlovo, a small mountain valley region on the northern edges of the central-eastern Balkan range, and Deliorman (lit. "Wild Forest," mod. Ludogorie),[1] a much larger, hilly, wooded plateau to the north of Gerlovo, were under-populated and underinstitutionalized (the presence of the rising Ottoman state being minimal), but by the end of the following century the areas were densely populated, with Muslims constituting a solid majority. The two regions came to be firmly incorporated into the Ottoman territorial-administrative framework, in which three urban centers, two well-estab-lished and one emerging, served as strongholds of Ottoman provincial authority through which the imperial center in Istanbul projected its power.

The Ottoman central state had a particular interest in asserting its con-trol in the region. From the late fifteenth through the mid-sixteenth cen-turies the area's countryside witnessed an influx of large groups of mostly semi-nomadic (Muslim) Turcomans and heterodox dervishes; the der-vishes usually serving the semi-nomadic Turcomans as spiritual guides and generally harboring attitudes of opposition toward the centralizing Ottoman state. Some of these migrants came from Thrace and the eastern Rhodope Mountains, to which their forefathers had come from Anatolia in the late fourteenth and fifteenth centuries. Others migrated directly from Anatolia, in the context of the evolving Ottoman-Safavid conflict,

---

[1] Deliorman is etymologically connected to the Cuman-Kipchak "Teleorman," which has the same meaning. Note the existence of the modern Romanian province Teleorman (and the eponymous river) on the left bank of the Danube; see T. Kowalski, J. Reychmann, and A. Zajaczkowski, "Deli-Orman,"*EI²*. In Ottoman administrative sources from the sixteenth century it also appears as "Divane Orman" (again carrying the same mean-ing), while in Ottoman narrative sources of the late fifteenth and sixteenth centuries the region is often referred to as "Ağaç Denizi" (lit. "Sea of Trees"). The modern appellation Ludogorie is a Bulgarian calque of Deliorman, introduced in 1950.

being either forcibly deported to the Balkans or fleeing from Selim I's (r. 1512–20) and Süleyman I's (r. 1520–66) persecutions of "heterodox" and largely semi-nomadic Turcomans as perceived sympathizers, on Ottoman soil, of the newly founded (Shiʻi) Safavid Empire of Iran. While largely depopulated as of the late fifteenth century, Deliorman had a history of sheltering all kinds of religio-political dissidents[2] – it was from there that Sheykh Bedreddin, the great Ottoman religious rebel and reformer, incited his revolt against the dynasty in 1416.

Thus, as Deliorman and Gerlovo's countryside was being repopulated by groups potentially not quite amenable to the centralizing drive of the rising, sedentary, and increasingly self-consciously Sunni, Ottoman imperial bureaucratic regime, the Ottoman state undertook to encourage the growth of urban centers to strengthen its control over what was theretofore an internal Ottoman "no man's land." The most decisive development in this respect was the foundation of the city of Hezargrad (mod. Razgrad) in 1533 by the mighty grand vizier Ibrahim Pasha, who provided for the town's rapid growth through the establishment of a richly endowed pious foundation (Ar. waqf; Tr. vakıf) which would finance the construction and maintenance of a congregational mosque, a madrasa, a soup kitchen, and other typical Ottoman (and Islamic) urban institutions that would turn the new city into a stronghold of Ottoman Sunni "orthodoxy." Soon after its foundation, Hezargrad was made the center of a newly carved-out provincial district and equipped with a judge and the appropriate military-administrative personnel. Concurrently, Shumnu (also Şumnu, mod. Shumen) – a medieval Bulgarian fortress town to the southeast of Hezargrad which had been captured by the Ottomans in 1388–9 and destroyed by the crusaders of Varna in 1444 – was rebuilt and developed into an Ottoman provincial district center. By 1579, Eski Cuma (mod. Târgovishte), to the west of Hezargrad and Shumnu, had emerged as a new Ottoman provincial district center, to be recognized as a town by the Ottoman authorities in the first half of the seventeenth century.

Supporting urban development was not the only tool that the Ottoman central state utilized to bring the area under its control. Employing judicious, flexible, and accomodationist taxation policies, the state encouraged the gradual sedentarization and agrarianization of the incoming Turcoman semi-nomads and dervishes (and their immediate descendants). Most notably, it initially accorded them favorable tax exemptions and related privileges based on their status as semi-nomads and/or dervishes, which would gradually be withdrawn in the course of the

---

[2] "Deli-Orman", EI².

sixteenth century. Thus, while at the turn of the century most of the Muslim residents in the countryside enjoyed one or another "special taxation status," by 1579 the overwhelming majority of rural Muslims had been "tamed" and "disciplined," having been converted to regular, sedentary, and mostly agriculturalist re'aya (tax-paying subjects), with dervishes settled in convents and (supposedly) praying for the well-being of the dynasty. Similar policies applied to rural Christians; significant numbers of Christians from the area or brought in from elsewhere (usually with no previous permanent residence) were likewise gradually tied to the land.

The present work is thus essentially a double case study. On the one hand, it explores the formation of one of the most numerous, compact (and in this case, Turkish-speaking) Muslim communities in the Balkans; one characterized, moreover, by a very significant "heterodox," non-Sunni element – the Alevi-Bektashis of today. It can thus be compared to other significant Muslim communities that developed elsewhere in the peninsula, such as those in Thrace, the Rhodope Mountains, Albania, and Bosnia. Arguing for a nuanced view of the formation of these communities, the present study emphasizes the importance of regional differentiation, as each of these communities followed separate trajectories that make the search for a common model precarious. In this regard, it explores the interplay between Turcoman colonization, conversion to Islam, the articulation of confessional identities, and Ottoman policies of centralization and regional development in the formation of the Muslim community in Deliorman and Gerlovo.

No less importantly, the present work is a regional case study of "the process of imperial construction"[3] whereby from the mid-fifteenth through the sixteenth centuries the Ottoman polity made the definitive transition from a frontier principality to a centralized bureaucratic empire. In the process, groups that had played paramount roles in the rise of the Ottoman frontier principality, such as Ottoman frontier-lord families, semi-nomadic Turcoman warriors, and non-Sharia-minded dervishes, came to be gradually displaced and marginalized by the emerging imperial regime's development of its institutional instrumentarium, which came to rely upon regular army units more tightly answerable to the center, a new military-administrative service class of largely *kul*/slave origin, a rapidly developing professional palace bureaucracy, and the rising *ulema* (Ar. *ulama*) class of *medrese* (Ar. *madrasa*)-trained religious

---

[3] I borrow the phrase from Cemal Kafadar, *Between Two Worlds: The Construction of the Ottoman State* (Berkeley, Los Angeles, and London: University of California Press, 1995), 31.

scholars who endorsed scriptural, Sharia-minded Islam and would staff the Ottoman judiciary and educational system. The semi-nomadic Turcomans and "heterodox" dervishes in Deliorman and Gerlovo who were "tamed" by the late sixteenth century were very much descendants of those original "masters of the frontier zone" who had made formative contributions to the success of the Ottoman frontier principality, having acted as members of a power-sharing partnership with the early Ottoman dynasty. The study thus aims to demonstrate how this "process of imperial construction" played out in a distant province, highlighting also the changing balance between the "wanderers" and the "settlers" – i.e. the itinerants and the (semi-) nomads and the sedentarists, respectively – in the decisive favor of the latter, the triumph of the cereal/agricultural economy over pastoral nomadism, and the relationship between confessional/religious identity and imperial policy.

Both dimensions of the book as a case study – the rise of the Ottoman imperial centralized state and the formation of a regional Muslim community in the northeastern Balkans – may be situated in the wider Islamic world and Eurasian context. The past several decades have witnessed the articulation of conceptualizations of "early modern Eurasia" as a distinct zone, from Western Europe to East Asia, whose historical development from *c.* 1450 to *c.* 1800 represented a global moment in world history and was characterized by a number of "unifying features," be they "parallelisms" or causally linked "interconnections."[4] Linking local or regional, contingent events and processes to macro-historical themes within the framework of evolving paradigms such as "integrative history" and "connected histories," scholars such as Joseph Fletcher, Sanjay Subrahmanyam, Jerry Bentley, and Victor Lieberman have elaborated upon a number of such unifying features: "a sustained movement from local fragmentation to political consolidation" that entailed a "drive towards centralization and the growth of coercive state apparatuses," imperial expansion and the reformulation of ideas of universal sovereignty within the context of heightened apocalyptic and millenarian sensibilities (especially *c.* 1450–*c.* 1600), religious revival and reformations, large-scale migrations and overall population growth (*c.* 1450–*c.* 1550), rural unrest and the growth of regional cities, intensified exploitation of natural environments, technological diffusions

---

[4] Joseph Fletcher defines "interconnections" as "historical phenomena in which there is contact linking two or more societies," and "historical parallelisms" as "roughly contemporaneous similar developments in the world's various societies," ibid., "Integrative History: Parallels and Interconnections in the Early Modern Period," in *Studies on Chinese and Islamic Inner Asia*, article no. X, ed. Beatrice Forbes Manz (Aldershot: Ashgate Variorum, 1995), 2–4.

and global cultural exchanges, and a generally "quickening tempo of history."[5]

Within the same interpretive framework, Charles Parker has highlighted the process of globalization of universal religious systems, especially Christianity and Islam.[6] The early modern period witnessed the Islamic world's significant expansion along its frontier zones, which entailed the formation of distinct new regional Islamic cultures. Beyond the confines of the Balkans and the Ottoman Empire, the formation of the Muslim community in early modern Ottoman Deliorman and Gerlovo may thus be productively compared to similar processes in other areas across early modern Eurasia such as Bengal and the lands of the Golden Horde.[7] By providing a focused, regional perspective, the study aims to offer valuable insights on "the indigenization of Islam" – the process by which Islam, in its diverse doctrinal and socio-cultural manifestations, became part and parcel of a regional landscape; in this case, that of the Balkans.

Geographical Scope

The present study's geographical scope is largely defined by the use of Ottoman tax registers that constitute the main source base for exploring demographic and socio-economic change. The area studied is a part of the northeastern Balkans that included the Ottoman districts (*kazas*) of Chernovi (mod. Cherven, Ruse province) and Shumnu in the eastern part of the Ottoman province (*sancak/liva*) of Niğbolu (mod. Nikopol)

---

[5] This list of selected "unifying features" is based on my reading of the work of the scholars referred to. For a more detailed analysis, see Fletcher, "Integrative History: Parallels and Interconnections in the Early Modern Period"; Sanjay Subrahmanyam, "Connected Histories: Notes towards a Reconfiguration of Early Modern Eurasia," *Modern Asian Studies* 31, no. 3 (1997): 735–762; Jerry H. Bentley, "Early Modern Europe and the Early Modern World," in *Between the Middle Ages and Modernity: Individual and Community in the Early Modern World*, ed. Charles H. Parker and Jerry Bentley (Lanham, MD: Rowman and Littlefield, 2007), 13–31; and Victor Lieberman, "Transcending East–West Dichotomies: State and Culture Formation in Six Ostensibly Disparate Areas," *Modern Asian Studies* 31, no. 3 (1997): 463–546. For a concise, but insightful discussion of Ottoman empire building within this early modern Eurasian conceptual framework, see Kaya Şahin, *Empire and Power in the Reign of Süleyman: Narrating the Sixteenth-Century Ottoman World* (New York: Cambridge University Press, 2013), 6–12.
[6] Charles H. Parker, *Global Interactions in the Early Modern Age, 1400–1800* (Cambridge: Cambridge University Press, 2010), 183–206.
[7] Richard Eaton, *The Rise of Islam and the Bengal Frontier, 1204–1760* (Berkeley, CA: University of California Press, 1993); Devin DeWeese, *Islamization and Native Religion in the Golden Horde: Baba Tükles and Conversion to Islam in Historical and Epic Tradition* (University Park, PA: The Pennsylvania State University Press, 1994). See also Rian Thum, *The Sacred Routes of Uyghur History* (Cambridge, MA: Harvard University Press, 2014).

as of the first decades of the sixteenth century,[8] thus containing most of the historical-geographic region of Deliorman as well as Gerlovo (Ott. Gerilova) in its entirety.

This area thus stretches from the Danube River – roughly between modern Ruse (Ott. Rus, Rusçuk) and Tutrakan in the northwest to the Balkan range in the southeast – just to the south of modern Târgovishte and Shumen. At the northwestern end, along the Danube, lies a several kilometer-wide strip of flat land. Moving to the southeast, the larger part of the area studied is dominated by Deliorman – the hilly and wooded plateau roughly delineated by the Danube to the northwest, the Ruse-Varna line to the southwest, and the relatively arid steppe-like plain of Dobrudja to the east.[9] With an average altitude of 300m, but reaching 485m, Deliorman, like the rest of the area under discussion, enjoys considerable yearly precipitation (around 550–600mm per year); however, due to its karst limestone and loess base, its aboveground water resources are limited, small creeks and rivers often losing their way in the loess sediments. This lack, at least in the pre-modern era, demanded the digging of wells and tapping of karst springs to ensure a satisfactory water supply.[10] Until the nineteenth century most of Deliorman was covered by oak, ash, elm, and maple trees.[11]

To the south of Deliorman rises the Shumen plateau as well as the hilly area around Târgovishte. The southernmost part of the area under discussion is occupied by Gerlovo – a hilly, fertile valley on the northern edges of the central-eastern Balkan range, formed by the Golyama Kamchiya (Ticha) River and a number of small tributaries.[12] With an

[8] While the area under discussion as reflected in Ottoman tax registers remained roughly the same from the late fifteenth century through the sixteenth centuries, the territorial-administrative divisions within this area did change with time. See section 4.2 in Chapter 4.

[9] Wolfgang Stubenrauch, *Kulturgeographie des Deli-Orman (Nordostbulgarien)* (Berlin: Komissionsverlag von J. Engelhorns Nachf. Stuttgart, 1933), 7–9. This definition of Deliorman's boundaries is largely based on the geomorphological features of the area. *C.* 1640 the famous Ottoman scholar Katip Çelebi defined Deliorman as the area between (or around) Shumnu (Shumen), Silistre (Silistra), and Hezargrad (Razgrad), Mustafa Ben Abdalla Hadschi Chalfa [Katip Çelebi], *Rumeli und Bosna, geographisch beschrieben*, trans. Joseph von Hammer (Vienna, Verlag des Kunst- und Industrie-Comptoirs, 1812), 38.

[10] Stubenrauch, *Kulturgeographie*, 10–13; V. Marinov, *Deli-Orman (iuzhna chast): oblastno geografsko izuchvane* (Sofia: n.p., 1941), 27–36.

[11] While the region saw the conversion of some forest areas into arable land in relation to the growth of the settlement network from the early sixteenth century onward, deforestation intensified in the nineteenth century; nowadays most of the "Wild Forest" has been converted into arable land, the remaining forest consisting mostly of oak trees; Stubenrauch, *Kulturgeographie*, 13–19; Marinov, *Deli-Orman*, 45–48.

[12] Gerlovo is rimmed by the Balkan range to the south, the smaller Preslav Mountain to the north and northeast, and the Omurtag Heights to the northwest; V. Marinov, *Gerlovo: oblastno geografsko izuchvane* (Sofia: n.p., 1936), 5–12. *C.* 1640 Katip Çelebi defined it as the area between Shumnu and the Balkan range, thus not much differently from modern definitions; Hadschi Chalfa, *Rumeli und Bosna*, 38.

altitude of 250–400m and a temperate continental climate, it is differentiated from Deliorman mainly by its much richer aboveground water resources.

Thus delineated, the region under investigation roughly covers the modern Bulgarian provinces of Ruse, Razgrad, Shumen, and Târgovishte, as well as a portion of the modern Bulgarian province of Silistra (Ott. Silistre). A small part of Deliorman remains left out in the neighboring Ottoman province of Silistre. While the area described above is the main focus of the present study, frequent references will be made to other parts of the eastern Balkans, above all Thrace and Dobrudja, as they relate to both the demographic and religio-cultural aspects of early modern Deliorman and Gerlovo's development.

Early Modern Ottoman Deliorman and Gerlovo in the Scholarly Literature

The formation of the Muslim community in early modern Ottoman Deliorman and Gerlovo, like that of those in the eastern Balkans in general, remains little-researched. A few late nineteenth- and early twentieth-century demographic/ethnographic studies written by Bulgarian scholars who lacked the relevant training and access to Ottoman sources attempted to explain why northeastern Bulgaria was predominantly populated by Turks at the time of the proclamation of the Bulgarian principality in 1878. In an unfinished article, M. Drinov, relying mostly on Western narrative sources, traced the demographic development of northeastern Bulgaria up to the mid-sixteenth century, arguing that until the late fifteenth century the region was still largely populated by Christian Bulgarians, while for the sixteenth century he analyzed Bulgarian accounts of forced Islamization and ethnic assimilation now proven to be spurious.[13] Other similar works do not throw much light on the history of the region, except in pointing to some interesting oral traditions.[14]

The first Ottomanist to advance a hypothesis about the origins of Deliorman's heterodox Muslim population – usually referred to as Kızılbaş (as well as Alevi-Bektashi) today[15] – for which the region has

---

[13] Marin Drinov, "Istorichesko osvetlenie vârhu statistikata na narodnostite v iztochnata chast na bâlgarskoto kniazhestvo," *Periodichesko Spisanie* 7 (1884): 1–24, and 8 (1884): 68–75. On the so-called Bulgarian "domestic sources" on conversion to Islam, see the relevant discussion in Chapter 1.

[14] Liubomir Miletich, *Staroto bâlgarsko naselenie v severoiztochna Bâlgaria* (Sofia: Bâlgarsko Knizhovno Druzhestvo, 1902); Stefan Bobchev, "Za deliormanskite turtsi i za kâzâl-bashite," *Sbornik na BAN* 24 (1929): 1–16; Vasil Marinov, *Deli-Orman* and *Gerlovo*.

[15] *Kızılbaş*, lit. "Red Head(s)," is the designation accorded to the followers of the Safavid order in the time of the Safavid Sheykh Haydar (in office, 1460–88) who introduced the famous

been well known in the modern age, was Franz Babinger – one of the founding fathers of Ottoman studies. He claimed, without adequate substantiation, that the Kızılbaş in Bulgaria, Deliorman included, were descendants of adherents of the "Safaviyya" (Ger. "Sefewijje"), which he seems to have conceptualized in the narrower sense of adherents of the Safavid order, but which could also be understood more broadly in the sense of sympathizers of the newly established Safavid regime in Iran (1501) who had fled from Anatolia in the context of the Ottoman-Safavid conflict in the sixteenth century.[16] There the issue long rested, but later research on the revolt of Sheykh Bedreddin in the early fifteenth century and the letters of the judge of Sofia, Sheykh Bali Efendi, to the grand vizier and the sultan in the 1540s, which point to the presence of adherents of Bedreddin's movement in Deliorman,[17] has induced some scholars to assume that the heterodox population in the area largely had its origins in that movement, and not in the Ottoman-Safavid conflict.[18] In the past few decades this view has been expressed in specialized studies as well as in general histories of the Ottoman Empire.[19] Most recently,

---

twelve-gored scarlet cap (known as *taj-ı Haydari*) as the order's common headgear. Through most of the sixteenth century, starting with Haydar's son – Shah Ismail I (r. 1501–24) – the founder of the Safavid Empire of Iran, the term *Kızılbaş*, especially from the point of view of the Ottoman state and establishment, was used to refer to the Safavid dynasty, state, and Safavid subjects in general, but also to designate perceived supporters of the Safavid cause on Ottoman soil. The latter, however, were not necessarily strict adherents of the Safavid order's theology and practices, but were those perceived as sympathetic toward the Safavid regime for a variety of reasons. For more details, see Chapters 1, 2, 4, and 6. On the modern usage of *Kızılbaş*, *Alevi*, and *Bektashi* as identity designations among heterodox Muslims in Bulgaria, see Hande Sözer, *Managing Invisibility: Dissimulation and Identity Maintenance among Alevi Bulgarian Turks* (Leiden: Brill, 2014).

[16] Franz Babinger, "Der Islam in Kleinasien," *ZDMG* 76 (1922): 140.

[17] See V. Minorsky, "Shaykh Bali Efendi on the Safavids," *BSOAS* 20 (1957): 437–451, and Andreas Tietze, "Sheykh Bali Efendi's Report on the Followers of Sheykh Bedreddin," *OA* 7–8 (1988): 115–122.

[18] Note also T. Kowalski's comments on the elements of Ponto-Caspian Turkic dialects found in the dialect spoken in the northeastern Balkans, thus highlighting the importance of pre-Ottoman Turcoman migrations from the Ponto-Caspian steppe, ibid. *Les Turcs et la langue Turc de la Bulgarie de Nord-Est* (Krakow, 1993). For more on these pre-Ottoman migrations, see Chapter 3, section 3.2.1.

[19] For example, in A. Y. Ocak, *Osmanlı Toplumunda Zındıklar ve Mülhidler (15.–17. Yüzyıllar)*, 4th ed. (Istanbul: Tarih Vakfı, 2013), hereafter *Zındıklar*,196–197, 212–216, and H. İnalcık, *The Ottoman Empire: The Classical Age, 1300–1600* (London: Weidenfeld and Nicolson, 1973), 190; hereafter *Classical Age*. On the basis of modern ethnographic and anthropological evidence, F. DeJong has questioned Babinger's thesis, arguing that the Kızılbaş of Deliorman must have their origins in "pre-Safavid" Kızılbaş sects [*sic*] in Bulgaria (by which he seems to mean pre-sixteenth century "heterodox" groups in the eastern Balkans) which could have undergone "Safavization" in the sixteenth century. Comparing the practices and beliefs of modern Kızılbaş-Alevi-Bektashi communities in Bulgaria to those of the Tahtacı tribe in eastern Anatolia (which he sees as having most faithfully preserved the traditions of the "Safavid Kızılbaş") he concludes

Nevena Gramatikova, in several fine works devoted to the history of the heterodox Muslim communities in Bulgaria, emphasized the importance of the heterodox collectivity of the Abdals of Rum of Otman Baba (d. 1478) and his successors – the sixteenth-century saints Akyazılı Baba and Demir Baba (the latter being the great sixteenth-century regional saint of Deliorman) – for the formation of the heterodox Muslim communities in the eastern and specifically the northeastern Balkans.[20] Gramatikova also places the development of heterodox Muslim communities in the eastern Balkans in the context of the Ottoman-Safavid conflict and notes that these communities were in all probability augmented by the migration of Safavid sympathizers onto Ottoman Anatolian soil into the Balkans in the sixteenth century (which, in turn, affected these communities' nature).

However, none of the studies referred to above has specifically focused on Deliorman and Gerlovo, neither has any of them utilized a diverse enough spectrum of sources, including Ottoman administrative sources (especially tax registers), to provide a more detailed picture of the relevant processes of demographic, socio-economic, and religious change in the countryside.[21] As for urban growth, one study of considerable scholarly

that, as heterodox groups in the Rhodope Mountains and Gerlovo "have more elements of ritual in common with the Tahtacıs," they are more likely to have their origins in the Safavid Kızılbaş, as compared to the "Kızılbaş" of Deliorman and Dobrudja; DeJong, "Problems Concerning the Origins of the Qızılbāş in Bulgaria: remnants of the Safaviyya?," in *Convegno sul tema: la Shi'a nell'Impero Ottomano* (Rome: Accademia Nazionale Dei Linzei, 1993), 203–215, esp. 214–215.

20 Most importantly, *Neortodoksalniiat Isliam v bâlgarskite zemi. Minalo i sâvremennost* (Sofia: Gutenberg, 2011). Her analysis of Demir Baba's *vita* is the only in-depth and competent study of this source, but its focus differs substantially from the related analysis in Chapter 6 of the present work. In her work Gramatikova has not utilized any of the major sixteenth-century tax registers for Deliorman and Gerlovo. Demir Baba's mausoleum/convent complex is the subject of a couple of now-outdated articles, most notably Franz Babinger, "Das Bektaschikloster Demir Baba," *Westasiatische Studien* 34 (1931): 8–93. Otman Baba, not a Deliorman saint *per se*, but critically important to the present study as he was the actual founder of the Abdals of Rum as a distinct dervish collectivity in the eastern Balkans and was Demir Baba's "spiritual grandfather," is the focus of two good modern scholarly articles: Halil İnalcık, "Dervish and Sultan: An Analysis of Otman Baba Vilayetnamesi," in ibid., *The Middle East and the Balkans under the Ottoman Empire: Essays on Economy and Society* (Bloomington: Indiana University Press, 1993), 19–36, and Nevena Gramatikova, "Otman Baba – One of the Spiritual Patrons of Islamic Heterodoxy in Bulgarian Lands," *Études Balkaniques* 3 (2002): 71–102. Otman Baba has also received some attention in the works of Ahmet Yaşar Ocak and Ahmet Karamustafa, most notably Ocak, *Osmanlı İmparatorluğunda Marjinal Sûfilik: Kalenderîler (XIV.–XVII. Yüzyıllar)* (Ankara: Türk Tarih Kurumu, 1992), hereafter *Kalenderîler*, and Karamustafa, *God's Unruly Friends: Dervish Groups in the Islamic Middle Period, 1200–1550* (Salt Lake City: University of Utah Press, 1994).

21 One should note Machiel Kiel's "Anatolia Transplanted? Patterns of Demographic, Ethnic and Religious Changes in the District of Tozluk (N.E. Bulgaria), 1479–1873," *Anatolica* 17 (1991): 1–29. This important article focuses on the small region of Tozluk, just to the west of Gerlovo, and deals with Turcoman settlement and colonization in the

value is Machiel Kiel's article, which briefly sketches Hezargrad's rise in the sixteenth century as a center of "orthodox" Sunni Islamic culture, as opposed to rural surroundings already populated by large "heterodox" groups.[22]

Overview of the Sources

The present study utilizes a wide array of mostly Ottoman sources which may be divided typologically into administrative, narrative, and legal.[23]

By far, the most important body of Ottoman administrative sources is a series of *tapu tahrir* tax registers (*tapu tahrir defterleri*) for the area under discussion.[24] Compiled in the fifteenth and sixteenth centuries, these registers survey tax-revenue sources, including land and agricultural produce in the countryside and taxable urban properties and enterprises (e.g. town markets, artisanal shops, or public bath-houses). They can be detailed (*mufassal*) or synoptic (*icmal*). Detailed registers include the names of taxpayers (adult Muslim and non-Muslim males – married household heads or bachelors – but also those of non-Muslim, usually Christian, widows registered as household heads) as well as a detailed breakdown of tax-revenue amounts for each settlement. Taxpayers, together with their families, were defined as *re'aya* (lit. "flock"), and were registered separately by religious affiliation and by specific local community when relevant (e.g. a Muslim or Christian neighborhood in a town, but also nomadic or semi-nomadic groups). Some *re'aya* had special (privileged) taxation status usually related to some specific duties they performed (e.g. auxiliary military personnel of semi-nomadic provenance, mountain-pass guards, rice cultivators who acted as suppliers for the state, etc.).

Synoptic registers usually contain only summary household and bachelor numbers as well as the total tax amounts assigned for each settlement. Most of the land was defined as state-controlled (*miri*) and tax

---

countryside, thus complementing the present study. However, it is based almost exclusively on Ottoman tax registers and covers, in summary fashion, a much longer period.

[22] Machiel Kiel, "Hrâzgrad-Hezargrad-Razgrad. The Vicissitudes of a Turkish Town in Bulgaria," *Turcica* 21–23 (1991): 495–569. Kiel places an emphasis on Hezargrad's architectural history, while also providing an overview of the town's demographic development, well-grounded in Ottoman tax registers; however, he does not utilize Ibrahim Pasha's important pious endowment charter (*vakfiye*) of 1533.

[23] Whereby such a distinction may not always be quite neat. For example, Ottoman law codes can be seen as legal-administrative sources. Unfortunately, Islamic court registers (*şer'iye sicil defterleri*) are not extant for the area of study and so have not been researched.

[24] The study also utilizes some tax registers for other areas in the Balkans, notably Thrace and Dobrudja.

revenue accruing from it was apportioned into small, medium, and large revenue grants assigned in lieu of a salary to state functionaries, usually defined as the ruling *askeri* class (lit. the "military" class, but which included bureaucrats and members of the learned hierarchy). The most numerous, small benefices (*timars*) were usually assigned to members of the provincial *sipahi* cavalry, fortress garrison members, and low-level administrative and judiciary personnel; mid-sized benefices (*ze'amets*) to mid-ranking provincial military commanders; and large benefices (*has*, pl. *havass*) belonged to the sultan, members of the dynasty, high state dignitaries, and provincial governors. Apart from *miri* lands, these registers include pious endowment (*evkaf*) properties (with the respective taxpayers, the accrued tax revenue, and the beneficiaries of the endowment) as well as freehold properties (*mülk*, pl. *emlak*). While many such registers included properties of all three kinds (*miri*, *evkaf*, and *emlak*), some covered only *miri* lands with their respective revenue grants (often referred to as *timar tahrir defterleri*) or only covered pious endowments and freehold properties (referred to as *evkaf ve emlak tahrir defterleri*).[25]

Related to these registers are provincial law codes (*sancak kanunnameleri*), usually included in tax registers, which not only reflect the normative aspects of taxation and various socio-economic activities, but also may contain references to forced deportations and migrations of Turcoman nomads from Anatolia to the Balkans in the sixteenth century.[26] To these sources, one should add pious endowment charters (*vakfiyes*) as well as "registers of important affairs" containing outgoing imperial orders (*mühimme defterleri*).

As for narrative sources, the study utilizes a variety of works of Ottoman historiography: chronicles of the Ottoman dynasty (*Tevarih-i Al-i Osman*) and narratives of specific military campaigns and heroic deeds (*gazavatnameler*), as well as the account of the famous seventeenth-century Ottoman traveler Evliya Çelebi. Hagiographic accounts (*vitae*, *velayetnameler*, *menakıbnameler*) of heterodox Muslim saints, especially those of Otman Baba and Demir Baba, are utilized to explore the nature of their respective saintly cults and the values and worldviews of the respective hagiographic communities, but also to offer an alternative perspective on historical events and processes.[27]

---

[25] For a detailed discussion of the Ottoman land regime and methods of land surveying in the fifteenth and sixteenth centuries, see *An Economic and Social History of the Ottoman Empire, 1300–1914*, ed. Halil İnalcık and Donald Quataert (Cambridge: Cambridge University Press, 1994), 103–178.

[26] On the nature of Ottoman provincial law codes, see Heath Lowry, "The Ottoman *Liva Kanunname*s contained in the *Defter-i Hakani*," *OA* 2 (1981): 43–74.

[27] The nature of specific narrative sources will be further discussed below upon their introduction.

Lastly, the study utilizes Ottoman *fatwa* (Tr. *fetva*) collections, especially those of early modern Ottoman *şeyhülislam*s (the heads of the Ottoman judicial/religious hierarchy), which highlight important aspects of the process of conversion to Islam as well as the development of confessional identities.

In addition to Ottoman sources, the study makes use of some Byzantine, Slavic, and Western chronicles and travel accounts.

Apart from the basic division into administrative, narrative/literary, and legal, at least two other divisions among sources could be made. First, from the perspective of authorial provenance, one may distinguish between sources that were products of the state and/or clearly endorsed the dynastic and state perspective, as opposed to sources emanating from non-state actors, who could be individuals or groups that espoused varied and changing attitudes toward the evolving Ottoman dynastic project. Thus, Ottoman administrative documents and dynasty-centered chronicles would fall in the former category, while hagiographic accounts of heterodox saints and sources of non-Ottoman provenance in the latter.

In addition, sources could be divided into those that shed light above all on administrative, demographic, and socio-economic change (mostly Ottoman administrative sources) and religio-cultural and socio-cultural developments (narrative/literary sources, as well as *fatwa* collections).

This study seeks to integrate in a balanced way the major aspects of demographic and socio-economic change on the one hand and religio-political and cultural developments on the other, but also to bring together the perspectives of the imperial center and those of non-state actors, thus exploring the interplay between the global and the local, the imperial and the regional, as well as the urban and the rural.

The book consists of seven chapters. Chapter 1 serves as an expanded introduction that provides a brief overview of Ottoman history through the sixteenth century and discusses theoretical and comparative aspects of the Ottoman transformation from a frontier principality to a centralized bureaucratic empire, together with a historiographical analysis of the formation of Muslim communities in the Balkans. Chapter 2 analyzes the broader aspects of Turcoman colonization in the Ottoman Balkans through the early sixteenth century and also contains case studies of the lives of two prominent Balkan Muslim heterodox saints from the mid-fourteenth through the fifteenth century – Seyyid Ali Sultan (Kızıl Deli) and Otman Baba – based largely on their respective hagiographical accounts. Chapter 3 discusses the pre-Ottoman and early Ottoman northeastern Balkans (through the fifteenth century). Chapters 4 and 5 are devoted to the demographic and socio-economic development of Deliorman, Gerlovo, and adjacent areas in the rural countryside and the urban centers, respectively. Chapter 6 analyzes select aspects of religion, culture, and authority in Deliorman and Gerlovo, largely through the lenses of Demir Baba's *vita*. Chapter 7 concludes with a discussion of two major conceptual and historiographic issues – conversion of Islam and confessionalization – within the regional context of the present study.

1   The Broad Historical Context: The Rise of the Ottoman Empire and the Formation of Muslim Communities in the Balkans as an Integral Part of the Ottomanization of the Region

1.1   The Rise of the Ottomans, *c.* 1300–*c.* 1550: An Overview

The rise of the Ottoman polity and its transformation from a petty principality in northwestern Anatolia at the beginning of the fourteenth century into a multi-ethnic, multi-religious empire controlling most of Anatolia, the Balkans, and the Arab lands by the mid-sixteenth century is one of the most fascinating topics in late medieval and early modern history. The first two major theories explaining early Ottoman success were those of Paul Wittek[1] and M.F. Köprülü.[2] Wittek's analysis has been viewed as placing a singular emphasis on religious fervor and the quest for "holy war" (*gaza*) as the driving motive of Turcoman warriors in Anatolia in setting out to conquer neighboring Christian territories. Köprülü, by contrast, painted a broad canvas of the socio-economic conditions in thirteenth- and fourteenth-century Anatolia, pointing to the Ottomans' favorable geographical location, the principle of unigeniture in dynastic succession, the Ottoman expansion in the Balkans, the role of specific social groups (such as the chivalric urban Muslim *ahi* brotherhoods), and the institutional and administrative legacy of highly developed Muslim states such as the Seljukid and Ilkhanid polities as the major factors contributing to the Ottomans' early rise.[3] The eminent Ottomanist Halil İnalcık produced something of a synthesis of these two approaches, according the spirit of *gaza* its due without failing to situate the Ottomans' early rapid expansion into the broader context of the prevailing political, socio-economic, and cultural conditions in Anatolia

---

[1] Paul Wittek, *The Rise of the Ottoman Empire* (London: The Royal Asiatic Society, 1938).
[2] M. Fuat Köprülü, *Les Origines de l'Empire Ottoman* (Paris: Boccard, 1935), published in English as *The Origins of the Ottoman Empire*, ed. and trans. Gary Leiser (Albany, NY: SUNY Press, 1992).
[3] Ibid., 111–117.

14

and the Balkans.[4] Later, Rudi Lindner emphasized the Ottoman principality's successful transition from a pastoral nomadic venture to a sedentary enterprise (conditioned largely by ecological factors within the
socio-political context of fourteenth-century Bythinia).[5] Cemal Kafadar
explored the Ottomans' successful navigation of fluid identities in the
Anatolian and Balkan frontier zones in engineering the transition from
a frontier polity to a centralizing empire.[6] Heath Lowry characterized
the early Ottoman enterprise as a pragmatic "predatory confederation"
driven more by conquest and profit than religious fervor and co-opting
non-Muslims in the newly conquered Christian territories.[7]

The Ottoman emirate emerged *c.* 1300 as one of a few dozen similar
petty Anatolian Turcoman states which came into being between 1260
and 1320 amidst the political fragmentation resulting from the weakening of the two major established state actors dominant in the peninsula – Byzantium and the Seljuk Sultanate of Rum. Bordering the
Byzantine Empire in Anatolia's northwest corner, the Ottoman enterprise remained for decades in the shadow of several western Anatolian
Turcoman maritime principalities active in Levantine trade and politics, which exacted tribute from both the Latin sea powers (Venice and
Genoa) and Byzantium, and carried out raids in the Aegean islands and
the Balkan mainland in the 1330s and 1340s. Most notably, the Emirate
of Aydın, led by the able naval commander Umur Bey, played a crucial
role in Byzantium's Age of Civil Wars (1321–54); Umur Bey's intervention in 1342–6 decisively helped one of the contending parties, which
was led by the future Emperor John VI Cantacuzene (r. 1347–54).[8]

The gradual decline of these petty maritime states, prompted by the
crusading efforts of Venice and the Papacy in 1334 and 1344, as well as
the Ottoman annexation of the neighboring emirate of Karesi (*c.* 1345)
that gave the fledgling Ottoman principality access to the Dardanelles
via the Marmara sea-shore, made the Ottomans the sole power-broker
among the western Anatolian emirates with whom Byzantium and
the Levantine sea-powers could negotiate.[9] As John VI Cantacuzene

---

[4] Halil İnalcık, "The Emergence of the Ottomans" and "The Rise of the Ottoman Empire,"
in *The Cambridge History of Islam*, ed. P.M. Holt, K.S. Lambton, and Bernard Lewis,
vol. 1 (Cambridge: Cambridge University Press, 1970), 263–291, 295–323.

[5] Rudi Paul Lindner, *Nomads and Ottomans in Medieval Anatolia* (Bloomington, IN:
Indiana University Press, 1983), esp. chapter one.

[6] Kafadar, *Between Two Worlds.*

[7] Heath W. Lowry, *The Nature of the Early Ottoman State* (Albany, NY: SUNY Press, 2003).

[8] See Paul Lemerle, *L'émirat d'Aydin, Byzance et l'Occident* (Paris: Presses Universitaires de
France, 1957).

[9] See E. Zachariadou, *Trade and Crusade: Venetian Crete and the Emirates of Menteshe
and Aydin, 1300–1415* (Venice: Instituto Ellenico di Studi Bizantini e Post-Bizantini di
Venezia, 1983), 21–44.

concluded an alliance with the Ottoman emir Orhan, giving the latter his daughter in marriage in 1346, the Ottomans took advantage of Byzantine factional struggles and established a firm foothold in the Gallipoli Peninsula between 1352 and 1354.[10] Traditionally considered to be a turning point in the history of both the Balkans and the Ottoman state, this development pointed to a clear difference between the Ottomans and other Anatolian emirates with respect to their ambitions. While warriors of western Anatolian Turcoman maritime principalities such as Saruhan and Aydın had embarked upon a number of expeditions in the Balkan mainland in the preceding decades, they had never attempted to establish a lasting presence there – neither by capturing a stronghold nor by planting colonists – but rather contented themselves with pillaging the countryside and capturing slaves. However, the Ottoman base on the European side of the Dardanelles was used to initiate a massive territorial expansion that would bring most of the eastern Balkans under direct Ottoman control by the end of the century.

That expansion was made possible on account of both the political and territorial fragmentation in the Balkans and specific Ottoman methods of conquest characterized by the careful use and distribution of various military resources, diplomatic skill, and accomodationist policies in the newly conquered territories.[11] The Ottoman conquest of the eastern Balkans (i.e. most of modern continental Greece and Bulgaria) proceeded in distinct phases. Ottoman forces, mostly warriors of fortune, first raided and conquered most of Byzantine and Bulgarian Thrace in the late 1350s and 1360s, including Adrianople. The crushing defeat inflicted upon a Serbian princely coalition at the Battle of Maritsa (Chernomen) in Thrace in 1371 enabled the Ottomans to impose vassalage upon a number of Balkan states (including Byzantium), while proceeding with the direct annexation of some parts of the peninsula. The combined approach of direct annexation and the imposition of vassalage that entailed the payment of hefty tributes and the procurement of Balkan vassal troops wisely used by the Ottomans in their expansionist campaigns against rival Turcoman polities in Anatolia, gradually withered the resistance of the Balkan states.[12] After the failure of the second and last attempt of a west Balkan princely coalition to stop

---

[10] Donald Nicol, *The Last Centuries of Byzantium, 1261–1453,* 2nd edn. (Cambridge: Cambridge University Press, 1993), 203–205.

[11] See H. İnalcık's seminal article "Ottoman Methods of Conquest," *Studia Islamica* 2 (1954): 103–129.

[12] For an excellent discussion of the relationship between the Ottomans and their Balkan vassals, see Khristo Matanov and Rumiana Mikhneva, *Ot Galipoli do Lepanto: Balkanite, Evropa i osmanskoto nashestvie* (Sofia: Nauka i Izkustvo, 1988), 52–81.

Ottoman expansion at the Battle of Kosovo Polje in 1389, Bayezid I (r. 1389–1402) proceeded with the swift annexation of most of the eastern Balkans. These conquests included the three Bulgarian states north of the Balkan range, several of the Serbian principalities in Macedonia which had formed as a result of the disintegration of Stefan Dušan's (r. 1331–55) Serbian Empire, as well as Thessaly, and Wallachia became an Ottoman vassal.[13]

It should be noted that while Bayezid I pursued a similar expansionist policy in Anatolia, Ottoman expansion encountered much more substantial difficulties there: first, because of the general prohibition that Islamic law imposed on fighting against fellow Muslims, which rendered such an expansion highly problematic from a religio-political point of view; second, due to the fact that many rival Turcoman principalities were better established and possessed superior claims to legitimacy by way of their achievements and dynastic pedigrees.[14] On the other hand, expansion in infidel territories was religiously commendable and brought the Ottomans considerable prestige among their Turcoman rivals.

While the Ottoman defeat in the hands of Tamerlane at Ankara in 1402[15] undid most of Bayezid I's conquests in Anatolia, its effect on the Ottoman domains in the Balkans was not nearly as dramatic. Most of the Ottoman Balkan territories remained under relatively stable control during the Ottoman interregnum (1402–13) that followed the Ankara debacle;[16] the relative political stability in the Balkans and the economic resources which these lands provided helped the Ottoman dynasty survive the greatest cataclysm in its early history and resume expansion in both the Balkans and Anatolia thereafter.

After Mehmed I (r. 1413–21) managed to restore the unity and stability of the Ottoman state, fending off a number of challenges, including

---

[13] Matanov and Mikhneva, *Ot Galipoli do Lepanto*, 84–96.

[14] On the Ottomans' relations with other Anatolian emirates, see Feridun Emecen, *İlk Osmanlılar ve Batı Anadolu Beylikler Dünyası* (Istanbul: Kitabevi, 2001). One of the legal solutions in the context of Islamic law that the Ottomans advanced to justify their aggressive actions against their Muslim neighbors was that the latter impeded the Ottomans' "holy war" campaigns in the Christian Balkans.

[15] The standard study on Timur (Tamerlane) is Beatrice Forbes Manz, *The Rise and Rule of Tamerlane* (Cambridge and New York: Cambridge University Press, 1989). Two detailed studies on Timur's involvement in Anatolia are Klaus-Peter Matschke, *Die Schlacht bei Ankara und das Schicksal von Byzanz* (Weimar: Herman Böhlaus Nachfolger, 1981), and Marie-Mathilde Alexandrescu-Dersca, *La campagne de Timur en Anatolie, 1402*, 2nd edn. (London: Variorum Reprints, 1977).

[16] The most authoritative treatment of the Ottoman interregnum is Dimitris Kastritsis, *The Sons of Bayezid: Empire Buildidng and Representation in the Ottoman Civil War of 1402–1413* (Leiden and Boston: Brill, 2007).

Sheykh Bedreddin's revolt in 1416, his successor Murad II (r. 1421–44, 1446–51), building upon his father's achievement, re-annexed a number of territories lost after the Battle of Ankara, such as the western Anatolian principalities of Saruhan, Aydın, and Germiyan, as well as Salonica in the Balkans. Murad II also neutralized several challenges to his throne, tightened the Ottomans' grip over Serbia (which resulted in a temporary annexation from 1439 to 1444), and repelled one last major crusading effort as he defeated the Crusaders' army at Varna in 1444, thus all but conclusively sealing the fate of the peninsula and positioning it firmly under Ottoman control.

Mehmed II the Conqueror's mature reign (1451–81) is often seen as a turning point in the Ottoman polity's definitive transformation from a frontier principality into a centralized empire. His most celebrated, symbolically and ideologically loaded achievement was the conquest of Constantinople in 1453, which facilitated the political and economic integration of the Ottoman state's Balkan and Anatolian domains. The conquest of a millennium-old, truly imperial metropolis provided a huge boost to Ottoman dynastic legitimacy and prestige within and without the Islamic world and furnished the dynasty with a number of related imperial claims – most notably, the claim to the legacy of Roman-Byzantine imperial universalism.[17]

Mehmed II's numerous campaigns of conquest led to further Ottoman expansion in both the east and the west. In the Balkans, Serbia was finally conquered in the late 1450s (with Belgrade remaining under Hungarian control), as was the Morea. Bosnia was annexed in 1463, and all of Albania was brought under Ottoman control by the late 1470s. In Anatolia, Mehmed II's greatest achievements were the annexation of the Empire of Trebizond in 1461 as well as the conquest of the central Anatolian principality of Karaman, following a decisive defeat of the Aqqoyunlu sovereign of Iran, Uzun Hasan, in 1473.

As will be discussed in more detail in the following section, one of the most important aspects of Mehmed II's achievement and legacy were his centralizing reforms. These entailed the definitive emergence of the main institutions of the central administration, including the Imperial Council headed by the grand vizier, and the financial administration headed by the *defterdar*(s), a more elaborate provincial administration, the further strengthening of the Janissary corps and the *timar*-holding provincial *sipahi* cavalry, and the rise of the *medrese*-trained learned class (the *ulema*) which came to staff the emerging Ottoman judiciary and *medrese* educational system.

---

[17] İnalcık, "The Rise of the Ottoman Empire," 295–297.

Usually seen as a "weaker" ruler,[18] Bayezid II (r. 1481–1512) could not emulate his father's spectacular military successes as his reign was dominated by two major crises: the struggle with his brother Cem, who continued to pose a threat as a viable pretender to the throne in exile until his death in 1495, and the emerging Safavid threat that took definitive shape once Shah Ismail proclaimed the foundation of the Safavid state in 1501. Nevertheless, Bayezid II's rule may be seen as a period of consolidation of Mehmed II's reform legacy. While some of the excesses of his father's reforms that had engendered widespread discontent (such as the confiscation of *waqf* and freehold properties) were amended in favor of a more accommodationist policy line targeting the integration of potentially recalcitrant groups, Bayezid II's regime continued the overall direction of Mehmed II's centralizing reforms and did not hesitate to deal heavy-handedly with perceived overt challenges to Ottoman authority and legitimacy, such as the activities of some antinomian dervish groups (as discussed in Chapter 2). To the extent possible, Bayezid II also continued the territorial consolidation of the Empire, most notably drawing Moldavia firmly into the Ottoman orbit and conquering the fortresses of Akkerman and Kilia (today Ukr. Bilhorod-Dnistrovskyi and Kiliya) in 1484, which further solidified Ottoman control over the Black Sea region, turning it into an "Ottoman lake." Bayezid II's ostensibly cautious approach to the emerging Safavid challenge in the first decade of the sixteenth century brought about his deposition by his son Selim I in 1512.

The reigns of Selim I (1512–20) and Süleyman I (1520–66) are traditionally seen as the period in which the Ottoman imperial bureaucratic regime attained its mature form. This entailed the further growth and consolidation of the Ottoman central and provincial administration under the control of the sultan's patrimonial household, including the further development of the Imperial Council and the scribal service (and the related bureaucratic practices) at the imperial court and the crystallization of the Ottoman provincial territorial-administrative regime; the further strengthening of both the *kapıkulu* "slave" military units (such as the Janissaries and the Cavalry of the Porte) and the provincial *sipahi* cavalry; as well as the consolidation of the *ulema*'s position as a leading prop and agent of the new imperial regime that also helped to articulate Ottoman religio-political ideology. This internal consolidation was paralleled and facilitated by the Ottoman state's successful handling of external

---

[18] For a critique of the perception of Bayezid II as a "softie," see Derin Terzioğlu, "Sufis in the Age of State-Building and Confessionalization," in *The Ottoman World*, ed. Christine Woodhead (London and New York: Routledge, 2011), 93–94.

challenges, most notably Selim I's victory over the Safavids at Chaldiran in 1514 and the 1517 conquest of the Mamluk domains, including Egypt, Syria, Palestine, and the Hijaz (thus making the Ottoman sultan the "protector" of the Holy Cities of Mecca and Medina), as well as Süleyman's subsequent annexations of Iraq (1534–5) and Hungary (1541). By the middle of Süleyman I's reign, the Ottoman polity could confidently claim the status of the premier imperial power in the Islamic world.

Excursus: The Ottoman-Safavid Conflict

The conflict between the Ottoman Empire and the Safavid state (1501–1722) dominated Ottoman (as well as Safavid) politics during the first half of the sixteenth century, before largely subsiding thereafter.[19] The Safavid state had its origins in the Sufi order founded in Ardabil (NW Iran) *c.* 1301 by Sheykh Safi al-Din (1252–1334) which developed as a traditional (and "non-heterodox"), hereditary urban religious association until the mid-fifteenth century, gradually increasing its religio-political influence and socio-economic resources so that in the first half of the fifteenth century the current head of the order, Sheykh Ibrahim (in office, 1429–47), was perceived by contemporary observers as the "lord of Ardabil" and had the appearance of a *padişah*.[20] Tensions around the succession of the new sheykh in 1447 led to the expulsion from Ardabil of Junayd, son of Sheykh Ibrahim. Junayd spent years as a wandering warrior-dervish in northwestern Iran (Azerbaijan), northern Syria, and central and eastern Anatolia, developing a militant religio-political movement with prominent messianic and millenarian overtones, including his claims to descent from Ali and to being divine; these claims appear to have been widely accepted by his followers, mostly militant Turcoman nomads with strong "extremist" Shi'ite leanings (*ghuluww*).[21] Junayd also

[19] While the late sixteenth and early seventeenth centuries featured some major Ottoman-Safavid military encounters, such as the wars of 1578–90 and 1603–18, these did not carry the aura of intense religio-political and confessional opposition of the first half of the sixteenth century.

[20] Monika Gronke, *Derwische im Vorhof der Macht: Sozial- und Wirtschaftsgeschichte Nordwestirans im 13. und 14. Jahrhundert* (Stuttgart: Franz Steiner, 1993), 354, 357. See also Michel Mazzaoui, *The Origins of the Ṣafawids: Šīʿism, Ṣūfism, and the Ġulāt* (Wiesbaden: Franz Steiner, 1972), 52–58.

[21] Junayd was the first among the Safavid sheykhs to make clear claims to Alid descent, which strengthened his messianic (*mahdistic*) claims. Both the anti-Safavid Fadlallah b. Ruzbihan Khunji who served under Uzun Hasan's son Sultan Yaqub (r. 1478–90) and Caterino Zeno, the high-profile Venetian ambassador to Uzun Hasan's court in the 1470s, report that Junayd's followers regarded him, as well as his son Haydar, to be divines and/or prophets; V. Minorsky, *Persia in A.D. 1478–1490: An Abridged Translation of Fadlallah b. Ruzbihan Khunji's Tarikh-i 'Alam-Ara-yi Amini* (London: Luzac & Co., 1957), 65–67, hereafter Khunji/Minorsky, *Tarikh*; Caterino Zeno, "Travels in Persia," in *A Narrative of Italian Travels in Persia in the Fifteenth and Sixteenth Centuries*, trans. and ed. Charles Grey, *Works Issued by the Hakluyt Society*, vol. 159 (New York: Burt Franklin, 1878), 43.

attracted the support of the Aqqoyunlu sovereign of Iran Uzun Hasan (r. 1453–78) and accepted his sister in marriage before devoting the last years of his life to *gaza* against infidels (especially Circassians) in the Caucasus, where he met his death in 1460.

Junayd must have built a viable organization, as the movement continued to expand under the (initially formal) leadership of his son Haydar, born just after the former's death; Haydar took control of Ardabil in 1470 with Uzun Hasan's support and accepted the latter's daughter in marriage.[22] In the 1480s, he would head three major *gaza* campaigns against Christian-populated territories in the Caucasus, on the last of which, in 1488, he met his death, much like his father had.

It was Haydar's son Ismail (b. 1487) who, emerging from the Aqqoyunlu civil war in the 1490s with dual claims to legitimacy – as both the leader of the Safavid organization and Uzun Hasan's direct descendant – proclaimed himself the ruler of a new state in Tabriz in 1501, declaring Twelver Shi'ism the official state religion. Building upon the religious claims of his father and grandfather, but also having received a formal instruction in the Imamite doctrine,[23] Ismail claimed to be the Mahdi and the Hidden Imam (the Twelfth Imam who would reappear from his occultation as an eschatological deliverer at the End of Time).[24] By 1510 he had consolidated his control over Iran, having eliminated rival Aqqoyunlu princes and defeated the Özbeg ruler Muhammad Shaybani Khan to gain control over Khorasan.[25] The transition to Imamite Shi'ism as the official religion of state in Iran (as opposed to the "extremist" variety espoused by his Turcoman followers) provided convincing legitimization of Ismail's claims to religio-political charismatic leadership, but would also facilitate the transformation of the Safavid conquest movement into a fully fledged, sedentary, urban-based state regime.

It is impossible to overestimate the religio-political and military challenge that the new Safavid state posed to Ottoman sovereignty and legitimacy. Ismail's pronounced *mahdistic* appeal, strengthened by the resounding initial success of his regime, presented the numerous,

[22] Khunji/Minorsky, *Tarikh*, 67; Zeno, "Travels in Persia," 44.
[23] See the contemporary anonymous Safavid chronicle translated by E. Denison Ross under the title "The Early Years of Shah Ismail, Founder of the Safavi Dynasty," *Journal of the Royal Asiatic Society* 28 (1896): 287–288.
[24] On Ismail's religio-political claims as reflected in his poetry, see Minorsky's seminal article "The Poetry of Shah Ismail I," *BSOAS* 10/4 (1942): 1006a–1053a.
[25] For a more detailed overview of these events, see John E. Woods, *The Aqquyunlu: Clan, Confederation, Empire: A Study in 15th/9th Century Turco-Iranian Politics* (Minneapolis, MN: Bibliotheca Islamica, 1976), 163–172 and Adel Allouche, *The Origins and Development of the Ottoman-Safavid Conflict (906–962/1500–1555)* (Berlin: Klaus Schwartz, 1983), 85–95.

semi-nomadic Turcomans (and some sedentary populations) in Anatolia with a viable and attractive alternative to the increasingly centralizing, expansionist Ottoman regime[26] Much of Anatolia had been incorporated into the Ottoman domains only recently (and tenuously), or was yet to be conquered. Ismail's new empire also represented the recrudesence of a powerful imperial neighbor to the east, capable of pursuing a distinctly anti-Ottoman mode of relations with Western Christendom, especially with the Republic of Venice, and indeed a number of cooperative efforts between the two sides would be negotiated.[27]

The emerging Safavid threat provoked a comprehensive Ottoman reaction. On the political and military level, the Ottoman-Safavid conflict developed on several planes. First, while Bayezid II had taken some measures against Anatolian sympathizers of the Safavid cause, including deportations to the Morea in the Balkans,[28] his ostensibly cautious approach provoked his son Selim (who closely monitored developments in central and eastern Anatolia as Ottoman prince-governor of Trabzon) to take control by deposing his father in 1512, much as a reaction to a major anti-Ottoman rebellion in Anatolia.[29] Selim I and Süleyman I also led a number of major military campaigns against the Safavids, most notably: in 1514, whereby Selim I dealt a crushing blow to Ismail's army at Chaldiran in eastern Anatolia (followed by the Ottoman annexation of large parts of eastern Anatolia, including the buffer principality of Dülkadır in 1515); the campaign of 1534–5, which ended with the

[26] According to the only existing near-contemporary estimate, given by Venetian *bailos* (ambassadors) in early sixteenth-century Istanbul, around four-fifths of the Anatolian population had Shi'ite leanings; Franz Babinger, "Marino Sanuto's Tagebücher als Qwelle zur Geschichte der Safawijja," in *A Volume of Oriental Studies presented to Edward G. Browne*, ed. T.W. Arnold and Reynold A. Nicholson (Cambridge: Cambridge University Press, 1922), 34–35.

[27] Indeed, early Western European representations of Ismail sought to identify him as the equivalent of Prester John – the enemy of the Turks/Muslims and a friend of the Christians, who could help the latter fend off the Turkish threat; see Palmira Brummett, "The Myth of Shah Ismail Safavi: Political Rhetoric and 'Divine' Kingship," in *Medieval Christian Perceptions of Islam: A Book of Essays*, ed. John Victor Toland (New York and London: Garland Publishing, 1996), 331–359. On Safavid-Venetian relations during this period, see Laurence Lockhart, "European Contacts with Persia, 1350–1736," in *The Cambridge History of Iran*, vol. 6, 373–411.

[28] Hoca Sadeddin, *Tacü't-Tevarih* (Istanbul: Tabhane-i Amire, 1862–3), vol. 2, 127. On other related measures taken by Bayezid II, see *II. Bayezid Dönemine Ait 906/1501 Tarihli Ahkâm Defteri*, ed. Ilhan Şahin and Feridun Emecen (Istanbul: Türk Dünyası Araştırmaları Vakfı, 1994), xxiv–xxv, as well as orders Nos. 27, 71, 111, 281, 330, 453, and 454.

[29] On Selim's accession, see H. Erdem Çıpa, *The Making of Selim: Succession, Legitimacy, and Memory in the Early Modern Ottoman World* (Bloomington, IN: Indiana University Press, 2017), and M. Çağatay Uluçay, "Yavuz Sultan Selim Nasıl Padişah Oldu?," *TD* 6, no. 9 (1954): 53–90, 7, no. 10 (1954): 117–142, and 8, nos. 11–12 (1955): 185–200.

Ottoman conquest of Iraq; as well as the more inconclusive campaigns of 1548–9 and 1553–4, the latter leading to the Treaty of Amasya (1555) that ended Safavid-Ottoman hostilities for more than two decades.

Direct military confrontations were paralleled by (and interacted with) Ottoman mass persecutions of perceived Safavid sympathizers on Ottoman soil in the context of a series of anti-Ottoman rebellions in Ottoman Anatolia.[30] The first of these, led by the son of a prominent Safavid agent who came to be known as Shah Kulu, erupted in the province of Teke (south-central Anatolia) in early 1511, and drew the support of much of the rural population, including some members of the provincial Ottoman military.[31] It took the lives of a governor-general of Anatolia, grand vizier Hadım Ali Pasha, and Shah Kulu himself, before being brutally suppressed by the newly enthroned Selim I in 1512.[32] A number of revolts shook Anatolia in the following two decades – the most important being those of Sheykh Celal in 1519–20, that in Bozok in 1526, and the one led by Kalender Shah in 1527 (all three in central Anatolia), as well as several uprisings in south and southeast Anatolia from 1526 to 1529.[33] While contemporary sources do not point clearly to any substantive Safavid involvement in the organization of these rebellions, most of the participants likely had sympathies for the Safavid cause. Yet, some of these revolts' leaders, such as Sheykh Celal and, before him, Shah Kulu, likely put forward their own claims to *mahdihood*, and Kalender Shah propagated his own divine charisma, claiming descent from Hacı Bektaş Veli (d. 1271), a celebrated saintly figure and the eponym of what eventually became one of the most popular dervish orders in the Ottoman Empire that would espouse some pro-Alid/Shiʻite tenets and integrate "heterodox" groups in both Anatolia and the Balkans.[34] These revolts also highlighted the heightened apocalyptic spirit of the age, resembling in many ways the revolt led by Ismail himself in 1499–1501, while not having the elaborate claims to legitimacy and organizational network of the Safavid revolutionary movement and its leaders.

[30] The best work on these rebellions and the related Ottoman persecutions is Hanna Sohrweide, "Der Sieg der Safaviden in Persien und seine Rückwirkungen auf die Schiiten Anatoliens im 16. Jahrhundert," *Der Islam* 41 (1965): 95–223.

[31] Hoca Sadeddin, *Tacü't-Tevarih*, vol. 2, 163; Sohrweide, "Der Sieg der Safaviden," 147.

[32] The figure of 40,000 people who allegedly became the victims of Selim I's persecutions of Kızılbaş on Ottoman soil in the context of this rebellion is found in contemporary and later Ottoman chronicles; however, on the symbolic meaning of the figure "40" (and by extension, "40,000") in Turco-Islamic tradition, see Abdülkadir Karahan, "İslamiyette 40 Adedi Hakkında," *Türk Dili ve Edebiyatı Dergisi* 4, no. 3 (1951): 265–273.

[33] For a detailed discussion, see Sohrweide, "Der Sieg der Safaviden," 164–186, Remzi Kılıç, *Kanuni Devri Osmanlı-İran Münasebetleri (1520–1566)* (Istanbul: IQ Kültür Sanat Yayıncılık, 2006), 144–151.

[34] Sohrweide, "Der Sieg der Safaviden," 164–186.

The Ottoman-Safavid conflict also engendered a significant redefinition of Ottoman dynastic ideology and religio-political claims. The Safavid state was defined as "heretical" and so were the alleged Safavid supporters on Ottoman soil, justifying the latter's persecution on religious grounds in numerous *fatwa*s and treatises authored by members of the Ottoman *ulema*, with the Ottoman dynasty and state coming to define themselves as guardians of "true Islam."[35]

1.2   The Ottoman Transformation from a Frontier Principality to an Imperial Bureaucratic Regime

The transformation of the Ottoman polity from a frontier principality into a bureaucratic imperial regime has already received considerable attention from a conceptual point of view, while its nature and mechanics still await further research. The most compelling theoretical conceptualization of the phenomenon is perhaps that of Ira Lapidus. In his analysis of tribe and state formation in Islamic history, Lapidus sees tribal chieftaincies and empires as the two major types of political organization, "often on the same territory, competing for power and legitimacy" and points out that "although tribes and empires represent, in one sense, an evolutionary sequence, once the sequence had been fully realized, the issue became one of the construction, deconstruction, and reconstruction of tribal chieftaincies and imperial entities."[36] He presents three basic modalities in the relationship between tribal chieftaincies and empires:

(1) the organization of conquest movements leading to state formation in stateless regions or to the reorganization of states in regions that already have a history of states or empires; (2) the transformation of conquest states into routinized states or imperial governments; and (3) the relation of routinized or institutionalized empires to the tribal populations within and outside their boundaries.[37]

Lapidus distinguishes between two basic types of conquest movements – those organized by religious chieftaincies led by a charismatic religio-political leader, such as the Arab conquest movement of the seventh century as well as those of the Fatimids, the Almoravids, the Almohads, and the Safavids, and conquest movements presided over by warrior chieftaincies "supported by a lineage, clan or *comitatus* – a band of warriors who in turn won the allegiance of other such warrior units and thereby dominated

---

[35] See related discussion in Chapter 7.
[36] Ira Lapidus, "Tribes and State Formation in Islamic History," in *Tribes and State Formation in the Middle East*, ed. Philip S. Khoury and Joseph Kostiner (Berkeley, Los Angeles, and London: University of California Press, 1990), 27–28.
[37] Ibid., 28.

a subject population."[38] In this context, the early Ottoman enterprise can be seen as a version of the second type: like other warrior chieftaincies, it was "conceived in kinship and genealogical terms, but the actual units of social organization were based on loyalty to successful warrior chieftains." However, it had an important religious dimension: "[T]he Sufi *babas* who led warrior bands in the conquest of Asia Minor and the Balkans represented a variant type of warrior chieftaincy with religious appeal."[39]

Such conquest-oriented chieftaincies, usually originating from milieux in which warfare was endemic and led by, or at least harnessing the energies of, nomadic or semi-nomadic warriors, would eventually, when successful, extend to lands populated by settled agricultural and urban populations.[40] This would most often lead to a complementary symbiotic relationship between "aggressive pastoralists" and "vulnerable agriculturalists" (and similarly vulnerable urban craftsmen and traders); the "defeated" groups would "have an interest in dealing with a single authority, which in turn has an interest in their own survival and their taxable prosperity."[41] These chieftaincies would thus emerge as power-sharing partnerships "involving pastoral nomads on the margins of cultivation, semisedentarized (especially agriculturalist) tribesmen, occasionally urban dwellers, and a ruler or chief domiciled in a town or in the countryside."[42]

Expanding conquest-oriented chieftaincies were, however, intrinsically fragile. Not possessing the institutional instrumentarium to handle the increasing population and land resources under their control, they would either disintegrate, usually shortly after the peak of expansion (thus suffering an "Ibn Khaldunian apocalypse"), or would manage to meet the need to centralize authority by evolving into fully fledged imperial bureaucratic states.[43]

The most important aspects of such a transition from a conquest-oriented chieftaincy to a routinized imperial state would be the replacement of nomadic warriors by more reliable and dependent client or slave forces (the latter being the so-called "*mamluk* option"),[44] the growth of a

[38] Ibid., 29.
[39] Ibid., 33.
[40] Philip Khoury and Joseph Kostiner, "Introduction: Tribes and the Complexities of State Formation in the Middle East," in *Tribes and State Formation in the Middle East*, 8; Allen Johnson and Timothy Earle, *The Evolution of Human Societies: From Foraging Group to Agrarian State* (Stanford, CA: Stanford University Press, 1987), 21–22.
[41] Ernest Gellner, "Tribalism and the State in the Middle East," in *Tribes and State Formation in the Middle East*, 111–112.
[42] Khoury and Kostiner, "Introduction," 8.
[43] Ibid., 10–12.
[44] On the "*mamluk* option" see Gellner, "Tribalism and the State," 113–114, and Patricia Crone, *Slaves on Horses: The Evolution of the Islamic Polity* (Cambridge: Cambridge University Press, 1980).

bureaucracy whose administrative-scribal cadres were commonly drawn from the conquered sedentary populations, a change in the concept of the ruler and the principles by which his rule was legitimized,[45] as well as the rise of a high-cultural, "scriptural" religion[46] whose clerisy would participate in the formulation of imperial ideology (and often in bureaucratic institutions).

Once routinized imperial bureaucratic regimes are essentially established – whereby the largely informal, oral transmission-based authority of the chief that relied on the personal loyalty and solidarity of his followers is replaced by the formal, impersonal authority of the imperial bureaucratic state, maintained by highly differentiated and specialized administrative institutions (as well as armed forces) whose main medium of communication is written documentation – the state would strive to limit the freedom and mobility of tribal pastoral nomads.[47] This could happen by pushing them out of the domains of the state, or making them accept the sovereignty of the state without immediately and dramatically affecting their lifestyle and subsistence patterns. The bureaucratic imperial state could allow some degree of autonomy to tribes while recognizing (pro-actively) or "appointing" some tribal chiefs as such and demanding military service from them (and their tribes); it could also co-opt pastoral nomads in smaller groups by exacting from them military or other (e.g. logistic) services – usually providing pay or tax privileges to increase their dependence.[48] The most radical mode of incorporating tribal pastoral nomads within an imperial bureaucratic regime was their sedentarization. This end could be achieved by regulating and limiting nomads' transhumance routes and/or increasing their tax burden, thus making pastoral nomadism an increasingly less feasible subsistence pattern, or through support for infrastructural projects (e.g. irrigation systems) which would make agriculture a more attractive economic alternative. Importantly, successful sedentarization depended on the nomads' migration into ecological zones that favored agriculture.[49]

However, the pre-modern imperial state was hardly able to completely incorporate tribal pastoral nomads into its structures. Resistance and protest to such incorporation and "taming" could take various forms: attempts

[45] Lapidus, "Tribes and State Formation in Islamic History," 34–36.

[46] As opposed to the "popular," often "undisciplined" religiosity espoused by tribal nomadic groups.

[47] Rıza Yıldırım, "Turkomans Between Two Empires: The Origins of the Qizilbash Identity in Anatolia (1447–1514)," Ph.D. diss., Bilkent University, 2008, 47–49.

[48] On different forms of pastoral nomads' submission to and dependence on sedentary societies, see Anatoly Khazanov, *Nomads and the Outside World*, 2nd edn. (Madison, WI: University of Wisconsin Press, 1994), 212–221.

[49] Ibid., 198–202.

at the preservation of autonomy on the part of "quasi-aristocratic" families of (semi-) nomadic origin, migration and evasion of taxation by tribal pastoral (semi-) nomads of humbler status, open revolt against the centralizing state which might also favor the cause of another polity that could provide an "alternative" (e.g. as the Safavid state did in early sixteenth-century Ottoman Anatolia), or an insurrection that could lead to the emergence of a new polity, such as the First Saudi State in 1744.[50]

The model outlined above is largely useful with regard to the Ottoman polity through the mid-sixteenth century. Emerging at the turn of the fourteenth century (as one of a number of similar polities) in a milieu characterized by weakened statehood, the Ottomans made the transition from a warrior chieftaincy or a frontier proto-state to an imperial bureaucratic regime. Lindner has demonstrated that the migration of the "tribe of Osman" (understood above all in political terms) to Bithynia (NW Anatolia) – an area in an ecological zone that favored agriculture over pastoral nomadism – conditioned Osman's so-called tribe's gradual sedentarization, which, in turn, triggered a process of transformation that featured most of the elements of transition from warrior chieftaincy to bureaucratic empire as outlined above,[51] during which the Ottomans could learn from well-established examples such as the Seljukid, Byzantine, and Ilkhanid state traditions.[52] As the Ottoman polity expanded to include sedentary populations and grew in both territorial size and socio-political and socio-economic complexity, tribal organization proved increasingly inadequate.[53]

In his innovative interpretation of pre-modern Ottoman history, Baki Tezcan views the Ottoman transformation as one from "feudal kingdom" to "patrimonial empire," with the Ottoman rulers making the transition from being a "marcher-lord" to a "great lord," and finally, to a patrimonial sovereign, "the emperor of his [political] slaves"; conquest was a political necessity for the Ottomans, as it could guarantee the dynasty's survival and success vis-à-vis competing Turcoman dynastic enterprises in the early Ottoman centuries.[54]

---

[50] Lapidus, "Tribes and State Formation in Islamic History," 38–44; Yıldırım, "Turkomans," 129–149.

[51] Lindner, *Nomads and Ottomans*, 29–34.

[52] Cemal Kafadar has argued that in comparison to all the contemporary Turcoman principalities that emerged as "heirs to the political culture of Seljukid Anatolia ... the Ottomans were much more experimental in reshaping it to need, much more creative in their bricolage of different traditions, be they Turkic, Islamic, or Byzantine," *Between Two Worlds*, 121.

[53] Lindner, *Nomads and Ottomans*, 35.

[54] Baki Tezcan, *The Second Ottoman Empire: Political and Social Transformation in the Early Modern World* (New York: Cambridge University Press, 2010), 81–93.

It has been noted that the Ottoman polity exhibited some signs of institutional complexity early in its history[55] – in the 1320s and 1330s the Ottomans were already minting coins and utilizing the services of scribal cadres versed in the tradition of sedentary states.[56] Orhan had members of the non-tribal *yaya* infantry corps fighting on his side at the Battle of Pelekanon in 1329.[57] In Kafadar's view it was "the crisis of the 1360s and the 1370s" which may have induced the introduction of further institutional features that would become part and parcel of the later Ottoman imperial order: the establishment of the Janissary corps (initially staffed by slaves acquired in warfare), the appointment of the first *kadı ʿasker* (military judge) as well as the drawing into Ottoman service of members of established families of scholar-administrators such as Çandarlı Kara Halil Pasha who served Murad I as vizier whereby "three generations of this family monopolized top offices of the administration and played a major role in the building of sophisticated structures of governing that buttressed the centralizing tendency of the Ottoman polity."[58] To this one should add the development of the *timar* institution and the provincial *sipahi* cavalry (as well as the provincial tax surveys) whose importance to Ottoman centralization has sometimes been left in the shadow of the emergence of the Janissary corps and the introduction of the *devshirme* levy, while they played an instrumental role in projecting Ottoman control in the provinces. *Timar*-holding *sipahi*s were not only participants in military campaigns, but also served as representatives of state authority at the provincial (including village) level.[59]

---

[55] The following comments on aspects of Ottoman centralization up to 1453 are not meant to be exhaustive. For a more detailed analysis, see Kafadar, *Between Two Worlds*, 118–150, and especially Yıldırım, "Turkomans," 87–120.

[56] Kafadar, *Between Two Worlds*, 123; Lowry, *The Nature of the Early Ottoman State*, 73–78.

[57] Feridun Emecen, "Yaya ve Müsellem," in *TDVİA*, vol. 43, 354; Lindner, *Nomads and Ottomans*, 31–32.

[58] Kafadar, *Between Two Worlds*, 138–143; Kafadar suggests that the crisis of the 1360s and 1370s was related to the Ottomans' temporary loss of Gallipoli, which may have loosened the bonds between the dynasty and the conquering *gazi*s in Thrace who had been originally commissioned by the Ottoman dynasty, but could have started entertaining notions of independence.

[59] It is hard to date precisely the visible functional emergence of the *timar* system, the *sipahi* cavalry, and the provincial tax surveys (*vilayet tahriri*). İnalcık points to traces of the *timar* system as early as in the reign of Orhan (1324–52). The oldest preserved *timar* register from 1430–1 contains clear signs of earlier registrations of *timar*-holding *sipahi*s (and the related sources of tax income, i.e. mostly peasant taxpayers and cultivated land) and attests that the *timar* system had certainly acquired a visibly "developed" form at the time of the register's composition; see İnalcık, "Timar," in *EI*²; ibid. (ed.), *Hicrî 835 Tarihli Sûret-i Defter-i Sancak-ı Arvanid* (Ankara: Türk Tarih Kurumu, 1954), xi–xxxvi; and ibid., "Ottoman Methods of Conquest," 109.

By the late fourteenth century, the Ottoman ruler could style himself *sultanu'r-Rum* ("Sultan of Anatolia," in this context)[60] and Murad II would experiment with titles such as *sultanu'l-Islam ve'l-müslimin* ("Sultan of Islam and the Muslims") as of 1430–1,[61] and *khalifat rabb al-'alemin* ("the Caliph of the Lord of the Worlds") and *ẓill Allah fi'l-arḍ* ("the Shadow of God on Earth") in 1444.[62]

While various aspects of the Ottoman "centralizing thrust"[63] manifested themselves from the 1320s onwards, the conquest of Constantinople and Mehmed II's mature reign (1451–81) are "usually taken as the turning point that finally transformed the Ottoman state from a frontier polity, in which the sultan was only 'first among equals,' into a centralized bureaucratic empire with an absolutist ethos."[64] Derin Terzioğlu has argued that: "[I]n many ways... it fell to Mehmed's much less charismatic son and successor Bayezid II (r. 1481–1512) to sort out the institutional arrangements that would sustain this newly forged empire."[65] Such an argument should be qualified in turn as both the "institutional arrangements" and their practical application, including the strength of Ottoman central authority in the provinces, continued to evolve after Bayezid II's death, well into, and even after, Süleyman I's reign. Kaya Şahin has emphasized the central importance of the first half of the sixteenth century for Ottoman empire-building,[66] and Cornell Fleischer has demonstrated the limits of Ottoman central authority in provincial settings in the early 1520s,[67] while also commenting on Süleyman I's reign that "in the spheres of intellectual and cultural life and social and administrative structuring, the period is more remarkable for rapid change, for innovation that is often extreme, and for an experimentation that often verges on the *ad hoc*."[68]

---

[60] See Halil İnalcık, "Osmanlı Sultanlarının Unvanları (Titülatür) ve Egemenlik Kavramı," *Doğu Batı. Makaleler II* (Ankara: Doğu Batı Yayınları, 2008), 188–189.

[61] This title is found at the very beginning of the tax register referred to above in fn. 59.

[62] The document in which these titles are used is a slave manumission deed (*azadname*) dated the last ten days of Şa'ban, AH 848 (mid-December, AD 1444), a month after the Battle of Varna, TSMA E. 5566, published by İnalcık in *Fatih Devri Üzerinde Tetkikler ve Vesikalar* (Ankara: Türk Tarih Kurumu, 1954), 215–217, facsimile on plate No. 6.

[63] Kafadar, *Between Two Worlds*, 121.

[64] Terzioğlu, "Sufis," 92. On the limitations of Mehmed II's reforms, see also Oktay Özel, "Limits of the Almighty: Mehmed II's 'Land Reform' Revisited," *JESHO* 42, no. 2 (1999): 226–246.

[65] Terzioğlu, "Sufis," 92.

[66] Şahin, *Empire and Power in the Reign of Süleyman*, 10–11.

[67] Cornell Fleischer, "On Gender and Servitude, c. 1520: Two Petitions of the Kul Kızı of Bergama to Sultan Süleyman," unpublished paper.

[68] Cornell Fleischer, "The Lawgiver as Messiah: The Making of the Imperial Image in the Reign of Süleyman," in *Soliman le Magnifique et son temps*, ed. Gilles Veinstein (Paris: Documentation Française, 1992), 159.

Thus Mehmed II's reign should not be seen as the end of transition from frontier polity to centralized empire, but rather a period that set the mechanisms that would govern the further transformation and consolidation of the Ottoman imperial regime – a process that would extend at least to the mid-sixteenth century.

1.3   The Formation of Muslim Communities in the Ottoman Balkans in Historiography and Memory*

The presence of sizable Muslim communities is indisputably one of the most prominent aspects of the Ottoman legacy in today's Balkans. While Ottoman rule in Anatolia, and later in the greater part of the Middle East, may be seen as a continuation and development of already existing political, cultural, and religious traditions, the centuries of Ottoman dominance in the predominantly Orthodox Christian Balkans have often been viewed as a period of unseen oppression and a major "civilizational change" which ran counter to the region's traditions and acted as a potent impediment to its "natural" development and overall progress.[69] Hence, it should not be seen as a surprise that Christian majorities in the modern Balkan nation-states that formed in the nineteenth and early twentieth centuries have continuously expressed negative attitudes toward the Muslim communities in their countries, often seeing them as "foreign bodies" formed mostly by descendants of local converts to Islam – historical "traitors" or "victims" of violent campaigns of forced conversion to Islam and ethno-linguistic assimilation directed by the Ottoman state.[70]

The historiography of the formation of Muslim communities in the Ottoman Balkans has, until recently, been dominated by the nationalist historiographies of the Ottoman successor states in the Balkans and the Republic of Turkey. The majority of the history writing on Muslim

---

[*] This section is a revised and abridged version of pages 31–43 in my "Emergence and Historical Development of Muslim Communities in the Ottoman Balkans: Historical and Historiographical Remarks," in *Beyond Mosque, Church and State: Alternative Narratives of the Nation in the Balkans*, ed. Theodora Dragostinova and Yana Hashamova (Budapest and New York: Central European University Press, 2016), 31–56.

[69] Such attitudes have been ubiquitous in nationalist Balkan historiographies and public opinion. For the purposes of the present discussion, it suffices to give the titles of two works by prominent Bulgarian scholars: Ivan Snegarov, *Turskoto vladichestvo – prechka za kulturnoto razvitie na bâlgarskiia narod i drugite balkanski narodi* (The Turkish Rule: An Impediment to the Cultural Development of the Bulgarian and the Other Balkan Peoples) (Sofia: BAN, 1958) and Petâr Petrov, *Po sledite na nasilieto* (On the Traces of Violence), 2 vols. (Sofia: Nauka i Izkustvo, 1987).

[70] Such notions have been employed to justify the harsh treatment of Balkan Muslims in the modern age, and even their "de-Islamization," a relevant example being the Bulgarian "Revival Process" in the 1980s.

communities in the peninsula has to be placed in the context of the development of politicized, mythical representations of the region's past as part of the forging of modern Balkan national identities, the history of Muslim communities in the Ottoman Balkans being situated within the general treatment of the Ottoman period and its legacy.

Mythicized representations in scholarly works have trickled down to dominate school textbooks and inform popular perceptions of Ottoman rule and its historical impact. In the national historiographies of the three largest Balkan countries dominated by Orthodox Christian majorities – Greece, Bulgaria, and Serbia – Ottoman rule has been traditionally conceptualized as an era of oppression, humiliation, and resistance, whereby the "glorious" pre-Ottoman statehood and cultural traditions of these respective "nations" were suppressed by the "aggressive" and "culturally inferior" Ottomans. The centuries of Ottoman rule proved to be a test of the resilience of these "nations," which re-emerged in the age of "national revival" in the late eighteenth and nineteenth centuries. While Ottoman rule in the Balkans has usually not been conceptualized as colonial domination in the "modern" (or rather, "early modern") sense associated with European trans-oceanic colonization,[71] Balkan nationalist master narratives of Ottoman rule resemble post-colonial representations of European colonial rule in many non-Western nationalist historiographies in their rendering Ottoman domination as the middle element in a tripartite periodization of national history. Such a periodization usually features a glorious ancient (or "classical") past, a "dark" middle period of foreign domination, and an era of "national revival" in which the shackles of foreign oppression are broken and the "nation" re-emerges, drawing on both its ancient glory and its historical resilience to foreign rule.[72]

In terms of myth typology, the most important generic myth type in Balkan nationalist historiographies regarding Ottoman rule is that of *martyrium*, which, as Pål Kolstø has argued, represents a "cluster of myths … that focus on the defeat and victimization of the group," whereby "the nation is presented as the perennial target of discrimination and persecution," it "functions as a boundary-defining myth" and invests the oppressed groups with the aura of moral superiority vis-à-vis their oppressors.[73] A complementary myth is that of the perennial resistance of

[71] Charles Verlinden, *The Beginnings of Modern Colonization: Eleven Essays with an Introduction*, trans. Yvonne Freccero (Ithaca, NY: Cornell University Press, 1970), ix–xxi.

[72] Partha Chatterjee, *The Nation and Its Fragments: Colonial and Postcolonial Histories* (Princeton, NJ: Princeton University Press, 1993), 102.

[73] Pål Kolstø, "Introduction: Assessing the Role of Historical Myths in Modern Society," in *Myths and Boundaries in South-Eastern Europe*, ed. Pål Kolstø (London: Hurst & Company, 2005), 21.

the Balkan Christians who actively engaged in military activities aimed at driving out the Ottoman (usually conceptualized as "Turkish") aggressors from the very first decades of Ottoman involvement in the Balkans. Staunch resistance to conversion (to Islam) under the leadership of the Orthodox Church was a passive counterpart of armed resistance, which preserved not only religious but also "national" identities.[74]

Anti-Ottoman mythicized historical narratives have tended to minimize the importance of Turcoman colonization in the Balkans to both counter modern Turkish irredentist myths and open the door for the possible (re-) assimilation (or "(re-) integration") of Muslim communities into the fold of modern Balkan Christian nations. In parts of the Balkans such as Bosnia, with its polymorphic cultural and political reality, the Ottoman past and the formation of Muslim communities have often found their place in competing parallel mythicized narratives which accord varying emphases on historical continuity and discontinuity and pronounce differing historical judgments regarding the Ottoman legacy in general as well as demographic change, particularly in relation to one's modern ethno-national identity.[75] In their presentations of Ottoman rule in the Balkans, Turkish historians have traditionally emphasized the notions of Ottoman paternalistic tolerance, a just and stable Ottoman socio-political order, and the autonomy of non-Muslim religious communities, even though the latter were discriminated vis-à-vis Ottoman Muslims.[76]

Balkan national historiographies have paid uneven attention to the processes of Turcoman colonization, conversion to Islam, ethno-religious change, and the Islamization of cultural space in the early modern Ottoman Balkans. Comparing Albanian and Bulgarian national historiographies, for example, scholars in Bulgaria (with its 12 percent-strong Muslim minority) have produced scores of works on ethno-religious change in the Ottoman period, usually based on limited Ottoman archival material and sometimes drawing on highly dubious "domestic sources," while conversion to Islam in Albania, which ultimately transformed the country into a predominantly Muslim one, has not attracted comparable attention on the part of Albanian scholars.[77] This can be largely attributed to the different role that Islam played in the nation-building of different modern Balkan states.

---

[74] George Arnakis, "The Role of Religion in the Development of Balkan Nationalism," in *The Balkans in Transition: Essays on the Development of Balkan Life and Politics since the Eighteenth Century*, ed. Charles and Barbara Jelavich (Berkeley, CA: University of California Press, 1963), 115–144, esp. 116–117, 126–133.

[75] Srećko Džaja, "Bosnian Historical Reality and Its Reflection in Myth," in *Myths and Boundaries in South-Eastern Europe*, 105–107.

[76] İnalcık, *Classical Age*, 7.

[77] One exception is Selami Pulaha, *Aspects de démographie historique de contrées albanaises pendant les XVe–XVIe siècles* (Tirana: 8 Nëntori, 1984).

Of the regions that host the most compact and numerically significant Muslim communities in the modern Balkans – Albania, Kosovo, Bosnia, Thrace, parts of Macedonia, the Rhodope Mountains, and northeastern Bulgaria (including Deliorman, Gerlovo, and Dobrudja) – only the case of Bosnian Islamization may be said to have been extensively researched and discussed in a relatively detached manner, largely thanks to the efforts of numerous outstanding representatives of modern Bosnian historiography.[78] Several modern Macedonian historians have also made substantial and meaningful contributions to the study of ethno-religious change and the development of Islamic culture in the lands of modern Macedonia.[79] Modern Turkish historiography, while much better grounded in terms of access to and usage of Ottoman primary sources, has produced a fairly limited amount of work on the formation of Muslim communities in the Balkans.

Lastly, for a variety of reasons, including the scarcity of adequately trained specialists and restricted access to archival and manuscript collections during the Cold War era, western scholars have also shown limited attention to the study of Muslim communities in the Ottoman Balkans. Their treatments have sometimes followed a distinctly "enlightening" approach,[80] exerting efforts to "correct" the distortions of well-established politico-historical myths in Balkan nationalist historiographies. This tendency has strengthened since the end of the Cold War, when not only more scholars from Western Europe and North America, but also a number of researchers within the Balkans have produced works that have parted with the traditional mythicizing approaches of Balkan nationalist historiographies.[81] Some of these works have alternatively followed a functionalist approach in treating myth-making as an inevitable

---

[78] Adem Handžić, "O islamizaciji u sjeveroistočnoj Bosni u XV i XVI vijeku," *POF* 16–17 (1966–1967): 5–48; M. Hadžijahić, "Turska komponenta u etnogenezi bosanskih muslimana," *Pregled* 18 (1966): 405–502; ibid., "Sinkretistički elementi u islamu u Bosni i Hercegovini," *POF* 28–29 (1978-9): 301–329; Nedim Filipović, "Napomene o islamizaciji u Bosni i Hercegovini u XV vijeku," *Godišnjak Akademije Nauka i Umjetnosti Bosne i Hercegovine 7, Centar na Balkanološka Ispitivanija* 5 (1970): 141–167; Srećko Džaja, *Konfessionalität und Nationalität Bosniens und der Herzegovina. Vorempanzipatorische Phase, 1463–1804* (Munich: Oldenborg, 1984).

[79] Aleksandar Stojanovski, *Gradovite na Makedonija od krajot na XIV do XVII vek: Demografski Proučuvanja* (Skopje: Zavod za Unapreduvanje na Stopanstvoto vo SRM "Samoupravna Praktika," 1981); Metodija Sokoloski, "Islamizacija u Makedoniji u XV i XVI veku," *IČ* 22 (1975): 75–89; Nijazi Limanoski, *Islamizacijata i etničkite promeni vo Makedonija* (Skopje: Makedonska Kniga, 1993).

[80] Kolstø, "Introduction," 2.

[81] A good example is Bulgarian post-Cold War Ottomanist historiography, which, being influenced by the process of democratization as well as eased access to archival and manuscript collections, has produced a number of studies that question some well-ingrained theses on the period of Ottoman rule in Bulgaria.

element of human existence[82] and emphasizing the impact such myths had on strengthening the coherence of emerging Balkan nations in the nineteenth and twentieth centuries.[83]

1.3.1 Major Theories of the Formation and Development of Muslim Communities in the Ottoman Balkans

As outlined above, most major scholarly arguments regarding the formation of Muslim communities in the Balkans have been heavily influenced by modern political concerns, often taking extreme forms emanating from widely diverging conceptualizations of Ottoman rule in the Balkans, seen by some as a "catastrophe" and by others as a "blessing."[84] A major division has developed around the relative emphasis on the role of Turcoman Muslim colonization of Anatolian provenance and conversion to Islam of local Balkan populations as the major factors in ethnoreligious change. The former has been heavily emphasized by Turkish scholars[85] while conversion to Islam has been favored by Balkan scholars, whereby yet another division has developed – between the proponents of forcible conversion directed by the Ottoman state (either through brute force, or via "indirect pressure") and voluntary conversion influenced by a number of factors, such as the quest for social and economic advancement, but also in the context of the growth of syncretic tendencies in the development of Balkan Islam.

   Conversion-Oriented Explanations By far the most extreme "theory" explaining the formation of Muslim communities in the Ottoman Balkans focuses on "conversion by the sword." Favored by a number of Balkan historians and still enjoying widespread popular reception, it views the formation of Muslim communities as the result of a series of state-organized punitive actions, whereby the Ottoman state aimed

[82] Kolstø, "Introduction," 2–3.
[83] Maria Todorova, "Conversion to Islam as a Trope in Bulgarian Historiography, Fiction and Film," in *Balkan Identities: Nation and Memory*, ed. Maria Todorova (New York: New York University Press, 2004), 129–157.
[84] Machiel Kiel, *Art and Society in Bulgaria in the Turkish Period* (Assen: Van Gorcum, 1985), 33–55; Anton Minkov, *Conversion to Islam in the Balkans: Kisve Bahası Petitions and Ottoman Social Life, 1670–1730* (Leiden: Brill, 2004), 1–8.
[85] Most notably Ömer Lütfi Barkan, "Osmanlı İmparatorluğunda Bir İskân ve Kolonizasyon Metodu Olarak Vakıflar ve Temlikler," *VD* 2 (1942): 279–386 (hereafter "Vakıflar ve Temlikler") and "Osmanlı İmparatorluğunda Bir İskân ve Kolonizasyon Metodu Olarak Sürgünler," *İÜİFM* 11 (1949–50): 524–69; 13 (1951–2): 56–78; 17 (1953–4): 209–37 (hereafter "Sürgünler"); M.T. Gökbilgin, *Rumeli'de Yürükler, Tatarlar ve Evlâd-ı Fâtihan* (Istanbul: Istanbul Üniversitesi Edebiyat Fakültesi Yayınları, 1957); Feridun Emecen, Yusuf Halaçoğlu, and İlhan Şahin, "Turkish Settlements in Rumelia (Bulgaria) in the 15th and 16th Centuries: Town and Village Population," *IJTS* 4 (1990): 23–40. To a lesser degree, İnalcık, "Ottoman Methods of Conquest."

at the conversion of large (Christian) population groups to strengthen its authority. This narrative jibes with general popular perceptions of Ottoman rule as oppressive and intolerant. It has been emphasized above all by Bulgarian scholars[86] who have traditionally resorted to the use of a small number of "domestic Slavic sources,"[87] now known to be nineteenth- and early twentieth-century fabrications,[88] that tell the story of violent conversions carried out by Ottoman troops, mostly in the Rhodope Mountains, in the sixteenth and seventeenth centuries. This trope has been used more generally to explain the presence of Muslim communities in the wider Balkans. The *devshirme* (child-levy) has also often been interwoven within this framework as a coordinated effort on the part of the Ottoman state to weaken non-Muslim communities on the way to the further Islamization of the region.[89] The conceptualization of Christian neo-martyrs as heroes who died for their faith resisting forced conversion to Islam has been another important trope that became part and parcel of Balkan historical consciousness – regardless of the fact that the mentioned neo-martyrs were usually recent converts who had apostatized.[90]

Another popular historiographical perception features the notion of "indirect pressure" – by imposing a higher tax burden on non-Muslims and usually denying them access to political and administrative offices, the Ottoman state, the argument goes, purposefully created conditions

---

[86] Bistra Cvetkova, *Geroichnata sâprotiva na bâlgarite protiv turskoto nashestvie* (The Heroic Resistance of the Bulgarians against the Turkish Invasion) (Sofia: Narodna Prosveta, 1960); Petâr Petrov, *Asimilatsionnata politika na turskite zavoevateli* (The Assimilatory Policy of the Turkish Conquerors) (Sofia: Izdatelstvo na Bâlgarskata Komunisticheska Partiia, 1964); Georgi Neshev, "Die bulgarische Kultur und die osmanische Eroberung," *Bulgarian Historical Review* 2 (1974): 46–61.

[87] The most important among these "domestic sources" are the so-called *Belovo Chronicle*, the *Batkun Chronicle*, Metodi Draginov's *Chronicle*, and the *Historical Notebook*, all of them "discovered" and published by patriotic Bulgarians in the nineteenth and early twentieth centuries. While these sources were supposedly written by contemporary observers of the "tragic events" in the seventeenth and eighteenth centuries, the originals were claimed to have been "lost" in one way or another. The published texts contain gross mistakes, such as the wrong names of Ottoman sultans. The texts of all these seemingly fabricated chronicles may be found in a collection of narrative sources on Bulgarian history, *Pisakhme da se znae* (*We Wrote it Down, So That It Be Known*), ed. V. Nachev and N. Fermandzhiev (Sofia: Izdatelstvo na Otechestveniia Front, 1984).

[88] Iliia Todorov, "Letopisniiat razkaz na Pop Metodi Draginov," *Starobâlgarska Literatura* 16 (1984): 62–75; Antonina Zhelyazkova, "The Problem of the Authenticity of Some Domestic Sources, Deeply Rooted in Bulgarian Historiography," *Études Balkaniques* 4 (1990): 105–111.

[89] Arnakis, "The Role of Religion in the Development of Balkan Nationalism," 120–124.

[90] The issue has most recently been critically evaluated by Tijana Krstić, *Contested Conversions to Islam: Narratives of Religious Change in the Early Modern Ottoman Empire* (Stanford, CA: Stanford University Press, 2011), 121–164.

that would reduce Balkan non-Muslims to gradually accepting Islam.[91] However, these forms of discrimination against non-Muslims were not devised by the Ottomans and have their roots in early Islamic history[92]. They could hardly produce visible results within a reasonable period of time, and there are no significant traces of any such "planning" in Ottoman sources. While the political and socio-economic discrimination against religious minorities was an integral feature of pre-modern Islamic societies (with parallels elsewhere, including medieval and early modern Europe), it was not a systematic policy meant to induce non-Muslims to convert. Such conceptualizations of conversion to Islam in the Ottoman Balkans as a result of direct or indirect pressure tend to attribute to the pre-modern Ottomans a nation-state-like proclivity to homogenize society, as well as social and cultural space.

Other scholars have viewed conversion to Islam above all as a natural voluntary choice, motivated by the quest for socio-economic advancement and facilitated by the relative ease with which one might convert to Islam. Conversion, therefore, was a gradual process that developed as a result of the interaction between the presence of the Ottoman state and incoming settlers from Anatolia and the specific political, socio-economic, and religio-cultural conditions in different parts of the Balkans.[93] This

[91] Nikolai Todorov, "Za demografskoto sâstoyanie na balkanskiia poluostrov prez XVI–XVI vek," *Godishnik na Sofiiskiia Universitet – Filosofsko-istoricheski Fakultet,* 52 (1959): 193–225 and *The Balkan City: Socio-Economic and Demographic Development, 1400–1900,* trans. P. Sugar (Seattle, WA: University of Washington Press, 1983), 47–51; Maria Todorova, "Identity (Trans)Formation among Bulgarian Muslims," in *The Myth of "Ethnic Conflict": Politics, Economics, and "Cultural"Violence,* ed. B. Crawford and R. Lipschutz (Berkeley, CA: University of California at Berkeley, International and Area Studies, 1998), 473. This argument has also been developed by Karl Binswanger in his *Untersuchungen zum Status der Nichtmuslime im Osmanischen Reich des 16. Jahrhunderts: mit einer Neudefinition des Begriffes "Dhimma"* (Munich: R. Trofenik, 1977).
[92] Whereby "[R]eading the relevant material in the Muslim sources one has frequently the impression that the humiliation of the unbeliever is more important than his conversion," Yohanan Friedmann, *Tolerance and Coercion in Islam: Interfaith Relations in the Muslim Tradition* (Cambridge: Cambridge University Press, 2003), 37.
[93] Kiel, *Art and Society,* ibid., "Tatar Pazarcık. The Development of an Ottoman Town in Central Bulgaria or the Story of How the Bulgarians Conquered Upper Thrace without Firing a Shot," in *Das Osmanische Reich in seinen Archivalien und Croniken, Nejat Göyünç zu ehren,* ed. Klaus Kreiser and Christoph Neumann (Istanbul: In Kommission bei Franz Steiner Verlag, Stuttgart, 1997), 31–67; "Razprostranenie na Isliama v balgarskoto selo prez osmanskata epoha (15‑18 V.): kolonizatsiia i isliamizatsiia," in *Miusiulumanskata kultura po bâlgarskite zemi,* vol.1, ed. R. Gradeva and S. Ivanova (Sofia: IMIR, 1998), 56–126; "The Ottoman Imperial Registers: Central Greece and Northern Bulgaria in 15th–19th Century: The Demographic Development of the Two Areas Compared," in *Reconstructing Past Population Trends in Mediterranean Europe (3000 B.C.–A.D. 1800),* ed. John Bintliff and Kostas Sbonias (Oxford: Oxbow, 1999), 195–218; Evgeni Radushev, *Pomatsite: Khristianstvo i Isliam v zapadnite Rodopi s dolinata na reka Mesta, XV – 30-te godini na XVIII-ti vek,* 2 vols. (Sofia: NBKM, 2005); Minkov, *Conversion to Islam.*

explanation of conversion to Islam[94] recalls Nock's notion of "adhesion" (as differentiated from "conversion," which he defines as the definite crossing of spiritual boundaries), which relates to more pragmatic attempts at achieving a status change conditioned by "natural needs."[95] Scholars working in this vein have also highlighted the role of Islamic institutions (especially urban charitable trusts – *waqf*s) in creating a proper milieu for Balkan non-Muslims' conversion to Islam.

Finally, some scholars have stressed the proselytizing role of non-state actors, especially dervishes, and the related syncretic practices that included dual worship sites and the mingling of local pre-Ottoman religious traditions with practices and beliefs associated with popular Islam.[96]

Colonization-Oriented Conceptualizations Turcoman colonization as the major explanation of the formation of Balkan Muslim communities has been emphasized above all by Turkish scholars who have accordingly tended to downplay the impact of conversion to Islam.[97] Ö.L. Barkan has highlighted the role of "colonizing dervishes" in sparsely populated areas of the Balkans that led to the emergence of hundreds of new Turcoman villages with the active direction and support of the Ottoman state.[98] He has also stressed the importance of forced deportations (*sürgün*) whereby the Ottoman state would resettle Turcoman populations from Anatolia to the Balkans in order to ease population pressure in Anatolia and/or to uproot politically troublesome populations that did or could pose a challenge to Ottoman authority. Such interpretations have been duly criticized for their attribution to the Ottoman state of excessive power and the ability to control Turcoman migration and colonization.[99] The

[94] Also featured in Richard W. Bulliet's now classic *Conversion to Islam in the Medieval Period: An Essay in Quantitative History* (Cambridge, MA: Harvard University Press, 1979).

[95] A.D. Nock, *Conversion: The Old and New in Religion from Alexander the Great to Augustine of Hippo* (Oxford: Oxford University Press, 1933), 7–10. See also Jessica Coope's valuable comments on conversion as "a shift to a new cultural and a social identity," rather than "a transformation of the inner self," "Religious and Cultural Conversion to Islam in Ninth-Century Umayyad Cordoba," *Journal of World History* 4 no. 1 (1993): 47.

[96] Frederick W. Hasluck, *Christianity and Islam under the Sultans*, 2 vols. (Oxford: Oxford University Press, 1929); Michel Balivet, "Deux Partisans de la fusion religieuse des chrétiens et des musulmans au XVIe siècle: Le turc Bedreddin de Simavna et le grec Georges de Trebizond," *Byzantina* 10 (1980): 363–396; Ahmet Yaşar Ocak, "Bâzı Menâkıbnâmelere Göre XIII.–XIV. Yüzyıllardaki İhtidâlarda Hederodoks Şeyh ve Dervişlerin Rolü," *OA* 2 (1981): 31–42. On this, see also the relevant discussion in Chapter 7.

[97] Barkan, "Vakıflar ve Temlikler" and "Sürgünler." A more detailed discussion of Barkan's arguments follows in Chapter 2.

[98] Ibid., "Vakıflar ve Temlikler," 279–386.

[99] Zhelyazkova, Antonina, "Islamization in the Balkans as an Historiographical Problem: The Southeast-European Perspective," in *The Ottomans and the Balkans: A Discussion of Historiography*, ed. Fikret Adanir and Suraiya Faroqhi (Leiden, Boston, and Köln: Brill, 2002), 231–232; Tsvetana Georgieva, *Prostranstvo i prostranstva na bâlgarite, XV–XVI vek* (Sofia: IMIR, 1999), 154–155.

assumption that all Anatolian migrants into the Balkans were "pure" Muslim Turks is also problematic, neglecting the issue of ethno-religious assimilation of the non-Muslim populations in Anatolia that dominated the peninsula before the late eleventh century. Gökbilgin has made important contributions to the study of semi-nomadic *yürük* coloniza-tion in the Balkans, again closely associating it with state initiative and control.[100]

1.3.2 Assessment of the Theories on the Formation of Muslim Communities in the Ottoman Balkans

The theories discussed above have been conditioned by both the socio-political and historiographic milieux in which various scholars of the Ottoman Balkans produced their works as well as by the nature of the sources which they utilized. Thus, the use of Ottoman administrative documents (especially Ottoman tax registers), largely dominant in the past several decades, has facilitated the development of arguments favor-ing conversion to Islam in a quest for advancing one's socio-economic status, as well as the role of the state as the major actor in the process of Turcoman colonization in the Balkans. Scholars who have relied mostly on narrative sources, especially on those related to dervish groups, have put forward valuable arguments about the formation of a distinctly "Balkan" Islam that incorporated pre-Ottoman Balkan beliefs and prac-tices and thus significantly facilitated the spread of Islam in the Ottoman Balkans (both in the sense of Islamization of space and individual con-versions to Islam).

I would like to make three major methodological points regarding the study of Muslim communities in the early modern Ottoman Balkans. First, despite the efforts of generations of scholars, much of the exist-ing voluminous Ottoman source material has remained insufficiently studied, or plainly untouched. This is especially true in the case of the seventeenth and eighteenth centuries, which likely saw an upsurge in the numbers of converts in most of the Balkans.

Second, the importance of regional differentiation within the peninsula should not be neglected. If one puts aside urban Islamization, one may observe that the most numerous and compact Muslim communities in the early modern Ottoman Balkans formed in specific parts of the peninsula at different times, under different historical conditions, and often due to different factors. Thus, while the Islamization of Bosnia's countryside took place largely in the late fifteenth and sixteenth centuries, the conversion

---

[100] Gökbilgin, *Rumeli'de Yürükler.*

of most of the population in Albania is traditionally assumed to not have taken place before the second half of the seventeenth and the eighteenth centuries, while the larger part of nearby Serbia never experienced the formation of significant Muslim communities, like most of modern western Bulgaria. Along different lines, the initial formation of Muslim communities in the eastern Balkans seems to have been conditioned above all by Turcoman colonization (largely due to the geographic proximity to Anatolia and the nature of the early Ottoman conquests), while conversion to Islam was the dominant factor in the formation of Muslim communities in the western Balkans (most notably in Bosnia and Albania). This also accounts for the fact that Muslim communities in the eastern Balkans are predominantly Turkish-speaking, while those in the western Balkans retained their respective pre-Ottoman languages. In effect, one may speak of a "mosaic of enclaves" dominated by Muslim communities that formed in different ways and in different historical periods.

Third, Islam in the Ottoman Balkans, just as elsewhere, was not a uniform phenomenon – conceptually, doctrinally, or in terms of practice. From the early years of Islamic history a multiplicity of voices and interpretations developed. Unlike in Christendom, for example, there has never been a viable attempt to formulate and enforce a unified statement of doctrine and practice. Indeed, this diversity became part and parcel of the development of Islam. In the Ottoman context one may distinguish between urban and rural Islam, stress the development of Sufi Islam, and point to the rise of practices and beliefs that were considered heretical by the Ottoman state and the *ulema* establishment – especially those associated with antinomian, non-conformist dervish groups.[101] Just as elsewhere on the periphery of the Islamic world, Islamic culture in the Balkans developed as a result of a two-way cross-fertilization – while the region became an integral part of *Pax Islamica*, "Balkan Islam" came to develop its own distinctive regional coloring, a process often referred to as "the indigenization of Islam." It is not only that Balkan Islam integrated local, pre-Ottoman religio-cultural elements, which can be observed, for example, in the emergence of sites of dual (Christian and Muslim) worship (especially dervish saints' mausolea); the Balkans came to be internalized as part of the Ottoman (and Islamic) world in both the emerging "mainstream" Ottoman historiography and in "alternative" narratives reflecting the sensibilities of groups associated with the initial Muslim conquest of the region – Ottoman frontier lords, antinomian dervishes, and semi-nomadic Turcomans.[102] While initially the

---

[101] On these, see the relevant discussions in Chapters 2 and 6.
[102] Krstić, *Contested Conversions*, 42–45.

presence of Islam was much associated with newcomers from Anatolia, by the mid-sixteenth century it had become a culturally internalized part of the Balkan religio-cultural landscape. Local-born Muslims (many of whom with pre-Ottoman Balkan roots) participated in and patronized urban Islamic culture, and the Sufi cult of saints was able to produce its own leading figures – the most prominent example being the sixteenth-century Rum Abdal (later Alevi-Bektashi) saint Demir Baba, born in Deliorman.

It is thus important to be cautious with any generalizations about the formation and historical development of Muslim communities in the early modern Ottoman Balkans. Unfortunately, such generalizations abound in scholarly works, with scholars tending to make arguments about the whole region based on a geographically and typologically limited source base, extending conclusions made about geographically limited areas of inquiry to the wider Balkans. In this relation, continuous work on regional and comparative case studies that utilize typologically diverse sources seems to be the most methodologically sound avenue of research at this stage of the development of the field.

2   Colonization, Settlement, and Faith in the Balkans in the Early Ottoman Period (*c.* 1352 to Early Sixteenth Century)

"*Sen bir şehirlüsün, padişah benem.*"

"You are a city-dweller, I am the *padişah*."

Otman Baba to Mehmed II[1]

2.1   Colonization and Settlement in the Early Ottoman Balkans: Historical and Historiographic Overview

Was there a "systematic" policy of settlement and colonization in the Balkans pursued by the Ottoman state? How did it change through the period under discussion? What about other important agents in this process (e.g. semi-nomadic Turcomans and heterodox "colonizing dervishes") and their relation to the Ottoman state? What was the connection between Islam and colonization, and what were the "varieties of Islam" espoused by the colonizers?

Such questions relate directly to the nature of both the early Ottoman state and the current state of Ottomanist historiography. This chapter will start with a general assessment of Turcoman colonization and settlement in the Ottoman Balkans from the fourteenth through the early sixteenth centuries and then focus upon the role of religion and specifically that of certain "heterodox" dervish groups in this process.

A good starting point for the present discussion is the influential work of Ömer Lütfi Barkan (1902–79), one of the most prominent Turkish historians in the early decades of the Turkish Republic and author of numerous influential studies in Ottoman socio-economic history. He was the first to clearly problematize and conceptualize some of the most important questions of settlement and colonization, focusing on the related roles of the Ottoman state and non-state actors.

---

[1] *OBV*, 253.

Barkan's work substantially followed the lead of M.F. Köprülü, the first great Turkish republican historian, a student of late medieval Anatolia who, like most early republican historians, worked to enhance the legitimacy of the fledgling Turkish nation-state and facilitate the consolidation of Turkish national and ethnic identity through his writings. Köprülü strove to demonstrate the role of ethnic Turks as active historical agents, worthy "makers of history," and even "founders of world civilizations," often in response to western scholarly works that undermined the role of Turks (sometimes derisively conceptualized as "Asiatics") in the rise and development of the Ottoman Empire.[2] To this Barkan forcefully added another major emphasis: the definitive role of the state in the socioeconomic development of the Ottoman domains. This emphasis has trickled into many later studies produced by both Turkish historians, whose link to early republican historiography is obviously more direct, and those of western scholars whom most primary sources of Ottoman provenance have presented with an emphatically state-centered perspective.[3]

Barkan laid out his major theses on Turcoman colonization in Anatolia and the Balkans in two lengthy articles published in Turkish: "Pious Endowments and Land Deeds as a Means of Settlement and Colonization in the Ottoman Empire," in which he emphasized the role of "colonizing dervishes" in the conquest and early development of the Ottoman Balkans, and "Deportations as a Means of Settlement and Colonization in the Ottoman Empire."[4]

As the latter work addresses more generally Turcoman colonization in the early Ottoman Balkans it is appropriate to discuss it first. Using as a point of departure well-documented deportations from Anatolia to the newly

---

[2] Until the mid-1930s, the most significant work on the emergence of the Ottoman state was H.A. Gibbons' *The Foundation of the Ottoman Empire: A History of the Osmanlis up to the Death of Bayezid I, 1300–1403* (New York: The Century Co., 1916). Gibbons would not identify the rise of a world empire like the Ottoman with the "simple-minded Osmanlis"; instead, he posited that under the leadership of Osman and his successors a "new race" emerged in Anatolia and the Balkans, "a race formed by the fusion of elements already existing at the place of birth," whereby it was local converts, chiefly of Greek origin, and thus heirs to the great Roman-Byzantine cultural and administrative tradition, who were essentially the makers of the new empire; ibid., 18, 49–53. One of Köprülü's best-known works, *Les Origines de l'Empire Ottoman*, was a direct response to Gibbons' claims.

[3] Such a perspective is not necessarily "wrong." Despite some scholars' understandable reaction against the overwhelming centrality of the state in Ottomanist historiography, it is worth considering Suraiya Faroqhi's argument that, nevertheless, and especially in comparison to late medieval and early modern Europe, the state did play a leading role in most aspects of socio-economic change in Ottoman society. See her *Der Bektaschi-Orden in Anatolien (vom späten fünfzehnten Jahrhundert bis 1826)* (Vienna: Verlag des Instituts für Orientalistik der Universität Wien, 1981), 2–3. The need for a nuanced and balanced approach is obvious, however.

[4] "Vakıflar ve Temlikler," and "Sürgünler."

conquered island of Cyprus in 1571–2,[5] Barkan argued that the Ottoman state's policy of forced population transfers as a means of resettlement and repopulation extended back to the mid-fourteenth century and traced this policy through the sixteenth century with an emphasis on the Ottoman Balkans. While acknowledging the importance of voluntary or spontaneous migrations from Anatolia to the Balkans,[6] he emphasized the notion of the all-powerful Ottoman state, which directed various population groups en masse and in a "systematic" manner to different parts of the empire, like "balls on a pool table,"[7] with the overarching aim of easing population pressure and enhancing political stability and economic productivity.

Relying on well-known passages in late fifteenth- and sixteenth-century Ottoman chronicles, Barkan places the beginnings of the "comprehensive" Ottoman policy of resettlement of nomadic masses of Turcomans (or sometimes Tatars) in the very first years following the conquest of Gallipoli by Orhan's son Süleyman Pasha in 1352–4, when Süleyman Pasha himself called for the transfer of Turcomans from western Anatolia to newly conquered areas in the Balkans.[8] He then follows this policy in the late fourteenth and the early fifteenth centuries, pointing to examples (again drawn mostly from later Ottoman chronicles) of whole nomadic populations being moved from Anatolia to the Balkans, often under the leadership of tribal chiefs, to fulfill the objectives outlined above. Thus, semi-nomadic Turcoman *yürüks* were resettled from Saruhan in western Anatolia as colonists to Serres (Siroz) and Manastır in Macedonia *c.* 1385[9] and to the region of Filibe (Plovdiv) in Thrace at the turn of the fifteenth century as a punishment for their opposition to a state-imposed monopoly on salt production and trade.[10] Similarly, nomadic Crimean Tatars (who had crossed into the Balkans) were deported by Sultan Bayezid I to the area of Filibe to prevent potential political resistance,[11] Tatars from İskilip in Anatolia were moved to the same region by Sultan Mehmed I in 1418.[12]

---

[5] Barkan, "Sürgünler" (I): 548–561.
[6] Barkan, "Sürgünler" (I): 544; (II): 59–61.
[7] Barkan, "Sürgünler" (II), 66; (III) 224–225.
[8] Barkan, "Sürgünler" (II), 56, 59–63.
[9] Barkan, "Sürgünler" (II): 67–68; Aşıkpaşazade, *Âşıkpaşazâde Tarihi (Osmanlı Tarihi [1285–1502])*, ed. N. Öztürk (Istanbul: Bilge Kültür Sanat, 2013), 84–85; *Oruç Beğ Tarihi (Osmanlı Tarihi [1288–1502])*, ed. N. Öztürk (Istanbul: Bilge Kültür Sanat, 2014), 28. For a more detailed discussion of *yürüks*, see M. Tayyib Gökbilgin, *Rumeli'de Yürükler*.
[10] Barkan, "Sürgünler," (II), 69–77. The earliest major Ottoman chronicle that recounts this story is *Âşıkpaşazâde Tarihi*, 100.
[11] Barkan, "Sürgünler," (III): 211–212; İbn Kemal (Kemalpaşazade), *Tevârih-i Âl-i Osman. IV. Defter*, ed. Koji İmazawa (Ankara: Türk Tarih Kurumu, 2000), 327–331.
[12] Barkan, "Sürgünler," (III): 209–211, *Âşıkpaşazâde Tarihi*, 121–122, *Oruç Beğ Tarihi*, 47. This latter deportation of Tatars to the region of Filibe is considered to have led to the foundation of the town of Tatar Pazarcık (mod. Pazardzhik).

In Barkan's view, the state's purposeful transfers of nomadic populations to distant but agriculturally more productive lands also aimed at their gradual agrarianization and sedentarization, which was of primary importance to the Ottoman centralization program as it promised greater political stability and higher tax revenue.[13] Indeed, migration to agriculturally more productive areas was a prominent factor which, as R.P. Lindner has shown, paved the way to "the tribe of Osman's" gradual transition from nomadic to sedentary life – a development central to the Ottoman state's very establishment and subsequent growth.[14]

Another aspect of Barkan's analysis is the reshuffling of military and political elites from Anatolia to the Balkans and vice versa as a method of preventing the potential emergence of bases of resistance to Ottoman rule. Relying mostly on Ottoman tax registers, he points to transfers of Anatolian *sipahi*s to Rumelia and Balkan Christian *sipahi*s to Anatolia in the reigns of Murad II and Mehmed II, sometimes together with the peasants pertaining to their *timars*.[15]

Finally, Barkan mentions the resettlement of rebellious heterodox groups that bears a direct relationship to the focus of this study – for example, the deportation of Kızılbaş (and perceivedly pro-Safavid) populations from the provinces of Teke and Hamid in western Anatolia to the Morea in 1502,[16] as well as the deportation of more than 1,000 households from Anatolia to the district of Pravadi in the province of Silistre (northeastern Balkans) in the early sixteenth century.[17]

A major argument advanced by Barkan is that, with the exception of Bosnia, population transfers from Anatolia were the dominant factor in the formation of Muslim communities in the Balkans. He thus downplays the importance of conversion to Islam of the local Balkan population and the related potential ethno-linguistic assimilation.[18]

Barkan's other article introduced above discusses the activities of "colonizing dervishes" as one of the major factors that could rationally explain the rapid rise and expansion of the early Ottoman state, pointing out their Turkish and Muslim identity and stressing the state's support for these colonizing enterprises through grants of land, the establishment

[13] Barkan, "Sürgünler," (II): 65–66.
[14] Lindner, *Nomads and Ottomans*, 29–38.
[15] Barkan, "Sürgünler" (III), 214–217, 220–224, 228.
[16] Ibid., 228.
[17] Ibid., 225. In the latter case the deportees' association with the Ottoman-Safavid conflict is implicit.
[18] Barkan, "Sürgünler" (II), 230–231. The same argument is seconded by İnalcık in his influential article "Ottoman Methods of Conquest," 125.

of pious endowments, and/or the conferral of related tax exemptions and privileges.[19]

While he does not dwell extensively on the specific religious identity of these dervishes, Barkan suggests that they were neither the mendicant antinomian dervishes who wandered semi-naked from place to place, consumed intoxicants, shaved all their facial hair, and subsisted mainly on charity; nor those who established themselves in the urban centers; nor the kind of contemplative, passive mystics as Sufi dervishes have often been conceptualized.[20] Instead, they were warrior-dervishes (*gazi-dervişler, alp-erenler*) who placed themselves at the forefront of the conquest and colonization effort, often being also communal heads or clan leaders (*cemaat beğleri*).[21] They tended to found their convents (*zaviyes, tekyes*) in desolate and empty areas in the countryside, often deliberately searching for such areas to be "opened" to Islam, upon which their convents, with the backing and under the control of the state, would serve as centers for spiritual support, but also cater to the worldly needs of new Turcoman settlers first in Anatolia and later in the Balkans by providing shelter and food to strangers (*ayende ve revendeye hizmet etmek*).[22] The emerging network of dervish convents in the Balkans thus came to constitute one important level of the institutional infrastructure that would facilitate the colonization and socio-economic utilization of the newly conquered Balkan lands, which Barkan romantically conceptualized as "another America."[23] Providing numerous examples derived from Ottoman tax registers, Barkan depicts the mechanism through which these convents would often form the nuclei of new villages. The convents founded by colonizing dervishes would normally be actively engaged in agriculture, animal husbandry, the repair of roads, and the construction of watermills.[24] Dervish colonizers also served as mountain-pass guards and relay-station (*menzilhane*) personnel.[25] This process would continue in desolate or underpopulated lands long after the formal conquest of the respective territories (termed by Barkan as "internal colonization"), especially in Ottoman Rumeli.[26]

---

[19] The phenomenon of "colonizing dervishes" in frontier zones was certainly not untypical of other pre-modern Islamic world contexts. See, for example Eaton's discussion on dervish colonization at the other end of the Islamic world, in late medieval Bengal, *The Rise of Islam and the Bengal Frontier*, 71–94.

[20] Barkan, "Vakıflar ve Temlikler," 285.

[21] Ibid., 295, 296.

[22] Ibid., 292.

[23] Ibid., 284–285.

[24] Ibid., 284–285, 293–294, 296

[25] Ibid., 293, 299–302.

[26] Ibid., 299.

Barkan's major arguments regarding the early Ottoman policies of colonization and settlement in the Balkans have been criticized both for his tendency to ascribe an overarching role to the state in the process (and thus an anachronistic level of centralization of state authority) and for his emphasis on these developments' exclusively Muslim-Turkish character and the related nature of the formation of Muslim communities in the Ottoman Balkans.

His thesis regarding forced deportations as a means of resettlement and repopulation is based on a limited number of examples backed by Ottoman administrative sources and chronicles from the mid-fifteenth century onwards, whence he deductively develops the larger argument that forced deportations were characteristic of Ottoman realities throughout the first three centuries in Ottoman history and most probably represented the most influential factor in the process of resettlement and colonization. This argument is especially problematic for the first century or so of Ottoman rule in the Balkans for which contemporary documentary evidence is scant. Even the limited number of examples in this period of purposeful resettlement from Anatolia to the Balkans, especially those of nomadic and semi-nomadic groups, that one could glean from later Ottoman chronicles do not unequivocally confirm the state's paramount role in the process. Subsequently, İnalcık somewhat modified Barkan's argument by asserting that "in the first decades of their conquests the Ottomans were undoubtedly encouraging voluntary emigration into the Balkans of the people who were daily coming into their territories from all parts of Anatolia and the rest of the Islamic world."[27]

As for Barkan's thesis on the "colonizing dervishes," he does not discuss in detail their religious identity and how the varieties of Islam they embraced related to their approach to colonization. For him, these were a kind of pro-active, energetic pioneers of the frontier, active mostly among semi-nomadic populations, who somehow decided to settle in newly conquered lands and practise agriculture, with the active encouragement and patronage of the Ottoman state. How and why they made that transition to sedentary life and the evolving dynamics of their relations with the rising Ottoman dynasty and state in the process are issues upon which he avoids dwelling.[28]

---

[27] İnalcık, "Ottoman Methods of Conquest," 128.

[28] While, unfortunately, most scholars have remained content with reiterating Barkan's major arguments, a recent work that builds upon his theses, but makes important original contributions in the form of two case studies of prominent colonizing dervish figures in late medieval Anatolia, is Ahmet Yaşar Ocak, *Ortaçağ Anadolu'sunda İki Büyük Yerleşimci/Kolonizatör Derviş: Dede Garkın ve Emîrci Sultan, Vefaiyye ve Yeseviyye Gerçeği* (Istanbul: Dergah Yayınları, 2014), hereafter *Dede Garkın ve Emîrci Sultan*.

An important issue that bears upon Barkan's arguments is his relatively uncritical use of Ottoman chronicles. The character and nature of the mainstream Ottoman historiographic tradition is of utmost importance, especially as it is our major source for the history of the Ottoman domains before the mid-fifteenth century. As Heath Lowry has aptly argued, the Ottoman chronicle tradition started coalescing in the late fifteenth and further developed in the sixteenth century, a period when the Ottoman dynasty had already emerged as the unchallenged leader of a fast-growing and maturing imperial enterprise; it thus presents a "sanitized version" of early Ottoman history which tends to minimize the role of non-state actors in the early development of the Ottoman project, and specifically in the shaping of the early Ottoman Balkans.[29] In other words, the mainstream Ottoman historiographic tradition essentially de-emphasizes the frontier nature of the early Ottoman state, which was characterized by a low degree of institutionalization and centralized state control, a "liquidity and fluidity of identities" which were continuously renegotiated,[30] the presence of multiple agents that shaped the early Ottoman involvement in the Balkans (as well as in Anatolia), and, very likely, significant spontaneous and voluntary migrations of semi-nomadic as well as sedentary population groups from Anatolia into the Balkans.

It should not come as a surprise then that in contrast with this historiographic tradition, an alternative history of the early Ottoman enterprise authored by the Greek-Italian Theodore Spandounes in the early sixteenth century, sees "Ottomano" (i.e. Osman) as only one of four "lords of the Turks" along the Byzantine frontier in Anatolia in the late thirteenth century, the other three being "Michauli," "Turachan," and "Evrenes." None of them being "more than a petty chieftain," "one day they assembled together to elect one lord from among them" and chose "Ottomano" on account of his "authority, courage and strength of character."[31] Indeed, members of the families of Köse Mihal, Turahan, and Evrenos (known later as the Mihaloğulları, the Turahanoğulları, and the Evrenosoğulları[32]), together with some others, such as the Timurtaşoğulları and the Malkoçoğulları, played a paramount role in the Ottoman conquest of the Balkans in the second half of the fourteenth century, as well as in the peninsula's administration in the fifteenth

---

[29] Heath Lowry, *The Shaping of the Ottoman Balkans, 1350–1550: The Conquest, Settlement and Infrastructural Development of Northern Greece* (Istanbul: Bahçeşehir University Publications, 2008), 63.

[30] Kafadar, *Between Two Worlds*, 28.

[31] Theodore Spandounes, *On the Origins of the Ottoman Emperors*, tr. Donald Nicol (Cambridge: Cambridge University Press, 1997), 15–16, see also Lowry, *The Nature of the Early Ottoman State*, 55–94.

[32] "-oğulları" stands for "sons/descendants of."

century. They acted as "frontier lords" (*uc beyleri*) and featured as commanders of light cavalry units (*akıncılar*) manned mostly by Turcoman nomads. Even the later, dynasty-centered, Ottoman chronicles provide sufficient references as to the large degree of autonomy that these frontier lords exercised in the areas in the Balkans that they had conquered and that had been granted to them by the Ottoman rulers as marches (*uc*) to administer in the second half of the fourteenth and the early fifteenth centuries. That these marcher lords saw themselves and were seen as near-equals to the Ottoman dynasty in the first century and a half of Ottoman history is also confirmed by the titles ascribed to them, such as *malik al-ghuzat* ("Lord of the Gazis") which did not differ substantially from the titulature employed by the members of the dynasty during that period.[33] In effect, these families formed the core of the "warrior quasi-nobility" of the early Ottoman state. Conquering strategic locations along the main roads in the Balkans, they established themselves in their strongholds and ruled them de facto as small frontier principalities, while at the same time playing an important role in Ottoman dynastic struggles (especially during the Ottoman Time of Troubles, 1402–13), as well as in major Ottoman military campaigns.[34] As members of these families were also granted large tracts of land as private property (*mülk*), they also established numerous pious foundations (*waqfs*) which contributed significantly to the infrastructural development of their respective areas of influence. One may point to the role played by Gazi Evrenos and his descendants in the development of northern Greece (Macedonia), where they presided over the building of mosque complexes, soup kitchens, baths, and dervish lodges,[35] as well as the Mihaloğulları's similar contribution to the development of towns and their hinterlands in northern Bulgaria (especially Plevne and Tırnova).[36] Their leadership in conquest campaigns and the riches that the latter promised must have attracted numerous warriors of (semi-)nomadic Turcoman origin in the first century of the history of the Ottoman Balkans, and the contributions to the infrastructural development in various areas of the peninsula that members of these families made undoubtedly facilitated further migrations.

It was only during Mehmed II's reign that the leading members of these families were effectively assimilated into the mainstream Ottoman

---

[33] See, for example, the titulature used in Gazi Evrenos' early fifteenth-century tombstone inscription, Lowry, *The Nature of the Early Ottoman State*, 60–61.

[34] Mariya Kiprovska, "The Military Organization of the Akıncıs in Ottoman Rumelia," M.A. thesis, Bilkent University, 2004, 17–28.

[35] Lowry, *The Shaping*, and Heath Lowry and İsmail Erünsal, *The Evrenos Dynasty of Yenice-i Vardar: Notes and Documents* (Istanbul: Bahçeşehir University Publications, 2010).

[36] M.T. Gökbilgin, "Mihaloğulları," *İA*.

military and administrative structures, usually by granting them successive offices as provincial governors along the borders of the Ottoman Balkans, which deprived them of their strong local power bases.[37] Yet scions of these families continued to occupy important military and administrative positions in the Ottoman Balkans through the sixteenth century.

2.2 The Abdals of Rum(eli) and their Allies: Heterodox Islam, Turcoman Colonization, and Legitimacy (Late Fourteenth–Early Sixteenth Centuries)

After this overview of the general nature and role of Turcoman colonization in the early Ottoman Balkans, it is appropriate to discuss in some detail the role of "colonizer-dervishes" in the same context. Many of them not only founded dervish convents in isolated places in newly conquered areas, which often became the nuclei of new rural settlements,[38] but also participated in conquest campaigns and actively popularized the spirit of *gaza* among semi-nomadic Turcomans. Thus, a discussion of the nature of Islam they propagated among their followers (including potential local converts to Islam) and their related claims to religio-political legitimacy, especially vis-à-vis the evolving Ottoman political ideology, is also appropriate for a proper understanding of the processes under discussion.

While Barkan generally avoids an in-depth discussion of their religious beliefs and practices, but states categorically that they were not of the antinomian mendicant variety,[39] the research of scholars such as Köprülü and Ocak[40] has demonstrated that for the most part these colonizing dervishes were, in fact, largely itinerant, non-Sharia-minded, and "deviant" from the perspective of "mainstream," Sharia-regulated, urban-based Islam.[41] They generally maintained an oppositional, "antinomian" stance

---

[37] Kiprovska, "The Military Organization," 29–41.

[38] Barkan, "Vakıflar ve Temlikler," 294–300.

[39] Ibid., 285; Barkan, however, does refer to Köprülü's argument that some of those mendicant, non-Sharia-minded dervishes could, in fact, abandon the practices of itinerancy and celibacy, form families, and settle in sparsely populated areas.

[40] Köprülü, *The Origins of the Ottoman Empire*, 103–107; Ocak, *Kalenderîler*, 215–217; ibid. *Dede Garkın ve Emîrci Sultan*.

[41] It should be remembered that "high" and "popular," "mainstream" and "deviant" Islam were not closed off from one another, but rather found themselves in continuous interaction. On the conceptual and methodological problems stemming from the assumption of a watertight separation between low/popular and high/learned/normative Islam, see Karamustafa, *God's Unruly Friends*, 9–11. For a further discussion of this two-tiered model in the study of religion, see Peter Brown, *The Cult of Saints: Its Rise and Function in Latin Christianity* (Chicago and London: The University of Chicago Press, 2015), enlarged edn., 12–22.

vis-à-vis centralized (or centralizing) state authority that sought to promote a societal order characterized by political authority concentrated in urban centers and supported by scriptural, "Sharia-minded" Islamic tradition and its functionaries (the urban, *medrese*-trained, *ulema* class), its main economic base being agriculture practiced by sedentary peasants. These dervishes engaged, to various degrees and in various forms, in renunciatory and ascetic practices as a form of protest against mainstream, "conformist" Islam, and could espouse religious ideas that would earn them the obloquy of heresy (e.g. the concepts of incarnation [*hulul*] and metempsychosis [Ar. *tanasukh*, Tr. *tenasüh*]).

The question of the social and cultural origins of these dervish groups, as well as their taxonomy and classification, is extremely complicated. Possessing a number of major common characteristics, they were nevertheless typologically diverse, both in terms of their religio-cultural origins and leanings and with respect to the functional nature of their activities. All of this certainly makes it even harder to produce a single (and satisfactory) "umbrella" term to characterize them all.

Mostly of Turcoman origin, these non-Sharia-minded dervishes migrated into the Anatolian (and later, Balkan) countryside via at least two main channels. First, many Turcoman *babas* started pouring into the peninsula as a part of the grand-scale process of Oghuz migrations from Central Asia through Iran and, from the second half of the eleventh century onward, into Anatolia. Some were also tribal leaders, while others migrated with their families in search for better economic opportunities and with the ambition of gaining influence through their teachings in the new lands affected by Turcoman conquests and migrations. The process, which continued through the thirteenth century, was intensified by the Mongol invasion in Anatolia of the 1240s, which precipitated the decline of the Seljuk Sultanate of Rum (*c.* 1081–1307), the only major Muslim polity in the peninsula that pursued the establishment of a centralist, citied, and sedentary political order along the lines of the Perso-Islamic state tradition.[42]

It has been generally accepted that Oghuz Turcomans embraced Islam en masse, starting in tenth-century Central Asia, largely via the channel of popular mysticism. This simplified mysticism, most strongly associated with Ahmed Yesevi (d. 1167), was characterized by a less demanding ritual practice incorporating pre-Islamic Turcoman traditions (including shamanism, as well as nature and ancestral cults) and

---

[42] On the general character of this process, see Irène Mélikoff, *Hadji Bektach: un mythe et ses avatars* (Leiden, Boston, and Köln: Brill, 1998), 25–50 and Ocak, *Dede Garkın ve Emîrci Sultan*, 25–32.

an emphasis on the purity and sincerity of belief, thus more easily winning the hearts of Turcoman nomads and comporting with their ethics of tribal solidarity.[43] Of central importance in this context was the (Sufi) cult of saints, whereby the wonders and good deeds worked by *ata*s or *baba*s (both having the generic meaning of "father") who carried the aura of holy men largely facilitated the transition from shamanistic practices to that of simplified Islamic mysticism.[44]

The other major channel through which non-Sharia-minded, "non-conformist" dervishes entered Anatolia, is associated with the rise of a new current in Islamic mysticism (*tasawwuf*) that emerged in the early thirteenth century in some of the Islamic world's "core areas" (especially Iran, Syria, Iraq, and Egypt).[45] Influenced by the Malamatiyya movement and its renunciant, inner-worldly piety that emerged in ninth- and tenth-century Khorasan,[46] as well as by some non-Islamic traditions, such as Buddhism, Manicheism, and Christianity, this "New Renunciation" emerged as a form of social protest against "mainstream," "world-embracing," largely urban Islamic mysticism (institutionalized in Sufi *tariqa*s, or brotherhoods), which had become well integrated into the Sharia-regulated social order that viewed "this-worldly oriented" human society as "the true arena of salvational

---

[43] The classic work on the Islamization of the Turcomans in Central Asia and the figure of Ahmed Yesevi is M.F. Köprülü, *Türk Edebiyatında İlk Mutasavvıflar* (Istanbul: Matba'a-i Amire, 1918); English translation: *Early Mystics in Turkish Literature*, trans. and ed. Gary Leiser and Robert Dankoff (London and New York: Routledge, 2006). One of Köprülü's major arguments is that the legacy of Ahmed Yesevi directly influenced the development of popular mystical Islam in Anatolia, and specifically the later Bektashi heterodox tradition. This argument has been questioned by recent research. See Ahmet Karamustafa, "Yesevilik, Melametilik, Kalenderilik, Vefa'ilik ve Anadolu Tasavvufunun Kökenleri Sorunu," in *Osmanlı Toplumunda Tasavvuf ve Sufiler*, ed. Ahmet Yaşar Ocak (Ankara: Türk Tarih Kurumu, 2006), 71–77; Devin DeWeese, "Foreword," *Early Mystics*, xix. On the concept of "Islamized shamanism" ("Le chamanisme islamisé"), see Mélikoff, *Hadji Bektach*, 1–24. A good overview of pre- and non-Islamic influences on the development of popular (heterodox) mysticism among the Turkic peoples, with an emphasis on Anatolia, is A.Y. Ocak, *Alevî ve Bektaşî İnançlarının İslam Öncesi Temelleri* (Istanbul: İletişim Yayınları, 2000); see also Gramatikova, *Neortodoksalniiat Isliam*, 87–94.

[44] The pioneering study on this subject is Ignaz Goldziher, "The Veneration of Saints in Islam," in Goldziher, *Muslim Studies*, ed. S.M. Stern, trans. C.R. Barber and S.M. Stern, vol. 2 (London: George Allen & Unwin, 1971), 255–342; originally published in German as *Muhammedanische Studien* (Halle: Niemeyer, 1889–1890); a recent authoritative work is John Renard, *Friends of God: Islamic Images of Piety, Commitment, and Sainthood* (Berkeley, Los Angeles and London, 2008). See also Ahmet Karamustafa, *Sufism: The Formative Period* (Berkeley, CA: University of California Press, 2007), 143–171.

[45] The two major works on this phenomenon are Ocak, *Kalenderîler*, and Karamustafa, *God's Unruly Friends*. Ocak uses the term "Kalenderi," the name of one of the most prominent among these renunciant groups, to describe the whole movement. However, this choice of terminology may be too narrow and potentially misleading. I prefer to use the term "new renunciation," which I borrow from Karamustafa's study, to refer to the movement at large.

[46] See Hamid Algar, "Malāmatiyya," *EI²*.

activity."[47] Attracting recruits from various social strata, including the respectable urban classes, the "New Renunciation" emphasized rejection of society and was characterized by a combination of asceticism – expressed through voluntary poverty, mendicancy, itinerancy, celibacy, and self-inflicted pain,[48] and antinomianism, which entailed the emphatic disregard for accepted social and Sharia-prescribed norms and the embracement of socially liminal practices like the cultivation of bizarre appearance (especially wandering semi-naked and practising the "four blows" [chahar darb], namely the shaving off of the hair, moustache, beard, and eyebrows, or at least some of these); the use of strange equipment (e.g. metal pendants); self-laceration and self-cauterization; and the consumption of intoxicants and hallucinogens.[49] These renunciants could see themselves as "divinely pulled" ecstatics (majdhubs), for whom divine attraction (jadhba) obviated the requirement of conforming to mainstream social, legal, and religious norms. They thus emerged "dead to society,"[50] consciously placing themselves beyond the pale of social respectability. Their blatant social deviance also entailed a radical re-interpretation of some central concepts in Islam and Islamic mysticism in particular, such as the passing away of the self (fana') and sainthood (walaya), and made recourse to openly heretical ideas such as reincarnation (hulul) and metempsychosis (tanasukh).[51] While the most important renunciant groups of this mold formed under prominent and forceful personalities such as Jamal al-Din Savi (d. c. 1232), the founder of the Qalandariyya in Syria, and Qutb al-Din Haydar (d. 1221) who founded the Haydariyya in Khorasan, these were relatively loose dervish collectivities that did not possess the level of institutionalization characteristic of "mainstream," socially respectable urban tariqas.[52]

Turcomans originating from Central Asia and representatives of the "New Renunciation" movement had started interacting outside of Anatolia. Some of those who joined the Qalandariyya in Syria were new Turcoman arrivals via Iran and Anatolia[53] and Turcoman babas had been subject to Malamati, Haydari, Qalandari, and similar influences in

---

[47] Karamustafa, God's Unruly Friends, 25–31. For Ocak's interpretation of this movement's origins, see Kalenderîler, 1–25; on the possible non-Islamic influences on this "new renunciation" movement, see ibid., 6–11.

[48] Karamustafa, God's Unruly Friends, 14–17.

[49] Ibid., 17–23; Ocak, Kalenderîler, 161–182.

[50] Karamustafa, God's Unruly Friends, 17, 21–23.

[51] Ibid., 21–23; Ocak, Kalenderîler, 147–155.

[52] Karamustafa aptly describes the relationship between "New Renunciation" groups and institutionalized tariqas as that between "rebellious offspring" and "socially conformist parents," God's Unruly Friends, 91.

[53] Ocak, Kalenderîler, 37–39.

Khorasan, hence many of the non-conformist, largely itinerant dervishes who traversed Anatolia in the thirteenth and fourteenth century came to be known as *Horasan erenleri* ("the Sufis of Khorasan"), the designation coming to denote a mode of dervish piety, not necessarily geographical origin.[54] However, the two currents – Oghuz Turcoman mysticism and the "New Renunciation" – came to interact more comprehensively (and to a considerable degree fuse) on Anatolian soil as the Mongol advance in the first half of the thirteenth century pushed numerous dervishes of both molds into the peninsula. While this interaction did not necessarily produce a single, unified mode of dervish piety, it conditioned the range of the most prominent practices and beliefs among dervish groups in Anatolia from the thirteenth (and in the Balkans, from the mid-fourteenth) through the fifteenth century.

A central event in this process was the so-called Babai Revolt of *c.* 1239–40. Led by two Vefa'i sheykhs, Baba İlyas Horasani and Baba İshak, the Babai Revolt took place in the context of the deep socio-economic crisis in the Seljuk sultanate of Anatolia after the death of sultan Ala al-Din Kayqubad I (r. 1220–37).[55] Conditioned by various demographic, socio-economic, political, and religious factors, including population pressure due to the incoming masses of Turcoman nomads and semi-nomads as a result of the Mongols' westward expansion, tensions and struggles over land resources between pastoralist Turcoman nomads and sedentary agricultural populations, as well as religious differences between urban elites and tribal Turcomans, the revolt spread quickly in central and southeastern Anatolia.[56] Not primarily a religious conflict,[57] it was largely an uprising of mostly non-sedentary, non-conformist, and non-Sharia-minded Turcoman groups against a centralizing state pursuing the consolidation of a Sharia-regulated, sedentary regime. Its most important feature was its messianic character; while no evidence points to outright *mahdistic* claims, Baba İlyas claimed to be a prophet and

---

[54] Ibid., 23–25; Köprülü, *Early Mystics*, 23.
[55] The most comprehensive treatment of the revolt is A.Y. Ocak, *Babaîler İsyanı: Aleviliğin Tarihsel Altyapısı Yahut Anadolu'da İslam-Türk Heterodoksisinin Teşekkülü*, 2nd rev. and enl. ed. (Istanbul: Dergah Yayınları, 1996); French ed., *La revolte de Baba Resul, ou, la formation de l'hétérodoxie musulmane en Anatolie au XIIIe siècle* (Ankara: Türk Tarih Kurumu, 1989); the most important primary source on the rebellion is Baba İlyas' *vita* composed c. 1358-9 by his grandson Elvan Çelebi, *Menâkıbu'l-Kudsiyye fî Menâsıbi'l-Ünsiyye (Baba İlyas-ı Horasani ve Sülâlesinin Menkabevî Tarihi)*, ed. İsmail Erünsal and Ahmet Yaşar Ocak (Istanbul: İstanbul Üniversitesi Edebiyat Fakültesi Matbaası, 1984).
[56] Ocak, *Babaîler İsyanı*, 2nd edn., 53–68.
[57] Ocak notes the participation of some sedentary, possibly "Sunni," as well as non-Muslim groups; ibid., "Babaîler İsyanından Kızılbaşlığa: Anadolu'da İslâm Heterodoksisinin Doğuş ve Gelişim Tarihine Kısa Bir Bakış," *Belleten* 64, No. 239 (April 2000): 135–137.

promised his followers deliverance from all the ills caused by the despotism of the Seljuk elites.[58] Though eventually suppressed (with its leaders having perished), the revolt served to solidify various non-Sharia-minded groups under a common cause into a loosely defined "Babai" religio-political movement,[59] which spread into the newly forming Turcoman frontier principalities in the second half of the thirteenth century, where they found fertile ground for their missionary activities among the Turcoman (semi-) nomadic populations.[60]

While different appellations describing these non-conformist, non-Sharia-minded dervishes were in circulation in late medieval Anatolia, by the fifteenth century most of them came to be best known by the collective term *abdal*s,[61] and more specifically as the *abdal*s of Rum (*abdalan-ı Rum, Rum abdalları*). The most celebrated early use of the term *abdalan-ı Rum* as an "umbrella" term is that of the great late-fifteenth century Ottoman chronicler Aşıkpaşazade who describes them as one of the four major popular groups, "well-known among the travelers" in Anatolia in the fourteenth and early fifteenth centuries.[62] Importantly, the term *Rum* (or *Urum*) *abdalları* is employed as a self-identification in sources emanating from dervish communities as well.[63] Ocak has aptly termed these *abdals of Rum* (in the general, "catch-all" sense) as second- and

---

[58] Ocak, *Babaîler İsyanı*, 2nd ed., 153–156.
[59] Ocak, "Babaîler İsyanından Kızılbaşlığa," 135–142. Importantly, a major early Ottoman chronicle composed two and a half centuries after the revolt, explicitly refers to the followers of Baba İlyas as *babayiler* (the Babais), *Oruç Beğ Tarihi*, 12.
[60] Ocak, *Babaîler İsyanı*, 2nd edn., 175–216.
[61] The most likely earliest use of the term *abdal* as a collective designation in the Anatolian context is to be found in Elvan Çelebi's *Menâkıbu'l-Kudsiyye*, 166. For an overview of the term in the late medieval context, see M.F. Köprülü, "Abdal," in *Türk Halk Edebiyatı Ansiklopedisi*, fsc. 1 (Istanbul: Türkiyat Enstitüsü, 1935), 23–56, esp. 23–38. In classical Islamic mysticism (*taṣawwuf*) theory the original meaning of *abdāl* is that of "substitute," "lieutenant"of God (from *badal*, pl. *abdāl*, note also cognate *badīl*, pl. *budalā*); *abdal* is also one of the stations in the Sufi hierarchy of saints who serve as God's lieutenants on earth to preserve the order of the universe in the context of the theory of *rijāl al-ghayb* that was articulated most eloquently by al-Tirmidhi and Ibn 'Arabi; see I. Goldziher, "Abdāl," *EI²*; Süleyman Uludağ, "Ricâlullah," "Ricâlü'l-Gayb," *TDVİA*, v. 35, 80–83. In this meaning *abdāl* relates to *qutb* (pole/axis, Tr. *ḳutb*), the pivot of this hierarchy. Some antinomian *majdhūb* (Tr. *meczūb*) saints like Otman Baba, to be discussed below, would claim *qutb* status. As for individual designations for dervishes, usually employed post nominally, the most widespread ones were *baba*, *abdāl*, *dede*, and *sulṭān* (e.g. Emirci Sultan, Kumral Abdal).
[62] *Âşıkpaşazâde Tarihi*, 307; the other three groups being the Gazis of Rum (*Gāziyān-ı Rūm*), the Ahis of Rum (*Aḥiyān-ı Rūm*) and the "sisters/women" of Rum (*Bācıyān-ı Rūm*). Importantly, Hatayi (i.e. Shah Ismail I Safavi) makes a similar categorization in his own poetry (not mentioning *bacıyan*), *Il canzoniere di Şah Ismail Hatai*, ed. Tourkhan Gandjei (Naples: Instituto Universitari Orientale, 1959), 15.
[63] For example, in the *velayetname* of Hacı Bektaş, composed in the late fifteenth century, he is presented as being sent to Anatolia by Ahmed Yesevi and "appointed" the head of the *abdals* of Rum ("Rum abdalları"), *Vilayet-name: Manakıb-ı Hünkar Hacı Bektaş-ı Veli*,

third-generation Babais.[64] Other, largely synonymous collective des-ignations such as *torlak*s, *ışık*s, or simply "dervishes" (*dervişan*) were in use as well.[65] While numerous late fifteenth- and sixteenth-century sources employ the appellation *abdalan-ı Rum* as a collective, umbrella term, especially in reference to the fourteenth and fifteenth centuries, this catch-all usage should be distinguished from the more restricted use referring to a specific and distinct non-conformist and antinomian der-vish collectivity referred to as *Abdalan-ı Rum* (or *Rum Abdalları*) and associated specifically with the prominent fifteenth-century renunciants Otman Baba and Sheykh Şücaüddin Veli. The Abdals of Rum (and more specifically those of "Otman Baba's branch") of the late fifteenth and sixteenth centuries were distinguished from other similar groups such as the Kalenderis, Haydaris, Camis, Edhemis, etc. in some prominent sixteenth-century (Ottoman and Western) sources.[66]

Importantly, operating in the Anatolian and Balkan frontier zones had a substantial, and largely transformative, impact on the life of these non-Sharia minded, non-conformist dervishes in the period of the crumbling

ed. Abdülbaki Gölpınarlı (Istanbul, İnkılap Kitabevi, 1958), 16; in the early sixteenth-century *vita* of Kaygusuz Abdal, an early fifteenth-century Anatolian saint and a disciple of Abdal Musa, whereby both were instrumental in developing the cult of Hacı Bektaş, Abdal Musa is presented as a leader of "Urum abdalları," *Kaygusuz Abdal (Alâeddin Gaybî) Menâkıbnâmesi*, ed. Abdurrahman Güzel, (Ankara: Türk Tarih Kurumu, 1999), 130. Similarly, the late sixteenth-/early seventeenth-century mystical poet Virani Baba (Virani Abdal) exclaims in one of his poems: "*Biz Ûrûm abdâlıyız, sultânımızdır Murtezâ*" ("We are the *abdals* of Rum, our 'sultan' is Murteza [i.e. Ali]"), and "*Biz Ûrûm abdâlıyız, serdârımız Kızıl Deli*" ("We are the *abdals* of Rum, our commander is Kızıl Deli"), the reference in the second example is to the great fourteenth-century dervish warrior-saint Kızıl Deli, to be discussed below, who took an active part in the Ottoman conquest of the Balkans, Saadettin Nüzhet Ergun, *Bektaşi Şairleri ve Nefesleri* (Istanbul: İstanbul Maarif Kitaphanesi, 1955), vol. 1, 214, 225.

[64] Ocak, *Babaîler İsyanı*, 2nd edn., 217–226.

[65] For the usage of these designations as collective umbrella terms in late fifteenth/early sixteenth-century Ottoman chronicles, see *Âşıkpaşazâde Tarihi*, 63–4, 279, 315; *Oruç Beğ Tarihi*, 134, 145; Mevlânâ Mehmed Neşrî, *Cihânnümâ [Osmanlı Tarihi (1288–1485)]*, ed. N. Öztürk (Istanbul: Bilge Kültür Sanat, 2013), 88, 284, 340; *Anonim Tevârîh-i Âl-i Osman. F. Giese Neşri*, ed. Nihat Azamat (Istanbul: Edebiyat Fakültesi Basımevi, 1992), 43. As will be shown below, especially in Chapter 4, these terms came to enjoy wide cir-culation in Ottoman administrative sources too. It should be noted that, again, just as in the case of *Abdâlân-ı Rûm*, some of these, especially *Torlak*s and *Dervîşân*, could be used as denoting specific dervish collectivities. See footnote immediately following.

[66] On these various groups and their representation in sixteenth-century Ottoman and western narratives, see Karamustafa, *God's Unruly Friends*, 65–84, and Ocak, *Kalenderîler*, 103–120. To make the distinction easier to identify, I use "abdals of Rum" when refer-ring to the catch-all usage in reference to the fourteenth and (early) fifteenth centuries, and "Abdals of Rum" when referring to the more specific collectivity (especially its branch associated with Otman Baba) from the late fifteenth century through the six-teenth and seventeenth centuries. Ocak similarly distinguishes between the catch-all and specific usages, *Kalenderîler*, 85–93.

Seljuk state (*c.* 1240s–1307) and the so-called *beylik* (principalities) period (late thirteenth to mid-fifteenth centuries). Unlike the "core areas" of the Islamic world, where, despite the tribulations of the epoch, there existed relatively strong and deeply-rooted traditions of centralized government, based in urban centers and usually operating according to the tenets of mainstream Islamic political and legal theory, the Anatolian and Balkan frontier zones, geographically situated between the core areas of the Islamic and the Christian worlds, were characterized by a low level of institutionalization, centralization, and hierarchical organization, not only politically, but also from a socio-economic, cultural, and religious perspective. In a way, this was "the land of opportunity" for "the non-mainstream-minded," that is, the "undisciplined" from the perspective of the established order in the "core zones." The frontier zone would naturally attract Turcoman (semi-)nomads – whom Anatolia, on the westernmost end of the Eurasian steppe corridor, also presented with favorable ecological conditions – as well as antinomian mystics, many of whom were already well integrated within nomadic groups. For all of these, the frontier zone accorded the opportunity to excel in *gaza* against the infidels and to partake in the redistribution of resources (land and booty) that accrued from successful conquests. In this process, most of the *abdal*s in fourteenth-century Anatolia, many of whom originally followed an itinerant and celibate lifestyle, established close relations with the ruling elites of the emerging Turcoman frontier principalities as evidenced in early Ottoman chronicles, Ottoman administrative documents, and some major heterodox saints' *vitae*. This de facto political union between heterodox dervishes, frontier lords, and Turcoman warriors at large in the frontier zone had three major aspects: the dervishes' religio-political support for the Ottoman and other frontier state enterprises;[67] their actual participation in *gaza*; and their participation in the process of settlement and colonization in the frontier zone (as demonstrated by Barkan).

Presented in early Ottoman chronicles as saintly figures (*azizler*) who actively supported the dynasty and prayed for Ottoman success,[68] heterodox dervishes also exerted their missionary efforts among Turcoman *gazi*s to raise the latter's fighting spirit and reaffirm the ideal of holy war.

Probably the most prominent example in the early Ottoman historiographic tradition that highlights the close connection between

---

[67] While our source base regarding the other Anatolian frontier principalities in the *beylik* period is very limited, there are no substantial reasons not to assume that the relationship between heterodox dervishes, political and military elites, and Turcoman warriors there was much different than in the Ottoman frontier state.

[68] *Âşıkpaşazâde Tarihi*, 305, *Oruç Beğ Tarihi*, 16, 22, Neşrî, *Cihânnümâ*, 388–389.

early Ottoman expansionism and heterodox dervishes is the relation
between Sheykh Ede Bali, a Vefa'i-Babai mystic, and the eponym of
the dynasty, Osman (r. 1299–1324). Ede Bali is portrayed as giving
his daughter in marriage to Osman and, in interpreting a dream that
Osman had, predicting the future growth of the fledgling Ottoman
state into a world empire.[69] While the historical veracity of the nature
of Sheykh Ede Bali's connection to Osman may be questioned, the
dream legend can be read as a compact of sovereignty and Ede Bali
as a "notary" of its contractual character who provided that contract
with legitimacy in the public sphere, as acknowledged by the late fifteenth-century Ottoman historiographic tradition which strove to
elaborate on the legitimacy of a rapidly centralizing Ottoman state
already centered in a true imperial metropolis.[70] This connection is
most emphatically expressed by Aşıkpaşazade, himself a dervish-*gazi*
of illustrious pedigree, who presents one of the disciples of Ede Bali
as saying to Osman: "Hey, Osman Gazi, you were given the emperor-
ship! You need to thank us," whereupon Ede Bali and his disciples ask
Osman to donate them some land.[71]

Warrior-dervishes' actual participation in conquest campaigns is
likewise well evidenced in early Ottoman historiography. Geyiklü Baba
participated in the conquest of Bursa (1326) and conquered with his
disciples a place named Kızıl Kilise,[72] and Abdal Musa, together with
Abdal Murad, Doğlu Baba, and Sheykh Mahmud likewise participated
in the conquest of Bursa,[73] Kumral Baba also excelled in the early
conquests.[74]

In exchange for their support, the early Ottoman rulers donated
these dervishes money and land which they endowed with pious foundation (*waqf*) status, endorsing the construction of convents. In that,
they were following a model established by the Seljuks of Anatolia.[75] To

[69] *Âşıkpaşazâde Tarihi*, 12, *Oruç Beğ Tarihi*, 13–14, Neşrî, *Cihânnümâ*, 40–41.
[70] Kafadar, *Between Two Worlds*, 132–133; see also Roy Motahedeh, *Loyalty and Leadership in an Early Islamic Society* (Princeton, NJ: Princeton University Press, 1980), 69–70.
[71] "*Ey 'Osmān Gāzī! Saña pādişāhlık verildi. Bize daḫi şükrāne gerek,*" *Âşıkpaşazâde Tarihi*, 12; the great early-sixteenth-century Ottoman jurist and historian, Ibn-i Kemal (Kemalpaşazade) mentions a certain Kumral Baba who confirmed Ede Bali's "good news," İbn-i Kemal, *Tevârih-i Âl-i Osman. I. Defter*, ed. Şerafettin Turan (Ankara: Türk Tarih Kurumu, 1970), 95.
[72] Hoca Sadeddin, *Tacü't-Tevarih*, vol. 2, 406, see Ocak, *Kalenderîler*, 89.
[73] Hoca Sadeddin, *Tacü't-Tevarih*, vol. 2, 406–7, *Âşıkpaşazâde Tarihi*, 41–2.
[74] İbn-i Kemal, *Tevârih-i Âl-i Osman. I. Defter*, 88–90.
[75] For example, fourteenth-century documents provide concrete evidence that Emirci Sultan, a thirteenth-century colonizing dervish in Anatolia, was granted a pious endow-ment by the Seljuk state; Ocak, *Dede Garkın ve Emîrci Sultan*, 198–201, 216–221, 257–273.

give a few examples derived from Ottoman chronicles, Osman endowed land to Ede Bali[76] as well as to Kumral Baba,[77] Orhan supported the construction of a *zaviye* for Geyiklü Baba with whom he was in close relations (*muhabbet*); Murad I followed in his steps by building a lodge for Postinpuş Baba in Yenişehir; and Bayezid I did the same for Ebu İshak Han.[78]

Non-Sharia-minded dervishes of the Rum *abdal* mold featured as key agents in both war-making and colonization from the very start of the Ottoman expansion in the Balkans in the mid-fourteenth century.[79] While Ottoman chronicles provide few references, Ottoman tax registers and some pious endowment charters (*vakfiyes*) from the fifteenth and sixteenth centuries open up a window into the role that such dervishes played in this process, first in the south and southeast Balkans – in Thrace and the eastern foothills of the Rhodope Mountains (especially the region known as Tanrıdağı) – and to the west into Macedonia, and later, in tune with the course of Ottoman expansion, in the northern Balkans as well, much along the lines of Barkan's research discussed above.[80] While usually dating from the late fifteenth century onwards, these administrative documents contain the registrations of hundreds of dervish lodges founded in the Balkans from the late fourteenth century onwards, often indicating the date of foundation. Often the beneficiaries of pious endowments established for them by the Ottoman dynasty and Balkan frontier lords,[81] the colonizing dervishes would settle on and cultivate the lands set aside for them. These pious endowments were usually hereditary, to be managed in succession by the descendants (biological or spiritual) of the founding dervishes. For example, the reign of Murad I (1362–89) saw the foundation of the *zaviye* of Abdal Cüneyd (with its pious endowment),[82] and that of Timur Han Sheykh (or Sheykh Timur

---

[76] *Âşıkpaşazâde Tarihi*, 12–13.

[77] İbn-i Kemal, *Tevârih-i Âl-i Osman. I. Defter*, 91.

[78] *Âşıkpaşazâde Tarihi*, 301–302.

[79] Lowry, *The Shaping*, 66.

[80] Barkan, "Vakıflar ve Temlikler"; see also E.H. Ayverdi, *Avrupa'da Osmanlı Mimari Eserleri* (Istanbul: Istanbul Fethi Cemiyeti, 1978–1982), 6 books in 4 volumes, esp. books 4–6; M.T. Gökbilgin, *XV–XVI Asırlarda Edirne ve Paşa Livası: Vakıflar-Mülkler-Mukataalar* (Istanbul: Üçler Basımevi, 1952); H. Lowry, *The Shaping* and *In the Footsteps of the Ottomans: A Search for Sacred Spaces and Architectural Monuments in Northern Greece* (Istanbul: Bahçeşehir University Press, 2009); M. Kiel, "A Monument of Early Ottoman Architecture in Bulgaria: The Bektaşi Tekke of Kıdemli Baba Sultan at Kalugerovo – Nova Zagora," *Belleten* 25 (1971): 53–60.

[81] For a good example of frontier lord patronage of dervish convents, see Mariya Kiprovska, "The Mihaloğlu Family: Gazi Warriors and Patrons of Dervish Hospices," *OA* 32 (2008): 193–222; Lowry and Erünsal, *The Evrenos Dynasty*.

[82] BOA TD 370, p. 30.

Han)[83] in the vicinity of Dimetoka (Didymoteicho), as well as the one of Ahi Musa in Malkara,[84] all in Thrace. Some of these lodges grew to be large settlements – by 1530 the *zaviye* of Sheykh Timur Han had 290 dervishes and servants (*hidmetkaran*), of whom 236 were married.[85] The most famous of these dervish convents that emerged in the age of the Ottomans' initial expansion into the Balkans came to be the one founded in 1402 by Kızıl Deli, the prominent heterodox warrior-saint in whose name, as will be discussed below, one of the most important heterodox saintly *vitae* was composed in the late fifteenth century.

Importantly, the very act of conquest engendered a strong claim to control, ownership rights over, and a quest to develop the conquered lands on the part of the conquerors. Thus, settling, cultivating, and maintaining control over the (once infidel) land was a physical as well as political expression and realization of the claim to successful participation in *gaza* and the concomitantly accruing religio-political legitimacy.

To the extent that most of the *abdals* of Rum were substantially influenced by pastoral nomadism and the New Renunciation movement, including the latter's world-rejecting tendencies underscored by renunciant practices such as itinerancy, mendicancy, voluntary poverty, and celibacy, participation in conquest and expansion in the frontier zone brought about significant changes, giving a major impetus to the rise of world-affirming attitudes and a tendency toward sedentarization (including the practice of agriculture and the embracing of family life). Most of the dervishes who participated in conquest and colonization ceased to be (if they ever had been) "dead to the world," and while most of them retained their confrontationist, "antinomian" attitude toward the traditional, politically centralized, urban-based, and Sharia-regulated order of the "core zones" of the Islamic world, many of them came to be active agents, together with frontier lords and Turcoman warriors, in the building of a new, albeit transient, *nomos* – that of the frontier zone. In a sense, the period from the late thirteenth to the mid-fifteenth century was one in which these participants in the conquest and colonization of Anatolia and the Balkans – non-Sharia-minded dervishes, frontier lords, and nomadic Turcoman warriors – were "masters of the frontier zone." The Ottoman dynasty was an integral part of this picture as long as the early Ottoman rulers and warrior princes retained the nature of frontier

---

[83] More properly, the hereditary *waqf* of Timur Han Sheykh was founded in the *mezra'a* of Elmalı in the sub-district of Karaca Halil, pertaining to Dimetoka. BOA TD 370, p. 33, Gökbilgin, *XV–XVI Asırlarda*, 174–5, Barkan, "Vakıflar ve Temlikler," 338–339.

[84] According to its extant pious endowment charter, Gökbilgin, *XV–XVI Asırlarda*, 173–174.

[85] BOA TD 370, p. 33.

lords. This situation started changing slowly, but visibly from the 1370s during the reign of Murad I,[86] with the gradual building of an institutional instrumentarium that would pave the way for the development of the centralizing, bureaucratic Ottoman state: a nascent central administrative apparatus, the introduction of tax surveys, the creation of non-nomadic armed units more tightly answerable to the political center (the Janissary corps and the provincial *sipahi* cavalry), as well as the cultivation of urban "high" Islamic culture and an indigenous Ottoman *ulema*. The transformation of the Ottoman polity from a frontier-zone conquest principality into a centralizing state endorsing a largely sedentary, agrarian socio-economic order gained definitive momentum in the last years of Murad II's reign and especially during that of his son Mehmed II, whose centralizing reforms were further developed and intensified by his successors. Landmark achievements in this regard were the acquisition of a true imperial metropolis (Constantinople); the emergence of a strong (by the standards of the time) central administrative apparatus centered in the royal court; and the erection of a more effective provincial administration that further limited the powers of the frontier lords. The ability of the central state to carry out its policies was strengthened by the further rise of centrally controlled military units – an enlarged Janissary corps and provincial *sipahi* cavalry, and the six cavalry regiments of the Porte. The rise of the *ulema* that staffed the emerging judicial administration and *medrese* educational system in both the capital and the provinces also came to strengthen "learned," Sharia-based, urban Islam. One of the most important reform measures effected by Mehmed II was the confiscation of pious endowments (*evkaf*) and freehold (*mülk*) property in order to expand the central state's tax base and thus finance the regular army units and the administration. This measure, which substantially affected both frontier lord families and dervish groups that had received lands as a reward for their efforts in early conquest and colonization, did not last long; but, together with Mehmed II's other reform policies, most of which were continued, it pointed clearly to the overall direction of change. With the gradual transformation of the Anatolian and Balkan frontier zones into "core lands," the original "masters of the frontier zone" were themselves being reduced to "centrifugal forces"[87] that would

---

[86] See also Kafadar, *Between Two Worlds*, 139–140.

[87] This is a paraphrase of Cemal Kafadar's apt concept of "centrifugal tendencies" in the context of the transformation of the Ottoman principality into a sedentary, bureaucratic empire, *Between Two Worlds*, 139. Kafadar sees heterodox dervishes, pastoralist Turcoman warriors, and frontier lord families forming an (informal) "coalition" of centrifugal forces that would resist the centralizing drive of the Ottoman state, ibid., 149–150.

have to cope with their changing, increasingly marginalized position in the newly emerging Ottoman imperial order.

Not surprisingly, a prominent feature of this transformation was the emergence of clusters of competing narratives of the rise of the Ottoman enterprise in the fourteenth and fifteenth centuries. While in this textual battle over the memory of the past (as well as the present order), the new (imperial) Ottoman historiography of the late fifteenth and sixteenth centuries strove to furnish an ideological, but also historical, legitimization for the centralizing Ottoman dynastic state, the parallel explosive growth of "alternative accounts," above all *vitae* of heterodox saints,[88] appeared very much as a defense of the legitimacy of those rapidly displaced and marginalized "centrifugal forces." These "alternative accounts" endorsed the values and ethos of the frontier zone by highlighting heterodox dervishes, frontier lords, and Turcoman pastoralists' accumulated historical and cultural capital stemming from their formative contributions to the early success of the Ottoman project.

2.3 Conquest, Colonization, and Authority in the Early Ottoman Balkans in the Light of Heterodox Hagiographic Works: The *Velayetname*s of Seyyid Ali Sultan (Kızıl Deli) and Otman Baba

Written roughly at the same time in the late fifteenth to early sixteenth centuries,[89] the *vitae* of two major heterodox saints who, together with their associates and followers, participated actively in the conquest, colonization, and overall political and relgio-cultural development of the

---

[88] While the focus here is on the *vitae* of Balkan heterodox saints, among the most important late fifteenth- and early sixteenth-century *vitae* of Anatolia-centered saints are those of Hacı Bektaş Veli, Hacım Sultan, Abdal Musa, Kaygusuz Abdal, and Sultan Şücaüddin Veli; for a good overview, see Ocak, *Alevî ve Bektaşî İnançlarının İslam Öncesi Temelleri*, 31–43, and *Kültir Tarihi Kaynağı Olarak Menâkıbnâmeler: Metodolojik bir Yaklaşım* (Ankara: Türk Tarih Kurumu, 1992), hereafter *Menâkıbnâmeler*. While all these *vitae* were eventually claimed by the Bektashi hagiographic tradition in the context of the Bektashi order's rise from the sixteenth century onward, it should be remembered that such claims do not necessarily reflect the historical context in which these works were composed. Another important "alternative account" of the epoch is Suzi Çelebi's "Gazavat-Name" of Mihaloğlu Ali Bey, the tale of the legendary conquest exploits of one of the most prominent Ottoman frontier commanders of the fifteenth century and scion of the great Balkan frontier lord family of Mihaloğulları; see Agah Sırrı Levend, *Gazavât-Nâmeler ve Mihaloğlu Ali Bey'in Gazavât-Nâmesi* (Ankara: Türk Tarih Kurumu, 1956).

[89] Otman Baba's *vita* is dated by its author AH 888/AD 1483–4, *OBV*, 276; Kızıl Deli's *velayetname* was likely written around the turn of the sixteenth century, based on its philological characteristics, the intellectual and theological influences evident in the work, and certain references to actual historical events; see Rıza Yıldırım, *Seyyid Ali Sultan (Kızıl Deli) ve Velâyetnâmesi* (Ankara: Türk Tarih Kurumu, 2007), 50–54.

Ottoman Balkans focus on two distinct periods in the history of the early Ottoman state. Seyyid Ali Sultan (also known as Kızıl Deli) and his fellow warrior-dervishes participated in the conquest of the Balkans in the second half of the fourteenth century – when heterodox dervishes, Balkan frontier lords, and Turcoman nomadic warriors still acted in co-operation with the fledgling Ottoman dynasty. Otman Baba's *vita* concentrates on the period of Mehmed II's centralizing reforms – the period in which these "masters of the frontier zone" were being reduced to "centrifugal forces" in the context of Ottoman centralization. An itinerant mystic who likely came to the Balkans in the 1440s and spent the rest of his life there until his death in 1478, Otman gained numerous followers and founded what could be termed "Otman Baba's branch of the Abdals of Rum" – a collectivity that would be prominent especially in the eastern Balkans in the subsequent centuries. Demir Baba, the great sixteenth-century regional saint of Deliorman, may be seen as Otman Baba's spiritual grandson, being (like Otman Baba) the supreme leader, "the pole of poles" (*kutbü'l-aktab*) of the Abdals of Rum in his time and following Otman Baba's "way."

While the "historicity" of hagiographic works has traditionally been questioned, largely on account of the presence of numerous fantastic wonder-working stories, these two *vitae* present historical narratives that nevertheless correspond closely to the timeline of events as established in non-hagiographic sources.[90] They have the overarching objective to establish the authority and saintly aura of their subjects, but also advance specific religio-political and ideological claims that legitimize the socio-political role and position of the dervish groups and their allies within the respective "hagiographic communities."

2.3.1   Kızıl Deli, Rüstem Gazi, and the Conquest of the Balkans

Seyyid Ali Sultan's anonymous *vita* tells the story of Kızıl Deli and his associates as conquerors and colonizers of the Balkans in the second half of the fourteenth century.[91] The main objective of putting the saint's wondrous story to paper is stated in the very first lines of the work:

---

[90] On the "historicity" of Islamic historiographic works and their value as historical sources, see Renard, *Friends of God*, 256–257; on the same issue in the early modern Ottoman context see Ocak, *Menâkıbnâmeler*, 65–69 and Yıldırım, *Seyyid Ali Sultan*, 37–45. As the two *velayetname*s' narratives follow closely actual historical events Ocak would classify them as "historical *vitae*" ("tarihi gerçeklere dayanan menkabeler"), *Menâkıbnâmeler*, 34.

[91] I am using the text as published by Yıldırım in *Seyyid Ali Sultan*. Yıldırım's monograph contains two appendices: a transliteration of the text of the *velayetname* (161–184) under the title *Hâza Velâyetnâme-i Seyyid Ali Sultan* as well as a facsimile of a late recension of

Let it henceforth be known how the *gazi*-dervishes who conquered Rumeli strove in the "way," fastening firmly the belts of their zeal, and produced numerous proofs and wonders, thus becoming manifest to many.[92]

The *vita* consists of two main parts. In the first, much longer section, the author narrates the participation of Kızıl Deli and his associates in the conquest of the Balkans; the second recounts mostly the life of Seyyid Rüstem Gazi, Kızıl Deli's leading associate, after the *gazi*-dervishes' withdrawal from military campaigns, when Seyyid Rüstem returns to a life of seclusion in the convent he founds in the newly conquered lands.

The narrative begins with Sultan Bayezid (or alternatively, Orhan)[93] who has long coveted the conquest of the Balkans (Rumeli), but whose many efforts had borne no fruit. Then, while engaged in prayer on a Friday night, the Prophet Muhammad appears to him in a dream and announces that God has answered his prayers: forty dervishes (*erenler*), "friends of God"[94] led by Seyyid Ali Sultan, himself of the holy line-age of the Prophet,[95] would soon come from Khorasan to help him in his endeavor as the conquest of Rumeli was in their powers; apart from Seyyid Ali Sultan himself, the Ottoman ruler is advised to show special attention and respect to another of the forty heroes – Seyyid Rüstem Gazi, famed for his knowledge and virtue.[96]

The Prophet then appears to the Forty as they perform their rites in their hermit cells in Khorasan and commands them to set out for Anatolia to the convent of Seyyid Hacı Bektaş who would gird them with swords and direct them to the Ottoman sultan.[97] Upon arrival, Hacı Bektaş assigns specific offices to some of them: Seyyid Ali Sultan

---

the work in Ottoman Turkish (187–230). Hereafter I refer to the text as *VSAS*, offering references to both the transliteration and the original text.

[92] "*Ammā ba'd ma'lūm ola ki Rumili'n feth eyleyen gāzī-erenleri ne vechle tarîkde cehd eyleyüb gayret kemeriñ meyānlarına muḥkem bend ederek bürhān ve kerāmetler iẓhār üdub cihānda nice erlere mu'ayyen ve ẓāhir oldılar,*" *VSAS*, 161/187.

[93] Of the extant several recensions of the *vita*, the one preserved in Cairo refers to Orhan as the current Ottoman ruler, the others, preserved in Turkey, to Bayezid I. Obviously, the Cairo version stands closer to historical chronology; the references to Bayezid in the other recensions may be attributed to a conflation of historical events or a sheer mistake on the part of later copyists; Yıldırım, *Seyyid Ali Sultan*, 45–48.

[94] The term used here is *veliyyullah* (Ar. *wālī Allāh*), lit. "friend of God." On the concepts of *wālī* (pl. *awliyā'*, Tr. *evliya*) and *walāya*, usually rendered in English as "saint" and "saint-hood" respectively; see Renard, *Friends of God*, 259–281. *Erenler*, lit. "those who have arrived [at the divine truth]," was used as a common designation for (ecstatic) mystics in late medieval and early modern Anatolia and the Balkans.

[95] *Seyyid* (Ar. *sayyid*) is a standard designation for somebody of the Prophet's lineage; by the late medieval period it would connote descent from the Prophet specifically through the line of Imam Husayn, while *şerîf* (Ar. *sharīf*) – through the line of Imam Hasan. However, this distinction was not made uniformly.

[96] *VSAS*, 161–162/188–189.

[97] Ibid., 162/190–191.

is appointed commander (*serdar*), Seyyid Rüstem Gazi military judge (*kadı ʿasker*), Abdüssamed Fakih imam; those not given specific appointments are simply girt with swords and all are sent on their way.[98]

Upon their arrival in the Ottoman court a council is convened with all the leading Ottoman commanders in attendance. Seyyid Rüstem presents his plan for the conquest of Rumeli and assigns different commanders specific tasks: the (Ottoman) sultan will advance on the left wing, Saruca Pasha in the middle, and the forty *gazi*-dervishes together with Süleyman Pasha (son of Orhan) on the right wing.[99] The plan is accepted and put into effect – the sultan advances with his forces and captures seven fortresses, apparently still on the Asia Minor side of the Dardanelles, taking 7,000 captives and ample booty to the *gazi*s' delight.[100] The *gazi*-dervishes, for their part, cross the Dardanelles into Rumeli to "clean the land from infidelity."[101] They conquer the strategic fortress of Gallipoli, being aided by an earthquake caused by Seyyid Ali's roaring battle cry, which severely damages the stronghold; many infidels lose their lives, some survivors accept Islam, and others agree to pay tribute (*harac*).[102] Thereupon, the Prophet appears again to the Ottoman sultan and instructs him that a certain amount of the captured booty should be directed to the treasury (*beytü'l-mal-ı Müslimin*) and that Seyyid Rüstem Gazi is the one who knows the exact proportion and should be appointed to administer this tax. The sultan sends a messenger laden with gifts to Seyyid Rüstem and the latter accepts the duty, specifying that it is one fifth of the booty that should be collected for the treasury (i.e. the canonical *khums*), and specifically one in five captives (the Ottoman *pencik*, which became the first source of recruitment for the Janissary corps).[103]

The dervishes then move north and west and conquer several fortresses in Thrace, including Edirne, whereafter they proceed further north to cross the Balkan range into Deliorman and Dobrudja and take Shumnu, Ruschuk, and the fortress of Silistre on the Danube. On the way back

[98] Ibid., 162–163/190–191.
[99] Ibid., 164/193–194.
[100] Ibid., 164/194.
[101] Ibid., 164–165/194–195.
[102] Ibid., 165/195. Importantly, the *vita* makes reference to an earthquake (albeit caused by supernatural forces) that facilitated the conquest of Gallipoli; thus the text stands closer to contemporary Byzantine sources which mention a powerful earthquake presented as the main reason for the conquest in 1354. "Mainstream" Ottoman chronicles attribute Ottoman victory solely to the bravery of the Ottoman *gazi*s and the grace of God. For references to contemporary Byzantine sources (esp. Gregoras and Cantacuzene), see Nicol, *The Last Centuries of Byzantium*, 241–242; for the rendition of early Ottoman chronicles, see *Âşıkpaşazâde Tarihi*, 65–70; Neşrî, *Cihânnümâ*, 74–76; *Oruç Beğ Tarihi*, 19–21; *Anonim Tevârîh-i Âl-i Osman*, 17–19.
[103] *VSAS*, 165–167/196–199.

south they conquer Yanbolu (modern Yambol in Thrace) and reach "the mountains of Kırcaali."[104] Thereupon, Seyyid Ali convenes his associates to a "high council" ('ali divan) and appoints one of the warriors – an indefatiguable gazi named Evrenos (i.e. the famous Ottoman Balkan frontier lord) – commander (ser'asker) to lead the conquest of an unnamed fortress; Seyyid Ali Sultan promises to come to Gazi Evrenos' help in case Evrenos needed it.[105] Indeed, when Evrenos gets himself into trouble fighting an infidel warrior, he calls Seyyid Ali, who miraculously appears, aids Evrenos in the ultimate conquest of the fortress, and urges him to continue his gaza campaigns in the Mediterranean (read: Aegean) region so that the Prophet may be pleased.[106]

With this, the gazi-dervishes' conquest campaigns end. Compared to the standard narrative of late fifteenth-century and later Ottoman chronicles, Kızıl Deli's vita presents a compressed version of select Ottoman conquests, starting with the Gallipoli Peninsula (1352–4) and a number of Byzantine fortresses in Thrace in the late 1350s and 1360s. The theatre of campaigns then abruptly moves to the northeastern Balkans, echoing the campaign of Çandarlı Ali Pasha in 1388–9.[107]

The most characteristic feature of the velayetname's presentation of the early Ottoman conquests in the Balkans is the unconditional centrality of Seyyid Ali Sultan, Seyyid Rüstem, and their gazi-dervish associates. The Ottoman ruler, while recognized as such, never appears actively campaigning in Rumeli – it is the gazi-dervishes who came from Khorasan at the urging of the Prophet and received the blessing of Hacı Bektaş to lead the warriors for the faith. The only member of the dynasty referred to as an active participant is Süleyman Pasha – mentioned once when Seyyid

---

[104] Ibid., 172–174/210–214.

[105] Ibid., 175/215-216; considering the closeness between the warrior dervishes and a conquering frontier lord like Evrenos as presented in the vita one may consider Irène Beldiceanu-Steinherr's argument about the eminent proximity between the images of Kızıl Deli and Hacı İlbeği (in the light of Ottoman chronicles), the leader of the Karesi gazis who joined the Ottomans upon the Ottoman incorporation of Karesi, which lends further credence to the assumption of the alliance of dervishes and pastoralist Turcoman warriors in the frontier zone. Beldiceanu-Steinherr suggests that Kızıl Deli and Hacı İlbeği may indeed have been one and the same person, "La vita de Seyyid 'Ali Sultan et la conquête de la Thrace par les Turcs," in Proceedings of the 27th International Congress of Orientalists ... 1967, ed. D. Sinor (Wiesbaden: Otto Harrasowitz, 1971), 275–276; and, "La conquête d'Adrianople par les Turcs; la pénétration turque en Thrace et la valeur de chroniques Ottomanes," Travaux et Memoires I (1965): 439–461, esp. 446–452. See also Kafadar, Between Two Worlds, 117.

[106] VSAS, 175–178/216–220.

[107] On this campaign, see Machiel Kiel, "Mevlana Neşrî and the Towns of Medieval Bulgaria: Historical and Topographical Notes" in Studies in Ottoman History in Honour of Professor V.L. Ménage, ed. C. Heywood and C. Imber (Istanbul: The Isis Press, 1994), 165–187.

Rüstem Gazi laid out his plan for invading the peninsula and a second time to mark his death as a martyr for the faith at Bolayır.[108] By contrast, Gazi Evrenos is accorded a visibly more important role, being appointed a commander by Seyyid Ali Sultan.

In this context, a closely related and intriguing feature of the *velayetname*'s narrative (typical also of Otman Baba's *vita*) is the intentional blurring of the boundaries between spiritual and worldly (i.e. political and military) authority, and specifically the boundaries between the sphere of authority of the *gazi*-dervishes on the one hand, and the sultan, the dynasty, and Ottoman military commanders, on the other. One example of this is the use of the appellation "sultan" for Seyyid Ali. With respect to the Ottoman dynasty, the title is usually used to denote a sovereign ruler or, in some cases, a male member of the dynasty when used prenominally. In Sufi circles, especially in the Ottoman context, it is usually used post-nominally – most often for prominent saintly figures, a good example being Seyyid Ali Sultan himself. This use of the title could be interpreted as indicative of a mystic's spiritual power, or simply as a term of affection.[109] The usage of the term in reference to Seyyid Ali in the *vita* goes well beyond that, however. Describing the conquest of Dimetoka in Thrace, the narrator recounts how the Christian inhabitants of the city came to the "Sultan of Rum Seyyid Ali Sultan" to ask for mercy and protection.[110] This usage echoes similar titles employed by Bayezid I and Mehmed II.[111] Similarly, three infidel captives convert to Islam "in the presence of the sultan" (*huzur-ı sultanda*) following the capture of Bolayır by the *gazi*-dervishes, whereby the "sultan" (i.e. Seyyid Ali) also orders that their relatives come and convert in his presence as well.[112] Finally, when Seyyid Rüstem Gazi is ordered by Kızıl Deli (Seyyid Ali Sultan) to post their banner on a fortress they conquered, Seyyid Rüstem does this "as required in accordance with the sultanic order" (*ber muceb-i emr-i sultani*) – a phrase uniformly employed in early modern Ottoman bureaucratic practice.[113] If one also remembers that Kızıl

---

[108] *VSAS*, 168/202. Alternatively, the mainstream Ottoman chronicle tradition casts Süleyman Pasha as the leader of the early Ottoman Balkan conquests and has him dying after falling from his horse while hunting. *Âşıkpaşazâde Tarihi*, 70; Neşrî, *Cihânnümâ*, 79; *Oruç Beğ Tarihi*, 21.

[109] See J.H. Kramers, "Sulṭān," *EI²*.

[110] "huzur-ı Sultan-ı Rum Seyyid Ali Sultan hazretlerine geldiler," *VSAS*, 172/211.

[111] Bayezid I is known to have used the title *sulṭānü'r-Rūm*, which can be translated as "Sultan of the former (Eastern) Roman domains"; following the conquest of Constantinople in 1453, Mehmed II used the title "*ḳayser-i Rūm* (lit. "Roman caesar/emperor"; or, in context, "emperor of the former (Eastern) Roman domains"); İnalcık, "Osmanlı Sultanlarının Unvanları," 188–189.

[112] "*Sulṭān anlarıñ gelmesini nuṭuḳ buyurdu*," *VSAS*, 168/202.

[113] *VSAS*, 171/208. Compare also the use of the title *hünkar* (sovereign) widely used in Ottoman administrative tradition and chronicles for Ottoman rulers, but also in reference to Sufi saints, most notably in the case of Hünkar Hacı Bektaş Veli.

Deli and Seyyid Rüstem were "appointed" by Hacı Bektaş as *serdar-ı Rum* (commander of Rum) and *kadı ʻasker* (military judge – then the highest office in the Ottoman judiciary), respectively, this intentionally ambivalent use of titulature, together with the presentation of the *gazi*-dervishes as the ultimate leaders in the Ottoman conquest movement, appears clearly to allude to an alternative claim to authority and legitimacy that would strengthen the position of heterodox dervish groups and their allies at a time when the Ottoman central state headed by the dynasty was making definitive strides in establishing its paramount position vis-à-vis other forces in the late fifteenth and the early sixteenth centuries. It is also worth noting the story of Seyyid Ali Sultan's transfer of military command to Gazi Evrenos and the fact that Seyyid Rüstem's appointment to administer the collection of *pencik* in the newly conquered territories in the Balkans is clearly reminiscent of the figure of a certain Mevlana Kara Rüstem in the Ottoman chronicle tradition: an *alim* from Karaman (the heartland of the old Seljuk sultanate of Rum) who introduced Çandarlı Kara Halil Pasha, then Ottoman *kadı ʻasker*, to the notion of the canonical *khums* (i.e. the Ottoman *pencik*) levy on booty and slaves and who was appointed to supervise its collection.[114]

In his discussion of the conquest of thirteenth-century Bengal by Muslim Turks Richard Eaton has noted the articulation of competing monarchic and Sufi models of authority and legitimacy in Perso-Islamic religio-political culture; "sultans and Sufis had inherited models of authority that, though embedded in a shared pool of symbols, made quite different assumptions about the world and the place that God, kings, and saints occupied in it."[115] While in the fifteenth- and sixteenth-century Ottoman hagiographic tradition titles more often associated with the authority of temporal, monarchic rulers (e.g. *sultan, hünkar*) were claimed for Sufi saints, in some other contemporary Ottoman sources titles typically associated with Sufi authority could be claimed by or for temporal rulers. For example, in his epic-in-verse *Kutb-Name*, composed in 1503 and dedicated to Bayezid II, Firdevsi-i Rumi claimed for the Ottoman ruler the title of *kutb* (hence the title of the work), which usually denotes the "pole" in a hierarchy of saints in Sufi theory.[116]

---

[114] *Âşıkpaşazâde Tarihi*, 75–76; Neşrî, *Cihânnümâ*, 83–84; *Oruç Beğ Tarihi*, 24–25, 33; *Anonim Tevârîh-i Âl-i Osman*, 24–25, 33; Yıldırım, *Seyyid Ali Sultan*, 66–71.

[115] Eaton, *The Rise of Islam and the Bengal Frontier*, 30–32.

[116] See Firdevsî-i Rumî, *Kutb-Nâme*, ed. İbrahim Olgun and İsmet Parmaksızoğlu (Ankara: Türk Tarih Kurumu, 1980). For more on *kutb*, see the following section on Otman Baba in this chapter.

After their last campaign of conquest, the forty *gazi*-dervishes bid farewell to one another and set out "to search for a place to settle."[117] Seyyid Rüstem Gazi arrives at Cebel-i Megair in Thrace, where he would build his convent, and sends a letter to the Ottoman sultan to ask that this land be endowed to him for the purpose. Shortly thereafter the sultan sees Seyyid Rüstem in a dream and, having woken up, miraculously discovers Rüstem's letter on his pillow. As it is the custom (*adet üzere*), he draws an imperial order (*hatt-ı hümayun*) and a land title-deed (*sened*) and sends a messenger to deliver it to Seyyid Rüstem, who extends his prayers for the well-being of the Ottoman state (*Devlet-i Aliyye hakkında hayır du'alar*). After completing seven years of seclusion, Rüstem sets out to open up space for his convent by cutting the trees around with his axe.[118] When a local Ottoman governor (*bey*) questions his actions, addressing him derogatorily as *torlak*, Rüstem defends his claim to the land: "This is the place that I conquered with my own sword!"[119] Asked to produce a proof for this he does not make recourse to the land-deed conferred to him by the Ottoman ruler, but instead produces a miracle making the rocks around move toward him.[120] Having attracted several disciples, he builds his *tekye*, acquires a pair of draft animals and the necessary tools, and starts cultivating the land.[121] As he and his disciples need to mill the grains they produce, Rüstem Gazi chooses a place for a mill, brings masons to build it, and, when told that there is no water to power the mill, he pokes the ground with his staff, whereupon fresh water miraculously springs up and sets the mill stones in motion.[122] Following this, the *vita* ends with a defense of the *gazi*-dervishes from those who deny their miracles and attribute various sins to them, pointing also to Seyyid Rüstem's year of death as AH 824/AD 1421.[123]

Thus, the second part of the *vita* presents settlement and colonization as a natural follow-up of conquest, which entailed the utilization of newly conquered lands through the practice of agriculture. Seyyid Rüstem's post-conquest activities as cast in the *velayetname* offer an image of the life of *gazi*-dervishes as colonizers which is largely in tune with early Ottoman chronicles and is confirmed, often to the minutest detail, by fifteenth- and sixteenth-century Ottoman tax registers which feature

---

[117] *VSAS*, 179/220.
[118] Ibid., 179–180/221–221.
[119] "*Bu yer benim kılıncım ile fetḥ eylediğim yerdir*," *VSAS*, 180–181/223.
[120] *VSAS*, 181/223–224.
[121] Ibid., 181/225.
[122] Ibid., 181–182/226–227; the miraculous discovery of water is one of the most characteristic abilities attributed to heterodox saints, especially in the Ottoman context, see Ocak, *Alevî ve Bektaşî İnançlarının İslam Öncesi Temelleri*, 273–275.
[123] *VSAS*, 183–184/230.

voluminous evidence of dervishes settling on lands endowed to them by the state and engaging in agriculture, serving travelers (*ayende ve revende*) and often described as engaged in prayers (*du'a-guyan*) for the well-being of the Ottoman ruler and state.

Extant Ottoman sources offer limited and chronologically late evidence regarding a convent associated with Seyyid Rüstem. An Ottoman tax register from the 1830s and the poet Keçeci-Zade İzzet Molla's near-contemporary collection of poems attest to the existence of a *zaviye* of Rüstem Baba in Keşan province in Thrace, close to the northern shore of the Gulf of Saroz, across the Gallipoli Peninsula.[124] A recent field expedition discovered the gravestones of residents of the *zaviye* from the late eighteenth and early nineteenth centuries referring to its founder as "Rüstem Baba Sultan" and "*kutbü'l-'arifin* [the pole/chief of the wise men] Rüstem Baba."[125]

Conversely, while the *velayetname* only hints that Kızıl Deli may have established a *zaviye*, there exists voluminous Ottoman archival material that allows us to trace the growth of the saint's mausoleum/convent complex near Dimetoka in Thrace from its establishment around the turn of the fifteenth century to the last decades of the Empire.[126] One reason for this is that the convent was integrated into the convent network of the newly institutionalized Bektashi order. The figure widely associated with the institutionalization of the order and its rise to prominence, Balım Sultan, spent years in Kızıl Deli's convent before becoming the head of the convent of Hacı Bektaş in Suluca Karahöyük in Anatolia in the early sixteenth century. By the following century Kızıl

---

[124] Keçeci-Zade İzzet Molla (1786–1829) wrote his *divan Mihnet-Keşan* much inspired by his exile to Keşan in 1823–4. In his poems he recounts at length his visit to the convent of Rüstem Baba, presenting a short history of his exploits, very much in tune with Seyyid Ali Sultan's *vita*, and provides a description of the current state of the convent complex, including the kitchen, the guest-house, the mill, etc. See Ali Emre Özyıldırım, *Keçeci-Zâde İzzet Molla and Mihnet-Keşân* (Cambridge, MA: Harvard University, Department of Near Eastern Languages and Civilizations, 2007), vol. 2, 163–172, and Ratip Kazancıgil, "Mihnetkeşan ve Rüstem Baba Dergahı," *Yöre* 37–38 (April–May 2003): 19–26. An Ottoman tax register, BOA MAD 9771, containing pious endowment records from the 1830s also refers to the *zaviye* of Rüstem Baba; Yıldırım, *Seyyid Ali Sultan*, 72–73. *The Yearbook of Edirne* for 1310 A.H., also mentions the *tekye* of Rüstem Baba (in the province of Keşan), it refers to Rüstem as a dervish who came from Khorasan *c.* AH 800/AD 1397–8 in the reign of Bayezid I, participated in the conquests and established his convent in AH 804/AD 1401–2, dying in AH 824, *Edirne Salnamesi: 1310 Sene-i Hicriyesine Mahsus* (Edirne: Matba'a-i Vilayet, 1310/1893), 628.

[125] Yıldırım, *Seyyid Ali Sultan*, 73; Ayhan Tunca, "Rüstem Baba Dergahı'na Bir Araştırma Gezisi," *Yöre* 37–38 (April–May 2003): 27–30.

[126] See the collection of Ottoman archival documents regarding the shrine complex of Kızıl Deli, *Osmanlı Arşiv Belegelerinde Kızıldeli (Seyyid Ali Sultan) Zaviyesi (1401–1852)*, ed. Gıyasettin Aytaş, Ali Sinan Bilgili, and Selahattin Tozlu, (Ankara: Gazi Üniversitesi Türk Kültürü ve Hacı Bektaş Veli Araştırma Merkezi, 2010).

Deli had become one of the great figures in the "Bektashi pantheon of saints," occupying the second position in that "pantheon," immediately after Hacı Bektaş himself. Accordingly, the shrine complex itself came to be regarded as one of the most important Bektashi cultic centers.[127] It is not necessary to trace this development here in detail,[128] but it suffices to refer to a few Ottoman documents that shed light on the early development of Kızıl Deli's pious endowment. The earliest preserved written document (*biti*) regarding Kızıl Deli dates from 1412 and was issued in Edirne by prince Musa, one of the contenders for the throne during the Ottoman civil war (1402–13).[129] The document, whose wording suggests that Kızıl Deli was still alive, asserts that the village of Sheykh Kızıl Deli had been endowed and exempted from taxes by previous Ottoman rulers (*beys*) and confirms these privileges. The earliest preserved tax registration of the pious endowment of Kızıl Deli dates from 1456, listing several *mezra'as* (agricultural sites) and a *derbend* (mountain pass) village as part of the endowment.[130] A later one, from 1485–6, states explicitly that the endowment properties had previously been confiscated by Mehmed II but were restored by Bayezid II. It refers to the endowment specifically as hereditary (*vakıf-ı evladlık*) and gives the names of five "sons" (read: descendants) of Kızıl Deli who hold the endowment jointly, whereby the *zaviye* was expected to serve travellers and passers-by.[131] Ottoman tax registrations of the first half of the sixteenth century already present the *zaviye* of Kızıl Deli as one of the most richly endowed in the Ottoman Balkans, controlling a number of villages and *mezra'as*;[132] a registration from the second half of the

---

[127] Köprülü uses the term "Bektaşi panteonu" in reference to all heterodox saints that had been appropriated by the Bektashi tradition by the mid-seventeenth century, M.F. Köprülü, "Bektaş, Hacı Bektaş Veli," *İA*, vol. 2, 461; Zeynep Yürekli employs the term more narrowly in reference to ten heterodox saints and two prophets who were the patron saints of the twelve offices in Bektashi convents, *Architecture and Hagiography in the Ottoman Empire: The Politics of Bektashi Shrines in the Classical Age* (Surrey, UK, and Burlington, VT: Ashgate, 2012), 38.

[128] See Irène Beldiceanu-Steinherr, "Seyyid 'Ali Sultan d'après les registres ottomans: L'installation de l'Islam hétérodoxe en Thrace," in *The Via Egnatia under Ottoman Rule (1380–1699)*, ed. Elizabeth Zachariadou (Rethymnon: Crete Univesity Press, 1996), 45–66; Ali Sinan Bilgili, "Osmanlı Arşiv Belgelerine Göre Kızıldeli (Seyyid Ali Sultan) Zaviyesi (1401–1826)," *TKHBVAD* 53 (2010): 89–114; and Suraiya Faroqhi, "Agricultural Activities in a Bektaşi Center: The Tekke of Kızıl Deli, 1750–1830," *Südost-Forschungen* 35 (1976): 69–96.

[129] BOA Ali Emiri Tasnifi, Musa Çelebi No. 1 (AH 815/AD 1412), also published in *Osmanlı Arşiv Belgelerinde Kızıldeli*, 16.

[130] Atatürk Kitaplığı MC O/89, p. 10, published in *Osmanlı Arşiv Belgelerinde Kızıldeli*, 18.

[131] BOA TD 20, pp. 264–265, published in *Osmanlı Arşiv Belegelerinde Kızıldeli*, 19–22.

[132] BOA TD 77 (AD 1519), pp. 185–187, 251–253; BOA TD 370 (AD 1530), pp. 25, 33, published in *Osmanlı Arşiv Belegelerinde Kızıldeli*, 25–29, 31–33.

same century points out that a property deed had been issued to the *zaviye* in the year AH 804/AD 1402.[133]

While tax registers were produced strictly for bureaucratic use, the lore of Kızıl Deli, Seyyid Rüstem Gazi, and their associates was likely transmitted to a larger audience among many incomers from Anatolia – mostly semi-nomadic Turcomans who recognized heterodox, non-Sharia-minded dervishes as their spiritual guides and had come to the Balkans either as conquerors or, in the post-conquest era, as migrants who sought better opportunities. The post-conquest activities of Seyyid Rüstem as described in the *vita* thus provided a model to be followed by those incomers. This model, communicated both in the form of popular lore and through the personal example of dervish-colonizers in real life, must have played a substantial role in those Turcomans' gradual sedentarization and agrarianization. Not surprisingly then, the centralizing state would encourage dervish colonization through endowing land and/or providing tax exemptions, as sedentarization was a leading imperative for the Ottoman dynasty in the transformation of the Ottoman enterprise from a conquest movement into a bureaucratic, imperial state. The state could thus both maximize its tax revenues and minimize the potentiality of semi-nomadic Turcoman groups' posing a threat in times they were less and less needed as military personnel, being replaced by regular military forces such as the provincial *sipahi* cavalry and the Janissaries. The downside for the dervishes and the Turcoman warriors was that they were thus losing their privileged position in the Ottoman project.

2.3.2   Otman Baba

Composed in the same epoch as the *velayetname* of Kızıl Deli, Otman Baba's *vita*, however, differs in many ways from the former. While Kızıl Deli's *vita* was authored anonymously up to a century after the deaths of Kızıl Deli and Rüstem Gazi, the author of Otman Baba's hagiographical account, Küçük Abdal, spent much of his life as a disciple and lieutenant (*halife*) of Otman Baba and managed to complete the work by 1483, within five years of the saint's death. It is one of the two most voluminous works in what would later be seen as the "Bektashi-Alevi" hagiographic tradition (the other being the *velayetname* of Hacı Bektaş). If Kızıl Deli's *velayetname* provides enough clues to the heterodox Kalenderi/Babai-type profile of its main protagonists, but does not dwell *in extenso* upon

---

[133] BOA TD 470 (AD 1568–9), 625, published in *Osmanlı Arşiv Belegelerinde Kızıldeli*, 42–43. For the later development of the convent, see Suraiya Faroqhi, "Agricultural Activities," 69–96.

their religious identity, Otman Baba's *vita* clearly identifies the saint and his followers as "Abdals of Rum" and contains long expositions of what one may call Rum Abdal ideology and theology. While up to the time of Otman Baba the appelation"abdals of Rum" was used as an umbrella term for most heterodox dervish groups in Anatolia and the Balkans (certainly, this is the meaning which Aşıkpaşazade attributes to it), under the leadership of Otman Baba it became the designation of a large movement in the eastern Balkans which emerged as a distinct heterodox collectivity distinguishable from other antinomian, non-Sharia-minded dervish groups.[134] This movement would have at least two subsequent leaders in the eastern Balkans in the late fifteenth and sixteenth centuries (Akyazılı Baba and Demir Baba) who, just like Otman Baba, claimed the dignity of "pole of poles" (*kutbü'l-aktab*) and avowed to follow his "way." The *velayetname* also recognizes the existence of a specific Rum Abdal community in Anatolia, largely consolidated around the cult of the early fifteenth-century Anatolian Abdal saint Şücaüddin Veli whose *vita* was composed in the mid-fifteenth century.[135]

The rise of "Otman Baba's branch of the Abdals of Rum" as well as its fraternal counterpart in Anatolia may be seen as a part and parcel of a more general process of differentiation of heterodox dervish collectivities, which entailed the articulation of separate communal identities – the most prominent related example being the rise of the Bektashi community, especially from the early sixteenth century onwards.

The *velayetname* presents Otman Baba as a typical itinerant heterodox dervish. Nearly all place names and historical events are easily identifiable, and the author impresses with his detailed knowledge of fifteenth-century Ottoman political and social developments.

While mostly devoted to Otman Baba's activities in the Balkans, the *vita* informs us that he came to Anatolia from the "East" (*maşrik tarafından*) at the time of Timur's invasion,[136] and spent several decades in Asia Minor passing through Germiyan and Saruhan, then traveling to Bursa and İznik as well as the Anatolian Black Sea coast, whereafter he crossed into the Balkans, most probably in the mid-1440s, to spend the rest of his life there. In the Balkans, Otman Baba travels mostly in the eastern part of the peninsula, most often in upper Thrace and Tanrıdağı, he also crosses the Balkan range on multiple occasions into

---

[134] Karamustafa, *God's Unruly Friends*, 46.
[135] Şücaüddin Veli's *velayetname* has been recently published, together with an analysis of the work and its main subject, by Yağmur Say, *Kalenderi, Alevi ve Bektaşi Kültünde Önemli Bir Alp-Eren Gazi: Şucâ'eddîn Velî (Sultan Varlığı) ve Velâyetnâmesi* (Ankara: Eskişehir Valiliği, 2010).
[136] *OBV*, 17.

the northeastern Balkans, including the regions of Gerlovo, Deliorman (Ağaç Denizi), Dobrudja, and the Balkan Black Sea coast, including Kaligra (Kaliakra) with its famous convent of Sarı Saltık, Varna, Balçık Hisarı (modern Balchik), and Misivri (mod. Nessebar). He traverses Aegean Thrace and Macedonia, including the towns of Yenice-i Karasu (mod. Genisea), Yenice-i Vardar (mod. Giannitsa), and Siroz (mod. Serres). His peregrinations also bring him to Vidin and Semendire (Smederevo) in the central and western Balkans. While mostly itinerant, on several occasions he would spend a whole year each at places like Pravadi (modern Provadia, near Varna) and Akça Kazanlık (mod. Kazanlık at the foot of the central Balkan range). Otman visits Edirne and Istanbul on multiple occasions, and toward the end of his life he spends around two years in Istanbul (c. 1474–6) before going back to Thrace, where he dies in 1478 near Hasköy (Haskovo) in the foothills of the eastern Rhodopes, likely as a centenarian.

While in his early career in Anatolia, Otman Baba seems to have traveled alone, in the Balkans he gradually recruited a large following of itinerant dervishes who accompanied him and whose number could have reached 300 toward the end of his life. He and his followers are identified as Abdals of Rum (*Rum Abdalları*), and their lifestyle and appearance, including the famous *chahar darb*, clearly identify them as mendicant dervishes of the New Renunciation mold.[137]

Unlike most other Ottoman heterodox Muslim hagiographic works, the *vita* of Otman Baba contains ample hagiological material,[138] as it articulates a theory of sainthood, including the relationship between (the ages of) prophecy and sainthood, and the nature, function, and role of the"pole of poles" (*kutbü'l-aktab*, or just *kutb*). As the cycle of prophecy (Ar. *nubuwwa*, Tr. *nübüvvet*) was sealed by the Prophet Muhammad, the cycle of sainthood (Ar. *walaya*, Tr. *velayet*) was initiated by his son-in-law and cousin Ali b. Abi Talib.[139] While prophecy was manifest and visible (*izhar itdi*), sainthood is esoteric and hidden (*batın*),[140] thus being an inner dimension, custodian (*nigah-daştı*), and shepherd (*çoban*) of prophecy.[141] Denial of sainthood automatically entails denial

---

[137] At one point in the *velayetname* Otman Baba himself exclaims: "*Bir bölük Ḫorāsān tenbelleriyüz*," OBV, 213.
[138] Muslim hagiographical literature contains three main types of material: hagiographical – dealing with the spiritual and moral qualities of the saint, most emphatically exemplified in the legendary stories about his "marvels" (*kerāmāt*), biohagiographical – providing information on the saint's personal and public life, and hagiological – discussing elements of doctrine and other theoretical considerations; Renard, *Friends of God*, 241–42.
[139] OBV, 3; Karamustafa, *God's Unruly Friends*, 47.
[140] OBV, 3.
[141] OBV, 3, 8; Karamustafa, *God's Unruly Friends*, 47.

of prophecy and amounts to a declaration of unbelief.[142] Thus the "mystery of Muhammad" (*sırr-ı Muhammed*) was preserved and perpetuated by a hierarchy of saints who are in control of everything and known only to God, and not to people.[143] These "hidden men" are saints who have been appointed by God to uphold the corporeal and spiritual order of the universe in the age of sainthood. Saints fall into two broad categories: ecstatic (*divane şeklü, meczub*) and licit (*meşruʿ*).[144] While the *vita* presents both types as "perfect," it gives preference to the ecstatic saints who were in a constant state of enthasis (Ar. *jadhba*, Tr. *cezbe*) and could occupy the highest position in the hierarchy – the "pole of poles."[145]

As *kutb*, Otman Baba is the lieutenant (or deputy) of God (*halife-i Hüda*), and has perfect command of esoteric knowledge, he can see and control all things (*sahib-i tasarruf-ı eşyadur*); being invisible to anybody but God (unless he chooses to disclose his identity), he provides guidance to believers.[146] The *kutb* has two "witnesses" (*tanık*s), one of whom is his "accepted disciple" (*mürid-i makbul*) who will succeed him on the throne of poleship; these Three are followed in importance by the Seven, the Forty, the 300, and the 1,000, each (smaller) group being a part of the subsequent (larger) group.[147] This is indeed a version of the Sufi theory of "the hidden men" (Ar. *rijal al-ghayb*, Tr. *rical-ı gayb*), most powerfully developed by Ibn Arabi (d. 1240).[148]

The *vita* points to two saints who were *kutb*s in Anatolia in their respective times – Hacı Bektaş, and later, at the time of Sultan Bayezid I and Timur's invasion in Anatolia, Sultan Şüca (Şücaüddin Veli). It also recounts the story of Sultan Şüca's warning Sultan Bayezid to leave Anatolia upon Timur's invasion and his refusal to accept a money gift from the Ottoman ruler.[149] As we shall see, these two tropes are also introduced in the *velayetname* as elements of Otman Baba's behavior

---

[142] *OBV*, 10, 32, 87, 118; Karamustafa, *God's Unruly Friends*, 47.
[143] *OBV*, 10.
[144] *OBV*, 13–14; Karamustafa, *God's Unruly Friends*, 47.
[145] *OBV*, 13; Karamustafa, *God's Unruly Friends*, 47.
[146] *OBV*, 12, 40.
[147] Ibid., 44.
[148] There exist different taxonomies of this hierarchy of hidden saints, the most widespread one features 300 *akhyar* (the "virtuous" ones), 40 *abdal*, seven *budala* (both *abdal* and *budala* may be translated as "substitutes"), four *awtad* (pegs), of whom three are *naqib*s (leaders) and one is the pole; Uludağ, "Ricâlü'l-Gayb." On Ibn 'Arabi's classic exposition of this theory, see Michel Chodkiewicz, *Seal of the Saints: Prophethood and Sainthood in the Doctrine of Ibn 'Arabi*, tr. Liadain Sherrard (Cambridge: The Islamic Texts Society, 1993), 74–116, on the theory's rendition by Abd al-Rahman Jami (d. 1492), see İnalcık, "Dervish and Sultan," 21–22. See also I. Goldziher, "Abdâl" and "Awtâd," *EI²*.
[149] *OBV*, 12.

vis-à-vis Sultan Mehmed II – underscoring both the *kutb*'s miraculous ability to predict the future and his political non-conformism.

Otman Baba's identity as *kutb* also carries visible messianic and especially millenarian overtones. These could often be an integral element of the concept of poleship in popular heterodox Sufism, whereby the *kutb* may be seen by his followers as a savior figure who would deliver them from oppression and bring justice, especially in times of perceived crisis.[150] Otman Baba claims to be the one who descends on earth once every 1,000 years to show compassion to all God's creatures.[151] While he does not make the outright claim of being the Mahdi, he is referred to as having the qualities of the Mahdi of the Age (*mehdi-i zaman sıfatlu*) and to ride his horse in a Mahdi-like (*mehdi-var*) fashion.[152] Among Otman's most radical claims are his embracing Mansur al-Hallaj's celebrated assertion to be the Divine Truth (or the Divine Absolute) – "*ana'l haqq*" (Tr. "*ene'l hak*")[153] – thus proclaiming the unity of God and man, as well as his claims to be the incarnation (*hulul*) of a number of celebrated prophetic and saintly figures: the prophets Adam, Moses, Jesus, and Muhammad[154] as well as Ali (more indirectly), Hüseyin, Mansur al-Hallaj, Sarı Saltık, and Hacı Bektaş in the age of sainthood.[155] The *vita* emphatically underscores the importance of the historical role of Ali, Hasan and Hüseyin, and the Holy Family (*ehl-i beyt*) and the need for them to be deeply revered. Ali is presented as the initiator and the mystery of sainthood (*sırr-ı velayet*), a hero of *gaza* in the formative age of Islam, and the father (in union with the Prophet's daughter Fatima) of

---

[150] A.Y. Ocak, "Syncrétisme et esprit messianique: le concept de *qotb* et les chefs des mouvements messianiques aux époques seldjoukide et ottomane (XIIIe–XVIIe siècle)," in *Syncrétismes et hérésies dans l'Orient seldjoukide et ottoman (XIV-e-XVIIIe siècle): actes de colloque du collège de France, octobre 2001*, ed. Gilles Veinstein (Paris and Dudley, MA: Peeters, 2005), 249–257.

[151] *OBV*, 70, 212.

[152] Ibid., 248, 152, 155, 173.

[153] Ibid., 120, 146, 158–159, 181, 224, 253, 265. On the famous mystic who was executed in Baghdad in 922, see L. Massignon and L. Gardet, "al-Ḥallādj," *EI²*.

[154] The claim that Otman Baba was the incarnation of the prophets Adam, Moses, Jesus, and Muhammad is a staple occurrence in the *vita*; *OBV*, 16, 146, 160, 162, 165, 172, 181, 200, 265, 274.

[155] While according to the *velayetname* Otman Baba does not directly claim to be the incarnation of Ali, he is referred to as carrying Ali's sword on numerous occasions, *OBV*, 150, 155, 172, 178, 179, 181, 183, 184, 210. Otman Baba claims to be *sırr-ı Yezdan* (the mystery of God) – a designation often used for Ali in heterodox Sufi tradition, ibid., 146, 168, 172, 200, 274; he also refers to his detained disciples at Varna as "my Hasans and Hüseyins" ("*benüm Ḥasan ile Ḥüseyinlerüm*"), ibid. 150; praise in verse for Otman Baba also identifies him with Ali and the Light of Ali (*nūr-ı ʿAlī*), ibid. 254–257. On Otman Baba's incarnationist claims regarding Hüseyin, see ibid., 36, regarding Mansur al-Hallaj 120, regarding Sarı Saltık 23, 105, 110, 117, 180; regarding Hacı Bektaş 202, 242.

Imam Hasan who was poisoned and Imam Hüseyin who fell as a martyr at Karbala.[156] The relation to Mansur al-Hallaj underscores the organic ties between the latter's radical theology and Otman Baba's own religio-political views, while Otman's claims to be the incarnation of Sarı Saltık and Hacı Bektaş position him firmly as a preeminent saintly figure in the Anatolian and Balkan popular heterodox mystic tradition.

While reverence for Ali and the Holy Family and some of Otman Baba's other beliefs mentioned above were generally a part of the popular epic tradition and the heterodox milieu of late medieval Anatolia,[157] a specific and powerful influence on his theology, religio-political views, and practices was Hurufism. A messianic sect with a cabalistic inclination founded by Fazlallah Astarabadi who was executed on accusations of heresy by Timur in 1394, it quickly gained influence in Anatolia and the Balkans in the fifteenth century, largely among the already existing popular heterodox non-Sharia-minded groups. A major channel for the spread of Hurufi beliefs in Anatolia and the Balkans was Fazlallah's disciple Imad al-Din Nesimi who, according to tradition, made the *"ana'l haqq"* claim during the interrogations and torture leading to his execution in Aleppo in 1417 and whose mystical poetry in Turkish would make him one of the "seven great poets" (*yedi ulu ozan*) of the Anatolian and Balkan heterodox (later Bektashi/Kızılbaş/Alevi) literary tradition.[158] As Irène Mélikoff has argued, Nesimi's perceived proclamation of the *"ana'l-haqq"* claim at the time of his execution earned him the fame of a "national Mansur al-Hallaj" among the Turks.[159] Otman Baba's *velayetname* also connects al-Hallaj and Nesimi referring to the two of them as the "poles of (religious) knowledge" who paid with their lives for their heretical beliefs.[160] Apart from reverence for Ali and the Holy Family and al-Hallaj's heretical claims that are well established in Hurufi tradition, another aspect of Otman Baba's religious views and practices that may be seen as a direct influence from Hurufism is "the cult of seven," that number being central to Hurufi symbolism, cosmology, and iconography. Hurufis believed that the seven lines of hair and the seven holes on the human face[161] bore the signs of God's speech and could explain

---

[156] *OBV*, 6–9. Ali's role as a *gazi* is evidenced by references to his participation at the Battle of Uhud (AD 625) and the Battle of Khaybar (AD 629).
[157] Mélikoff, *Hadji Bektach*, 47–50.
[158] Mélikoff, *Hadji Bektach*, 122.
[159] Ibid., 122.
[160] *"Manṣūr ve Nesīmī gibi ʿālimler ki ʿilmüñ ḳuṭbları olmış iken şerīʿate muḫālif kelām itdükleri içün ḳatl idüp anları helāk itdiler."* In fact, this claim is imbedded in the speech of the leading *ulema* of Istanbul who complain to Sultan Mehmed II about Otman Baba's heretical beliefs, *OBV*, 219.
[161] The seven lines of hair being the hairline, the two eyebrows, and the two sets of eyelashes; the seven holes, the two eyes, the two ears, the two nostrils, and the mouth.

human nature; these attributes of the human face corresponded to the seven verses of the Qur'an's opening chapter (the *Fatiha*), the seven climes, the seven seas, the seven heavens, and the seven stars that were part of the terrestrial and cosmic order.[162] In the *velayetname*, we see Otman Baba repeating these claims almost verbatim at a gathering with his Abdals while wearing a seven-gored headpiece.[163] He introduces the seven services/posts (*yedi hizmet/yedi post*) in his dervish collectivity. The same emphasis is probably the best explanation for the heptagonal structure of Otman Baba's mausoleum (*türbe*), the same feature characterizing the mausolea of the three most important Rum Abdal saints of the eastern Balkans in the sixteenth century – Akyazılı Baba, Kademli Baba, and Demir Baba.[164] Otman Baba's "cult of seven" should thus be differentiated from the corresponding emphasis on the number twelve in the Bektashi tradition.

Otman Baba is presented as generally well received in villages and small towns where his radical propaganda could be attractive to those impoverished groups that bore the burden of increased taxation under Mehmed II's centralizing regime – people in villages and small towns would often ask for his blessing and offer sacrificial meals to him and his Abdal retinue.[165] However, the saint is most active among pastoral nomadic Turcomans, and specifically the *yürüks* whose main modes of subsistence were animal husbandry (especially sheep-breeding) and participation in raids along the Ottoman frontier with Christendom.[166] This largely explains his main area of activity – the eastern Balkans, which had a large concentration of *yürük* populations at the time – from Thrace, Tanrıdağı, and eastern Macedonia in the south through Gerlovo at the foothills of the Balkan range to Deliorman and Dobrudja in the north, reaching the Danube.[167] The *velayetname* points to numerous examples

---

[162] Fatih Usluer, *Hurufilik: İlk Elden Kaynaklarla Doğuşundan İtibaren* (Istanbul: Kabalcı Yayınevi: 2009), 209, 264–268, 277–285, 297–300; Shahzad Bashir, *Fazlallah Astarabadi and the Hurufis* (Oxford: Oneworld, 2005), 51–52. Mélikoff insists on a close connection between Hurufism and Ismailism and would also maintain that view with respect to Ismaili influences, via Hurufism, on Otman Baba, *Hadji Bektach*, 116–125; Irène Mélikoff, "Les voies de pénétration de l'hétérodoxie islamique en Thrace et dans les Balkans aux XIVe–XVe siècles," in *The Via Egnatia Under Ottoman Rule*, 160.

[163] "*Daḫi ol kān-ı velayet kendü mübarek eliyle ol yedi tergli tāc dikmiş idi. Ol arada mübarek eline ol yedi tergli tācı alup, ayıtdı kim: Ḫaṭ yedi, gök yedi, yir yedi, ve kevākib-i heft kim terbiyet-i eşyādur. Ve fātiḥa kim seb'u'l-meṣānīdür ki ümmü'l-Ḳur'āndur,*" OBV, 100.

[164] Mélikoff shares this view but connects it to Ismailism as well, *Hadji Bektach*, 125. For other hypotheses, see Kiprovska, "The Mihaloğlu Family," 210.

[165] *OBV*, 71–74, 81, 99, 106, 109, 114, 120.

[166] The *yürüks* will be discussed in more detail in Chapter 4, with a focus on Deliorman and Gerlovo. The most comprehensive coverage of this group continues to be Gökbilgin, *Rumeli'de Yürükler*.

[167] See Mélikoff, "Les voies," 159–170.

of "shepherds" becoming Otman's disciples and joining his Rum Abdal retinue;[168] one of his detractors calls him *"yürük kocası"* (i.e. a *yürük* elder); a *yürük* commander (*yürük subaşısı*) builds a convent in Thrace for a group of dervishes close to Otman Baba and becomes his follower.[169] All this is hardly surprising as Otman Baba's radical theology entails a lenient attitude toward the ritual prescriptions of the Sharia and contains clear messianic and millenarian overtones. Combined with his wonder-working abilities and his support for *gaza*, it fit well the "undisciplined religiosity"[170] of these semi-nomadic Turcoman populations (as opposed to "settled orthodoxy"). As the "pole of poles," the "lord of the two worlds" (*şah-ı dü cihan*) and the "mine of sainthood" (*kan-ı velayet*) who claimed to be in control of everything that happens on earth, Otman Baba posed a direct challenge to the legitimacy of the socio-political claims to authority of urban civilization, represented by Mehmed II's centralizing state. Among the main principles of his Rum Abdal doctrine was to reach out to and help the oppressed and helpless.[171] This strengthened the receptivity to his mission amongst social groups that felt gradually displaced and marginalized by the emerging Ottoman bureaucratic regime – like the Turcoman nomads, especially as *gaza* was increasingly becoming the preserve of the central state with its regular military units. Likewise, it is not surprising either that the *velayetname* casts a prominent member of one of the most distinguished Balkan frontier-lord families, the Mihaloğulları, as being close to Otman. While Kızıl Deli's *vita* praises Gazi Evrenos Bey as a champion of *gaza* and a *gaza* commander appointed by Kızıl Deli, Otman Baba's *velayetname* presents Mihaloğlu Ali Bey (d. 1507) – a grandson of the famous Gazi Mihal Bey[172] and a leading raider commander (*akıncı beği*) under Mehmed II and Bayezid II, who also served as provincial governor at various locations along the Ottoman Danubian frontier – as a relentless *gazi* who recognized Otman Baba as his spiritual guide and owed his success in his numerous campaigns in Hungary to the blessing of the saint. Mihaloğlu Ali Bey offers Otman Baba numerous gifts and on one occasion his *gazi*s convene in a council with Otman's Rum Abdals.[173] The close relationship between the

---

[168] *OBV*, 124, 131, 138.

[169] Ibid., 65, 94.

[170] I borrow the concept from Said Amir Arjomand, *The Shadow of God and the Hidden Imam: Religion, Political Order, and Societal Change in Shi'ite Iran from the Beginning to 1890* (Chicago and London: The University of Chicago Press, 1984), 67.

[171] İnalcık, "Dervish and Sultan," 23.

[172] On Mihaloğlu Ali Bey, see Olga Zirojević, "Smederevski sandžakbeg Ali-Beg Mihaloglu," *Zbornik za Istoriju. Matica Srpska* 3 (1971): 9–27; Levend, *Gazavāt-Nāmeler*, 187–195.

[173] The *velayetname* points to two occasions on which the two meet, once near Semendire (Smederevo, in northern Serbia) whose governor Ali Bey was at the time, whereby Otman Baba blessed Ali Bey's campaign against Hungary, whereafter Ali Bey, returning

two figures as suggested in the *vita* is corroborated by Ottoman archival evidence from the early sixteenth century that demonstrates that members of the Mihaloğlu family patronized Otman Baba's mausoleum/convent complex in Thrace, and the famous seventeenth-century Ottoman traveller Evliya Çelebi goes as far as to claim that the complex was indeed constructed by Ali Bey. While archival sources do not provide firm proof of this, Ali Bey may well have sponsored the construction of the mausoleum, and Evliya Çelebi's claims at least serve as evidence of the vivid memory of the bond between the two.[174]

One last group with which Otman Baba and his Abdals maintained close and cordial relations were the already mentioned "Abdals of Rum of Anatolia" who are referred to as "Sultan Şüca Abdalları."[175] While in Istanbul, Otman Baba and his disciples cross the Bosphorus to have a reunion of sorts with their Anatolian brethren at Üsküdar and, as it was the time of their festival (*kiçi bayram*) they went together to the tomb of Sultan Şücaüddin Veli (near Eskişehir in western Anatolia) and performed the "great pilgrimage" (*hacc-ı kebir*), which must mean that they paid a visit to the nearby shrine of Seyyid Gazi, which, as is known from sixteenth-century observers, was the major venue of communal gathering for the Rum Abdals at the time.[176] It is on this occasion that Otman Baba declares that there are two persons (i.e. leaders) in the whole creation, himself and Sultan Şücaüddin Veli, and enjoins his followers to revere the latter.[177] The close connection between the shrine of Seyyid Gazi, as well as Otman Baba and Şücaüddin Veli as patron-saints of the Abdals of Rum in the Ottoman domains is confirmed by Vahidi in whose 1522 treatise on dervish groups the Abdals of Rum are described as a distinct dervish

---

with a lot of booty, came to meet the saint, offered him a sacrificial meal (*kurban*) and gave him a horse as a gift; and the second time near Edirne where Ali Bey kissed the hand of the saint, offering him his sword and received Otman's blessing, after which Ali Bey's warriors gathered together with Otman Baba's Abdals; *OBV*, 73–74, 168–169.

[174] Evliya Çelebi, *Evliyâ Çelebi Seyahatnâmesi* (Istanbul: Yapı Kredi Yayınları, 2011), vol. 8, 344; Kiprovska, "The Mihaloğlu Family," 197.

[175] *OBV*, 244–251.

[176] Ibid., 249. It is not quite clear whether the great annual festival at the shrine of Seyyid Gazi, which coincided with the pilgrimage to Mecca, is meant here; the reference to "*kiçi bâyrâm/kiçi ḥacât*" rather suggests that it is the feast of breaking the fast that the author has in mind. On the festival at the shrine of Seyyid Gazi, see Yürekli, *Architecture and Hagiography*, 19–20, 42–47.

[177] "*Biz bu mülkde iki kişiyiz ki birimüz Ḥüssâm Şâh ve birimüze Şefkülli Beğ dirler... Şefkülli Beğ'i dost dutun ki ben size sevem daḥi*," *OBV*, 244. The passage also suggests that Otman Baba considered Şücaüddin Veli (Şefkülli Beğ) to be his guide; this connection has been preserved to the present day whereby modern Babai/Kızılbaş/Alevi followers of Otman Baba in the Balkans pay visits to Şücaüddin Veli's tomb and consider themselves subordinate to the "hearth" of Şücaüddin Veli in Anatolia (*Şücâ'üddîn Velî ocağı*), Mehmet Ersal, "Şücaeddin Veli Ocağı: Balkan Aleviliğindeki Yeri, Rolü ve Önemi," *TKHBVAD* 63 (2012), 207–230; Kiprovska, "The Mihaloğlu Family," 207.

collectivity whose members are reported as declaring: "We come from Rum... from the hearth of Sultan Seyyid Gazi. We are the Abdals of Rum with bodies covered with burn wounds. We are the disciples (*köçekler*) of Otman Baba carrying the staff of Şüca'[üddin Veli]."[178]

While Otman Baba's mission in the eastern Balkans enjoys popularity amongst pastoral Turcomans (especially *yürüks*) and frontier-lord families, villagers, and small-town residents, the *velayetname* exposes numerous and deep tensions between him and groups that either directly represented the Ottoman dynasty and state or were perceived as displaying a conformist attitude toward Mehmed II's regime. Among these groups one counts sheykhs (*meşayih*) associated with institutionalized, *tariqa* (Tr. *tarikat*) Sufism, the populace of the big cities – especially of Edirne and Istanbul – whom Otman addresses as "ugly townsmen,"[179] the urban *ulema* class in particular, and the Ottoman dynasty and its functionaries.

In his radical criticism of the representatives of institutionalized Sufism – those sheykhs who belong to a Sufi brotherhood (*sahib-i tarikat*), reside in Sufi hospices (*sahib-i tekye*), and wear the woollen cloak characteristic of Sufis (*sahib-i hırka*) – Otman Baba makes a clear distinction between these and true men of sainthood (with whom he identifies). The "people of *tarikat*" do not possess the quality of sainthood, which cannot be acquired through effort and striving – sainthood comes only by way of divine inspiration, God's "unveiling and miracles."[180] While the "men of the hospices" claim to be *evliya* among the gullible common folk, Otman Baba's *vita* exposes this as a lie: they could only acquire gnosis, or spiritual knowledge (*ma'rifet*), and are selling their "rotten knowledge" ("*çürük ma'rifet*") to the people, gathering disciples and claiming to be their spiritual guides.[181] Having embraced this world ("*dünyayı kabul edüp*"), they possess slaves and concubines, dress in nice clothes, and go out to hunt with fine Arabians and hounds.[182] As Ahmet Karamustafa has convincingly argued, this radical propaganda against respectable, institutionalized Sufism, which emanated from increasingly marginalized antinomian groups such as Otman Baba's Abdals of Rum, may be seen as a reaction to the firm and decisive incorporation of institutional Sufism into the fabric of everyday life, whereby *tarikat* Sufism enjoyed the support of

---

[178] *Vāhidī's Menākıb-i Hvoca-i Cihān ve Netīce-i Cān*, ed. Ahmet Karamustafa (Cambridge, MA: Department of Near Eastern Languages and Civilizations, Harvard University, 1993), f. 42b/128. Also cited in Yürekli, *Architecture and Hagiography*, 41.

[179] "*Bak bre, çirkin şehirlü*," "*Bak bre, çirkin gebe karınlu şehirlüsü*," *OBV*, 171, 160.

[180] *OBV*, 43, 45.

[181] Ibid., 11, 45.

[182] Ibid., 45.

the dynasty and state elites through the building of hospices and the establishment of pious endowments.[183] The process of marginalization and assimilation of antinomian mysticism into the Ottoman order had advanced well enough by the end of Otman Baba's life, that a figure like him – a vehemently non-conformist, itinerant dervish, who would have thrived in the frontier zone – was now more of an exception, a representative of a fading phenomenon. This may in turn serve to explain the acuteness of the *velayetname*'s criticism of what Otman Baba understood to be "conformist Sufis" whose rise was intertwined with the emergence of the Ottoman imperial order.

While spurning conformist Sufis in general, there is one (emerging) dervish group with which Otman seems to be in continuous competition and conflict. During his travels in Rumeli he repeatedly encounters a certain Mümin Dervish, a head of a hospice in Zağra (mod. Stara Zagora in Thrace), and his guide Bayezid Baba, who resides at a convent in Yenice-i Vardar. While Mümin Dervish and Bayezid Baba are not openly presented as "Bektashis" (the designation "Bektaşiler" is never used in the *velayetname*), they clearly adhere to the growing cult of Hacı Bektaş, as Bayezid Baba goes on a visit to the shrine of Hacı Bektaş in Suluca Karahöyük. Bayezid Baba also earns Otman Baba's censure when, after being accused of introducing "unlawful innovatitons" (*bid'at*) in Salonica, he obeys the city judge and *ulema* – something Otman Baba would never have done; Otman's fervent non-conformism is one more proof of his being the true "pole of poles."[184] Mümin Dervish repeatedly challenges Otman Baba's spiritual supremacy; on one occasion he even reports Otman to the governor of Varna for making the claim to being God, whereupon the governor orders the judge of nearby Pravadi (Provadia) to investigate the matter. As some of Otman's Abdals are detained and interrogated by the judge, Mümin Dervish tries to convert Otman Baba's disciples to his "way," claiming the support of the Ottoman authorities. In the end Otman Baba triumphs as his dervishes are exonerated.[185]

Another encounter with dervishes associated with Hacı Bektaş takes place in Istanbul toward the end of Otman's life (in the mid-1470s). This time, his rivals' affiliation is emphatically explicit – they are presented as "the dervishes of Hacı Bektaş" and their leader, a certain Mahmud Çelebi, as a lieutenant of Hacı Bektaş.[186] Having learned that Otman Baba

---

[183] Karamustafa, *God's Unruly Friends*, 90–96.
[184] *OBV*, 62–63.
[185] Ibid., 145–151.
[186] The dervish group is referred to as "*Ḥācı Bektāş Velī ḥażretlerinüñ dervīşleri*," and Mahmud Çelebi as "*ḥünkār ḥalīfesi*," *OBV*, 242.

is in town, Mahmud Çelebi, possibly a descendant of Hacı Bektaş and even a brother of Balım Sultan,[187] comes to pay his respects together with his followers. When Otman asks them who the *hünkar* ("sovereign") is, they reply, "It is our Hünkar Hacı Bektaş Veli." In response, Otman Baba asserts that he himself was the rock-dove who flew over seven seas, thus claiming to be Hacı Bektaş's reincarnation.[188] Otman is especially upset by Mahmud Çelebi's fine attire which reflects his embrace of worldly life and puts him in the group of those false mystics he frowns upon. Having been denounced as an impostor and a "hypocrite" (*münafık*)[189] and intimidated by Otman Baba, Mahmud Çelebi has to seek refuge in a nearby Edhemi hospice.[190]

Otman Baba's hostility toward the followers of Hacı Bektaş as the sole specific enemy dervish group in the *velayetname* deserves special attention. The established scholarly argument presents the history of Bektashism as divided into two main periods. Until the late fifteenth century it did not exist as an organized brotherhood (*tarikat*) but was a growing saintly cult.[191] From the early sixteenth century onwards, Balım

---

[187] Mahmud Çelebi is referred to as a descendant of Hacı Bektaş by Aşıkpaşazade, as well as in a *waqf* register entry regarding his convent in Istanbul, dated 1546. He and Balım Sultan may have had a common father by the name of Resul Çelebi; Yürekli, *Architecture and Hagiography*, 33–34.

[188] *OBV*, 242. The original motif of Hacı Bektaş who, transformed into a rock-dove, flew over seven seas to come to Anatolia is found in his *vita*, see *Velâyetnâme. Hacı Bektaş-ı Veli*, ed. Hamiye Duran (Ankara: Türkiye Diyanet Vakfı, 2014), 2nd edn., 178–179.

[189] Originating from the Prophet Muhammad's tensions with the "hypocrites" of Medina to whom the 63rd *sura* ("Sūrat al-Munāfiqūn") of the Qur'an is devoted, the concepts of hypocrisy (*nifāq*) and hypocrites (*munāfiqūn*) have been used to designate "half-hearted believers who outwardly profess Islam while their hearts harbor doubt or even unbelief;" C.P. Adlang, "Hypocrites and Hypocrisy," in *Encyclopaedia of the Qur'an*, vol. 2, 468–472. The use of "münafık" to describe Otman Baba's Bektashi enemies is thus not a random choice, especially in the context of the *velayetname*'s claim that he was the reincarnation of the Prophet Muhammad. On another plane, this accusation levied against Mahmud Çelebi could be read as a claim that the latter distorted and/or misappropriated the legacy of Hacı Bektaş (whose reincarnation Otman Baba also claimed to be).

[190] *OBV*, 242–243. The mention of an Edhemi hospice is a rare reference to a specific dervish group in the *velayetname*, other than the Bektashis and the Abdals of Rum. Among the nine major dervish groups in Ottoman society featured in Vahidi's 1522 treatise, they are one of three of which Vahidi approves, the rest are declared heretical; Karamustafa, *Vāhidī's Menākıb*, 191–197/ff. 105b–111b; ibid., "Kalenders, Abdals, Hayderis: The Formation of the Bektaşiye in the Sixteenth Century," in *Süleyman the Second and His Time*, ed. Halil İnalcık and Cemal Kafadar (Istanbul: The Isis Press, 1993), 125, and Süleyman Uludağ, "Edhemiyye," in *TDVİA*, vol. 10, 421.

[191] Ocak points out that in the early hagiographic literature associated with the cult of Hacı Bektaş and produced in the late fifteenth century, most notably the *velayetname* of Hacı Bektaş itself, the followers of the cult of Haci Bektaş are not referred to as a separate dervish group, even less so as an organized brotherhood; *Kalenderîler*, 203–207; see also Karamustafa, "Kalenders, Abdals, Hayderis," 122–123.

Sultan (d. 1516), capitalizing on the rapid growth of the cult of Hacı
Bektaş in the second half of the fifteenth century and the asserted connection between this cult and the Janissaries, laid the foundations of an
institutionalized Bektashi *tarikat* which came to be recognized and supported by the Ottoman dynasty, for which reason he became known in
the history of Bektashism as the second patron saint (*Pir-i Sani*) of the
order, after Hacı Bektaş himself.[192] Emerging as the most prominent case
of elaborate, large-scale, long-term institutionalization among heterodox
groups in the early modern Ottoman period, the Bektashi order would
gradually assimilate into itself other heterodox dervish groups, such as
the Abdals of Rum, the Kalenderis, the Haydaris, etc., over the course of
the sixteenth and seventeenth centuries.[193]

The *velayetname*'s reference to "the dervishes of Hacı Bektaş Veli" is
likely the earliest of this sort and the whole episode suggests that they
were already emerging as a distinct collectivity from the 1470s onward
and that their emergence, associated in the *velayetname* with their political and religious conformism, could be perceived as threatening to the
identity and independence of other heterodox groups, such as Otman
Baba's Abdals of Rum. It is Aşıkpaşazade's chronicle composed in the
late fifteenth century (but after Otman Baba's *velayetname*) that first
uses the designation "Bektashis" ("Bekdaşiler").[194] The *velayetname* is
also most likely the earliest source that suggests a connection between
the Janissaries and the cult of Hacı Bektaş; as the soldier (apparently a
Janissary) who accompanies Otman Baba to Istanbul on the orders of
Mehmed II claims that his headgear was modeled on that of Hacı Bektaş,
thus provoking Otman Baba to declare himself (as in his encounter with
Mahmud Çelebi) the incarnation of Hacı Bektaş (as well as of Ali).[195]
Importantly, Otman Baba's claim to be Hacı Bektaş's incarnation cannot
be seen as a proof of him being a "Bektashi." Rather, it should be placed
in the context of the *velayetname*'s assertions that Otman Baba was the

[192] John K. Birge, *The Bektashi Order of Dervishes*, (London: Luzac and Co., 1937), 56–58.
[193] Ocak, *Kalenderîler*, 199–209; Karamustafa, "Kalenders, Abdals, Hayderis," 121–129.
See also further discussion in Chapter 6.
[194] *Aşıkpaşazâde Tarihi*, 308–309. In the same passage Aşıkpaşazade also refers to Mahmud
Çelebi as a Bektashi leader and criticizes his "devilish customs," and especially his consumption of intoxicants.
[195] *OBV*, 202; Aşıkpaşazade denies the claim that the distinctive white Janissary cap (*ak
börk*) came from the "Bektashis," asserting that it appeared in Bilecik in the time of
Orhan Gazi (i.e. in the context of the early Ottoman *gaza* campaigns) and that it was a
sheykh by the name of Abdal Musa (indeed, the pre-eminent figure associated with the
rise of the cult of Hacı Bektaş and a prominent member of the later Bektashi "pantheon
of saints") who participated in many of these campaigns, befriended the Janissaries, and
took the cap design from them; *Âşıkpaşazâde Tarihi*, 308.

incarnation of close to a dozen of preeminent prophets and saints which could be seen as further proof of his unquestionable poleship.

The Ottoman *ulema* in Edirne and Istanbul are other prominent opponents of Otman Baba and his Abdals. Unlike "conformist" dervishes whom the *velayetname* casts as Otman's direct rivals, the tensions between the urban *ulema*, seen as closely associated with the (new) Ottoman centralizing order, and Otman Baba are more distant. Otman's provocative claims on his visits to the two cities would lead to the *ulema*'s subsequent accusations of heresy which would prompt the dynasty and its executives to act upon those accusations. Thus, on several visits to Edirne Otman Baba, accompanied by his "army of Abdals" (*leşker-i abdalan*), scandalizes the city residents by making the claim of *"ene'l-hak,"* being "God's mystery" (*sırr-ı Yezdan*), "Muhammad's mystery" (*sırr-ı Muhammed*) as well as the incarnation of Adam, Moses, Jesus, and Muhammad, whereby he is reported to the city judge for sedition and disregarding prayer.[196] Having been expelled several times from Edirne, Otman visits it once more to encounter the local Sharia-upholding *ulema* and (perceivedly "conformist") urban Sufi sheykhs[197] (*şeyh ü meşayih ve ta'ife-i ulema-i şeriat*) who question his Abdals about their true religious identity, accusing them of not belonging to any recognized religious community (*millet*) or "rite" (*mezheb*), to which they answer: "He [Otman Baba] is the mine of sainthood and the Axis Mundi of the whole world, the lord of the horizons and the guide of the Court... We are the army of the lord of sainthood and the Pole of Poles of the whole of existence, and we are his Forty, Seven, and Three. We are the Abdals of Rum and thus we became free from Satan's whispers and from all trickery and deceit, artifice and hypocrisy."[198] Thereupon the local *ulema* send a letter of complaint to Mehmed II who summons the saint to the capital. Otman Baba's encounters with the *ulema* of Istanbul during his two-year long stay there (*c.* 1474–6) follow a similar pattern. When two leading *alim*s, Molla Gürani and Molla Kırımi, approach Mehmed II and report to him about Otman Baba's disrespect for the Sharia and heretical claims – pointing out that even great scholars such as the "poles of knowledge" (*'ilmün kutbları*) Mansur

---

[196] Ibid., 155–163.
[197] Ibid., 189. The *velayetname* groups the urban mystics of Edirne together with the city's *ulema* as representatives of urban, Sharia-regulated order and enemies of Otman Baba who question the soundness of his beliefs.
[198] *"Ol kān-ı velāyet ve kutbü'l-aktāb-ı cihān ve server-i afāk ve mürşid-i bārgāhdur... Biz ol şāh-ı velāyet'üñ ve kutbü'l-aktāb-ı temāmetüñ leşkeri ve kırklarıyuz ve yedileri ve üçleriyüz ki abdālān-ı Rūm olup vesvās-ı şeytāndan ve hīle vü mekrden ve zerk [ü] riyādan āzād u fāriğ olduk,"* OBV, 190.

al-Hallaj and Nesimi paid with their lives for similar offenses – the sultan defends Otman Baba saying that he is a saintly man (*sahib-i velayet*) and the Pole of Poles.[199]

Otman Baba's relations with Mehmed II and the Ottoman dynasty are, in certain ways, the most important aspect of his life. Throughout the *velayetname*, Otman is presented as the possessor of power vastly superior to that of the dynasty; while the Ottoman sultan is a mere worldly ruler (*sultan-ı 'alem, dünya beği*),[200] Otman Baba is the "lord of the two worlds"[201] – all failures and achievements of the dynasty and state are the result of his blessing and support or lack thereof.[202] Upon Murad II's death, Mehmed, then prince-governor in Manisa, has a dream in which Otman Baba appears to him saying, "I have come to make you *padişah* of Rum."[203] Shortly thereafter Otman Baba prays on a hill overlooking Constantinople saying, "I have come to conquer this city."[204] Thereafter the saint encounters Mehmed II and his commander (later grand vizier) Mahmud Pasha in Istanbul and warns them not to undertake the siege of Belgrade they were contemplating. After the siege fails (1456), Otman Baba and the sultan meet again, Mehmed II kisses the saint's hand and recognizes his superiority, and upon being asked by Otman Baba who the *padişah* is (*Padişah kimdir?*), admits that Otman Baba is the true *padişah* and he, Mehmed II, is his obedient son.[205] This exchange is used to explain Mehmed II's later admiration for Otman Baba and his defense of the dervish against the *ulema*'s attacks. In his later career Otman continues to direct the fortunes of the Ottoman state and dynasty – it is his spiritual power that brings Mehmed II success in the Battle of Başkent/ Otlukbeli against the Aqqoyunlu Uzun Hasan in 1473; during the saint's long stay in Istanbul (*c*. 1474–6) the sultan, probably remembering the lesson of his failed Belgrad campaign, sends his commanders to ask for Otman's blessing for a particular military mission. Thus, when Süleyman Pasha fails to obtain it, he fails miserably in his campaign in Kara Boğdan

---

[199] *OBV*, 218–219. On Molla Gürani (d. 1488), the great Ottoman jurist and *müfti* of Istanbul under Mehmed II and Bayezid II, see M. Kamil Yaşaroğlu, "Molla Gürânî," *TDVİA*, vol. 30, 248–250. The claim that leading Ottoman religious scholars referred to two famous heretics (from the perspective of Sunni orthodoxy) as "the poles of (religious) knowledge" is highly dubious; it could be seen as an example of the time-honored polemic device of placing a tenuous claim in the mouth of an adversary to make that claim emphatically credible to the work's intended audience.

[200] For *sulṭān-ı 'ālem, dünyā beği*, *OBV*, 41, 233; İnalcık, "Dervish and Sultan," 24.

[201] I.e. *şāh-ı dü cihān, şāh-ı dü 'ālem, iki cihānuñ şāhı. OBV*, 54, 149, 224.

[202] Otman Baba would also uniformly reject gift offers from Mehmed II and state executives, *OBV*, 40, 214, 232–233; see also Karamustafa, *God's Unruly Friends*, 48.

[203] *Ve ben seni Rūm'a pādişāh eylemeye geldüm, OBV*, 18.

[204] *OBV*, 19.

[205] Ibid., 38–41.

(Moldavia); conversely, Ahmed Pasha receives Otman Baba's blessing and returns victorious from his campaign in the Crimea.[206] The interactions between dervish and sultan during Otman Baba's stay in Istanbul near the end of his life further assert the superior position of Otman Baba vis-à-vis Mehmed II and his worldly authority. In their last meeting held in the palace, Otman once again insists that he is the real holder of power. Making probably his most memorable religio-political claims vis-à-vis Mehmed II, Otman contends that he, and not the Ottoman sultan, is the real "Muhammed" (echoing his claim to be the incarnation of the Prophet Muhammad, but also implying a word-play with the sultan's name).[207] He then insists again on being the true *padişah*, as an urban dweller (*şehirlü*) such as Mehmed II could not have a legitimate claim to political authority.[208] A truly remarkable claim, this can be read as a textual expression of the last ripples of the Chinggisid moment,[209] the belief that mandate to political authority did not rest with "the settlers," the urban and, more generally, the sedentary classes, but with the "wanderers," the nomads and itinerants. Otman likewise berates Mehmed II for building and settling in a palace, thus hinting at his disappointment with the sultan's betrayal of the legacy of his forefathers.[210]

Be that as it may, at the end of his life Otman Baba is presented as suddenly abandoning his preference for the non-conformist, itinerant and mendicant lifestyle that he has practiced and advocated throughout his career. Following his last meeting with Mehmed II he leaves the capital and settles in northern Thrace, near the eastern slopes of the Rhodope Mountains, where he would die in 1478. Feeling that his life is nearing its end, he holds several "councils" with his Abdals to whom he offers words

[206] Ibid., 152–154, 225–28. The two commanders and respective military campaigns referred to here must be Hadım Süleyman Pasha – then governor-general of Rumelia, who was defeated in the Battle of Vaslui (January 10, 1475) by Stephen III the Great of Moldavia (r. 1457–1504), and grand vizier Gedik Ahmed Pasha – the conqueror of Kefe (Caffa) in the Crimea in June 1475.

[207] The assimilated "Mehmed" is the most widespread rendition of "Muhammad" in Turkish, Mehmed II's name could well have been pronounced "Mehemmed" or "Muhammed" in his own time as the orthography in contemporary Ottoman documents and chronicles suggests. The exact claim is: *"Sen Muḥammed nesne değilsüñ ki Muḥammed ve üç eri benem."* (*üç eri* here likely refers to Otman's claim to be also the incarnation of Adam, Moses, and Jesus, as they usually come "packaged" together with the Prophet Muhammad), *OBV*, 253.

[208] The exact claim is: *Sen bir şehirlüsüñ, pādişāh benem*, ("You are a city-dweller, I am the *padişah*!"), *OBV*, 253.

[209] I refer here to the most of Eurasia. In some increasingly isolated areas, notably the Crimea, Chinggisid notions of statehood and governance endured into the eighteenth century; Cornell Fleischer, *Bureaucrat and Intellectual in the Ottoman Empire: The Historian Mustafa Ali (1541–1600)* (Princeton, NJ: Princeton University Press, 1986), 275–277.

[210] *OBV*, 253.

of advice and admonition to keep them on the Straight Path. In what is meant to be his testament to his disciples in the private atmosphere of his last meetings with his most devout and loyal followers, Otman Baba commits an unexpected volte-face – he instructs his renunciant disciples to abandon their itinerant, mendicant lifestyle, and urges them to settle at that place (or else "he would beat them"), and to open space by cutting the trees around, to tend to gardens and orchards and make use of water-mills, and even build a city.[211] Could this be read as an admission on the part of Otman Baba (and the hagiographic community associated with him) that they were actually "losing the battle," i.e. that they had no other choice but to accept "the new rules of the game" as set by the increasingly assertive, centralizing and sedentarizing Ottoman state? Certainly, Otman Baba's last words of advice are a far cry from the claim that he had made to Mehmed II some time earlier: "You are a [mere] city-dweller, I am the *padişah!*"

While it is not easy to definitively account for this sudden change of direction, such a hypothesis appears plausible as Otman Baba's last testament may reflect the Ottoman state's growing pressure toward sedentarization and the realization that settling down and devoting oneself to materially productive activity could be the only way to (partially) preserve the Rum Abdals' position and influence, especially in the context of the growing tensions between the state and antinomian dervish groups. Alternatively, Otman Baba's followers might have taken the decision to settle shortly after their master's death and the saint's "last testament" episode in the *velayetname* may have been invented to retrospectively legitimize his followers' actions – either by the *vita*'s author, Küçük Abdal, especially if Otman Baba's convent was founded some time between his death (1478) and Mehmed II's death (1481), as discussed below, or by a later copyist. Be that as it may, later developments appear to validate this drive toward sedentarization.

While Mehmed II's successor, Bayezid II, undid one of his father's most controversial centralizing policy measures, the confiscation of *waqf* and free-hold property in the late 1470s, he did not change the general direction of reforms. Ottoman chronicles from the early sixteenth century provide evidence that the late fifteenth century saw an intensification of the tensions between non-Sharia-minded dervish groups and

---

[211] "*Pes öyle olsa ol günlerde bir gün ol kān-ı velāyet sohbet ü nasīḥātle abdāllara ayıtdı ki: sākınun ol Allāh'a ḫub dilenci şeyḫlerden olman ki sizi döğerim didi... ve yatduğıñuz yirde sinuñ yatun. Yoḫsa sizi döğerim didi;" Ve cevāba gelüp nuṭk-ı ḳadīmiñle ayıtdı ki: ben bu ulu derede ziyāret olurum. Ve sizüñ bunda değirmenleriñüz vardır. Daḫi şol ṭūrān kozları kesüb bāğ ü bāğçe eyleyün. Ve eliñüzi toprağa urup şol pıñarı şuna akıduñ, yerine şehr olsa gerekdür,*" OBV, 262, 261.

the state, which may be put in the context of the pressure the state (and the *ulema* class) put on such groups. The best known piece of evidence for this process is the well-known assassination attempt on Bayezid II. Returning from a military campaign in Albania in 1492, he was attacked by a dervish of Haydari (or alternatively, Kalenderi) appearance near Manastır (mod. Bitola in Macedonia). In the words of Oruç Beğ, "an accursed man of heresy and unbelief, clad in felt, of Haydari appearance, with rings on his neck and ears, uncircumcised, unclean and disheveled, followed the *padişah* on his way, and thinking it was the right opportunity, suddenly attacked him. Shouting 'I am the Mahdi,' and pulling a sword out of his felt cloak, he rushed to assault the *padişah*;" as the bodyguards of the sultan dispersed in a cowardly fashion, it was İskender Pasha who saved Bayezid's life by killing the assassin with his mace.[212] While there is no evidence of a direct relation between Otman Baba and the attacker, the dervish group to which the latter belonged seems to have been largely similar to Otman Baba's Abdals.

Two years later, very likely as a follow-up to the assassination attempt and in the context of a perceived general upsurge of heresy,[213] Bayezid II ordered the judge of Edirne İsa Fakih to investigate all "*abdal*s, dervishes, *ışık*s, and people of [heretical] innovation (*ehl-i bid'at*)" to the east of Filibe and Zağra (in Thrace), and punish those who were established to have uttered blasphemous words. The judge investigated the matter and brought several of the disciples of "the late possessed man Osman Dede" (likely our Otman Baba), who were executed; forty or fifty dervishes (presumably belonging to other dervish groups) were also subjected to interrogation and torture and subsequently proven guilty, two being hanged in accordance with the Sharia, and the rest were deported to Anatolia.[214] Relating to the same events, Spandounes adds that Bayezid ordered that "all these dervishes" be banned in the Empire.[215] As Ocak

---

[212] *Oruç Beğ Tarihi*, 133; İnalcık refers to a similar version of the event in *Die altosmanische anonymen Chroniken=Tavarih-i Al-i 'Usman*, ed. F. Giese (Breslau, 1922–1925), 126; ibid., "Dervish and Sultan," 32. While Oruç Beğ and the Anonymous Chronicle present the attacker as a Haydari dervish, other (later) chronicles present him alternatively as a "Kalender," Hoca Sadeddin, *Tacü't-Tevarih*, vol. 2, 71, "Kalenderi" in Solakzade, *Solakzade Tarihi* (Istanbul: Mahmud Bey Matba'ası, 1298/1880–1), 304 and "Torlak" ("torlacchi") in Spandounes, *On the Origins*, 138–139. Karamustafa argues that Spandounes' "Torlacchi" are the actual Kalenderis, *God's Unruly Friends*, 65–66.

[213] Immediately preceding the episode describing the persecution of antinomian dervishes, Oruç Bey tells the story of Mevlana Lütfi, a professor at the Muradiye *medrese* in Bursa who was executed on the sultan's orders for spreading heresy; as Oruç Bey remarks, such a thing reminding of Mansur al-Hallaj had not happened among the *ulema* in recent times, *Oruç Beğ Tarihi*, 145. On Mevlana Lütfi see also Ocak, *Zındıklar*, 239–268.

[214] *Oruç Beğ Tarihi*, 145. See also İnalcık, "Dervish and Sultan," 33.

[215] Spandounes, *On the Origins*, 138–139.

has commented, such measures – and especially the deportations of non-conformist dervishes to Anatolia – did not help much the Ottoman cause, as the deportees could only add to the tumult related to the rise of Safavid propaganda in Anatolia.[216] And those who stayed in the Balkans would readily bond with Anatolian sympathizers of Shah Ismail who would migrate to the Balkans (willingly or being forcibly deported by the Ottoman state) in the first half of the sixteenth century.[217] The political climate of the last decades of the fifteenth century may thus be one explanation for the fact that the next *kutb* of the Abdals of Rum of Otman Baba's branch, Akyazılı Baba, emerged only in the mid-1490s, seventeen years or so after Otman Baba's death, and he was established in the far northeast corner of the peninsula, in Dobrudja.[218]

Thus, whether they followed their master's advice or acted out of their own will, Otman Baba's Abdals' decision to settle and engage in agriculture may have been one, if not the only, effective way to escape persecution, as sedentarization could be read as a sign of submission from the perspective of the centralizing state. With time, the convent/mausoleum complex of Otman Baba came to be one of the most important cultic centers of heterodox Muslim communities in the Balkans (as it continues to be today).

The famous seventeenth-century Ottoman traveler Evliya Çelebi informs us that the mausoleum (*türbe*) of the saint (see Fig. 2.1) was built in AH 912/AD 1506–7[219] and a number of sixteenth-century Ottoman tax register entries throw additional light on the early history of the *zaviye*.

The earliest available Ottoman tax registration of the complex dates from AH 921/AD 1515–16.[220] The expository text reads as follows:

The *zaviye* of the late Osman Baba, in the district of Hasköy. According to the old [i.e. previous] register an order obeyed by the world was issued by the *padişah*, the refuge of the world, which made the *zaviye* authorized. It has been entered in the [old] register that it has been determined that they (?) exercise possession of his estate and *tekye* in the prescribed boundaries, and if sheep are brought from the vicinity to be sacrificed it should be seen to it that no tax-collector may

---

[216] Ocak, *Kalenderîler*, 125–126.

[217] İnalcık, "Dervish and Sultan," 33.

[218] On Akyazılı Baba, see Chapter 6.

[219] Evliya Çelebi claims to have read an inscription on Otman Baba's *tekye* (dated AH 912/ AD 1506–7) testifying that it was built by Mihaloğlu Ali Bey in memory of his grandfather Gazi Mihal Bey; the present-day inscription placed over the gate of the tomb has the same date, but no patrons, *Evliyâ Çelebi Seyahatnâmesi* vol. 8, 344; Kiprovska, "The Mihaloğlu Family," 197. Alternatively, the seventeenth-century Ottoman historian Edirneli Hibri asserts that the Malkoçoğulları, another prominent frontier lord dynasty, built the convent; M. Kiel, "Sarı Saltık ve Erken Bektaşilik Üzerine Notlar," *Türk Dünyası Araştırmaları Dergisi*, 2, no. 9 (1980), 32–33.

[220] BOA TD 50, pp. 130–131.

Figure 2.1 Mausoleum (*türbe*) of Otman Baba. Photograph by Mariya Kiprovska.

intervene and attempt to levy taxes [on the sheep]. Thereafter the late Sultan Bayezid Han issued another imperial edict, ordering that if anyone comes and questions the rights over the *tekye* and the orchards, gardens, and water-mills related to it by saying "this is my *waqf*," that person should be hindered and refuted in doing so.[221]

On the basis of this exposition it appears that the *zaviye* was first registered in the time of Mehmed II, most likely after Otman Baba's death, i.e. between 1478 and 1481, and its rights were then confirmed by an edict issued by Bayezid II. The entry goes on to list the resident dervishes and the pious endowment's properties in or near villages in the area, whose tax revenue was assigned for the support of the *zaviye*, including a water-mill, five orchards, and a rice-mill, with tax amounts in wheat, fruit, and rice specified accordingly. One of the orchards, close to the convent, was run by the Abdals themselves who turned it into a *timar*.[222] Some of these properties are stated to have been endowed by specific donors: İlyas Voyvoda, Benlü Hasan, Yunus Dede, and importantly, İskenderbeyoğlu Yahşi Bey, the nephew of Mihaloğlu Gazi Ali Bey (whom Otman Baba's *vita* presents as a follower and ally of the saint), and a prominent *akıncı* commander in his own right under Bayezid II, who bestowed the tax income of a rice-mill in the village of Konuş.[223] As for the convent's resident dervishes, it is striking that fourteen of the twenty are "sons of Abdullah," i.e. most likely converts, which does not fit well the assumption that Otman Baba's followers were mostly of Turcoman nomadic origin.[224] It should be remembered that the *yürük* communities that were a major source of followers for a figure like Otman Baba had a substantial potential to attract and assimilate converts, but this should not be essentialized.[225] It is also possible that many of Otman Baba's core disciples had dispersed for a time (or had been deported to Anatolia)

---

[221] "*Zāviye-i merḥūm 'Osmān Baba. Ḫāṣköy nevāhisinde ber mūceb-i defter-i 'atīḳ, ḥażret-i pādişāh-ı 'ālem-penāh hükm-i cihan-muṭā' erzānī ḳılmış yurdunu (?) ḥudūd ile ve tekyes-ini taṣarruf idüb iḳāmet ide eṭrāfdan gelen ḳurbān içün ḳoyuna 'āmil daḫl itmeye ve resm ṭāleb ḳılmaya naẓar ḳılınub muḳarrer ḳılındı deyü deftere ṣebt olunmuş. Ba'dehu merḥūm ve maġfūr lahu Sulṭān Bāyezīd Ḫān tekrār hükm-i şerīf ṣadaḳa idüb emr eylemişdir ki ẕikr olan tekye ve ana müte'alliḳ olan bāġa ve bāġçeye ve değirmana kimesne "vaḳfımdır" deyü nizā' iderse men' ve def' oluna deyü*," BOA TD 50, p. 130.

[222] "*Bāġçe. Abdāllar kendüler tīmār eylemişler. Tekye civārındadır.*" BOA TD 50, p. 131. *Timar* here is most probably used in one of its original meanings, i.e. the dervishes attended to the place by cultivating the land, and not in the meaning of an Ottoman revenue grant.

[223] BOA TD 50, p. 131; Kiprovska, "The Mihaloğlu Family," 197–198.

[224] However, such a concentration of converts in a dervish convent is truly exceptional, at least in the light of the present author's research. For a discussion on converts at dervish lodges, see Chapter 7.

[225] S. Dimitrov, "Za yurushkata organizatsiia i rolyata i v etnoasimilatsionnite protsesi," *Vekove* 1–2 (1982): 33–43.

during which time local converts may have joined the *zaviye* in the light of the accruing socio-economic advantages.

Subsequent sixteenth-century registrations show several tendencies: the number of the resident dervishes and servants of the *tekye* grows substantially, together with the convent's endowment, and the very high percentage of converts recorded in 1515–16 quickly declines. The summary registration from AH 937/AD 1530 confirms the status of the *zaviye* as a pious endowment, declaring it had sixty-nine dervishes and servants and was granted the income of three water-mills, a rice-mill and five gardens, with a total tax burden of 3,500 *akçe* and two *müd* of rice.[226] A later registration from Süleyman I's reign shows sixty-eight dervishes and servants (of whom twenty-three were "sons of Abdullah") and a recently formed small Gypsy community (nine registered adult males); the properties supporting the convent have been augmented to five water-mills, two rice mills and six gardens/orchards.[227] Finally, in 1579 we see the convent with forty-five dervishes and servants (five converts), the small Gypsy community unchanged in strength, and an expanded revenue base: four water-mills, two rice-mills and twelve orchards, with the one taken care by the Abdals themselves still in existence.[228] The names of the dervishes (across the successive tax registrations), among which such as Şah Kulu, Bektaş, Pir Ali, Ede Bali, Ismail, Ali, Hasan, and Hüseyin figure prominently, betray the convent's heterodox orientation and may also reflect pro-Safavid sympathies.[229]

Thus, Otman Baba's most visible legacy, his mausoleum/convent complex, developed as an agricultural center that hosted sedentary dervishes, much in tune with the general policy objectives of the centralizing Ottoman state.

★★★

The *vitae* of Seyyid Ali Sultan (Kızıl Deli) and Otman Baba thus point to two different modes in the evolution of heterodox, non-Sharia-minded dervish groups in the context of the Ottoman state's gradual transformation from a frontier polity into a centralized bureaucratic empire. Seyyid Ali, Rüstem Gazi, and associates participated in the conquest of the Balkans in the second half of the fourteenth century. Their settlement, which entailed the foundation of dervish convents and the practice of agriculture, was a natural follow-up of their participation in

---

[226] BOA TD 370, p. 341; *müd* is a measure for grain, a double handful (2–3 lbs.).

[227] BOA TD 385, pp. 365–366. This detailed register has not been dated precisely, but internal evidence suggests that it is most likely from *c.* 1535–45.

[228] BOA TD 581, pp. 444–445.

[229] E.g. in the BOA TD 385 registration, out of 68 dervishes four have "Şah Kulu" and five "Bektaş" as their proper names or patronymics.

conquest campaigns and was also a practical realization of their claim to successful participation in *gaza*. While not necessarily intentionally "conformist" (at least originally), their sedentarization and agrarianization thus appeared to fit the concurrent evolution of Ottoman society. This line of behavior was continued by their later followers in the context of the integration of the cult of Kızıl Deli into the developing Bektashi doctrine and the forging of strong bonds between the Bektashi order and the Ottoman imperial regime from the early sixteenth century onwards, despite Bektashism's "heterodox" aspects.

Otman Baba and his Abdals of Rum developed as a distinct dervish collectivity in the second half of the fifteenth century, when the Ottoman state was articulating the definitive mechanisms of transition to a centralized bureaucratic regime. While strongly supportive of *gaza*, as cast in Otman Baba's *velayetname*, and thus sharing in the spirit of the frontier zone, Otman and his disciples were not active participants in frontier warfare – increasingly the preserve of the emerging imperial state and its regular armed units – but rather roamed the countryside as itinerant dervishes of the New Renunciation mold. In the context of Mehmed II's and Bayezid II's centralizing reforms they would appear as lagging behind the pace of transformation of Ottoman state and society. Eventually, Otman Baba's followers would settle too, a process that started shortly after the saint's death and continued with force in the sixteenth century, as will be shown below in the specific context of Deliorman and Gerlovo. But their adaptation would certainly be less seamless, the result of a struggle for survival under the weight of changing historical circumstances.

3   The Northeastern Balkans from the Late
      Medieval Period to the Late Fifteenth
      Century: Pre-Ottoman Turcoman Invasions
      and Migrations, the Ottoman Conquest,
      and the "Turbulent" Fifteenth Century.
      Deliorman and Gerlovo as a "Special Case"

3.1   Introduction

Previously part of the Byzantine domains, the northeastern Balkans
came to be the heart of the newly founded First Bulgarian Kingdom
(681–1018). While the founders of this state were the Turkic Bulgars,
within a couple of centuries they came to be largely assimilated into the
Slavic majority in medieval Bulgaria. Bulgarian statehood was restored
in 1185 after almost two centuries of Byzantine domination until most
of the northeastern Balkans were conquered by the Ottomans during
Çandarlı Ali Pasha's campaign in 1388–9, and all medieval Bulgarian
lands north of the Balkan range came to be part of the Ottoman state
by 1396.[1]

  In the first century of Ottoman rule, the northeastern Balkans were
affected by state-sponsored foreign incursions – those of the Wallachian
*voevode*s to the north – especially those of Mircea I the Elder in the late
fourteenth and early fifteenth century and Vlad III Ţepeş (most notably
in 1461–2), as well as of western crusaders during the Crusade of Varna
(1444). The region was also much affected by the Ottoman civil war of
1402–13 and was the point of origin of the 1416 anti-Ottoman rebellion of the great religious rebel and reformer Sheykh Bedreddin. Thus,

---

[1] Toward the mid-fourteenth century, the Second Bulgarian Kingdom had split into
  three: the kingdoms of Vidin in the west, that of Turnovo in the center, and the semi-
  autonomous Despotate of Dobrudja in the east. The Kingdom of Vidin, which occupied
  the territory of modern northwestern Bulgaria as well as parts of modern Serbia, was
  the last of the three to be annexed by the Ottomans in 1396. All of Ottoman Gerlovo
  and most of Deliorman fell in the eastern part of the Kingdom of Turnovo, and most of
  Dobrudja in the eponymous Despotate.

from the late fourteenth and through most of the fifteenth centuries the northeastern Ottoman Balkans could be viewed as an arena of contested sovereignty and competing political and territorial claims in the context of the Ottomans' gradual expansion in Europe.

3.2   Turcoman Involvement in the Northeastern Balkans Prior to the Ottoman Conquest

3.2.1   *Pontic Turcoman Incursions into the Balkans in the Pre-Ottoman Period*

Apart from the Turkic Bulgars who carved out a state in the Balkans in the seventh century, the (northeastern) Balkans suffered numerous invasions by other nomadic Turkic peoples from the tenth through the twelfth century: the Pechenegs, the Uzes, and later the Cumans (Qipchaqs) – all originating from the Ponto-Caspian steppe.[2] For two centuries the Pechenegs engaged in a series of large-scale raids from the Pontic steppe to the south of the Danube (such as those in 934, 1027, 1032, 1033, 1035, and 1048), while also occasionally serving as mercenaries in the Bulgarian and Byzantine armies.[3] The Cumans – who eventually assimilated the Pechenegs and the Uzes – were the dominant presence in the northern Black Sea steppe from the early eleventh century to the Mongol invasions of 1223 and 1237–41. While playing a significant role in the establishment of the Second Bulgarian Kingdom (1185–1390s) and serving as mercenaries in the late medieval Balkan states, they too made numerous incursions into the Balkans from the eleventh through the mid-thirteenth centuries.[4] While these (non-Muslim) Turkic invaders did not engage in large-scale colonization and settlement in the Balkans, their incursions had a markedly negative impact on the demographic development of the northeastern Balkans (Dobrudja and Deliorman), whereby the area would remain severely underpopulated in the next

[2] These invasions were unlocked by the disintegration of the Khazar state *c.* 965; see Peter Golden, *An Introduction to the History of the Turkic Peoples* (Wiesbaden: Harrassowitz, 1992), 243–277.

[3] P. Diaconu, "The Petchenegs on the Lower Danube," in *Relations Between the Autochthonous Population and the Migratory Populations on the Territory of Romania*, ed. Miron Constantinescu, Ştefan Pascu, and Petre Diaconu (Bucharest: Editura Academiei RSR, 1975), 236–239.

[4] See Anna Comnena's (d. 1153) vivid descriptions of Cuman invasions in the Balkans and their devastating effect; *The Alexiad of the Princess Anna Comnena*, trans. Elizabeth A.S. Dawes (New York: Barnes & Noble, 1967), 130–132, 164–174, 246–247; for the Cumans' role in the establishment of the Second Bulgarian Kingdom as well as their involvement in other late medieval Balkan armies, see István Vásáry, *Cumans and Tatars: Oriental Military in the Pre-Ottoman Balkans, 1185–1365* (Cambridge: Cambridge University Press, 2005).

two to three centuries.[5] This underpopulation may have invited renewed settlement, such as the supposed migration of Anatolian Turcomans to Dobrudja under the leadership of Sarı Saltık in the 1260s, as well as in the Ottoman period.

3.2.2   The Migration of "Seljuk Turks" to Dobrudja and the Role of Sarı Saltık

The story of the migration of numerous nomadic Turcomans from Anatolia to the steppe of Dobrudja in the early 1260s under the leadership of a Turcoman heterodox dervish known as Sarı Saltık during the political struggles of the former Seljuk sultan Izz al-Din Kaykawus II (r. 1246–57, alone or jointly with his brothers Rukn al-Din Kılıc Arslan IV and Ala al-Din Kayqubad II) has been a subject of heated debates, largely due to historical sources that provide insufficient and often questionable or contradictory evidence. The most important evidence for what has been seen as the first large-scale migration of Turcomans from Anatolia into the Balkans is to be found in Yazıcızade Ali's Tevarih-i Al-i Selcuk (History of the House of Seljuk) composed for Sultan Murad II in 1424.[6] According to Yazıcızade Ali, after Izz al-Din Kaykawus II was ousted from power, he sought refuge at the court of Michael VIII Palaiologos (r. 1259–82) in Constantinople, and after spending some time there, asked the emperor in 1261–2 for a land where he and his Turcoman followers could settle. Michael VIII assented, indicating Dobrudja in the northeastern Balkans. While Izz al-Din spent more time in Constantinople before he finally found refuge with Berke, the khan of the Golden Horde in the Crimea, thousands of his Turcoman followers crossed the Bosphorus via Üsküdar (Skutari) and headed to Dobrudja where they founded two or three Muslim towns and 30 to 40 nomadic camps, the "holy man" Sarı Saltık crossing into Europe with them.[7]

This passage provided the main source base for Paul Wittek to develop the hypothesis that not only did the migration happen, but that the

---

[5] An excellent discussion on this issue based on archaeological evidence is to be found in G. Atanasov, "Etno-demografski promeni v Dobrudzha (X–XI v.)," IP 47/2 (1991), 75–84.

[6] While several recensions of the work have been preserved, I have utilized one of the versions available in the Topkapı Palace Museum Library in Istanbul, TSMK Revan No. 1390. Another recension (TSMK Revan No. 1391) has recently been published as Yazıcızade Ali, Tevârîh-i Âl-i Selçuk (Selçuklu Tarihi), ed. Abdullah Bakır (Istanbul: Çamlıca, 2009). Yazıcızāde 'Alī's work is considered to have been heavily influenced by Ibn Bībī's history of the Anatolian Seljuk state, composed in Persian in 1270, as well as Rashīd al-Dīn's Jāmi' al-Tawārīkh.

[7] Yazıcızade Ali, Tevārīh-i Āl-i Selcuk, TSMK, Revan No. 1390, ff. 233b–234a.

community of Christian Turks who live in parts of Dobrudja today, known as "Gagauz," has its origins in this event and indeed derived its very name from the name of the Seljuk sultan (Kaykawus = Gagauz).[8] Machiel Kiel adduces some additional evidence for the historicity of Sarı Saltık's mission in Dobrudja such as the mention of the city of Baba Saltık by the famous Maghribi traveler Ibn Battuta in 1331–2, which Kiel identifies with the city of Babadağ in northern Dobrudja, and the reference of the Arab geographer Abu'l-Fida, dated 1321, of Turkish Muslim inhabitants in the town of İsakçe (mod. Isaccea) in the same district.[9] Kiel also refers to a newly found source completed in 1315 by the Arab historian al-Saraj, which makes a clear mention of a Turkish saint by the name of Saltık al-Turki who was active and was later buried near İsakçe.[10] A.Y. Ocak has suggested that the migration of Turcomans led by Sarı Saltık was an offshoot of the Babai revolt of c. 1240; he has also described the spread of the cult of Sarı Saltık in the Balkans and Anatolia in the fifteenth and sixteenth centuries, asserting Sarı Saltık's identity as a heterodox ("Kalenderi") sheykh, who later became popular in Bektashi/Kizilbaş/Alevi circles.[11] Even though the historicity of Sarı Saltık and the story of the migration of Anatolian Turcomans to Dobrudja under his leadership has been questioned,[12] it has come to be widely accepted in Ottomanist historiography. While the demographic impact of this alleged migration is impossible to ascertain, the cult of the saint did indeed spread in both Anatolia and the Balkans in the following centuries, and he came to occupy an eminent position within the emerging pantheon of Balkan/Anatolian heterodox saints of the Kalenderi/Babai/Abdal mold (later assimilated into the Bektashi tradition). The memory of Sarı Saltık, further strengthened by the composition of a *vita* devoted to him in the

---

[8] See Wittek's two influential articles on the subject, "Les Gagaouzes = Les gens de Kaykaus," *Rocznik Orientalistyczny* 17 (1951–2), 12–24, and "Yazijioghlu Ali on the Christian Turks of the Dobruja," *BSOAS* 14 (1952), 639–668.

[9] Machiel Kiel, "Sarı Saltık: Pionier des Islam auf dem Balkan im 13. Jahrhundert," in *Aleviler/Alewiten: Kimlik ve Tarih/Identität und Geschichte*, ed. Ismail Engin and Erhard Franz, vol. 1 (Hamburg: Deutsches Orient-Institut, 2000), 255–256.

[10] Ibid., 261–266.

[11] A.Y. Ocak, *Sarı Saltık: Popüler İslam'ın Balkanlar'daki Destanî Öncüsü* (Ankara: Türk Tarih Kurumu, 2002), 76–78, 99–100, 103–125.

[12] Peter Mutafčiev, "Die angebliche Einwanderung von Seldschuk-Türken in die Dobrudscha im 13. Jahrhundert," *Spisanie ne Bâlgarskata Akademiia na Naukite (Klon Istoriko-Filologichen)* 56 (1943), 1–130. Mutafčiev was not trained as an Orientalist, but had a Byzantinist background. His critique of the related oriental sources is not entirely persuasive, but he does pose some relevant questions – most notably, whether Dobrudja was indeed under Byzantine control at the time, as well as the issue of the silence of contemporary Byzantine historians, especially Georges Pachymeres who must have resided in Constantinople at the time and could have made notice of the purported thousands of Turcomans crossing the Bosphorus.

late fifteenth century,[13] figures prominently in the hagiographic accounts of both Otman Baba and his "spiritual grandson" Demir Baba. In his *velayetname*, Otman claims to be Sarı Saltık's incarnation and pays a visit to the latter's convent in Dobrudja. This evolving memory could be seen as one more factor that could have strengthened the image of the northeastern Balkans as an attractive area to settle among heterodox Turcoman (semi-) nomads in the fifteenth and sixteenth centuries.

3.3   The Northeastern Ottoman Balkans in the "Turbulent" Fifteenth Century

3.3.1   *The Battle of Ankara and the Ottoman Interregnum*

The Ottomans' seemingly unstoppable expansion in both Anatolia and the Balkans in the late fourteenth century was halted by Timur's invasion of Anatolia which precipitated the greatest crisis in early Ottoman history. The Battle of Ankara in July 1402, in which the Ottomans were soundly defeated and their ruler was captured and died in captivity a few months later, had far-reaching consequences for the political development of Anatolia and the Balkans.[14] While Timur restored a number of Anatolian Turcoman principalities recently conquered by the Ottomans, he partitioned the remains of the Ottoman state in Anatolia and the Balkans among three of Bayezid I's sons as vassal rulers without designating any of them as successor to the throne of a unified Ottoman state. While not at odds with the Turco-Mongol tradition of dividing a patrimonium into appanages (*ulus*es) among the ruler's sons, the partition contradicted the already established principle of unigeniture in the Ottoman state, which differentiated it from traditional Turcoman polities and had played an important role in its success theretofore.[15] This largely conditioned the ensuing civil war (*Fetret Devri*, or "Time of Troubles") among Bayezid I's sons until 1413 when the Ottoman state was again reunited under Mehmed I.[16]

In the Balkans, the Ottoman defeat at Ankara ushered in a period of relief from Ottoman expansion for the first time in decades.[17] In a very

---

[13] *Saltuk-name: The Legend of Sarı Saltuk Collected from Oral Tradition by Ebu'l Hayr Rumi (Text in Facsimile with a Critical and Stylistic Analysis and Index by Fahir İz)*, 7 vols. (Cambridge, MA: Harvard University Department of Near Eastern Languages and Civilizations, 1974–84).

[14] On Timur's empire and the Battle of Ankara, see the literature referred to in fn. 15 in Chapter 1.

[15] On Ottoman dynastic succession, see Halil İnalcık, "The Ottoman Succession and Its Relation to the Turkish Concept of Sovereignty," in *The Middle East and the Balkans Under the Ottoman Empire* (Bloomington, IN: Indiana University Press, 1993), 37–69.

[16] For a detailed analysis of the Ottoman civil war, see Kastritsis, *The Sons of Bayezid*.

[17] Matanov and Mikhneva, *Ot Galipoli do Lepanto*, 144–152.

weak position, Süleyman Çelebi – Bayezid's son who had control over the Ottoman Balkans – signed the Treaty of Galata in early 1403, in accordance with which Byzantium regained its full independence as well as some important territories such as Chalcidice, Salonica, and lands along the western Black Sea coast; Venice was granted control of Athens and some other cities, while some Genoese colonies in the Aegean were also relieved of their vassalage.[18] Yet, the Bulgarian lands remained part of the Ottoman state, and the Serbian Despot Stephen Lazarević remained an Ottoman vassal.

As not all major actors in Balkan politics were satisfied with the Treaty of Galata, a Christian coalition was formed by the beginning of 1404.[19] Led by the Hungarian king Sigismund and including the Wallachian *voevode* Mircea the Elder, the Serbian Despot Stephen Lazarević, the king of Bosnia, and Constantine, the son of the last Bulgarian ruler of Vidin, it focused its activities above all in the northern Ottoman Balkans and Serbia.[20] For Lazarević it provided a chance to denounce his Ottoman vassalage, and for Constantine it was a hope for the restoration of the Bulgarian state.

Concerning the northeastern Balkans, the most important development in this context is Mircea's likely reconquest of much of Dobrudja, including the strategically important fortress of Silistra (Silistre) on the southern bank of the lower Danube;[21] an Ottoman attack on Silistra was successfully repulsed by Mircea (most likely *c*. 1405–6).[22] While not directly affecting the northeastern Balkans, the activities of the Bulgarian prince Constantine possibly temporarily established a measure of control over his father's former domains around Vidin *c*. 1403–4.[23] Several years

[18] G.T. Dennis, "The Byzantine-Turkish Treaty of 1403," *Orientalia Christiana Periodica* 33 (1967), 81–82. Importantly, in the Treaty of Galata, Süleyman is styled as "son of the Byzantine emperor." See also Matschke, *Die Schlacht*, 51–75.

[19] There exists no formal treaty or other such document that provides direct formal evidence for the existence of this coalition, but contemporary administrative and diplomatic documents emanating from Hungary and Wallachia, as well as some contemporary Slavic sources, provide sufficient evidence of its existence; Şerban Papacostea, "La Valachie et la crise de structure de l'Empire Ottoman (1402–1413)," *Revue Roumaine D'Histoire* 25, no. 1–2 (1986), 24.

[20] P. Petrov, "Antituretskaiia koalitsiia balkanskih stran v nachale XV veka," *Trudy 25-go Mezhdunarodnogo Kongresa Vostokovedov* (Moscow, 1962), 501–504.

[21] Papacostea, "La Valachie," 26. Papacostea refers to a deed of Mircea, dated 1406, in which he styles himself as ruler of all lands along the Danube up to the Black Sea and a master of Dristor (Silistra).

[22] Ibid., 26–27.

[23] In his letter to the Duke of Burgundy, dated April 1404, Sigismund reports of numerous successful attacks of his vassals Mircea of Wallachia and Constantine, referred to as "Emperor of Bulgaria," into the Ottoman domains south of the Danube; full text of letter in P. Petrov, "Vâstanieto na Konstantin i Fruzhin," *Izvestiia na Instituta po Istoriia* 9 (1960), 188–189.

later, in 1408, Constantine and his cousin Fruzhin (i.e. the sons of the two last rulers of the Bulgarian kingdoms of Vidin and Turnovo, respectively) led a revolt which affected most of the northern Ottoman Balkans; yet it was quashed by Süleyman, who defeated their army in the Morava valley.[24]

It was in this context that Musa – an Ottoman prince not included in Timur's original partition of the Ottoman domains – entered the Ottoman civil war, and his actions directly affected developments in the northeastern Balkans. Released by his brother Mehmed with the possible aim of weakening Süleyman's position in the Balkans, he travelled by sea from Sinop (on the southern Black Sea coast) to Wallachia in 1409 where he concluded a marriage alliance with Mircea the Elder and, aided by the latter and Stephen Lazarević, he invaded the lands south of the Danube and managed to gain the support of most Ottoman fortress commanders, Ottoman military revenue grant holders, and the local population (including many of the old Bulgarian boyars). Having crossed the Balkan range and occupied Edirne (Adrianople) and Gallipoli, Musa was defeated on the battlefield by Süleyman in June 1410, but it was Süleyman who finally lost the battle for the Ottoman Balkans, losing his life in 1411 after being gradually deserted by his troops.

Musa's career as a ruler in Rumelia was short;[25] he was soon betrayed and attacked by some of his Balkan allies who lent their support to Mehmed. While victorious against Mehmed near Sofia in 1413, Musa eventually fled the field, and was killed by his brother's men, which made Mehmed the sole ruler of all Ottoman domains. Beside the political turmoil and devastation caused by Musa's activities in the Ottoman Balkans, specifically in the north, his career is important in the present context as he appointed Sheykh Bedreddin – a charismatic Ottoman jurist and theologian, who would become even more prominent a few years later – to be his *kadı 'asker* (military judge). It is at this point that Bedreddin, whose ideas are considered to have contained important elements of religious and social egalitarianism, started building his own support base,

---

[24] V. Jagić, "Konstantin Filosof i njegov Život Stefana Lazarevića Despota Srpskoga," *Glasnik SUD* 42 (1875): 292. The *Vita* of Lazarević does not mention Fruzhin by name as a leader of the revolt, but only refers to him as a son of the Bulgarian tsar who joined his brother; a land deed by Sigismund awarding his expoits, confirms his participation. See full Latin text and Bulgarian translation in Petâr Nikov, "Turskoto zavladiavane na Bâlgaria i sâdbata na poslednite Shishmanovtsi," *IBID* 7–8 (1928), 91–92, 111–112.

[25] The most detailed account of Mūsā's short rule in the Balkans may be found in Nedim Filipović, *Princ Musa i Šejh Bedreddin* (Sarajevo: Svjetlost, 1971), 318–374. Filipović asserts that Mūsā won popular support both among the indigenous Christian population and the early Turcoman colonists in the region, as a defender of the rights of the middle and lower strata of society against the regime of his brother Süleyman who was supported by the Rumelian marcher lords (*uc beyleri*).

which would help him raise the banner of a rebellion against Mehmed I that originated in Deliorman.[26]

3.3.2   The Revolt of Sheykh Bedreddin

Eventually victorious over his brothers, Mehmed I faced a number of challenges in consolidating his power. Largely the result of the severe political and social crisis that developed in the Ottoman state during the interregnum, he faced opposition from two dynastic claimants to the throne[27] as well as several popular rebellions with strong social and religious appeal. Three rebellions were led by Sheykh Bedreddin and his disciples Börklüce Mustafa and Torlak Hu Kemal in 1416.[28] While the latter two centered their activities in western Anatolia (Torlak Hu Kemal in Saruhan, and Börklüce Mustafa in Aydın), Bedreddin himself raised the banner of revolt in Deliorman, whence it spread to other parts of the eastern Balkans before being quashed by Mehmed I at the end of the year. The same year also saw the rebellion of Cüneyd, the governor of Niğbolu, which significantly overlapped with that of Bedreddin in terms of area of activity and support base.[29]

One of the most interesting and enigmatic figures in early Ottoman history, Bedreddin (c. 1359–1416) does not fit the stereotype associated with the figure of a wandering charismatic heterodox dervish who channeled the popular appeal of mystical Islam into concrete political action. The son of an Ottoman *gazi* of the small town of Simavna[30] in newly conquered Ottoman Thrace and (possibly) a Greek mother, he received an elite education in Islamic law and theology in Konya, Tabriz, and

---

[26] Michel Balivet, *Islam mystique et révolution armée dans les Balkans Ottomans: vie de Cheikh Bedreddin le «Hallaj des Turcs» (1358/59–1416)* (Istanbul: The Isis Press, 1995), 66–69.

[27] These were a son of Emīr Süleymān, most probably named Orḫān, and Muṣṭāfā, a son of Bāyezīd who would become known as Düzme (False) Muṣṭāfā, in later Ottoman historiographic tradition. For a brief overview of Orḫān and Muṣṭāfā's activities during Meḥmed I's reign, see Imber, Colin imber, *The Ottoman Empire: 1300–1481* (Istanbul: The Isis Press, 1990), 77–78.

[28] On the dating of these events, see Balivet, *Islam mystique*, 80–81.

[29] The rebellious Cüneyd, former ruler of the Anatolian principality of Aydın who had been dispossessed by Bāyezīd I, enjoyed the support of Mircea the Elder and the False Muṣṭāfā, the pretender to the Ottoman throne who claimed to be Bayezid I's son. The most detailed source on Cüneyd's revolt is Doukas, *Decline and Fall of Byzantium to the Ottoman Turks*, trans. and ed. Harry Magoulias (Detroit, MI: Wayne State University Press, 1975), 122–123. Ottoman chronicles are much more obscure on the incident. Balivet has suggested that Cüneyd was a disciple of Sheykh Bedreddin, *Islam mystique*, 88–91.

[30] While Bedreddīn's father has traditionally been thought to have been a judge (*ḳāḍı*), more recent research demonstrates that he was indeed a *gāzī* (warrior for the faith); Orhan Şaik Gökyay, "Şeyh Bedreddin'in Babası Kadı Mı İdi?," *Tarih ve Toplum* 1, no. 2 (1984), 96–98.

Cairo. In Cairo he became exposed to the ideas of mystical Islam (*tasav-vuf*) under the guidance of the eminent Cairene Sufi sheykh Husayn Akhlati.[31] There he also won great fame as a theologian and jurist and the reigning Mamluk sultan appointed him mentor to his son and conferred upon him the title Shaykhu'l-Islam.[32]

According to Bedreddin's *vita*, on his return to Anatolia via Aleppo *c.* 1403–4, he passed through the recently restored principalities of Karaman and Germiyan before reaching the principality of Aydın on the Aegean shore; many local Turcomans, as well the rulers of the three principalities, became his disciples.[33] By 1405–6 he had returned to his parental home in Edirne where he spent several years before he became entangled in the Ottoman civil war, whereby, on account of his fame as a jurist, he was appointed military judge by Musa in the period 1411–13. After Musa's defeat, Bedreddin was banished to İznik (northwestern Anatolia) where he remained until 1416. As in the first half of that year, the anti-Ottoman rebellions of his disciples Börklüce Mustafa and Torlak Kemal in western Anatolia had gained momentum,[34] Bedreddin, follow-ing the route used by prince Musa in 1409, escaped to Wallachia via Sinop, whence he moved across the Danube to the regions of Deliorman (Ağaç Denizi) and Dobrudja.[35] There he managed to assemble a substan-tial and diverse group of followers in a major challenge to the authority of Mehmed I. While the revolt spread over much of the eastern Balkans

---

[31] The major source for Bedreddin's life is his *Menākıb* (*Vita*) composed by his grandson Ḥalīl b. İsmā'īl. It is the only near-contemporary source with respect to some important details about Bedreddin's origin, such as the origin of his mother and the claim that he was a descendant of the Anatolian Seljukid dynasty. Many later sources would reiterate these details largely relying on Ḥalīl b. İsmā'īl's work. On Bedreddin's early life accord-ing to his *vita* see Halil bin Ismail bin Şeyh Bedrüddin Mahmud, *Sımavna Kadısıoglu Şeyh Bedreddin Manâkıbı*, ed. Abdülbaki Gölpinarlı and İsmet Sungurbey (Istanbul: Eti Yayınevi, 1967), 4–11. For a modern discussion of Bedreddin's early life, see Balivet, *Islam Mystique*, 40–53, and Ocak, *Zındıklar*, 168–178.

[32] Ernst Werner, *Die Geburt einer Großmacht – Die Osmanen*, *(1300–1481)*, 4th edn. (Weimar: Hermann Böhlaus Nachfolger, 1985), 217–218.

[33] Halil b. İsmail, *Sımavna Kadısıoglu Şeyh Bedreddin Manâkıbı*, 86–89; Balivet, *Islam mys-tique*, 53–63. Ocak has argued that Bedreddin's actions during his trip through Anatolia, including the important contacts he made with nomadic Turcomans and local rulers, were informed by his pre-conceived revolutionary program aiming at a new social order, which would convert important ideas of mystical Islam into distinct political and social action; *Zındıklar*, 194–195.

[34] Mainstream Ottoman chronicles agree that the two revolts in Anatolia started upon the orders of Bedreddin. Bedreddin's *vita*, which generally tries to exonerate him of any unlawful activities against the legitimate Ottoman sultan, does not dwell upon this. See *Âşıkpaşazâde Tarihi*, 122–123; Neşrı, *Cihânnümâ*, 231–232; Oruc Beğ Tarihi, 47–49. Although the three chronicles are quite similar in this respect, Neşrî and Oruc Beğ are more assertive in pointing out the longstanding relationship between Bedreddin and Börklüce Muṣṭāfā. See also Ocak, *Zındıklar*, 189.

[35] *Âşıkpaşazâde Tarihi*, 123; Neşrı, *Cihânnümâ*, 231; *Oruc Beğ Tarihi*, 48–49.

within a few months, it was crushed by the end of the year, with its leader
tried and condemned to death in Serres (eastern Macedonia) in the presence of the sultan.[36]

The nature of Bedreddin's rebellion is difficult to assess in light of
the limited and sometimes contradictory evidence provided by contemporary and near-contemporary sources. While the near-contemporary
Byzantine historian Doukas offers a detailed description of Börklüce
Mustafa's revolt, presenting it as a typical messianic rebellion led by "a
simple-minded Turkish peasant" who preached that all property, except
for women, should be held in common and also insisted on the equality
between Muslims and Christians,[37] he makes no mention of Bedreddin's
revolt.[38] Ottoman chronicles tell of Börklüce Mustafa's claim to prophethood, and relate his rebellion to the suppression of Torlak Hu Kemal's
rising in neighboring Saruhan.[39] While the two Anatolian rebellions
much resemble one another, especially with respect to their leaders'
background and following (which must have included members of the
lower classes, mostly Muslims, but also probably some Christians), the
revolt instigated by their spiritual master differs in certain important
aspects. Besides the very different nature of Bedreddin's background
and personality, most Ottoman chronicles do not fail to point out that
after he traveled to Wallachia and crossed the Danube, establishing his
base in Deliorman, he relied on the support of some of his former political associates from his tenure as military judge in Rumelia under Musa,
including many members of the local Ottoman military establishment
whom he himself had awarded military revenue grants (*timar*s) during
his tenure as *kadı 'asker*. Yet, these allies seem to have deserted him after
they learned of his "vile plans" to march against the legitimate sultan and
claim the sultanate (possibly a sign that they had been assured of their
social position under Mehmed I's new regime). Clearly, Bedreddin's
revolt must have attracted the support of various social strata, including nomadic or semi-nomadic Turcomans and possibly some Christians;
Ottoman chronicles describe his agents as "sufis" (dervishes) who spread
around his ideas.[40]

---

[36] *Âşıkpaşazâde Tarihi*, 123; Neşrı, *Cihânnümâ*, 232; *Oruc Beğ Tarihi*, 49.

[37] Doukas, *Decline and Fall*, 119–122.

[38] For a possible explanation of this omission, see Ocak, *Zındıklar*, 192.

[39] *Âşıkpaşazâde Tarihi*, 124, Neşrı, *Cihânnümâ*, 232; Oruc Beğ Tarihi, 49. In addi-
tion, Bedreddīn's *Vita* is the single source that mentions a third related rebellion in
Anatolia, led by a certain Aygıloğlu; Halil b. İsmail, *Sımavna Kadısıoglu Şeyh Bedreddin
Manâkıbı*, 117.

[40] *Âşıkpaşazâde Tarihi*, 123, Neşrı, *Cihânnümâ*, 232; *Oruc Beğ Tarihi*, 48. For a related analysis see, Filipović, *Princ Musa i Šejh Bedreddin*, 558–559, 563–564.

The revolt has been variously interpreted as a quest for a new, egali-tarian and utopian social order,[41] as a centrifugal reaction of the domi-nant social forces in the Ottoman borderlands against the centralizing tendencies of Mehmed I's new regime,[42] or as an attempt at overthrow-ing the legitimate sultan (especially on account of Bedreddin's claims to Seljukid dynastic descent). Importantly, Bedreddin was executed on the last charge.[43] However, probably the most appropriate characterization of Bedreddin's revolt is that it was a typical messianic movement in a historical milieu (the deep Ottoman socio-political and economic crisis of the early fifteenth century) that was clearly conducive to such develop-ments.[44] In the context of the present study, it is of critical importance that Bedreddin's rebellion originated in Deliorman, and that in the fol-lowing decades and centuries his teachings attracted numerous adepts in both the Balkans and Anatolia. Neşri's early sixteenth-century chronicle refers to followers of Bedreddin still active in Deliorman and the judge of Sofia Sheykh Bali Efendi (d. 1553) points to Deliorman and Dobrudja as their main concentrations, claiming also that Bedreddin's "deputies" had spread "over the entire world."[45] While some of them retained their identity as "Bedreddinists" ("Bedreddinlüler"),[46] most must have min-gled with other "heterodox" Islamic groups and movements, such as the Rum Abdals, Bektashis, and the Kızılbaş.

3.3.3   The Crusade of Varna (1444), and the Invasion of Vlad III Țepeş South of the Danube (1461–1462)

The Crusade of Varna (1444) was the last major crusading campaign in the Ottoman Balkans.[47] It was precipitated by Wallachia's growing

---

[41] For a well-argued Marxist interpretation of Bedreddin's revolt, see Werner, *Die Geburt*, 217–234.

[42] This hypothesis has been advanced by a number of authors, but see especially İnalcık, *Classical Age*, 188. See also Filipović's analysis of Mūsā's regime in this direction, as many of Bedreddin's followers were Mūsā's supporters, *Prince Musa i Şeyh Bedreddin*, 318–320.

[43] *Âşıkpaşazâde Tarihi*, 124, Neşri, *Cihânnümâ*, 232; *Oruc Beğ Tarihi*, 49. A proof for this is that, as the Ottoman chronicles recount, the *fatwa* that condemned Bedreddin to death did not order the confiscation of his property. For a modern analysis, see Ocak, *Zındıklar*, 205.

[44] See the pertinent analysis of Ocak and that of Imber, who places Bedreddin's revolt in the general context of messianic movements in the Mediterranean in the late medieval and early modern periods; Ocak, *Zındıklar*, 197–203, Colin Imber, *The Ottoman Empire*, 83–84.

[45] Tietze, "Sheykh Bali Efendi's Report," 115–122; Neşrî, *Cihânnümâ*, 232.

[46] On modern Bedreddinist communities in Thrace, see Thierry Zarcone, "Nouvelles per-spectives dans les recherches sur les Kızılbaş-Alévis et les Bektachis de la Dobroudja, de Deliorman et de la Thrace orientale," *Anatolia Moderna* 4 (1992): 9–11.

[47] For a more detailed discussion of the crusade, see Colin Imber's "Introduction" in ibid., *The Crusade of Varna, 1443–45* (Aldershot, UK, and Burlington, VT: Ashgate, 2006), 1–39, as well as the literature cited therein.

dependence on the Ottoman state in the 1430s and the Ottoman annexation of the Serbian Despotate in 1438–9, which made the Ottomans direct neighbors of Hungary and Bosnia.[48] The most important development that prepared the soil for the emergence of a broad anti-Ottoman Christian coalition led by the Papacy was the Council of Ferrara-Florence in 1438–9 at the end of which Byzantium accepted the decree of union between the Orthodox and Roman Churches, thus recognizing Roman ecclesiastical primacy. The compensation for Byzantium's compromise would be a crusade that would oust the Ottomans from the Balkans. Delayed by a major dynastic crisis in Hungary that followed the death of King Albert II in 1440, by 1443 the crusade's organization was taking shape under the energetic efforts of Pope Eugenius IV and his newly appointed envoy to Hungary, Bohemia, and Poland, Cardinal Giuliano Cesarini, which led to the formation of a coalition that included the new king of Hungary and Poland, Władysław III Jagiełło, the *voevode* of Transylvania and prominent military commander John Hunyadi, and Venice.

The crusade would rely on a two-pronged attack: an allied land force would approach the Ottoman lands along the Danube, while a navy, composed of Papal, Venetian, and Burgundian vessels (later to be joined by Ragusan ships) would block the passage of Ottoman troops through the Straits.

Following an ill-timed expedition led by Hunyadi that reached the Zlatitsa Pass (central Balkan range) in December 1443 before retreating,[49] the first half of 1444 saw intensive preparations for a new campaign. Meanwhile Murad II sought a settlement with Władysław, Hunyadi, and the former Serbian Despot George Branković toward the beginning of the summer, which he secured in the Peace of Adrianople on June 12, 1444. While Branković was most interested in keeping the peace, as it stipulated the restoration of his Despotate, the other two Christian signatories – Władysław and Hunyadi – continued preparations for a major campaign. The Christian signatories were also encouraged by the Pope who absolved them from their oaths on the peace treaty, obviously without Murad II's knowledge. Preparations were further encouraged by the news of the allied fleet's arrival at the Dardanelles, and Murad II's abdication in favor of his 12-year-old son Mehmed II, following the conclusion of a new peace with the central Anatolian principality of Karaman.[50]

[48] Imber, *The Ottoman Empire*, 100–102, 115–119.
[49] Imber, *The Ottoman Empire*, 122–125.
[50] For an excellent analysis of these events, see İnalcık, *Fatih Devri*, 112–124.

The crusaders' army set out from Szeged in late September. After crossing the Danube at Orşova, conquering Vidin and unsuccessfully besieging Nicopolis (Niğbolu), they turned south to the old Bulgarian capital of Turnovo. When they found the nearby mountain passes of the Balkan range blocked, they crossed through the northeastern Balkans, passing by the southern edges of Deliorman and sacking the fortress of Shumnu on their way to Varna where, on November 10, 1444, they encountered Murad II's army in a decisive battle. The crusaders' defeat very much sealed the fate of the Balkans and precipitated the fall of Byzantium.[51]

Besides its great general political significance, the Crusade of Varna's impact on the demographic history of the northeastern Ottoman Balkans cannot be underestimated. Many villages were depopulated along the route of the two rival armies, and one of the western participants in the crusades, Jehan de Wavrin, who left a valuable account of the campaign, reports that "at least 12,000" local inhabitants of the northeastern Balkans (i.e. mostly Deliorman and Dobrudja) crossed the Danube into Wallachia in early 1445 together with some of the fleeing crusaders.[52] Another participant in the crusade, Andreas del Palatio, described the area between Varna and the Danube as "*desertum.*"[53]

The Crusade of Varna was not the last major disturbance in the fifteenth-century northeastern Ottoman Balkans. In 1461–2 the Wallachian *voevode* Vlad III Ţepeş ("the Impaler"), also known as Dracula (r. 1456–62), invaded the Ottoman lands south of the Danube (from Nicopolis to Isaccea) and afflicted enormous demographic losses to the area. According to his own letter to the Hungarian king in February 1462, he massacred more than 20,000 people – Turks and Bulgarians – before being deposed by the Ottoman ruler in a swift and successful punitive campaign.[54]

---

[51] The two most comprehensive accounts of the battle, an anonymous Ottoman account and the chronicle of Jehan de Wavrin, have been published in English by C. Imber, *The Crusade of Varna, 1443–1445* (London: Ashgate, 2006), 91–104, 131–137.

[52] Imber, ed., *The Crusade of Varna*, 158.

[53] S. Dimitrov, N. Zhechev, and V. Tonev, *Istoriia na Dobrudzha*, vol. 3 (Sofia: BAN, 1988), 16.

[54] Vlad III's famous letter was published by N. Iorga, *Scrisori de Boieri, Scrisori de Domni*, 3rd edn. (Valenii de Munte, 1932), 161–167. See also Doukas, *Decline and Fall*, 259–261. For a general analysis of these events, see Radu Florescu, "Vlad II Dracul and Vlad III Dracula's Military Campaigns in Bulgaria, 1443–1462," in *Dracula: Essays on the Life and Times of Vlad Ţepeş*, ed. K.W. Treptow (Boulder, CO: East European Monographs, 1991), 111–113.

3.4 Patterns of Demographic and Socio-Economic Development in Deliorman and Gerlovo in the Late Fifteenth Century. Deliorman and Gerlovo as a "Special Case"

In the context of the preceding overview of the late medieval history of the northeastern Balkans, an analysis of the earliest preserved tax register data for Deliorman and Gerlovo will shed light on the major aspects of the two regions' demographic and socio-economic structure toward the end of the fifteenth century, especially with respect to important developments such as depopulation and Turkic colonization. This analysis will thus help delineate many of the features of the two regions (and especially Deliorman) that made the area a "special case" in the demographic history of the wider Balkans – especially the sparse and unstable settlement network, and the nascent and limited nature of Turcoman colonization.[55] It would also be an appropriate point of departure for the discussion of the repopulation of the two regions in the sixteenth century.

As of the late fifteenth century (and through the sixteenth) the greater part of Deliorman, all of Gerlovo, and some adjacent areas constituted the eastern zone of the Ottoman province of Niğbolu (Nicopolis), which, in turn, occupied the central part of the former Bulgarian lands north of the Balkan range annexed by the Ottomans by the 1390s.[56] The main sources for the present demographic analysis are two large synoptic tax register (*icmal defteri*) fragments for the province of Niğbolu, dated *c.* 1479 and *c.* 1485,[57] respectively, as well as the oldest fully preserved

---

[55] In her monograph on the demographic and socio-economic history of the Bulgarian lands in the early modern Ottoman period, Tsvetana Georgieva has already referred to the northeastern Balkans as one of three "special cases" (the other two being the Drin river valley in Macedonia and parts of Vidin province). Georgieva focuses mostly on Dobrudja, utilizing S. Dimitrov's demographic analysis and does not make recourse to the tax registers for the province of Niğbolu utilized in this study; Georgieva, *Prostranstvo i prostranstva*, 123–130. However, as the earliest Ottoman tax register data for Dobrudja is from 1518 and reflects the process of ongoing Turcoman colonization (albeit of seemingly recent origin), it is not possible to make definitive arguments about Dobrudja's demographic situation in the late fifteenth century.

[56] To the west, the *sancak* of Niğbolu was flanked by that of Vidin, and to the east by the *sancak* of Silistre (Silistra). Being "pragmatic" and "efficient" conquerors, the Ottomans often preserved the boundaries of conquered polities, converting them into regular Ottoman provinces. Thus, the province of Niğbolu practically inherited the boundaries of the medieval Bulgarian kingdom of Turnovo. Similarly, the Ottoman province of Vidin was the territorial-administrative successor of the Bulgarian Kingdom of Vidin, and that of Silistra largely inherited the boundaries of the Despotate of Dobrudja.

[57] Both fragments are housed in the Ottoman archive of the National Library "Saints Cyril and Methodius" in Sofia. The *c.* 1479 register fragment, NBKM OAK 45/29 has been so dated mainly in relation to the temporary abolition of pious foundations by Meḥmed

(also synoptic) tax register for the province, which is clearly dated 1512, but is based on the data contained in the *c.* 1485 register, thus reflecting the demographic and socio-economic profile of the province as of the mid-1480s.[58] As the last source is complete, it is the one on which the present analysis is essentially based. It contains all revenue grants in the province held by members of the Ottoman dynasty and the Ottoman *'askeri* class (mostly members of the provincial *sipahi* cavalry and fortress garrisons, but also civic functionaries, such as provincial judges and scribes); a full listing of the pious endowment (*waqf*) holdings in the province (not preserved in the *c.* 1485 fragment); and a comprehensive listing of all sources of income (urban and rural) – with summary figures for the expected tax revenue from each source. The available summary registrations of taxpayers for every settlement – all adult males (heads of household and bachelors alike, Muslims and non-Muslims) as well as non-Muslim widows registered as heads of household – provide a clear picture of the settlement network and the basic demographic characteristics of the province.[59]

II (r. 1444–6, 1451–81) in the last years of his reign. On the dating, see S. Dimitrov, "Za datirovkata na niakoi osmanski registri ot XV vek," *IBID* 25 (1968): 241–247. The document has also been published in Ottoman Turkish, with Bulgarian translation by R. Stoykov in *TIBI*, vol 2, ed. N. Todorov and B. Nedkov (Sofia: BAN, 1966), 161–335. The second fragment – NBKM OAK 12/9, was published (in Bulgarian translation only) by Rumen Kovachev, *Opis na nikopolskiia sandzhak ot 80-te godini na XV vek* (Sofia: NBKM, 1997). For the dating of this register fragment, see Kovachev's introduction, 11–12.

[58] This hitherto unutilized register is housed in the Topkapı Palace Museum Archive in Istanbul under the call number D 167. Dated in the first ten days of Muharram 918 A.H. (19–29 March 1512 A.D.), TSMA D 167, f. 2b, it was thus composed shortly before Selīm I's accession on the 7th of Safar, 918 A.H. (April 24, 1512), i.e. during his march from Trabzon via the Crimea, Wallachia, and the northeastern Balkans, to Istanbul where he deposed his father, Bāyezīd II. It is thus also an important source for the history of Selīm's accession to the throne. In all probability, prince Selīm ordered this register's compilation as a way to assess the available human and tax revenue resources in the *sancak* of Niğbolu as he marched through the province. The register opens up with Selīm's revenue grants in the province (*ḥāṣṣhā-i Sulṭān Selīm*) and does not list such for his father Bāyezīd or any other member of the dynasty. In addition, many of the other registered revenue grants (especially the larger ones) do not come with their holders' names, but appear as currently "vacant," i.e. Selim most likely intended to distribute them to their new holders upon his anticipated accession to the throne. While it is not a direct copy of the the *c.* 1485 register (fragment) – the order of revenue grants and settlements is not the same – all demographic and tax revenue data match perfectly the corresponding data in the *c.* 1485 fragment. TSMA D 167 may thus have been based on an intermediate compilation of tax revenue and demographic data for the province, ultimately originating from the *c.* 1485 registration. On Selīm I's accession, see the literature cited in Chapter 1, fn. 29.

[59] For the purposes of this demographic analysis household numbers are used, the most widely accepted household multiplier of five, proposed by Barkan, has been utilized; i.e. one household is assumed to contain five souls on average. See Ö.L. Barkan, "Research

In the tax register dated 1512, but containing data pertaining to c. 1485, the area under discussion in this study – i.e. most of Deliorman, all of Gerlovo, and some adjacent areas – is apportioned into six districts, sub-provinces of the *sancak* of Niğbolu: Yer Gögi (Rus, Rusçuk, mod. Ruse); Krapich (mod. vil. of Krepcha, Ruse province); Chernovi (Çernovi, mod. vil. of Cherven, Ruse province) in the north; Shumnu (mod. Shumen); Gerilova (i.e. Gerlovo); and Ala Kilise (mod. town of Omurtag, Târgovishte province) in the south. These constitute what may be seen as the "eastern zone" of the province of Niğbolu north of the Balkan range.[60]

The tax register of 1512 reveals a characteristic picture of Deliorman (and to a lesser extent, Gerlovo), whereby Deliorman's most striking demographic characteristic as of the mid-1480s is that it was heavily depopulated – essentially desolate. Most of the 3,222 households

on the Ottoman Fiscal Surveys," in *Studies in the Economic History of the Middle East*, ed. M.A. Cook (Oxford: Oxford University Press, 1970), 168. On other household multiplier values, ranging from three to seven, see İnalcık's discussion in *An Economic and Social History of the Ottoman Empire*, 28–29.

[60] The *sancak* of Niğbolu is divided into twenty-five districts, or sub-provinces. Of these, nineteen are situated to the north of the Balkan range and would remain part of the province in the sixteenth century. The six districts south of the Balkan range would be removed in the sixteenth century. I group the nineteen districts of the province of Niğbolu "proper" into three zones of roughly similar size: the "eastern," containing the six districts already mentioned above; the "central," containing the districts of Niğbolu (Nicopolis, mod. Nikopol), Tırnova (mod. Veliko Turnovo), Lofça (mod. Lovech), Pilevne (mod. Pleven), Kurşuna (mod. vil. of Krushuna, Lovech province), and Gigan (mod. vil. of Gigen, Pleven province); and the "western" zone consisting of the districts of İvraca (mod. Vratsa), Nedeliçko (extinct or unidentifiable), Reseleç (mod. vil. of Reselets, Pleven province), Kieva (extinct or unidentifiable), Rahova (mod. town of Oryahovo, Vratsa province), Mramorniçe (extinct or unidentifiable), and Çibri (mod. vil. of Gorni Tsibar, Montana province). I will refer below to the "western" and "central" zones when comparing them to the "eastern" zone, which is the proper regional focus of this analysis (and the study at large). These districts are alternatively named *vilâyet*, *ze'âmet*, and *nâhiye*, all seemingly enjoying roughly the same territorial-administrative status. It is confusing that *vilâyet* and *nâhiye*, which have been employed in Ottoman bureaucratic practice as administrative-territorial units, have been mixed up with *ze'âmets*, which are normally meant to denote revenue grants only, and not administrative-territorial units. This fluidity in the administrative nomenclature at the time was an empire-wide phenomenon and would continue to exist, albeit in a less acute form, through most of the sixteenth century, until its last decades when the system of provincial-territorial organization would assume a more regularized shape in the form of four units, in descending order of size: *eyâlet* (governorate-general), *sancak/livâ*, *kazâ*, and *nâhiye*. As of 1516 the nineteen districts to the north of the Balkan range would be consolidated into 7 *kazâs* (judgeships), the "eastern" zone being encompassed by the *kazâs* of Chernovi to the north and Shumnu to the south; this and further administrative reorganizations are discussed in Chapter 4. However, the boundaries of the overall area under discussion remained largely unchanged throughout the sixteenth century.

For a related case study dealing with the same issue in contemporary Ottoman Anatolia, see Oktay Özel, "The Transformation of Provincial Administration in Anatolia: Observations on Amasya from 15th to 17th Centuries," in *The Ottoman*

registered in the whole area (the six mentioned districts in the "eastern zone") were settled along the edges of Deliorman proper: along or close to the Danube, including the towns of Yer Gögi, Tutrakan, as well as Chernovi, and in the south – along the northern slopes of the Balkan range – in the southern part of the district of Shumnu and in that of Gerlovo, which included most of the Muslim population of this part of the province of Niğbolu (still predominantly semi-nomadic Turcoman *yürük*s), and several large mountain pass (*derbend*) Christian villages that enjoyed special status and tax privileges[61] (see Table 3.1).

An overview of the settlement network reveals that the number of villages in the area was very small, a total of eighty-five across all six districts of Chernovi, Ala Kilise, Shumnu, Krapich, Yer Gögi, and Gerlovo. This is almost half as many that stood in the district of Tırnova (Turnovo) alone, and comparable to the number of villages in other individual districts in the central and western parts of the province, such as Lofça (Lovech) and İvraca (Vratsa). Another striking aspect is the disproportionately high number of *mezra'a*s, agricultural sites cultivated by laborers coming "from the outside," or by some tentatively registered residents, but not having the status of (established) villages.[62] The number of *mezra'a*s in the eastern zone as of the mid-1480s is thirty-six (almost half the number of registered villages) of which twenty-four had registered taxpayers. In comparison, the number of *mezra'a*s (with or without registered taxpayers) in the central zone of Niğbolu province did not constitute more than 10 percent of all registered locations, and in the western zone it was negligible. Most of these *mezra'a*s were to be found in the southernmost (mountainous) part of the region, the southern edge of the district of Shumnu, and in that of Gerilova (Gerlovo), just south of Deliorman proper. They were populated and/or cultivated mainly by *yürük*s, whose presence likely reflected an early stage of their sedentarization as well as the overall repopulation of the area. Tax registers from the first half of the sixteenth century show most of these *mezra'a*s graduating to the size and status of well-established villages.

As the overwhelming majority (85 percent) of registered Muslims in the eastern zone of the province of Niğbolu were *yürük*s living in Gerlovo

---

Empire: Myths, Realities, and 'Black Holes': Contributions in Honour of Colin Imber, ed. Eugenia Kermeli and Oktay Özel (Istanbul: The Isis Press, 2006), 60–69.

[61] On *derbend* villages, see the related discussion in Chapter 4.

[62] On *mezra'a*s, see Fikret Adanır, "Mezra'a: zu einem Problem der Siedlungs- und Agrargeschichte Südosteuropas im ausgehenden Mittlealter und in der Frühen Neuzeit," in *Deutschland und Europa in der Neuzeit: Festschrift für Karl Otmar Freiherr von Aretin zum 65. Geburtstag,* ed. Ralph Melville et al. (Stuttgart: Franz Steiner, 1988), 193–204.

Table 3.1 *Household distribution in the eastern zone of the province of Niğbolu in the 1480s (the districts of Chernovi, Yer Gögi, and Krapich in the north, and Shumnu, Gerilova, and Ala Kilise in the south)*

Sub-province	Muslims			Christians			Total	Totals	Percentage of Muslims
	Reg. Households	Others[63]	Total	Reg. Households	Widow households	Total			
Chernovi	0	18	18	753	36	789	807	2%
Yer Gögi	3	43	46	246	5	251	297	15.5%
Krapich	10	0	10	325	14	339	349	3%
Shumnu	63	323	386	880	41	921	1,307	29.5%
Gerilova	0	60	60	248	40	288	348	17%
Ala Kilise	0	114	114	0	0	0	114	100%
Totals	76	558	634	2,452	136	2,588	3,222	19.7%

[63] Almost exclusively *yürüks* and *yürük*-related groups.

Table 3.2 *Settlement distribution by type in the eastern zone of the province of Niğbolu in the mid-1480s*

Sub-province	Towns/District centers[64]	Villages	Mezra'as	
			With registered residents	Without registered residents
Çernovi	2	32	1	3
Yer Gögi	1	2	1	0
Krapich	1	11	0	0
Shumnu	1	31	17	4
Gerilova	1	9	5	5
Ala Kilise	No settlements – 114 "scattered" *yürük* households			
Totals	6	85	24	12

and the southernmost parts of the district of Shumnu (i.e. along the southern edges of Deliorman proper), the percentage of Muslims in the rural population in Deliorman, which would later become well known for the heavy presence of heterodox Muslim groups, was still far lower than the average for the whole province of Niğbolu. The most striking example of this is observed in the district of Chernovi in the heart of Deliorman, which had only eighteen Muslim households (all of them *yürük*) – found in a single *mezra'a*.[65] The same district counted 753 Christian households, most of them along the Danube and thus on the northern edge of Deliorman proper. As Table 3.3 demonstrates, while in the two southern districts of Shumnu and Gerilova the number of wholly Muslim settlements was about half of all settlements (including

---

[64] The settlements referred to as "towns" in Tables 3.2 and 3.3 are those designated as "nefs" (Ar. *nafs*) in TSMA D 167 and the extant late fifteenth-century register fragments preserved in Sofia. As discussed in Chapter 5, the term did not necessarily betray the well-established urban nature of these settlements, but rather denoted their status as administrative centers. Some of them would later appear as mere villages. Thus, in the eastern zone of the province of Niğbolu in the 1480s, the settlements of Krapich and Gerilova may be said to figure as "nefs" solely on account of being administrative centers. Yer Gögi (Rus) and Tutrakan on the Danube (and thus outside of the scope of the present study), as well as Cherven (in northern Deliorman) had the character of towns in the mid-1480s, just as Shumnu, on the southern edges of Deliorman. Chapter 5 offers a discussion on Shumnu and Cherven.

[65] The *mezra'a* of Vardun (mod. village of Vardun in the province of Târgovishte), TSMA D 167, 37b. While in TSMA D 167 it appears to belong to the sub-province of Tırnova (Turnovo), a comparison with NBKM Nk 12/9 – the register fragment preserved in the National Library in Sofia (and dated from the mid-1480s) shows clearly that it pertained to Chernovi, NBKM N k 12/9, f. 8a.

Table 3.3 *Settlement distribution by religious affiliation in the eastern zone of the province of Niğbolu in the mid-1480s*

Sub-province	Muslim	Mixed	Christian
Chernovi	1	0	35
Yer Gögi	1	1	2
Krapich	1	2	9
Shumnu	20	6	23
Gerilova	7	0	8
Ala Kilise	No permanent settlements		
Totals	30	9	77

mezra 'as with registered residents), in the northern districts of the eastern zone (Yer Gögi, Chernovi, and Krapich), the number of wholly Muslim (as well as mixed) settlements was negligible. An interesting case is the district (or sub-province) of Ala Kilise (mod. district of Omurtag) in the south, which had no registered settlements, containing only 114 "scattered" (*perakende*) *yürük* households.[66] This testifies to the efforts and capacity of the Ottoman state to keep track of and tax (semi-) nomadic (i.e. still largely unsettled) population groups in the region as early as in the late fifteenth century and runs counter to the theoretical supposition that the numerous nomadic or semi-nomadic taxpayers added to the Ottoman tax registers in the first half of the sixteenth century might have already been in the area without being registered by the Ottoman authorities.

This specific demographic situation in the eastern part of the province of Niğbolu may be explained by both the continuous Uze, Pecheneg, and Cuman raids into the Balkan northeast during the two to three centuries preceding the Ottoman conquest as well as the already discussed fifteenth-century developments in the area, all of which contributed to its depopulation.

At this point it is appropriate to address a major scholarly argument regarding the historical origins of the heterodox Muslim community in the Balkan northeast, which links those origins to the revolt of Sheykh Bedreddin in the early fifteenth century. A.Y. Ocak, relying on the writings of Ottoman intellectuals like Bali Efendi (d. 1553), the judge (*kadı*) of Sofia, strongly asserts that the heterodox (Kızılbaş, later Alevi-Bektashi) population of Deliorman represents the descendants of Sheykh

---

[66] TSMA D 167, f. 9a.

Bedreddin's followers.[67] While not focusing specifically on Bedreddin's rebellion, F. De Jong questions Babinger's argument that heterodox Muslim communities in the eastern Balkans were largely the product of migrations of adherents of the Safavid order in the context of the Ottoman-Safavid conflict of the first half of the sixteenth century. Based on a somewhat questionable comparison between the religio-cultural practices of the Kızılbaş of Deliorman and the Tahtacı tribe of eastern Anatolia, which he sees as closest to the Safavid Kızılbaş socio-cultural tradition, De Jong sees the Kızılbaş population of Deliorman as having little to do with Safavid religious traditions and thus rooted in pre-sixteenth-century developments. Conversely, as the modern Bektashi community of Gerlovo appears to have more in common in terms of rituals and beliefs with the Tahtacıs of eastern Anatolia, De Jong sees this latter community as more likely to have its origins in the Ottoman-Safavid conflict and to contain descendants of Safavid Turcoman sympathizers on Ottoman soil who migrated to the Balkans in the early sixteenth century.[68]

In the light of the analysis of the earliest fully preserved Ottoman tax register that covers the area under discussion and contains data pertaining to *c.* 1485, and comparing it with the detailed tax registers of the sixteenth century (discussed in the following chapter) during which rural Deliorman and Gerlovo experienced a dramatic population growth attributable mostly to incoming Turcoman migrants, it may be concluded that while Sheykh Bedreddin's legacy may have played (and likely did play) a role, the hypothesis positing a very strong degree of continuity between Bedreddin's activities in the region and the overall formation of the sizable heterodox Muslim community in Deliorman and Gerlovo is hardly supported by Ottoman tax register data.

It is possible however that some followers of Bedreddin's teachings migrated to Deliorman and Gerlovo from other parts of the Balkans, as well as, no less importantly, from Anatolia, as descendants of the original followers of Bedreddin (from his Anatolian period) and his disciples Börklüce Mustafa and Torlak Hu Kemal might have likewise found Deliorman (possibly connected with Bedreddin in sixteenth-century historical memory) an attractive place to find refuge in the context of sixteenth-century tumult in Asia Minor.

---

[67] Ocak, *Zındıklar*, 228–231. See also Minorsky, "Shaykh Bali Efendi," and Tietze, "Sheykh Bali Efendi's Report." İnalcık also argues that most of the heterodox population of Deliorman (and neighboring Dobrudja) had its origins in Bedreddin's movement, but does not substantiate his argument; İnalcik, *Classical Age*, 190.

[68] De Jong, "Problems."

4   The Repopulation of Deliorman and Gerlovo's Countryside in the Sixteenth Century

While late fifteenth-century Deliorman, Gerlovo, and adjacent areas possessed an established historical tradition of Turcoman presence and yet were largely underpopulated, the area experienced a dramatic population increase in the first half of the sixteenth century, very much leading to the foundational formation of its Muslim and predominantly Turkish-speaking community, followed by a demographic stabilization in the second half of the century. The countryside saw a veritable demographic explosion, whereby the overall registered rural population grew close to tenfold between the 1480s and the 1570s, with the corresponding increase in the rural Muslim population being around twentyfold. The most significant aspect of population growth of the countryside was the influx of Turcoman migrants from the southern Balkans (especially Thrace) and Anatolia, most of whom likely espoused religious views that fell in the realm of "heterodox" Islam, and who founded numerous new rural settlements. As will be discussed in the next chapter, this was paralleled by a vigorous expansion of the area's urban network continuously supported by the Ottoman state, whereby Deliorman's towns would develop as strongholds of Ottoman authority as well as (Ottoman) "Sunni orthodoxy" whose articulation was a process in the making.

The influx of Turcoman migrants in the northeast Balkans and in Deliorman and Gerlovo in particular relates to a matrix of issues that constitute a central aspect of expansion and state consolidation in the early Ottoman centuries. It should be placed in the context of both "internal" migrations of Turcomans within the Balkans from the second half of the fourteenth century onwards and the Ottoman-Safavid conflict, under which the persecutions of heterodox populations in Ottoman Anatolia led to state-sponsored deportations (*sürgün*) as well as spontaneous migrations (*göç*) of Anatolian newcomers into the Balkans.[1]

---

[1] For a general overview of migrations in the sixteenth-century Ottoman Empire, see Hüseyin Arslan, *Osmanlı'da Nüfus Hareketleri (XVI. Yüzyıl): Yönetim, Nüfus, Göçler, İskanlar, Sürgünler* (Istanbul: Kaknüs Yayınları, 2001).

These processes relate directly to Barkan's major arguments and also raise as issues two major dynamics. The first is the ongoing efforts of the Ottoman state to increase the degree of central control in the provinces, including control over semi-nomadic and nomadic groups and the latter's continuous contact with the local, largely settled (and predominantly Slavic-speaking) population that led to the gradual sedentarization of many Turcoman colonists who did not previously follow a strictly sedentary way of life.[2] Second is the "Islamization" of Deliorman and Gerlovo's countryside in its various manifestations. The most important distinction to be made in this regard is between the "Islamization of space" – i.e. the utilization of territories not yet firmly integrated within the Islamic world's socio-cultural and religious landscape, largely the result of Turcoman settlement and colonization as well as Ottoman urban development, and the "Islamization of people" – that is, the religious conversion of parts of the local, mostly Slavic-speaking and Orthodox Christian population, as well as the introduction of freed slaves, whose manumission was usually related to their conversion[3]. The former aspect of Islamization, that of space, will be discussed in this chapter, while conversion to Islam will be taken up in more detail in Chapter 7 as a part of an integrated analysis of religious conversion in both the rural countryside and the urban centers of Deliorman and Gerlovo. At this point, it should be noted that conversion to Islam in the countryside was not characterized by the high rates typical of urban centers; yet, given that the overwhelming part of the population lived in villages, the overall number of converts to Islam in the countryside was larger than that in the urban centers and thus was nevertheless demographically as well as culturally significant.

4.1   The Repopulation of Deliorman and Gerlovo in the Sixteenth Century – *sürgün* and *göç*, the Role of the State and its Limits

The discussion of the nature of Ottoman colonization in Chapter 2 outlined two main forms of population transfers: state-organized forced deportations (*sürgün*) and migrations (*göç*) not directly organized by the state but occasioned by broader political, socio-economic, and religio-cultural factors. Such migrations could take the form of mass flight or

---

[2] On this process in Ottoman Bulgaria, see Georgieva, *Prostranstvo i prostranstva*, 165–175; for a more general discussion of Ottoman policies of settling nomadic groups, see Cengiz Orhonlu, *Osmanlı İmparatorluğunda Aşiretleri İskân Teşebbüsü (1691–1696)* (Istanbul: İstanbul Üniversitesi Edebiyat Fakültesi Basımevi, 1963), 27–32.
[3] On this distinction, see Radushev, *Pomatsite*, vol. 1, 16–19.

migrations of individual families and smaller groups, including religio-politically conditioned colonization such as that carried out by coloniz-ing dervishes as discussed by Barkan.

The northeastern Balkans, and Deliorman and Gerlovo in particular, possessed several interrelated characteristics that could prove accom-modating to Turcoman (semi-nomadic) incomers. First, as of the late fifteenth century, the area (especially Deliorman) was underpopulated, difficult to access, and featured a low degree of central state control that could also offer at least temporary opportunities for tax evasion – all this could be an "attraction" for the "non-mainstream-minded" and "undis-ciplined" vis-à-vis the centralizing, sedentarizing Ottoman regime.

Second, Deliorman offered good conditions for sheep breeding, a traditional subsistence pattern for nomadic and semi-nomadic popula-tions. As Anthony Greenwood has demonstrated, Deliorman became so important in the state-organized system of meat provisioning for the imperial capital Istanbul (and Edirne) that by the second half of the six-teenth century one of the four meat-provisioning "seasons" within that system was named "Deliorman" (or *Divane Orman*) – the season during which many of the sheep driven to the two cities to secure the required mutton supply came from Deliorman.[4] This is confirmed by numer-ous contemporary imperial edicts contained in the registers of outgoing imperial orders (*mühimme defterleri*).[5] At the same time, the region had potential for agriculture as arable land could be opened up by clearing forest, very much in the way practiced by Seyyid Rüstem Gazi (and other colonizing dervishes). This potential would eventually be fulfilled in the sixteenth century (and later) in the context of the ongoing processes of sedentarization and agrarianization. As Machiel Kiel has commented, "[T]he greater part of the Deli Orman villages appear as clearing set-tlements (*Rodungssiedlungen*), with the fields radiating from the village and surrounded by the forest or the remains of it."[6] In the context of Deliorman's explosive demographic growth in the sixteenth century, this potential had to be utilized as "[I]n the dry and wooded area of the Deli Orman expansion of agriculture to feed the growing population was only possible by cutting down large parts of the forest."[7]

---

[4] Anthony Greenwood, "Istanbul's Meat Provisioning: A Study of the Celepkeşan System," Ph.D. diss., The University of Chicago, 1988, 122–123.
[5] To give a few examples: BOA MD 3, No. 1642 (gurre, Rebi'ü'l-evvel AH 968/November 20, 1560); BOA MD 22, No. 271 (15 Rebi'ü'l-ahir AH 981/August 14, 1573); BOA MD 35, No. 301 (29 Cemaziü'l-ahir AH 986/September 2, 1578); BOA MD 40, No. 479 (28 Şevval AH 987/December 18, 1579); BOA MD 42, No. 583 (11 Muharrem AH 989/February 15, 1581).
[6] Kiel, "Hrâzgrad-Hezargrad-Razgrad," 505.
[7] Ibid.

Third, Deliorman and Gerlovo already had well-established traditions of "heterodox" Islam in the fifteenth century and thus could be attractive to non-Sharia-minded Turcomans and dervishes. Deliorman was the place of origin of Sheykh Bedreddin's revolt in 1416, and as Mevlana Neşri reminds us, it still sheltered some of his adherents as of the early sixteenth century.[8] Deliorman and Gerlovo also figured prominently in Otman Baba's peregrinations.

What were the geographical origins of this influx of Turcomans? While the Ottoman chronicle tradition provides close to no clues, extant tax registers suggest two major channels of migration: from the southeastern Balkans, and from Anatolia, in the latter case in the form of mass flight and state-organized deportations in the context of the Safavid-Ottoman conflict and the related persecutions of heterodox, largely nomadic or semi-nomadic groups perceived as Safavid sympathizers.

The case of "internal" migrations within the Balkans is supported by two main clusters of evidence. First, the Ottoman tax registrations from the 1480s and the first half of the sixteenth century suggest a wave of Turcoman colonization and settlement, largely on the part of *yürük*s and related groups. This process had started by the 1480s and advanced from south to north: first along the northern slopes of the Balkan range (above all Gerlovo), and then with time, further northward into Deliorman proper, almost reaching the Danube by the mid-sixteenth century. The most likely origin of these *yürük* (and related or similar) groups is Thrace (and the eastern Rhodopes), right on the other side of the Balkan range.[9] Some settlement names, such as Filibelüler and Zağralı, also point in that direction.

The second, related cluster of evidence specifically concerns dervish colonization. As demonstrated below, tax registrations show clearly that a number of newly founded dervish lodge communities in Gerlovo and Deliorman originated specifically from Thrace and Tanrıdağı – like the

---

[8] Neşrî, *Cihânnümâ*, 232. Some of these "adherents of Bedreddîn" may have been new arrivals from elsewhere (e.g. Thrace or Anatolia) whom Neşrî could have associated with Bedreddîn on account of their perceived "heretical" ways. Bedreddîn's fame had spread in western and central Anatolia on account of his own activities as well as the revolts of his disciples Torlak Hû Kemâl and Börklüce Muṣṭāfā that paralleled Bedreddîn's uprising in 1416. Aşıkpaşazâde's history mentions Bedreddîn's followers (from Rûmeli) fighting on the side of the Safavid sheykh Junayd in Syria in the 1440s; *Âşıkpaşazade Tarihi*, 231. This passage falls in the section covering the years 1486–1502 whose authorship is debatable, but has been traditionally considered a part of the chronicle and was included in 'Alî Bey's edition, *Âşıkpaşazâde Tarihi* (Istanbul: Matba'a-i Amire, AH 1332/AD 1914), 266. Many of Bedreddîn's followers may have already been assimilated into other movements, such as the Safavid order of Ardabil and the Bektashis, Mazzaoui, *The Origins of the Safawids*, 62, or the Abdals of Rum – see related argument in Chapter 6.

[9] Thus following the "natural" routes of ("heterodox") Turcoman expansion in the Balkans, see Mélikoff, "Les voies."

community of Yolkulu Dede, which figures prominently in the *vita* of Demir Baba, the great sixteenth-century Rum Abdal saint of Deliorman; some "descendants" of Kızıl Deli; and the strikingly numerous "progeny" of Sheykh Timur Han that spread all over Deliorman and Gerlovo. The latter two figures, as discussed in Chapter 2, were among the prominent colonizers of the southeastern Balkans in the late fourteenth/early fifteenth century.

Placed in their proper historical context, these migrations of semi-nomadic Turcomans and heterodox dervishes from Thrace and Tanrıdağı to the northeastern Balkans may be related to the Ottoman state's concurrent centralizing drive whose impact was radiating from the capital, as well as to the related rise of Ottoman "Sunni orthodoxy" which prompted the suppression of non-Sharia-minded dervish groups like that of Otman Baba.

In addition to this "internal migration" within the Balkans one must consider a second wave – from Anatolia, in the context of the Safavid-Ottoman conflict. While contemporary sixteenth-century sources rarely specifically mention transfers of "Kızılbaş" from Anatolia to the northeastern Balkans, forced or "voluntary," they contain important clues in this direction. This supposition is further strengthened by the popularity of the poetry of Hatayi (Shah Ismail I Safavi) among the Abdals of Rum in the northeastern Balkans, as evidenced in Demir Baba's *vita*, as well as the predominance of "Kızılbaş" as a self-designation among the heterodox population of the northeastern Balkans in the modern age[10] and the related circulation of oral traditions pointing to Ottoman persecutions in Anatolia as the origin of the Kızılbaş community in Deliorman.[11]

The most massive wave of deportations to the wider northeastern Balkans has been categorically documented in a synoptic tax register for Ottoman Rumelia dated 1530, but largely utilizing demographic data from earlier registrations dated 1516 and 1518.[12]

---

[10] See Irène Mélikoff, "La communauté Kızılbaş du Deli Orman en Bulgarie," in ibid., *Sur les traces du soufisme turc: Recherches sur l'Islam populaire en Anatolie* (Istanbul: The Isis Press, 1992), 105–113. On the inclusion of Hatayi's poetry in Demir Baba's *vita*, see Chapter 6.

[11] One such oral tradition recorded in the early 1980s in Deliorman's village of Bisertsi (Ottoman-era Naṣrüddīn) recounts a purported meeting between the victorious Ottoman sultan "Yavuz Selīm" and the Safavid shah – the shah prostrated himself before Selīm and gave him his beautiful purple *kaftān* to evoke his mercy, Selīm ended the massacres of Kızılbaş and commuted due to deportations in the distant provinces of the Empire (implicitly including Deliorman). Sofiia Biserova, "Etnografski materiali za selo Bisertsi," in *Bâlgarskite aliani: sbornik etnografski materiali*, ed Ivanichka Georgieva (Sofia: Universitetsko Izdatelstvo "Sv. Kliment Ohridski," 1991), 50–51.

[12] BOA TD 370, also published in facsimile as *370 Numaralı Muhâsabe-i Vilâyet-i Rûm-ili Defteri (937/1530)* (Ankara: T.C. Başbakanlık Devlet Arşivleri Genel Müdürlüğü, 2002); the demographic data for the province of Niğbolu in TD 370 have been extracted from

According to the above-mentioned register, these transfers had a direct impact mostly on the province (*sancak*) of Silistre, dominated by the region of Dobrudja, which likely underwent a concurrent demographic transformation similar to that in Deliorman.[13] The register contains numerous references to "households of deportees" (*hane-i sürgünan*), the "community of deportees" (*cema'at-i sürgünan, sürgünan ta'ifesi*) scattered all across the (southern) part of the province in the sub-provinces of Varna, Pravadi, and Silistre.[14] While many of these deportee households may be seen scattered among numerous villages, the largest single concentration (as recorded in this register) is formed by a so-called "*ze'amet* of the deportees" (*ze'amet-i sürgünan*) in the sub-province (*kaza*) of Pravadi and consisting of 1,784 households of deportees originating from Anatolia, as clearly stated in the respective register entry.[15] While the entry dates from 1530 it mentions an earlier register (*defter-i köhne*) – the earliest extant (synoptic) register for the province of Silistre, dated AH 924/AD 1518 – which contains a similar, but shorter entry.[16] Most of the other references to deportees in the province of Silistre in the 1530 register have also been copied from the original 1518 Silistre register,[17] which would mean that these deportations must have started in the reign of Selim I (or possibly in the last years of the reign of Bayezid II, given the reference to "past sultans"); this dating fits well with contemporary political developments, especially Selim I's succession to the throne in 1512 in the context of Shah Kulu's rebellion and the persecutions that followed in Anatolia.

BOA MAD 11 of 1516, a detailed register whose second half, covering the eastern part of the province, including most of Deliorman, is missing. Yet, a comparison between the preserved half of BOA MAD 11 and the section for the province of Niğbolu in BOA TD 370 suggests that the former register was used for the compilation of the latter. Similarly, the section in BOA TD 370 covering the province of Silistre, which contains Deliorman's neighboring region of Dobrudja is related in a similar way to a (poorly preserved) synoptic register (BOA TD 65) for that province dated AH 924/AD 1518.

[13] Related comprehensive research on Dobrudja is unavailable, but see Kemal Karpat, "Dobruca," *TDVİA*, vol. 9, 482–486.

[14] BOA TD 370, pp. 384–387, 391, 394, 397, 399, 409, 411, 415–420, 422–444, 450, 452, 465–470.

[15] BOA TD 370, p. 436, "*Ze'āmet-i sürgünān ki gelüb dimekle ma'rūflardır. Zikr olan tā'ife bundan evvel Anadolu'dan Dobruca'ya sürgün gelüb…ve sā'ir 'avārız-ı dīvāniyyeden mu'āf ü müsellem olalar deyü, ve defter-i köhnede mukayyed olunub, ellerinde Selātīn-i māżiden ve Pādişāhımız Sultān Süleymān…mukayyed ve hükümları olduğu sebebden mu'āf kayd olunub… 'avārız-ı dīvāniyyeden mu'āf olalar.*"

[16] BOA TD 65, p. 30. This entry appears half-obliterated, but as the total tax revenue figure for the "*ze'amet* of the deportees" is the same in BOA TD 65 and BOA TD 370, it can be deduced that the entry in TD 370 conveys in essence the same information originally recorded in the 1518 register (BOA TD 65).

[17] This statement can be made to the extent to which the respective entries in BOA TD 65 are legible, given its poor condition.

The law codes for the province of Silistre contained in both registers shed further light on both the circumstances surrounding these forced deportations and the regulations that applied to the deportees. The most important regulation in the law code accompanying the 1518 register (copied almost verbatim in the 1530 register) reads as follows:

The [exiled] deportees (*sürgün ta'ifesi*) who have come from Anatolia and do not have relatives among the ones [previously] exiled, belong to [i.e. pay their taxes to] the village lord to whose village they first came and settled; thereafter a change of residence should not change these conditions [?]. And such a group that comes from Rum-ili or consists of [former] infidels who have accepted Islam [and thus mixed with the Muslim deportees from Anatolia] or is not related to the exiled and are [to be found] among them, should not be paid attention if they say "I am among the exiled;" those not entered in the new register should pay taxes to the lord of the village in which they settled. And if the deportation commander (*sürgün subaşısı*) says "They are among my deportees," attention should not be paid to him. But the ones who have come from Anatolia to the aforementioned province and are relatives of the exiled, are again considered deportees.[18]

This regulation and the data from the two registers suggest several tentative arguments regarding the nature of population movements, demographic change, and the related role of the Ottoman state in the process, not only within the northeastern Balkans, but also in the greater Balkan and empire-wide contexts.

First, it is clear that the Ottoman state resorted to the well-organized forced deportation of large groups of people from Anatolia to the province of Silistre, and specifically to the coastal provincial district of Varna and the district of Pravadi, immediately to its west. As Barkan has observed, the Ottoman state would typically resort to forced deportations in order to maximize socio-economic efficiency and tax revenue and/or to resettle actually or potentially rebellious population groups to neutralize challenges to Ottoman sovereignty. While the registers and law codes cited do not refer to specific reasons for the deportations, the years in which they were compiled (1518 and 1530, respectively) suggest strongly that these forced population transfers took place in direct relation to early sixteenth-century Anatolia's political climate: the opening phases of

---

[18] BOA TD 65, pp. 3–4: "*Ve sürgün tā'ifesinin Anadolu'dan göçüb gelenleri ki, sürgün akrabāsından olmayanlar, anlar kangi tīmārda mütemekkin ve mütevaṭṭın olalar, mütemekkin oldukları karye ṣāḥibiniŋ ol evvel kangi köye geldiyse anıŋ ola; soŋra tebdīl-i mekān etmekle tagyīr olmaya. Ve şol tā'ife ki Rumili'nden ola veya kāfirden imāna gele veya sürgünden gayriniŋ müte'allıkı ola ve sürgün arasında ola, anlarıŋ "Sürgünüm" dediğine 'amel olunmaya, defter-i cedīde mukayyed olmayanlar kangi köyde mütemekkinse rüsūmun köy ṣāḥibi ala, ve sürgün subaşısı "Benüm sürgünüm" dediğine 'amel olunmaya. Ammā Anadolu'dan gelüb livā-i mezkūreye gelüb akrabā-i sürgün yine sürgün kısmındadır,*" also published in transliteration in Ahmed Akgündüz, *Osmanlı Kanunnâmeleri ve Hukukî Tahlilleri*, vol. 3 (Istanbul: Fey Vakfı Yayınları, 1991), 467.

the Ottoman-Safavid conflict and the series of rebellions perceived by the Ottoman central government as pro-Safavid, such as those of Shah Kulu (1511–12), Sheykh Celal (1519), and Kalender Shah (1527). The related data in both registers also suggest that forced population transfers were likely recurrent events, rather than a one-time measure taken by the government.

Second, the quoted regulation provides clear evidence that the Ottoman state was not fully in control of certain processes related to the deportations it had ordered – more specifically, the "original" deportees were accompanied or followed by relatives (*akraba*) who were originally not supposed to be deported. The law code stipulates that these family members should also be considered deportees. This fits criticisms levelled against Barkan's views of an all-powerful Ottoman state, but provides yet one more example of the state's efforts and capacity to register and accommodate processes that it did not necessarily initiate and/or was not fully able to control.

Third, and also related to the consideration presented above, is the mention of groups of people originating from Rumelia (i.e. the Balkans) who mixed with the deportees from Anatolia. The two registers for the province of Silistre, like contemporary registers for neighboring Deliorman and Gerlovo, contain a number of toponymic appellations that suggest recent migrations from other parts of the Balkans, especially from Thrace, which had been colonized in the late fourteenth and fifteenth centuries.[19] The Ottoman administration, rather than directing these population movements, was exerting efforts to register taxpayers on the move in its quest to assert its authority and maximize tax revenues.

Lastly, as for the mention of converts to Islam who may have mixed with the deportees, these were likely local converts who claimed deportee status to enjoy the related tax exemptions. Alternatively, they may have come from farther away where they might have felt increasingly uncomfortable in a predominantly non-Muslim milieu.

How do these deportations to the province of Silistre relate to the repopulation of Deliorman (and Gerlovo) in the first half of the sixteenth century? A particular difficulty is posed because tax-register data for Deliorman do not provide comparably clear evidence of forced resettlement of population groups from Anatolia, the only exception being small groups of *Sürgünan-ı Acem* (lit. "Persian deportees") scattered in

---

[19] For example, the *mezraʿa* of Filibelüler in the *ḳażā* of Silistre, or that of Çirmenlü in the *ḳażā* of Aydos, and a number of settlements associated with Albanians: the villages of Arnavud Kuyusu and Arnavud Kuyusu-i Diğer in the *ḳażā*s of Varna and Pravadi, respectively, as well as Arnavud Pınarı in the *ḳażā* of Silistre; BOA TD 370, pp. 392, 448, 430, 438.

numerous provinces of Rumeli, the Hezargrad area included.[20] As the discussion of the above-presented early sixteenth-century law-code regulations for the province of Silistre has shown, the Ottoman state hardly had complete control over population movements from Anatolia to the Balkans or within the Balkans themselves. As Deliorman largely occupies the eastern part of the province of Niğbolu, neighboring that of Silistre (and a portion of historic Deliorman itself is to be found the province of Silistre),[21] one meaningful hypothesis could be that a significant part of the migrants who contributed to Deliorman's repopulation in the first half of the sixteenth century could have come from Anatolia (including deportees and their relatives) via the Black Sea coast areas of the province of Silistre in search of underpopulated areas befitting their way of life and in a quest to escape state control and taxation.

A copy of a law code, tentatively dated to the mid-sixteenth century, may shed more light on this possibility. A law code for the "Province of Nigbolu and others," collected in a compilation of Ottoman law codes from the second half of the same century, it includes a regulation very similar to the one discussed above for the province of Silistre, stipulating very much the same conditions applying to deportees from Anatolia and other migrating groups.[22] It could be argued, albeit tentatively, that the inclusion of this regulation in a law code for the province of Niğbolu may reflect such a spill-over of deportees from the province of Silistre to that of Niğbolu.

Indeed, the fact that there is no clear evidence of large population groups deported from Anatolia specifically to Deliorman in registers pertaining to the first half of the sixteenth century may be seen as fitting well with the general nature of Ottoman deportation policies. A brief look at the places to which the Ottoman central government would direct deportees on account of actual or perceived potential disobedience shows that preference was given to either islands hard for deportees to escape from, such as Rhodes and Cyprus (after the conquest of those two in 1521 and 1570–1, respectively), or, alternatively, coastal areas such as Modon (Methoni) and Koron (Koroni) in the Peloponesse and the northwest Black Sea coast in the province of Silistre, or along major trade routes[23] within easy reach of the

---

[20] BOA TD 309, pp. 70–71. This pious endowment register is dated AH 965/AD 1558.

[21] This part of Deliorman is not subject to detailed demographic analysis due to methodological considerations discussed in the introduction.

[22] This collection of Ottoman *ḳānūnnāme*s is housed in the National Library in Sofia, NBKM Or 73; the particular law code is found at 108a–120b; the specific regulation is on f. 117a.

[23] For example, the deportation of nomads from Saruhan in northwestern Anatolia to what became a settlement named Saruhan Bey (mod. Septemvri) in Thrace along the Via Militaris on the account of their opposition to regulations on salt production and trade imposed by Bāyezīd I, see *Āşıkpaşazâde Tarihi*, 100 and p. 43 above.

Ottoman authorities. Deliorman, being inland and characterized by a hilly, wooded terrain, was not such an area, and it is not hard to understand why large, compact masses of (potentially rebellious) deportees would not be deliberately directed there. It is also not hard to conceive that deportees, as well as other increasingly marginalized groups (religio-political "dissidents" of various types, subjects without permanent residence, etc.) would find a region like Deliorman a suitable place of refuge.[24]

Thus, any attempt to explain the repopulation of Deliorman in the sixteenth century necessitates paying considerable attention to non-state-controlled migrations. While often downplayed by statist-minded historians like Barkan, these should be accorded a greater importance than state-directed population transfers, given the early modern Ottoman state's limited ability to control population movements.

If explosive population growth that led to the formation of a sizable and stable Muslim community was one major change that Deliorman and Gerlovo experienced from the late fifteenth through the sixteenth centuries, another, concurrent and related transformation was the "disciplining" or "taming" of the nomadic or semi-nomadic Turcomans. As discussed in the following section, sixteenth-century tax-register data show that though the overwhelming majority of new Turcoman arrivals in the area enjoyed special tax exemptions relating to their semi-nomadic (*yürük* or similar) profile as of the late fifteenth century, by 1579 the dominant majority of rural Muslims were sedentary, regular (and presumably "obedient") *re'aya* – well established in their respective villages and engaged in agriculture (and, often, sheep rearing), without any privileged taxation status. An alternative perspective on this process from the point of view of some of those "disciplined" groups – as through the lens of Demir Baba's *velayetname* as discussed in Chapter 6 – would suggest that by the seventeenth century or so, such groups had also come to accept the legitimacy and the primacy of the Ottoman state.

4.2   Major Aspects of Rural Deliorman and Gerlovo's Demographic Transformation in the Sixteenth Century: Turcoman Repopulation, the Rise of *derbend* Villages, and Christian–Muslim Co-Existence in the Light of Ottoman Tax Registers

The following analysis of the broad demographic and socio-economic transformation of Deliorman and Gerlovo's countryside is largely based

---

[24] Or, as the authors of the article on "Deli-Orman" in *EI²* put it: "In the Ottoman period Deli-Orman was a place of refuge for all kinds of political and religious refugees."

on a series of five tax registers for the province of Niğbolu reflecting the area's development from the late fifteenth through the late sixteenth centuries as well as on contemporary Ottoman provincial law codes. The first two of these registers – one dated 1512[25] but reflecting a mid-1480s registration, and another from 1530, but based on a 1516 register[26] – are synoptic (icmal) and thus provide only summary taxpayer numbers including taxation status (Muslim and non-Muslim, householders and bachelors, groups with special obligations and tax privileges) as well as summary tax revenue figures for each settlement. The later three registers – from c. 1535,[27] c. 1550,[28] and 1579[29] are detailed (mufassal) and, in addition, list all taxpayers individually and furnish detailed tax revenue breakdowns, thus allowing for a more nuanced analysis of the development of the settlement network and individual and group sectarian identities,[30] including examining the questions of dervish colonization, subsistence patterns, and socio-economic development.[31]

While the overall boundaries of the area under consideration, as outlined in the Introduction, remained roughly the same, tax registers reflect evolving internal administrative subdivisions. Divided into six

---

[25] TSMA D 167, discussed in Chapter 3, section 3.4.

[26] BOA TD 370, see fn. 12 in this chapter.

[27] Tîmâr register BOA TD 439. An internal note on p. 93 (part of the original text) referring to an earlier villagers' petition dated the middle ten days of Safer AH 931 (December 12–21, 1524) furnishes the terminus post quem. The earliest marginal annotation on p. 72 (entered after the register's compilation) is dated the first ten days of Safer AH 955 (March 11–20, 1548) and may be accepted as the terminus ante quem. A comparison of BOA TD 439 to the other tax registers utilized in this study suggests that this register was most likely compiled c. 1535, but possibly a couple of years earlier. This register's first several pages are absent; a comparison to other sixteenth-century registers for the area suggests that several Christian villages along the Danube are thus missing, while the registration of all Muslim and mixed villages appears to be complete. Thus the data from this register regarding Christian villages should be accepted with some caution, but the missing information very likely would not change significantly the general picture as far as the area's Christian population is concerned, and not at all so regarding the Muslim population. For c. 1535, I also use a fragment of contemporary pious endowments (evkâf) register NBKM OAK 217/8, adding several waqf villages to complete the respective demographic calculations. On this latter source, see section 4.2.5.

[28] BOA TD 382, housed in the Prime Ministry Ottoman Archive in Istanbul; dating is based on internal evidence.

[29] TKG KK TTd 151, preserved in the Archive of the Directorate for Land Deeds and the Cadaster in Ankara. Several pious endowment (waqf) villages from TKG KK TTd 411, also dated 1579, have been added to the 1579 registration calculations to complete the demographic picture for the area in that year.

[30] While Ottoman tax registers explicitly distinguish between Muslims and non-Muslims, denoting also specific non-Muslim religious and confessional identities (Orthodox Christians, Catholics, Armenian Monophysites, Jews, etc.), they do not point clearly to Muslim taxpayers' sectarian or confessional identities. However, some details (e.g. taxpayers' names) may provide clues about Muslims' socio-cultural and sectarian identities. Muslim taxpayers' names also clearly point to converts to Islam. See discussion on conversion in Chapter 7.

[31] See also the discussion of synoptic and detailed tax registers in the Introduction.

smaller administrative districts in the late fifteenth century,[32] according to the registrations of 1530 (likely reflecting 1516 data), and c. 1535 the same area was consolidated into" two districts: the *kazas/nahiyes* of Chernovi and Shumnu. By the mid-sixteenth century, the area under discussion comprised three administrative districts (*nahiyes*), including the new district of Hezargrad carved out between those of Chernovi and Shumnu, and by the 1579, another district (*nahiye*), that of Eski Cuma, was formed out of the northwestern part of the district of Shumnu.[33]

4.2.1   The Development of the Settlement Network

The evolving number of rural settlements, including the changing figures for Muslim, Christian, and mixed settlements (i.e. having both Muslim and Christian residents), a general and somewhat cursory, yet telling measure, offers important insights into sixteenth-century Deliorman and Gerlovo's demographic transformation.

In the late fifteenth century,[34] the entire area had 112 rural settlements: 33 Muslim, 6 mixed, and 73 wholly Christian. A striking feature of the settlement distribution is the practical absence of Muslim settlements in the northern part of the area studied (the districts of Chernovi, Yer Gögi, and Krapich); one finds only one village and two temporary agricultural sites (*mezra'as*) with registered residents. The overwhelming majority of Muslim settlements are found in the southern districts of Shumnu and Gerilova (Gerlovo), along the northern slopes of the Balkan range that feature a terrain suitable to the typical subsistence patterns and lifestyle of semi-nomadic Turcoman groups, including animal husbandry (especially sheep breeding). Twenty-one of the thirty Muslim settlements in the two districts were *mezra'as* settled mostly by *yürüks* and related groups who enjoyed a special taxation status that included a number of tax exemptions that would induce their sedentarization.[35] The registration of 114 "scattered" (i.e. still not permanently settled) *yürük* households in the district of Ala Kilise testifies to the centralizing Ottoman state's efforts as well as actual capacity to integrate such groups

---

[32] See Chapter 3, section 3.4.

[33] While it is often assumed that the *nāḥiye* (county) was a subdivision of a *ḳażā* (judgeship) in the sixteenth century, in the tax registers utilized, the two are very much used interchangeably, meaning "a subdivision of a province" (*sancak/livā*). BOA TD 370 of 1530 has the districts of Chernovi and Shumnu defined as *ḳażā*s – direct subdivisions of the *sancak/livā* of Niğbolu – but the later sixteenth-century tax registers for the area use *nāḥiye* for the same districts.

[34] That is, on the basis of TSMA D 167.

[35] On *mezra'as* in this context, see also Chapter 3, section 3.4.

Table 4.1 *Settlement distribution in Deliorman and Gerlovo's countryside by religious affiliation in the mid-1480s (Chernovi, Yer Gögi, and Krapich in the north, Shumnu, Gerilova, and Ala Kilise in the south)*

Sub-province	Muslim	Mixed	Christian	Total
Chernovi	1	0	33	34
Yer Gögi	1	0	2	3
Krapich	1	1	9	11
Shumnu	23	5	21	49
Gerilova	7	0	8	15
Ala Kilise	114 scattered *yürük* households			0
Total	33	6	73	112

within its military, fiscal, and land regime and portended their being tied to the land in the coming decades.[36]

The settlement distribution as of 1516 reflects the early stage of the definitive demographic and ethno-religious transformation of the region. Already administratively consolidated into two *kaza*s – Chernovi in the north and Shumnu in the south – the area witnessed a dramatic increase in the overall number of settlements, due exclusively to the proliferation of Muslim settlements, the total increase being from 112 in the 1480s to 293 in 1516, and from 33 to 218 Muslim settlements, with 147 Muslim villages in the south (*kaza* of Shumnu) and 71 in the north (*kaza* of Chernovi). While the number of Muslim settlements increased almost fivefold in the south, the northern part of the region saw the actual beginning of mass colonization by Muslim settlers (71 settlements in 1516, as compared to only 3 in the 1480s). If Ottoman archival data of thirty years earlier pointed to the presence of Muslim settlers only in the southernmost part of what in 1516 was the *kaza* of Shumnu, in 1516 one witnesses the emergence of an increasingly dense (Muslim) settlement network in the north of the same *kaza* and in most of that of Chernovi, with the exception of the narrow flat strip of land along the Danube (which already had a number of large Christian villages as of the mid-1480s). It would be from these areas which saw an intense

---

[36] See also Chapter 3, section 3.4. The district of Ala Kilise would become known as Osman Pazarı from the seventeenth century onwards. In tune with the ongoing sedentarization of semi-nomadic groups, it would acquire an urban center, Osman Pazarı (mod. Omurtag), which M. Kiel traces back to the village of Arabacı Osman; Kiel, "Osmanpazarı," *TDVİA*, vol. 34, 1–2; see also BOA TD 370, p. 551; BOA TD 382, p. 597; TKG KK TTd 151, f. 210a.

Table 4.2 *Settlement distribution in Deliorman and Gerlovo's countryside by religious affiliation in 1516*

Sub-province	Muslim	Mixed	Christian	Total
Chernovi	71	9	31	111
Shumnu	147	9	26	182
Total	218	18	57	293

Table 4.3 *Settlement distribution in Deliorman and Gerlovo's countryside by religious affiliation c. 1535*

Sub-province	Muslim	Mixed	Christian	Total
Chernovi	113	16	35	164
Shumnu	195	12	27	234
Total	308	28	62	398

influx of Turcoman settlers – the northern part of the sub-province of Shumnu and the southern portion of that of Chernovi – that the new sub-province of Hezargrad would be carved out in the mid-sixteenth century. Importantly as well, the 1516 registration no longer features any settled *mezra'a*s (i.e. *mezra'a*s with registered taxpayers) – those listed as such earlier had turned into fully fledged villages.

As for the Christian settlement network, just as in the 1480s, it was concentrated in the southern and northernmost ends of the area under discussion, in the narrow flat strip along the Danube and along the foothills of the Balkan range (mostly in Gerlovo). While the number of wholly Christian villages dropped from 73 in the 1480s to 56 in 1516, this decrease was offset by the tripling of mixed villages (from 6 to 18), all of which but one[37] were essentially Christian settlements with up to 4 or 5 Muslim taxpayers (male heads of household or bachelors) – usually local converts. As further discussed in Chapter 7, these converts often found themselves in religious and social isolation, which could prompt them to migrate to nearby Muslim villages or the nearest urban center.

As of c. 1535 the total number of rural settlements had grown up by around a third to almost 400 – largely due to the rise in numbers of the Muslim and mixed villages by roughly a half (from 218 to 308 and 18 to

[37] Istroviçe, BOA TD 370, p. 557.

28, respectively), while the number of Christian settlements registered a modest growth from 57 to 62.

By the mid-sixteenth century, the area featured 574 rural settlements – almost double the number reflected in the 1516 registration – of which 466 were wholly Muslim, 59 Christian, and 49 mixed. In all the three sub-provinces in the region, including the new one centered in Hezargrad, the number of Muslim settlements was more than four times as high as that of the Christian and mixed villages combined (and for the *nahiye* of Shumnu, the ratio was 6:1).

The number of wholly or predominantly Christian villages had also risen significantly, possibly in tune with the general population growth in the Mediterranean basin in the first half of the century, though that increase was negligible compared to the Muslim settlement network's explosive expansion. However, the number of mixed villages had increased dramatically, almost matching that of exclusively Christian settlements. This relates to the rising prominence of conversion to Islam in the region, in the context of the overall growing presence of Islam and Muslims as a religio-cultural phenomenon. The continuous co-existence of Muslims and non-Muslims would make Islam increasingly a part and parcel of the local socio-cultural and religious landscape, better known and acceptable to the indigenous local Christian population.

The tax registration of *c.* 1550 thus represents the demographic explosion in Deliorman in full bloom. It is also the earliest that features newly appearing Muslim villages not founded by settlers from outside the region, but splitting off from pre-existing villages, as under an emerging population pressure settlers were searching for hitherto unused land in the area.[38] The total number of such villages for the three sub-provinces is 31, around 5 percent of all villages. All of these save one were new Muslim settlements that split off from villages founded by Turcoman settlers: 5 in the *nahiye* of Chernovi, 11 in that of Hezargrad, and 15 in that of Shumnu, which coincides with the areas of greatest growth of Turcoman population. In some cases not one, but two or three new villages would emerge, having separated from a larger rural settlement. Such is the case with the villages of Dobriçlüler,[39] Kasımlar, and Çanakçı Oğulları that separated from the village of Kruşova in the *nahiye* of Chernovi[40] and those of Süleyman Fakih and Tanburacı, offshoots of the

---

[38] On population pressure as a major factor in the more general demographic and socio-economic development of the early modern Ottoman Empire, see Michael Cook, *Population Pressure in Rural Anatolia* (London and New York: Cambridge University Press, 1972), and Barkan "Research on the Ottoman Fiscal Surveys," 163–171, as well as İnalcık's comments in *An Economic and Social History of the Ottoman Empire*, 29–31.
[39] The reading of this place name is uncertain.
[40] BOA TD 382, pp. 113, 115, 160–161, 169.

Table 4.4 *Settlement distribution in Deliorman and Gerlovo's countryside by religious affiliation c. 1550*

Sub-province	Muslim	Mixed	Christian	Total
Chernovi	90	8	21	119
Hezargrad	168	25	19	212
Shumnu	208	16	19	243
Total	466	49	59	574

village of Sarı Turgud in the *nahiye* of Hezargrad.[41] Both of the original "mother-villages" had appeared for the first time in the registration of 1516,[42] that of Kruşova had grown to have two separate neighborhoods (*mahalle*s) by 1550. The only non-Muslim exception among these newly emerged villages is the Christian Yenice (the name being of Turkish origin and broadly signifying a new settlement) in the *nahiye* of Shumnu. It had separated from the mixed village of Oraşniçe that already had a significant number of Muslims – this development in Oraşniçe possibly precipitated the emergence of the new exclusively Christian village.[43]

The further subdivision of growing Muslim villages in the region would continue during the second half of the century, as the 1579 tax registration shows, as did the proliferation of (previously exclusively Christian) mixed villages (usually due to the appearance of local converts). As of 1579, mixed (yet predominantly Christian) villages already outnumbered wholly Christian settlements.

At the same time, the second half of the sixteenth century was marked by an overall demographic stabilization. Both in terms of settlement distribution and total population numbers, Deliorman, Gerlovo, and the adjacent areas did not experience the kind of explosive transformation characteristic of the first half of the century. This can be explained by two major factors. First, demographic stabilization was a general feature of the history of the Mediterranean basin in this period.[44] Secondly, Ottoman-Safavid tensions and the related political instability in Anatolia visibly subsided following the Treaty of Amasya (1555), which could be

[41] Ibid., pp. 335–336.
[42] BOA TD 370, pp. 559–559.
[43] BOA TD 382, pp. 490–491, 594–595. The appearance of Muslims in Oraşniçe (some clearly identifiable as converts) seems to have been a very recent phenomenon, the *c.* 1535 registration has the village as wholly Christian, BOA TD 439, p. 202.
[44] For a discussion of similar processes in Ottoman Anatolia as well as the broader Mediterranean basin, see Suraiya Faroqhi, "Population Rise and Fall in Anatolia, 1550–1620," *Middle Eastern Studies* 15 (1979), 422–445, and the literature therein.

Table 4.5 *Settlement distribution in Deliorman and Gerlovo's countryside by religious affiliation in 1579*

Sub-province	Muslim	Mixed	Christian	Total
Chernovi	91	17	22	130
Hezargrad	165	30	17	212
Shumnu	181	17	13	211
Eski Cuma	26	5	2	33
Total	463	69	54	586

seen as a factor that limited potential population transfers or migrations from Anatolia.

4.2.2 Demographic Analysis by Settlement Size

While the preceding general analysis of the settlement network in Deliorman, Gerlovo, and the adjacent areas may furnish a broad idea of the dramatic demographic and ethno-religious transformation that the region experienced in the sixteenth century, a closer look at the distribution of rural settlements by size sheds further light on the nature of demographic dynamics, especially in relation to the settlement network's growth, decline, or stability over extended periods of time. For the purposes of this analysis, all rural settlements have been divided into five categories: very small villages (with populations of up to five households); small villages (6–20 households); mid-sized villages (21–40 households); large villages (41–80 households); and very large villages (exceeding 80 households).[45]

The first two categories of settlements – the "very small" and "small" villages – often reflect one of two opposite demographic tendencies. In the context of rapid demographic growth, these are usually newly founded settlements. Alternatively, the presence of small settlements can be a sign of a continuous demographic decline, leading to settlements' gradual disappearance. In the present case, it is clear that small sizes mostly signify newly founded settlements. Numerous small villages that appeared

---

[45] By applying this settlement categorization by size, I am following an already relatively well-established tradition in Balkan, and especially Bulgarian, demographic history of the Ottoman period. See Georgieva, *Prostranstvo i prostranstva*, 59–91, Todorov, "Za demografskoto sastoianie," 218, and Radushev, *Pomatsite*, vol. 1, 156–157. The present discussion of the nature of the different categories of settlements by size follows the general lines of Georgieva's analysis, *Prostranstvo i prostranstva*, 71–72.

in the region in the first half of the sixteenth century may easily be explicitly identified as new, being named after founders who may be individually identifiable as registered taxpayers. The process of transformation of *mezra'a*s into fully fledged villages points in the same direction. Medium settlement size may be associated with relative demographic stabilization (which may have been recently achieved and also be a sign of potential for further growth), and the last two categories ("large" and "very large" villages) characterize very stable and prosperous settlements, usually founded way back in time.

Without going into too much detail, the following could be said about the nature and dynamics of demographic change in the light of village-size distribution. In the early phases of Muslim colonization in the region, very small and small settlements constituted the overwhelming majority of Muslim settlements: 28 of 33 (85%) in the 1480s, when, as already mentioned, Turcoman colonization had affected only the southernmost part of the region, along the slopes of the Balkan range, and 191 of 218 (88%) in 1516, when the rest of the area under discussion (with the exception of the flat strip of land along the Danube) had started being settled in earnest by Muslim colonists. The even higher percentage of small Muslim villages in the 1516 registration may be clearly related to the recent influx of new settlers. The tendency remains largely unchanged *c.* 1535 with 244 out of 308 (79%) rural Muslim settlements being "very small" or "small" (up to 20 households).

The mid-sixteenth and especially late sixteenth-century registrations show a steady decrease in the percentage of very small and small Muslim settlements: 56% (257 of 460) in mid-century and 46% (207 of 449) in 1579, despite the continuing influx of new settlers between 1516 and the mid-sixteenth century and the emerging process of of larger villages splitting from the mid-sixteenth century onwards. Conversely, the portion of mid-sized and large villages grew steadily during the second half of the century, and while in the 1480s and in 1516 there was not a single "very large" Muslim settlement, in the mid-sixteenth century and 1579 registrations their number was eight and ten, respectively. While still representing a tiny fraction of the total, such very large Muslim villages already had a visible presence in the area's demographic landscape. These processes attest to the gradual stabilization of the Muslim settlement network in the second half of the century following the explosive influx of settlers in the first half of the century that spurred a colonization process that had initially led to the formation of hundreds of very small settlements very often named after the founder(s) of the village (e.g. Yunus Abdal, Taşkun Abdal, Hacı Salih, Rahim Oğulları, Kulfallar, etc.), where the original founder or first-generation descendants thereof are to be found in the detailed registers of *c.* 1535 and/or *c.* 1550; some settlement names betray belonging to nomadic pastoral groups (*obas*) that were undergoing sedentarization (e.g. Tuñrul Obası, Uruz Obası).[46]

As for the wholly Christian villages and mixed settlements, which were located primarily along the Danube or close to the Balkan range (i.e. in the northern- and southernmost extremities of the area under discussion), the percentages of very small and small villages declined steadily as well, but were much lower from the very beginning: 53% for Christian and 33% for mixed settlements in the 1480s; 23% for Christian and 11% for mixed villages in 1516; 27% for Christian and 7% for mixed villages *c.* 1535; 12% and 4% in mid-century; and 8% and 3% in 1579, respectively. Indeed, as of *c.* 1550 and 1579, the majority of mixed villages were "very large." "Large" and "very large" settlements taken together constituted the majority among wholly Christian settlements. This could be explained with the existence of a stable network of Christian settlements that pre-dated the advent of the Ottomans. While this network did likely suffer some initial disruption in the early decades of Ottoman rule in the context of the Ottoman conquest and developments in the "turbulent" fifteenth century, it seems to have survived well from pre-Ottoman times and to have quickly reconsolidated beginning in the early sixteenth century. The extant archival data does not show much change regarding the Christian (and "mixed," but predominantly Christian) settlement network itself. Despite the marked population growth in the sixteenth century, the number of Christian villages did not increase dramatically. It was largely old, most likely pre-Ottoman, settlements that grew in population. This trend goes against a popular thesis developed by Khristo Gandev that posited that the early centuries of Ottoman rule brought about a massive displacement of Christian populations from the fertile plains to the mountainous regions while the "conquerors" themselves settled in the more fertile lowlands.[47] This reflects, apart from the obvious

---

[46] Yunus Abdal, mod. Yonkovo (Razgrad province), BOA TD 439, p. 264, with three sons of Yūnus 'Abdāl listed, including Velī Dede, registered first as head of convent (*tekye-nişīn*); Taşkun Abdal, mod. Buynovitsa (Shumen province), with Taşkun Abdāl himself registered first, the settlement is first registered as a settled *mezra'a*, *c.* 1535, BOA TD 439, p. 205, fully fledged village named Taşkun *c.* 1550, BOA TD 382, pp. 587–588, whereby the founder Taşkun, still alive and again registered first, already has three sons registered as adult male taxpayers; Hacı Salih, mod. Veselets (Târgovishte province), BOA TD 439, p. 306, with "Mūsā, son of Hācı Şāliḥ" listed – this village was founded earlier, as it is present in the 1516 registration, BOA TD 370, p. 554; Rahim Oğulları (i.e. "the sons/descendants of Rahim"), unidentified in modern times, BOA TD 382, pp. 240–241, with "Yūsuf, son of Raḥīm" registered first, and three sons of Yūsuf following; Kulfallar, mod. Razvigorovo (Shumen province), BOA TD 439, p. 227, with "Kulfal, son of İbrāhīm," albeit not registered first. For Tuñrul Obası, see BOA TD 439, p. 213; Uruz Obası appears by that name in the 1516 registration, *c.* 1535 and in subsequent registration it appears as Uruzlar, thus losing the designation *oba*, BOA TD 370, p. 551; BOA TD 439, p. 263.

[47] Khristo Gandev, *Bâlgarskata narodnost prez 15-ti vek*, 2nd edn. (Sofia: Nauka i Izkustvo, 1989), 20–116.

nationalist bias of the author, the perception of lowlands as indisputably more agriculturally productive compared to hilly and mountainous terrains. However, the lowlands' agricultural advantage emerged only in the eighteenth and nineteenth centuries with the advent of new advances in agricultural technology and big farm agriculture that dramatically increased the productivity of farming in the lowlands.[48]

4.2.3   Demographic Analysis by Overall Population Size and Status of Taxpayers

The last quantitative measure that will be used to shed light on the demographic and ethno-religious transformation of Deliorman, Gerlovo, and the adjacent areas in the sixteenth century is the growth of overall population numbers and the related status of taxpayers. Contemporary registers clearly distinguish between regular tax-paying re'aya and numerous "privileged re'aya" groups which performed special services to the state and/or held a special socio-political or religious status enjoying accordingly specific tax exemptions duly articulated in contemporary Ottoman law codes.

Two main trends may be highlighted in this context. First, overall population growth is most spectacular in the first half of the sixteenth century (the total number of rural households, Muslim and non-Muslim alike, rising from 2,722 in the 1480s to 4,241 in 1516; 8,489 c. 1535; 19,915 c. 1550; and 25,305 in 1579). This dramatic demographic growth resulted above all from the increase in Muslim households: 615 in the 1480s; 2,476 in 1516; 4,712 c. 1535; 11,532 c. 1550; and 13,629 in 1579, due largely to the influx of Muslim settlers in the region as well as to natural population growth. Yet, the rural Christian population – concentrated mostly in districts adjacent to Deliorman proper, along the Danube in the north and on the slopes of the Balkan range (including Gerlovo and its vicinity) – rose dramatically too, if not as spectacularly. The impressive growth of the rural Christian population may be attributed to the general political stabilization in the area following the "turbulent" fifteenth century, natural population growth, possible (usually difficult to document) migrations from the outside, and importantly, the institution of mountain-pass (derbend) settlements, where resident village mountain-pass guards (derbendcis) had the right to carry weapons and enjoyed a number of tax privileges in exchange for the duties they performed.

---

[48] Georgieva, Prostranstvo i prostranstva, 66–67.

Table 4.6 *Population distribution by households in Deliorman and Gerlovo's countryside in the late fifteenth and sixteenth centuries*

Year	Reg. Muslim	Muslim with special status	Total Muslim	Reg. Christian	Christian *derbendcis*	Other Christian with special status	Total Christian	Total
1480s	68	547	615	1,914	193	0	2,107	2,722
1516	1,268	1,208	2,476	1,068	647	50	1,765	4,241
C. 1535	2,004	2,708	4,712	2,967	665	145	3,777	8,489
C. 1550	8,677	2,855	11,532	6,047	2,236	100	8,383	19,915
1579	11,433	2,196	13,629	8,184	3,407	85	11,676	25,305

Second, a process of major importance affecting the Muslim (largely Turcoman) population and the overall demographic, socio-political, and socio-economic transformation of the area under discussion was the gradual reduction of the share of rural Muslim taxpayers with special status in favor of regular *re'aya*. While among those with special status (i.e. enjoying some tax exemptions), there were some sons of *sipahi*s, village imams, old men (*pir-i fani*), and madmen (*mecnun*), the overwhelming majority of the rural Muslim *re'aya* with "special status" were groups of nomadic and semi-nomadic origin such as the *yürük*s, *yağcı*s (buttermakers), *güreci*s (colt-breeders), and *doğancı*s (falconers), who enjoyed tax exemptions in return for special military and logistic services to the state, as well as dervishes and descendants of the Prophet (*seyyid*s, *şerif*s). While in the 1480s only 11% of the registered rural Muslim taxpayers had the status of regular *re'aya* (the rest having "special status"), the percentage rose to 53% in 1516, then dropped slightly to 43% *c.* 1535, before settling at very high values in the second half of the sixteenth century: 75% *c.* 1550, and 84% by 1579.[49] The temporary percentage increase of rural Muslim *re'aya* with "special status" *c.* 1535 (mostly in the southern part of the area studied) may be indicative of fresh migrations from Anatolia in the context of continuing political instability in relation to anti-Ottoman rebellions (such as those of Sheykh Celal in 1519 and Kalender Shah of 1527) and the Ottoman state's ongoing persecutions of perceived sympathizers of the Safavid cause. In the context of the northeastern Balkans, however, Turcoman newcomers could be accommodated and encouraged to stay (and settle) by initially being accorded a favorable taxation status reflecting their semi-nomadic way of life.

The overall spectacular increase of the share of regular, settled *re'aya* among rural Muslims shows the success of the Ottoman state's quest to firmly tie to the land as regular (and "obedient") rural population groups originally not quite amenable to the state's centralizing and sedentarizing drive. This development observed in the northeastern Ottoman Balkans calls to attention the importance of the first half of the sixteenth century in the history of Ottoman empire-building and the consolidation of the Ottoman bureaucratic regime.[50]

[49] The same process could be observed just to the east of the area discussed here. Tax registrations for the district (*nāḥiye*) of Silistre (a part of the province [*sancak*] of the same name) which included a small part of Deliorman and parts of Dobrudja, reveal that the percentage of *yürük*s and related or similar groups of semi-nomadic *re'āyā* with special status fell from 55% to 13% between 1518 to 1569; Nikolay Antov, "The Ottoman State and Semi-Nomadic Groups along the Ottoman Danubian *Serhad* (Frontier Zone) in the Late 15th and the First Half of the 16th Centuries: Challenges and Policies," *Hungarian Studies* 27/2 (2013), 229–231.

[50] See Şahin's insightful comments on this issue, *Empire and Power*, 6–10.

4.2.4   Major Agents of Turcoman Colonization in the Countryside: yürüks and Other Nomadic or Semi-Nomadic Groups, Dervishes, and Descendants of the Prophet

Numerically the most prominent agents of Turcoman colonization in Deliorman, Gerlovo, and the adjacent areas, Turcoman semi-nomads were in large part organized in groups that performed special military or logistic duties for the Ottoman state in exchange for tax exemptions (most typically from "extraordinary taxes").

The yürüks, whose main productive occupation was sheep breeding and played an important role in the colonization of the Balkans, were organized in an auxiliary military contingent in units (ocaks) of 30; each ocak had five armed retainers (eşküncüs) who would go on campaign, and 25 yamaks (helpers, reservists, also referred to as ellicis).[51] Similar groups with logistic functions were the doğancıs (falconers), and the gürecis (colt breeders), and the yağcıs (butter makers) who supplied specified quantities of butter for the needs of the army as well as for waqf establishments such as the pious endowment of the imaret (soup kitchen) of Sultan Murad in Edirne.[52]

The steadily decreasing percentages of registered yürük and similar groups in the sixteenth century reflect the overall tendency of the Ottoman state to limit the privileges of these groups as they were gradually turned into regular rea'ya.

This process of gradual sedentarization and stripping away of tax and other privileges of yürüks may be observed in the case of many originally temporary settlements (settled mezra'as) in which the Ottoman state was registering yürüks in an attempt to tie them to the land and convert them into regular tax-paying, agricultural populations. In the 1480s, 23 of a total of 33 Muslim settlements in the whole region were settled

---

[51] On yürüks, see Gökbilgin, Rumeli'de Yürükler. Ellicis would support the eşküncüs by paying them the equivalent of the extraordinary tax burden ('avārız-ı dīvāniye), which was 50 (elli) akçe, see Ahmet Refik, Anadolu'da Türk Aşiretleri, 966–1200 (Istanbul: Devlet Matbaası, 1930), vi–vii, as well as the law code for yürüks ("Ḳānūnnāme-i Yürükān"), tentatively dated 1530, Ö. L. Barkan, XV ve XVI-ıncı Asırlarda Osmanlı İmparatorluğunda Zirai Ekonominin Hukuki ve Mali Esasları. Birinci Cilt: Kanunlar (Istanbul: Burhaneddin Matbaası, 1945), 260–261.

[52] The term güreci has often been transliterated as küreci, from küre (smelting furnace), and thus associated with mining. In the present context a more appropriate reading would be güre, meaning (wild) colt, hence güreci denotes colt/horse breeder who raised colts (up to three years old) later directed to the sultan's stables for military use; see "Güreci," in M. Z. Pakalın, Osmanlı Tarih Deyimleri ve Terimleri Sözlüğü (Istanbul: Milli Eğitim Basımevi, 1983), vol. 1, 689; Strashimir Dimitrov, "Novi danni za demografskite otnosheniia v iuzhna Dobrudzha prez pârvata polovina na XVI v.," Dobrudzha 14–16 (1997–9): 289; Antov, "The Ottoman State and Semi-nomadic Groups," 230.

*mezra'a*s with mostly *yürük*s and related groups (tentatively) settled on them. By the mid-sixteenth century, this phenomenon was a chapter of the past – those temporary settlements had become fully fledged Muslim villages, the majority of their residents usually being regular tax-paying *rea'ya*, while occasionally featuring limited numbers of *yürük*s or similar groups still enjoying certain tax privileges. The *mezra'a*s found in the registrations of *c.* 1550 and 1579 were agricultural sites worked by peasants from nearby well-established villages (whether Christian, Muslim, or mixed). To give a couple of examples, in the registration of the 1480s, one sees a *mezra'a* by the name of Kayalu Dere (Rocky Valley) in the sub-province of Shumnu with 14 *yürük*s registered on it; in 1516 it was already registered as a village (*karye*) with 34 *yürük*s and *ellici*s (and no regular *rea'ya* tax-payers); *c.* 1550 it had 39 regular *rea'ya* households, 30 regular tax-paying bachelors and only 5 *yürük* or *yürük*-related adult male residents; and in 1579, 68 regular *re'aya* households, 30 bachelors, 2 *güreci*s and 2 insolvents (*muflise*s).[53] The *mezra'a* of Ak Dere Yakası to the south of Shumnu had no registered tax-paying residents in the 1480s, but was worked by *yürük*s "from the outside" (*haricden yürükler ekerler*); in 1516 it was registered as a wholly Muslim village with 8 regular *rea'ya* households, 5 regular tax-paying bachelors and 16 *yürük*s and *güreci*s; and *c.* 1550, it was a mid-sized Muslim village with three quarters (*mahalle*s), 41 regular households, 19 bachelors, one descendant of the Prophet (*ehl-i Resul*) and only one *güreci*.[54]

As for the the new Muslim settlers in the countryside who were not specifically designated as belonging to any special groups (and had never had such status, like the 11 percent regular *re'aya* in the mid-1480s), while it is difficult to judge their nature (especially based on the synoptic registers from the mid-1480s and 1516/1530), the above-presented analysis of the development of the settlement network suggests that they were also likely largely (semi-) nomadic groups that typically formed originally small villages of 1–10 households in newly utilized areas that possessed fair conditions for practicing agriculture (together with sheep breeding) under the sedentarizing pressure imposed by the state and its taxation regime. These settlements would grow into fully fledged larger villages in the following decades, a pattern described by Cengiz Orhonlu in his study of Ottoman policies of settling tribal groups (albeit for a later period).[55]

---

[53] TSMA D 167, f. 3b; BOA TD 370, p. 551; BOA TD 382, pp. 601–602; TKG KK TTd 151, f. 178b.

[54] TSMA D 167, f. 37b; BOA TD 370, p. 554; BOA TD 382, pp. 589–590.

[55] Orhonlu, *Osmanlı İmparatorluğunda Aşiretleri İskân Teşebbüsü*, 32–35.

"Colonizing Dervishes"   At this stage, it is important to revisit the issue of "colonizing dervishes." Several general observations can be made on the development of dervish lodges in Deliorman, Gerlovo, and the adjacent areas and the role of dervishes in the region's repopulation and colonization.

First, the settlement of individuals and groups clearly identifiable as colonizing dervishes, following Barkan's conceptualization, should have started in the first decades of the sixteenth century, very much befitting the general context of the influx of Turcoman settlers in the region. While the *c.* 1485 tax registration betrays no presence and that of 1516 only a minimal presence of Sufi mystics, the detailed registration of *c.* 1535 is the earliest one that points to some substantial presence of dervishes and their lodges (*tekyes, zaviyes*).

Second, in harmony with the overall trend of repopulation and colonization of the region, the emergence of dervish lodges was initially more visible in the southern part of the area under discussion – starting with Gerlovo in the sub-province of Shumnu and spreading to the north.

Third, relatively few convents were registered as independent revenue-generating units. The emergence of most dervish lodges is usually traceable through the registrations of "lodge masters" (*zaviye-nişin, tekye-nişin, post-nişin*) accompanied by their subordinates (usually designated as "servants of the *tekye,*" *hıdmetkar-ı tekye*) incorporated into regular villages or in rarer cases, around *mezra'a*s. However, even when incorporated into villages, dervishes are often explicitly referred to as having founded or contributed to the foundation of such villages.

Fourth, in contrast to the emphasis placed by Barkan, very few lodges were part of pious endowments. They usually enjoyed some tax privileges, most often exemptions from extraordinary taxes (*avarız-ı divaniye ve tekalif-i örfiye*), but sometimes also from the land tax (*resm-i çift*). Thus, in terms of taxation, dervishes were usually treated as other groups of *rea'ya* with special status/duties: colt breeders, butter makers, mountain-pass guards, rice cultivators (*çeltükçü*s), miners (*madenci*s), etc. In some cases, though, certain dervishes managed to achieve greater concessions from the state, amounting to the right to appropriate much of the tax revenue of certain villages (especially when they were the recognized founders) to be used for the economic revival of a certain area and to provide support and hospitality to travelers or "passers-by" (*ayende ve revende*),[56] and in others dervishes could attain a permission to legally transform agricultural property into *waqf*. An Ottoman dignitary might also found a pious endowment with the purpose of supporting a rural dervish lodge.

---

[56] A lodge would normally offer hospitality (lodging and food) to a stranger for up to three days.

Last but not least, while some of these settlements featured recent converts to Islam (identifiable through the patronymic "Abdullah"), on no occasion may a dervish lodge be found in a mixed settlement (i.e. populated by both Muslims and Christians).[57] All the settlements in question were wholly Muslim.

All in all, the tax registration of *c.* 1535 contains 26 settlements (6 in the northern sub-province of Chernovi and 20 in southern sub-province of Shumnu) which had registered dervishes (usually as "lodge masters" and "lodge servants," less often just as *dede*s, or simply "dervishes"). Of these settlements, two were registered explicitly as *zaviye*s, and two as *mezra'a*s (all in the Shumnu sub-province); the rest were small villages. All six such settlements in the northern sub-province of Chernovi were most likely recently founded (it was specified that this was their first registration)[58] and of the twenty such settlements in the southern sub-province of Shumnu, only four may be traced back to the 1516 registration.

The registration of *c.* 1550 features 25 such settlements with registered dervishes (11 in the sub-province of Shumnu, 9 in the newly carved-out sub-province of Hezargrad, and 5 in the sub-province of Chernovi) and the registers of 1579 only 10 (3 in the sub-province of Shumnu, 4 in that of Hezargrad, 3 in that of Chernovi). In most cases these settlements can be traced back to the tax registration of *c.* 1535, while there are some new foundations.

A more careful examination of the records in the registration of *c.* 1535 shows a variety of forms in which dervishes and their colonizing efforts were treated or accommodated by the state through its taxation policies. At the simplest level, a group of dervishes could obtain an imperial order to facilitate the functioning of a newly founded *zaviye*, which would guarantee that their activities would not be obstructed and that the taxes they paid on agricultural produce would be kept minimal. Such was the case of the *zaviye* founded by Hafızoğlu Mehmed Dede (also known as Armudlu Pınarı) in Gerlovo, near the village of Sarı Yusuflu on the northern slopes of the Balkan range in the southernmost part of the sub-province of Shumnu, where the aforementioned Hafızoğlu Mehmed Dede and two other dervishes (*dede*s), Yusuf Dede and Dur Bali Dede, possessed a deed (*hüccet*) from the judge (*kadı*) of Shumnu and an imperial order against the interference of others in their activities. Being exempt from the land tax (*çift-resmi*), they paid only a lump sum of

---

[57] See related discussion in Chapter 7.
[58] Usually expressed by the Persianate phrase *ḫāric ez defter*, roughly *extra regesta*, i.e. "not in the [old, previous] register."

28 *akçe*s as a tax on their grain yield and orchard produce.[59] *Circa* 1550, the lodge had four dervishes registered: a lodge master (*tekye-nişin*) and three servants of the lodge (*hıdmetkar-ı tekye*), all the stipulations from the previous registration including the low 28-*akçe* tax burden were confirmed.[60] In the last registration for the century (1579), the lodge's personnel structure had been kept, with one important difference – one of the three servants of the lodge had the patronymic "Abdullah," i.e. he was very likely a recent convert to Islam; the yearly tax to be paid as a lump sum had been raised to 50 *akçe*.[61]

While the dervish lodge founded by Hafızoğlu Mehmed Dede remained a small establishment throughout the sixteenth century, other settlements founded by dervishes grew substantially and their founders managed to negotiate substantial tax privileges with the Ottoman state. Such is the case of the village of Şüca Dede in the sub-province of Chernovi, named after its eponymous founder. Its earliest registration of *c.* 1535 shows Şüca Dede (son of Orhan Dede) himself, three of his brothers (Hızır Dede, Alagöz, and İsa Bali) and five other residents. While Şüca Dede was registered as lodge master (*zaviye-nişin*) and was exempt from the land tax (*çift-resmi*), the others were entered as tax-paying *rea'ya*: four household heads and four adult bachelors who paid the land tax at a reduced rate, a total of 76 *akçe* for all eight registered together with the tithe (*öşür*) on their grain produce – 5 bushels (*kiles*) of wheat, 2 bushels of barley, and 3 of fodder – for a total of 77 *akçe*.[62]

Some 15 years later, the village's situation had changed substantially. Its population had grown dramatically. Apart from the lodge personnel – Şüca Dede himself still being the lodge master, and four servants of the lodge, all of them Şüca's sons – there were 14 regular heads of household (three of whom most likely recent converts) and 8 adult bachelors, some of whom could be recognized as Şüca Dede's nephews, one *ellici* (*yürük* reservist) and his son – a total of 29 registered adult males. The *c.* 1550 registration also includes a note stating that

---

[59] "*Zāviye-i Ḥāfıẓoğlu Meḥmed Dede, nām-ı dīğer Armudlu Pınarı, tābi'-i Şumnu. Meẕkūr Armudlu Pınarı'nıñ ḥudūdu içün Mevlānā Şumnu Ḳaḍısı[ndan] Meḥmed Dede ellerinde ḥüccetleri olub, ve kimesne daḫl eylemeye [deyü] aḥkām-ı hümāyūnları vardır,*" BOA TD 439, p. 303. The additions in square brackets may be suggested upon comparing this note with the similar one in the next registration of *c.* 1550 in BOA TD 382, p. 404. Ḥāfıẓoğlu Meḥmed Dede's lodge figures prominently in the *velayetname* of Demir Baba, wherein part of Demir Baba's parents' wedding festivities take place there. See the relevant discussion in Chapter 6.
[60] BOA TD 382, p. 404.
[61] TKG KK TTd 151, f. 246 a.
[62] BOA TD 439, p. 77; the village is registered as *Ḳarye-i Şüca Dede, ḫāric ez defter-i 'atīḳ, tābi'-i m, ān tīmār-ı m.*

the aforementioned Şüca Dede was a lodge master and presided over two convents (or one convent with two branches) in the area wherefore he could keep the canonical and customary taxes accruing from the village (mainly on land and agricultural produce) – a total of 514 *akçe* – and spend this tax revenue to support travellers who would stop by the two convents. Upon Şüca Dede's death, this right to the village's tax revenues would pass to one of his sons, provided that he be "upright and pious" (*salih ve mütedeyyin*), if none such was available, representatives of the area *ulema* and notables would take control of the operation of the convent, which clearly served as a stopping station for travelling Muslims and, very probably, new settlers to the area.[63] In the next registration of 1579, the village had kept its population, and its tax revenue increased to 1,000 *akçe*.[64]

A very similar case, again in the sub-province of Chernovi, is that of the village of Ali Baba, son of Tay (Dayı) Hızır, whose first registration again appears *c.* 1535. The village developed around the *zaviye* of the aforementioned Ali Baba, who, according to the next registration, received the rights to the tax income of the village in the same fashion as Şüca Dede. Just as in the case of Şuca Dede's establishment, in the *c.* 1550 registration, it was stipulated that upon the extinction of Ali Baba's line, the village would come under the control of the respected *ulema* and notables of the area.[65] In reality, this represents a mechanism for the eventual assimilation of convents (and villages) founded by heterodox dervishes into the control of the Sunni Ottoman state, through the (Sunni) *ulema*. While in the case of Şüca Dede, the name of the mystic and the remaining register data suggest strongly that this was a convent of dervishes of the non-Sharia-minded, *abdal*, variety (as discussed in Chapter 2), we can be quite sure about Ali Baba's convent: it was part of the community of the Rum Abdals of Otman Baba's branch. Ali Baba (and his father Tay Hızır) feature prominently in the *vita* of Demir

---

[63] "*Karye-i Şücā 'Dede, tābi'-i Çernovi. Meẕkūr Şücā' Dede tekye-nişīn olub, ve iki yerde zāviyesi olmağın, mutaṣarrıf olduğu karyeniñ ḥāṣıl olan rüsūm-ı şer'iyesin ve 'örfiyesin żabṭ idüb, āyende ve revendeye ṣarf ide deyü, defter-i 'atīkde meşrūḥ ve muḳayyed olub, ḥāliyā daḥi vukū'u üzere 'arż olundukda, ber-karār-ı sābik mukarrer buyurulmağın, defter-i cedīde kayd olundu. Ve meẕkūr Şücā' Dede każa-i baḥt itdükden soñra, mezkūruñ evlādından ṣāliḥ ve mütedeyyin kimesne olursa, ḥākim-i vakt olan efendiler [aña] tevcīh ideler. Ve eğer olmaz ise, 'ulemā-i ṣāliḥinden ve eşrāfdan her kime ki maḥall ve münāsib görürlerse aña tevcīh ideler. Ve karye-i meẕbūreniñ rüsūm-ı şer'iyesin ve 'örfiyesin żabṭ idüb, meẕbūr zāviyeye gelen āyende ve revendeye ṣarf ideler, ve karye-i meẕbūrenin vaki' olan beş yüz on dört akçe maktū'un her senede sipāhī[ye] eda ideler. Pādişāh-ı 'ālem-penāh ḥażretleriniñ izdiyād-ı eyyām-ı sa'ādetlerine du'āda olalar,*" BOA TD 382, p. 145.

[64] TKG KK TTd 151, ff. 65a–65b.

[65] TD 382, p. 151. This stipulation is almost *verbatim* the same as in the case of Şücā' Dede's village.

Baba. Tay Hızır was a close associate of Akyazılı Baba, the second *kutb* of Otman Baba's Rum Abdals (and Demir's predecessor), and Demir Baba himself visits Ali Baba's convent according to his *velayetname*.[66] While Şüca Dede had progeny, the tax registrations suggest that Ali Baba had no sons. It should not be surprising then that the last sixteenth-century registration, that of 1579, omits the stipulation of Ali Baba's line's hereditary rights over the convent-village (which was present in the *c.* 1550 registration) and declares that the establishment would fall under the control of the area's (Sunni) *ulema* (and notables) immediately upon Ali Baba's death.[67] While the state was initially accommodating toward these (heterodox) colonizing dervishes, it monitored their convents' development and bade its time to direct these convents into the control of the *ulema*. In the case of both convents (as in that of many similar others), the dervishes were enjoined "to pray for the prolongation of the felicitous days of the *padişah*, Refuge of the World."

As in the case of Şüca Dede, the village of Ali Baba had some (likely) recent converts (bearing the patronymic "Abdullah"): two unmarried adult men *c.* 1535, and two householders *c.* 1550, one of them traceable to the preceding registration. The register of *c.* 1550 also shows two freed slaves, one of whom was among the four servants of the lodge. By 1579 the number of recent converts had increased to six – two heads of household and four bachelors – out of 15 heads of household and 19 bachelors in total.[68]

Şüca Dede and Ali Baba were two dervishes who founded new villages organized around their lodges and managed to negotiate with the state de facto, but not unconditional, control over their respective villages. In some cases, such founding figures would try to achieve this authority by turning the village they had founded into a *waqf* (pious endowment), thus hoping to preclude substantial future interference on the part of the government. Such was the case of Mustafa Halife who came to Deliorman to found a new village whose first registration, like the preceding two examples, is of *c.* 1535. In the case of Mustafa Halife, we also know that he was of *yürük* origin, and more specifically from the *yürük*s of Tanrı Dağı, i.e. most probably from Aegean Thrace and the eastern

---

[66] See the relevant discussion in Chapter 6.
[67] "*Mezkūr 'Alī Baba fevt olduktan şoņra ḥākim-i vakt olan efendiler 'ulemā-i ṣāliḥinden her kim ki maḥall ve münāsib görürlerse, aña tevcīḥ ideler ve karye-i mezbūreniñ rüsūm-ı şer'iyyesin ve örfiyyesin żabṭ idüb, mezkūr zāviyeye gelen āyende ve revendeye ṣarf ideler, ve karye-i mezbūreniñ vāki' olan beş yüz akçe maktū'un her senede sipāhiye eda ideler. Pādişāh-ı 'ālempenāh ḥażretleriniñ izdiyād-ı eyyām-ı sa'ādetlerine du'āda olalar ber mūceb-i defter-i 'atīk,*" TKG KK TTd 151, ff. 62b–63a.
[68] BOA TD 439, p. 100; BOA TD 382, p. 151; TKG KK TTd 151, ff. 62b–63a

Rhodopes.[69] The village as it appears in its first registration consists of the family of Sheykh Mustafa – himself designated as a lodge master (*tekye-nişin*), with his six sons and a grandson – together with three butter makers pertaining to the endowment of the soup kitchen of Sultan Murad in Edirne. From the attached note it is clear that Sheykh Mustafa first managed to attain private property rights over the land on which he founded his village and then converted it into a pious endowment, whose tax revenue was assigned to the service of travelers who passed by his lodge.[70] The fact that Sheykh Mustafa managed to obtain private property rights over the land he settled on with his progeny may be also related to the state's efforts at the gradual sedentarization of nomadic and semi-nomadic groups. In an interesting (but not necessarily surprising) twist, though, in the next two registrations (*c.* 1550 and 1579), with Sheykh Mustafa no more among the living (but with many of his sons clearly identifiable), there are no traces of a functioning dervish lodge and a related *waqf*; the village – already double the size of the initial registration and pertaining to the new sub-province of Hezargrad, appears to be treated as a regular *re'aya* settlement.[71]

That not all such colonization-related activities and arrangements were durable is confirmed by another example, additionally important as the colonizers appear related to Kızıl Deli and his convent in Thrace. The *timar* register of *c.* 1535 contains a *mezra'a* named Pinar-ı Mehmed Dede (The Spring of Mehmed Dede), pertaining to the sub-province of Shumnu (in Gerlovo or the vicinity) and assigned to "Mehmed Dede, son [read "descendant"] of Kızıl Delü." The temporary settlement has as its residents the aforementioned Mehmed Dede – registered as a lodge master hailing from Tanrı Dağı, and his three sons: Sultan Kulu Dede, Bayram Dede and Doyran (?). They moved from the area of Dimetoka where they had held two *mezra'a*s, possessing a sultanic diploma (*berat-ı padişahi*), but apparently left and settled in the said *mezra'a* (Pınar-ı Mehmed Dede). They were expected to pay the tithe on their agricultural produce.[72]

As by 1535 the convent community of Kızıl Deli in Thrace was integrated into the rising Bektashi order, this may be seen as an attempt

---

[69] On the *yürük*s of Tanrı Dağı, see Gökbilgin, *Rumeli'de Yürükler*, 64–74.

[70] "*Mezkūr Şeyḫ Muṣṭāfā, Ṭanrı Dağı yürüklerinden olub, yürük yazan emīn ve kātib ellerine tezkīre virüb, mezkūr şeyḫ emlākın ve esbābın ve bāğın ve bāğçesin külliyen āyende ve revendeye içün hisbeten lillahi zevāyā idüb, vakf itmiş ki kendü evlādıyla ve ḥīş ile zevāyā-nişīn olmuşlardır, 'arż olundu,*" BOA TD 439, p. 90.

[71] BOA TD 382, p. 366; TKG KK TTd 151, f. 153 a. This, of course, does not necessarily signify the lodge's disappearance, but if it continued functioning, it was no longer recognized as such for taxation purposes.

[72] "*Mezra'a-i Pınār-ı Meḥmed Dede, tābi'-i m, ḫāric ez defter, tīmār-ı m. Meḥmed Dede, veled-i Ḳızıl Delü – ān Ṭanrı Dağı āmed. Sulṭān Ḳulu Dede [veled-i] Meḥmed Dede, Bayram*"

of Bektashi colonization in the northeast Balkans. The position of this new settlement in the *c.* 1535 tax register suggests that it fell in an area (Gerlovo) already colonized by Rum Abdals of Otman Baba's branch by the late 1520s.[73] The fact that there are no traces of Mehmed Dede and his sons in subsequent tax registrations may be telling. Was it that Bektashis were not welcome in "Rum Abdal territory?"[74]

Regarding larger groups of dervishes associated with a single progenitor or dervish community leader and a related center of activity, one should mention the "progeny of Sheykh Timur Khan" (*nesl-i Şeyh Timur Han*). Documents related to the pious endowment of the sheykh's *zaviye* indicate that he received a *mezra'a* and established himself in Thrace (in Elmalı, near Dimetoka) as early as the reign of Murad I (1362–89); this property was later converted into a *waqf* and that status was maintained as such by his progeny throughout the sixteenth and seventeenth centuries.[75] The sixteenth-century detailed tax registers show that individuals registered as "the progeny of Sheykh Timur Khan" spread in considerable numbers in Deliorman, Gerlovo, and the adjacent areas: 87 of them are to be found in the register of *c.* 1535 (47 in the northern sub-province of Chernovi, and 40 in the southern one of Shumnu); 82 in that of *c.* 1550 (15 in the sub-province of Chernovi, 19, in that of Hezargrad, and 48 in that of Shumnu); but only 19 in the tax registrations of 1579.[76]

Dede veled-i Mehmed Dede, Doyran [?] veled-i Mehmed Dede. Mezkūrlar Mehmed Dede Dimetoḳa ḳażāsından Ḳızıl Delü evlādından olub, Büyük Viran ve Turfillü [?] nām mezra'a berāt-ı pādişāhī ile mutaṣarrıfdır. El-ana mezra'a-i mezkūrede mütemekkin olub, zirā'at itdükleriniñ 'öşürlerin virürler. Ḥāṣıl: 200 [akçe];" BOA TD 439, p. 270. Fifteenth- and sixteenth-century tax registrations for Ḳızıl Deli's convent/mausoleum complex in Thrace confirm this entry's references to settlements in Thrace; Mehmed Dede and his sons, being descendants of Ḳızıl Deli, must have come from that dervish community. See the discussion on Ḳızıl Deli's convent in Thrace in Chapter 2 as well as BOA TD 370, p. 33. The latter entry has also been published by Barkan, "Vakıflar ve Temlikler," 339.

[73] It is hard to locate exactly the Spring of Mehmed Dede, but looking at the villages that surround it in the register, one may tentatively place it somewhere between the modern villages of Malko Selo (Sliven province) and Dâlgach (Târgovishte province), i.e. Gerlovo and the vicinity. The area contains a number of settlements founded in the first two or three decades of the sixteenth century by the latest and, in the light of Demir Baba's *vita*, were part of or closely related to the Rūm Abdāls of Otman Baba's branch, e.g. the community of Yolkulu Dede, the convent of Hafızoğlu Mehmed Dede, and the village of Topuzlar (mod. Topuzevo, Sliven Province). Demir Baba's *vita* casts the Bektashis as enemies of the Rūm Abdāls and even recounts the story of the dervishes of the convent of Ḳızıl Deli plotting to kill Demir Baba. See Chapter 6.

[74] Compare to the *vita* of Demir Baba, which tells the story of Demir's rivalry with a local (Deliorman) Bektashi leader, Ḥüseyin Baba. In the end, Demir Baba closes Ḥüseyin's lodge and causes the Bektashi's death. See Chapter 6.

[75] Gökbilgin, *XV–XV. Asırlarda Edirne*, 174–175; see also Barkan, "Vakıflar ve Temlikler," 338–339.

[76] As in the case of the lodge of Sheykh Muṣṭāfā Ḥalīfe that lost its status, the greatly reduced number of Timur Ḥān's descendants as of 1579 should not necessarily be read

Until mid-century these individuals seem to have been exempt from the *çift-resmi*, but in 1579 they paid 12 *akçes* (i.e. half the usual rate). This is in harmony with the general tendency of the gradual reduction of privileges for various (Muslim) groups that held any "special status" from the mid-sixteenth century onwards. We possess a clue that representatives of this group were to be found in the neighboring province (*sancak*) of Silistre, as a 1569 law code for that province points to Sheykh Timur Khan's progeny enjoying certain tax privileges.[77]

There are also examples of lodges in the region founded by dervishes whose direct connection to Anatolia is explicitly stated. Such is the story of Hüseyin Dede, son of Genc Baba. The pious endowment register of 1579 contains a *waqf* record of the lodge (*zaviye*) of Genc Baba, whereby it is stated that Genc Baba's "holiness" (*velayet*) became manifest (*zahir*) in Anatolia, after which his son Hüseyin Dede came to the village of Mirahor (mod. Velino, Shumen province) in the sub-province of Shumnu, and established a lodge named after his father. Being exempt from all taxes save for the canonic tithe, Hüseyin Dede would serve travelers and passers-by. After his death, four of his sons took over the *zaviye* and continued to operate it under the same conditions.[78]

As it can be seen, dervishes coming from either Thrace or Anatolia (those coming from Thrace largely the descendants of earlier Anatolian migrants), participated in the colonization of Deliorman and Gerlovo, engaging mainly in agriculture and providing hospitality to travelers and possibly new settlers in the area.

Going back to Barkan's related arguments, one may say that, based on the evidence presented above, the state played a less pronounced role in dervish colonization than Barkan would like to assert. The colonizing dervishes pro-actively negotiated various forms and degrees of tax privileges. However, while the Ottoman state seemed to play a more accommodationist role, adapting to the activities of colonizers, it ultimately

---

to mean they "disappeared," but that they were no longer recognized as having a privileged, tax-exempt status.

[77] Barkan, *Kanunlar*, 278, 285.

[78] "*Zāviye-i Genc Baba der ḳarye-i Mīrāḫōr, tābi'-i Şumnu. Ḫāric ez defter. Vilāyet-i Anadolu'da velāyeti zāhir olmuş Genc Baba nām dervişiñ oġlu Hüseyin Dede gelüb, Şumnu'ya tābi' merḳūm Mīrāḫōr nām ḳaryede zāviye binā idüb, āyende ve revendeye ḫıdmet itdüğü muḳābelede cem'-i rüsūmdan mu'āf olub, ancaḳ 'öşrüñ ḳarye-i meẕbūre sipāhisine edā ederken vefāt itdükden ṣoñra, meẕkūr Naṣūḥ ve Mürüvvet ve Muṣṭāfā ve Ṣāḥib Kerem ve Abdāl Muṣṭāfā nām dervişler evlādın olmaḳla ḥāliyā zāviye-i meẕbūreyi vech-i meşrūh üzere taṣarruf idüb, āyende ve revendeye ḫıdmet itdükleri muḳābelede rüsūmlarından mu'āf olub, 'öşürleriñ ḳarye-i meẕbūre sipāhisine edā idüb du'ā-i devām-ı devlet-i pādişāhī'ye iştigāllık olalar deyü defter-i cedīde ḳayd olundu,*" TKG KK TTd 411, f. 122 a. Barkan cites an almost identical record which he claims to have found in BOA TD 382, however, I have not been able to locate it in that register; Barkan, "Vakıflar ve Temlikler," 342.

succeeded in incorporating and integrating them into the existing (and evolving) Ottoman land regime, eventually tying them to the land, whereby many dervish convents engaged in agriculture would serve as anchors for village formation, thus contributing to the gradual sedentarization and agrarianization of semi-nomadic Turcomans as well. As in the earliest stages of the Ottomans' expansion in the Balkans and Anatolia, it was this ability to adapt and accommodate, but also to simultaneously set and develop the essential macropolitical mechanisms of control that very much lay at the root of Ottoman success.

Descendants of the Prophet   One last group of migrants to Deliorman and Gerlovo whose presence merits attention is descendants of the Prophet (*seyyids* and *şerifs*, or collectively, *sadat*) who enjoyed a special social and tax status. One sees them in large numbers in Deliorman and Gerlovo's countryside, as reflected in the *c.* 1535 tax registration which contains 213 such registered descendants of the Prophet (80 in the sub-province of Chernovi and 133 in that of Shumnu). Their number is lower *c.* 1550, 169 (30 in the sub-province of Chernovi, 74 in that of Hezargrad, and 65 in that of Shumnu). While they were spread among dozens of villages across the region, there are settlements in which their concentration was remarkable, such as the case of the village of Topuzlar (mod. Topuzevo, Sliven province) in Gerlovo. *Circa* 1535, it held 20 married descendants of the Prophet, together with 28 bachelors of the same distinction – the vast majority of the village population, as there were only three other heads of household (including one belonging to the progeny of Sheykh Timur Khan)[79]. Similarly, in the village of Mestan Demürciler in the sub-province of Chernovi (and later part of the sub-province of Hezargrad) half of the villagers (seven *şerifs* with their adult unmarried sons) belonged to the same group.[80] In both cases, however, the settlements existed as early as 1516, but had no registered descendants of the Prophet; therefore, the latter may not be (necessarily) credited with the foundation of these villages.[81] While the presence of *seyyids* and *şerifs* was typical of Ottoman urban milieux, their role in rural settlements has been less well researched. Their visible presence in the region may be seen in the specific context of rural Deliorman and Gerlovo's transformation in the sixteenth century whereby descendants of the Prophet, being also

[79] BOA TD 439, pp. 284–285. The founder of the village, a certain Topuz, may have been from a lineage related to that of Demir Baba in the light of the saint's *vita*. See the relevant discussion in Chapter 6.

[80] BOA TD 439, p. 85.

[81] BOA TD 370, pp. 551, 559. Or alternatively, their special status may have been entered in the registers later. BOA TD 370, which is largely based on data from 1516, contains only 3 *seyyids* in the sub-provinces of Chernovi and Shumnu.

descendants of Imam Ali and the Holy Family, could play much more important leadership roles in a heterodox milieu with visible pro-Alid tendencies.[82] Otman Baba and Demir Baba were *seyyid*s too in the light of the latter's *vita*.

4.2.5   Waqf *(Pious Endowment) Villages*

The rise of pious endowments in the sixteenth century was another factor that contributed significantly to the growth and consolidation of the rural settlement network in Deliorman, Gerlovo, and the adjacent regions (as it did elsewhere in the Empire). The discussion of Barkan's work on colonization in the Ottoman Balkans already touched upon the role of pious endowments in relation to the Islamization of territory and the settlement of new Turcoman colonists. Apart from colonizing dervishes who could seek to incorporate their convents within a pious endowment, the sixteenth century saw the spectacular rise of pious endowments founded by Ottoman grandees and notables at the central and provincial level. According to the tenets of Islamic law and within the context of Islamic tradition in general, *waqf*s were created to serve a "pious" end, usually the erection and upkeep of a mosque and/or educational and charitable institutions, such as *medrese*s and soup kitchens (*imaret*s), dervish convents, and/or the maintenance or repair of infrastructure (e.g. roads and bridges), with the overall objective of especially serving the poorer members of the *umma*.

While establishing a *waqf* was by and in itself a pious deed, scholars have discussed at length worldly motives which came into play, the two most conspicuous being to bolster one's prestige and legitimacy as well as to secure wealth for the founder's posterity (in the case of the so-called *evladlık*, or hereditary endowments, in which case the endowment charter stipulated that the chief *waqf* administrators (*mütevelli*s) should belong to the endower's line of descendants).[83]

Most of the arable land in the empire was, in principle, property of the Ottoman state and was registered formally as *miri* land. As pious endowments could not use *miri* land, those who sought to found *waqf*s that included land[84] were prompted to seek uncultivated wasteland not registered as *miri*, attain property rights over it by converting it into *mülk*

---

[82] On *seyyid*s and *şerif*s in the Ottoman Empire, see Rüya Kılıç, *Osmanlıda Seyyidler ve Şerifler* (Istanbul: Kitap Yayınevi, 2005).

[83] Vera Moutafchieva, *Agrarian Relations in the Ottoman Empire in the 15th and 16th Centuries* (Boulder, CO: East European Monographs, 1988), 96–98.

[84] *Waqf*s could utilize both urban (e.g. artisan shops) and rural property (land) as revenue-generating resources.

(i.e. private freehold), usually in exchange for the promise to "revive" the land and put it to good use, and then convert it into a *waqf*.[85] Thus, the revenue-generating portions of pious endowments often included *mezra'a*s that could later develop into fully fledged villages and/or villages that were created anew by bringing unregistered *rea'ya* to work the land. Modern scholarship has pointed to numerous examples that show that Ottoman *waqf* founders (as well freehold land owners) in the Empire at large, but especially in its Balkan domains, would bring slaves (who could later be manumitted), freed slaves, (*'atik*, or *mu'tak*), or people without permanent residence (*haymanes*) to populate their holdings, work the land, and generate tax revenue.[86] *Waqf* villages, whether newly founded or pre-existing, would often undergo dramatic expansion upon their incorporation into a pious endowment, largely due to the favorable tax status associated with *waqf* estates.

Late fifteenth-century Deliorman and Gerlovo featured no *waqf* settlements, but only two *waqf mezra'a*s with no registered taxpayers in the *vilayet* (sub-province) of Shumnu.[87] As of 1516, these two *mezra'a*s remained the only registered revenue-generating *waqf* units; the only development being that one of them (the *mezra'a* of İzlatar) already had some 16 adult males registered on it (eight regular *rea'ya* household heads, six bachelors, and two *ellici*s).[88]

---

[85] As discussed by Barkan, "Vakıflar ve Temlikler," 354–362, and Kiel, *Art and Society*, 101–105.

[86] Ö. L. Barkan, "XV. ve XVI. Asırlarda Osmanlı İmparatorluğunda Toprak İşçiliğinin Organizasyonu Şekilleri," *İÜİFM* 1, no. 1 (1939), 29–74; no. 2 (1939), 198–245; and no. 4 (1940), 397–477. Barkan's article deals primarily with slave labor (*kullar* and *ortakçı kullar*). The beginning of its third part (1, No. 4 [1940], 397–416) is devoted to the Balkans and provides numerous examples of the utilization of slave labor in freehold lands (*mülk*) and newly-founded *waqf*s, see 1, No. 4 (1940), 404–412 for examples of slaves and freed slaves settled in the lands of the *waqf*s of Evrenos Bey and Timurtaş Bey (Thrace) as well as in the freehold property of Miḫaloğlu Ġāzī 'Alī Bey around Plevne (Pleven) in modern northern Bulgaria in the fifteenth century. Kiel has also given a concrete example in this regard in relation to the development of Miḫaloğlu Ġāzī 'Alī Bey's domains, already transformed into a *waqf* by the mid-sixteenth century, whereby it was explicitly mentioned in the tax register that the land was populated by unregistered *re'āyā* (*haymanes*), Kiel, "Hrâzgrad-Hezargrad-Razgrad," 534. The example given by Kiel is to be found in BOA TD 382, p. 675. Gökbilgin gives numerous examples of *haymanes* being settled in *mülk* and *waqf* lands in the Balkans in the fifteenth and sixteenth centuries, to the degree that this could well be considered a common practice, especially in the case of repopulating hitherto abandoned agricultural lands. For the sixteenth century, see Gökbilgin, *XV. ve XVI asırlarda Edirne*, 489 (villages belonging to the *waqf*s of Sultan Selīm I), 498–499 (villages belonging to the *waqf*s of Devlet-Şāhī Sulṭān, sister of Sultan Süleyman I and wife of Rüstem Pasha, around Dimetoka in Thrace), 508–509 (villages belonging to the *waqf*s of Sokollu Mehmed Pasha in Thrace). For a general discussion on these issues, see also Moutafchieva, *Agrarian Relations*, 111–121.

[87] Neither of the *mezra'a*s of Dalḳaç and İzlatar had any registered settlers; the latter, it is specified, was worked by *yürük*s "from the outside"; TSMA D 167, f. 101b.

[88] BOA TD 370, p. 555. Regarding the other *mezra'a*, Dalḳaç, one can point to a village with the same name, Dalḳaç-ı Müslim (i.e. Muslim Dalḳaç), with some eight households

It was in the second quarter of the sixteenth century, in tune with other related processes of internal colonization and the growth and consolidation of the settlement network, that the region witnessed a rapid growth of the number and size of *waqf* settlements. A fragment of a pious-endowments register (*evkaf defteri*) for the northern Balkans dated *c.* 1535 sheds light upon three sizable *waqf*s, two founded for the benefit of the *umma* in Deliorman (i.e. not only the revenue-generating villages, but also the beneficiaries of the endowment lay in the area) and the third containing several revenue-generating villages in the region, with its revenue directed elsewhere.[89]

The most important of these is that of Grand Vizier (Pargalı, Maktul) Ibrahim Pasha, who served in that capacity from 1523 to 1536 when he was executed upon the orders of Süleyman I. While this pious endowment, founded in 1533, will be also discussed in the following chapter, in relation to the (re-) founding of the town of Hezargrad, it is worth a brief discussion here, as it lay in the heart of Deliorman and played an important role in the repopulation of the region. In the aforementioned *c.* 1535 register fragment, Ibrahim Pasha's *waqf* entry contains five villages[90] in the sub-province of Chernovi, which the grand vizier exchanged for some freehold (*mülk*) villages in his possession in the vicinity of Istanbul: the fully Muslim Yenice, also known as New Hezargrad (Hezargrad-ı Cedid, later simply Hezargrad), which would quickly grow to become a major urban center and the seat of a provincial district with a total of 106 households; the fully Christian Kayacık (later Kayacık Pınarı) with 224 households; the mixed, but predominantly Christian Dobrova (with 14 Muslim households, 4 of which were headed by converts to Islam, and more than 100 Christian households);[91] the fully

---

and five unmarried adult men registered. It is hard to establish whether these two were related; BOA TD 370, p. 554.

[89] NBKM OAK 217/8; preserved in the National Library in Sofia this fragment of *mülk* (freehold) and *waqf* holdings in northeastern Bulgaria may be safely dated *c.* 1535, certainly post-dating İbrāhīm Pasha's *vakfiye* of 1533 and pre-dating the grand vizier's death in 1536, as he is not mentioned as "deceased" (*merhūm*) which is explicitly mentioned about the late founders of other *waqf*s in the region. Thus it was compiled at roughly the same time as the *tīmār* register for the area BOA TD 439, preserved in Istanbul. NBKM OAK 217/8 is published in facsimile and Bulgarian translation in *TIBI*, vol. 3 (2 pts.) (Sofia: BAN, 1972), 427–473 (Bulgarian translation in Part One); 419–462 (facsimile in Part Two).

[90] The *c.* 1535 registration refers to four villages pertaining to Ibrahim Pasha's *waqf*, as Yenice and Kayacık were listed together. However, this must be an aberration as the pious-endowment charter (discussed in the following chapter) and later sixteenth-century tax registrations list these two villages separately, NBKM OAK 217/8, f. 11a, *TIBI*, vol. 3, 441.

[91] As this folio of the fragment has not been fully preserved, the exact number of Christians remains unknown.

Muslim Hasanlar (with 27 households); and the Christian Duymuşlar (later known as Arnavudlar, "Albanians") with 42 households.[92] Of these, Dobrova, Hasanlar and Duymuşlar may have existed before, as settlements with such names are mentioned in the 1516 registration.[93] If these were the same villages, they did undergo a dramatic transformation as a result of purposeful resettlement with the aim of increasing the revenue-generating capacity of the grand vizier's newly established pious endowment. Dobrova of 1516 was a small Muslim village, which added more than 100 Christian households; Hasanlar remained fully Muslim but more than doubled in size; and Duymuşlar was transformed from a very small Muslim village (of four households) in 1516 to a mid-sized Christian one, which may have been repopulated with Albanians, as its later name suggests, likely in relation to Ibrahim Pasha's Albanian origins.[94] That purposeful resettlement (of both Muslims and Christians) played an important, if not dominant, role in the initial development of Ibrahim Pasha's *waqf* villages in Deliorman is supported by a note at the end of the *c.* 1535 registration stipulating that of the 94,224 *akçe* total revenue of the *waqf*, 26,085 *akçe* paid by those without permanent residence (that is, up to their settlement in the area) were reserved for the imperial treasury, while the remainder was to be used for the maintenance of the mosque and the school (*medrese*) in Hezargrad.[95]

The second pious endowment was founded by Bali Bey, son of Yahya Pasha[96], the military commander (*subaşı*) of the fortified town of Tutrakan on the Danube, to support a dervish convent (*tekye*) built by him near the village of Sırneva in the sub-province of Chernovi. While detailed data on the *tekye* itself are not available, a note on Sırneva, registered with 90 Christian and one Muslim (convert) households, clearly states that, because the place

---

[92] *TIBI*, vol. 3, 441–449.

[93] BOA TD 370, p. 558. Hasanlar and Dobrova probably existed as early as in 1479 as a *mezra'a* named "Dobro Voda, with another name Hasanlar" found in the synoptic tax register fragment of that year (NBKM OAK 45/29); *TIBI*, vol 2, 234–235. In this registration, this *mezra'a* had 18 registered *yürük* households. As "Dobro Voda" could possibly be the later "Dobrova" (moreover, what later became the villages of Hasanlar and Dobrova are quite close to each other), it may be surmised that the two villages had their origins in this *mezra'a* and later separated.

[94] See also Kiel's related discussion, "Hrâzgrad-Hezargrad-Razgrad," 531–539.

[95] NBKM OAK 217/8, f. 17a, *TIBI*, vol. 3, 449. Gökbilgin has provided a similar example in villages belonging to the *waqf*s of Devlet-Şâhî Sultān in Thrace, in which a special tax levied on the *haymane*s (*resm-i haymane*) was reserved for the imperial treasury, *XV. ve XVI asırlarda Edirne*, 499.

[96] While it is not entirely clear, this may be a scion of the famous frontier lord family of Malkoçoğulları. It is known that Malkoçoğlu Dâmâd Yahyâ Pasha (d. 1507), who served as governor-general of Rumelia and Bosnia in the late fifteenth and early sixteenth centuries and established *waqf*s at numerous locations in the Balkans, including Skopje (where a neighborhood is now named after him), had a son, later famous as Sultānzāde

was dangerous and frequented by brigands, Bali Bey settled the village with unregistered infidel re'aya (haymane), whereby it thus became "safe for the passage of Muslims."[97] The other villages in the same waqf are in the sub-province of Shumnu: the former mezra'a of İzlatar, already a village with a total of 10 Muslim households, the newly registered village of Zaviye-i Seyyid Osman (organized around a dervish lodge founded by a descendant of the Prophet together with his brother, son, and nephews) and containing a total of around 20 Muslim and 10–15 non-Muslim households,[98] and the newly registered derbend (mountain pass) village of Volna[99] with 4 Muslim and at least 10 Christian households[100] all contain similar notes about pur-poseful resettlement as does a note at the end of the waqf entry concerning all of its villages.[101] As was usual with such newly founded waqf settlements, the assigned tax burden was much lower than that of the regular re'aya in well-established villages, and the new settlers were exempt from a number of taxes (especially from "extraordinary taxes").

The last pious endowment entered in the c. 1535 fragment is that of the soup kitchen (imaret) of the late Abdüsselam Bey (d. c. 1530), a for-mer chief treasurer (başdefterdar), in (Küçük) Çekmece near Istanbul.[102] This waqf included the large village of Novasel (of the sub-province of Shumnu), which was overwhelmingly Christian, with only two registered adult married Muslims, both of them converts to Islam.[103]

The following detailed (and complete) waqf registrations in the region (of c. 1550 and 1579)[104] show some changes with respect to waqfs and the related settlements, but largely confirm the situation as reflected in the c. 1535 fragment. The most important change as of c. 1550 is the appearance

Koca Bali Pasha who served as governor-general of Budin (Buda) in the 1540s. This possible connection is supported by the fact that some of the shops at the market of the town of Shumnu (Shumen) in the sixteenth century were part of the revenue-generating property of Yahyā Pasha's waqf in Skopje (as discussed in Chapter 5). In Demir Baba's velāyetnāme, a certain "Kara Malkoç" is among the distinguished guests at the wedding of the saint's parents. Some oral traditions present members of the Malkoçoğulları as sponsors of the construction of Demir Baba's mausoleum/convent complex, DBV, "Introduction," 11. It is thus possible that it was Koca Bali Pasha who built this tekye early in his career (possibly in the 1520s), before acquiring his later fame. See also Fahamettin Başar, "Malkoçoğulları," TDVİA, vol. 27, 537–538.

[97] TIBI, vol. 3, 462.
[98] The marital status of the non-Muslim taxpayers in this village is not clearly specified.
[99] The reading of this place name is uncertain.
[100] The folio containing the registration of this village is not fully preserved.
[101] TIBI, vol. 3, 463–466.
[102] On 'Abdüsselām Bey, see Mehmed Süreyya, Sicill-i Osmani, vol. 1, ed. Nuri Akbayar and Seyyid Ali Kahraman (Istanbul: Tarih Vakfi, 1996), 139. The registration mentions "Çekmece" only; most probably it refers to Küçük Çekmece, where 'Abdüsselām Bey died.
[103] TIBI, vol. 3, 457–459.
[104] Contained in BOA TD 382 and TKG KK TTd 411.

of ten villages belonging to the endowment of the congregational mosque of Üsküdar, built by Süleyman I's daughter Mihrimah Sultan in the 1540s; seven of these were *derbend* villages.[105] The newly carved-out sub-province of Hezargrad contained the villages of Ibrahim Pasha's endowment centered in Hezargrad as well as Sırneva belonging to the endowment of the *tekye* of Bali Bey, and included one more village (Çereşova Pınarı) which was part of grand vizier Rüstem Pasha's endowment.[106] The sub-province of Shumnu featured two *waqf* villages and one *mezra'a*, all part of the late Sultan Bayezid II's endowments, the abovementioned İzlatar, which had changed hands; the village of Kuru Dere; and the cited *mezra'a* of Dalkaç.[107] The *waqf* register of 1579 shows roughly the same picture with several villages having been transferred to different pious endowments, a phenomenon largely characteristic of the Ottoman *waqf*-related land regime. One important new development was the addition of one more dervish lodge – that of the already mentioned Genç Baba.

4.2.6   Derbend Villages

A very sizable part of the rural Christian population in the area under discussion was concentrated in the so-called *derbend* (mountain pass) villages, in which many or all male household heads had the official status of *derbendci* (lit. mountain-pass guards) and enjoyed tax privileges (usually exemption from extraordinary taxes and sometimes lower land/head tax [*ispençe*]).[108] *Derbendci*s also had the right to carry weapons, a clear mark of higher social status among the tax-paying population (the *re'aya*) – especially among non-Muslims.

Most likely of Turco-Mongol origin and transmitted to the Ottomans from the Ilkhanid-dominated late Anatolian Seljuk state and some Anatolian Turcoman principalities in the late thirteenth and fourteenth centuries, the *derbend* institution aimed at securing the road network at sensitive points; receiving *derbend* status upon being judged by the authorities to be located at such sensitive or "dangerous" places – mostly mountain passes, but also river fords and bridges – these villages would serve to strengthen social order and stimulate trade.[109]

---

[105] BOA TD 382, pp. 813–836.
[106] Ibid., pp. 841–867; the villages belonging to the endowment of Ibrahim Pasha already numbered eight as some of the original villages had split.
[107] Ibid., pp. 868–869.
[108] Either all male household heads in a village, or a specified number were accorded *derbendci* status – usually 30, 60, or 90, whereby the rest would have the status of regular *re'āyā*. On *ispençe*, see related comments in Chapter 7, section 7.1.3.
[109] Cengiz Orhonlu, *Osmanlı İmparatorluğunda Derbend Teşkilâtı* (Istanbul: Istanbul Üniversitesi Edebiyat Fakültesi Yayınları, 1967), 11–21.

Derbend villages are found in the earliest extant Ottoman tax register (from the early 1430s), and *derbend* service was carried out predominantly by Muslims in Anatolia and Christians in the Balkans, although conversion to Islam would not change one's *derbendci* status.[110] In the fifteenth and especially during the sixteenth and seventeenth centuries, in addition to many already existing villages that were granted *derbend* status, numerous *derbend* villages were founded from scratch; the Ottoman government would urge local representatives of state authority (usually judges) to gather people not entered in the tax registers theretofore (*haymane, haymanegan*) and settle them at places along trade routes that were considered both insufficiently secure and of strategic significance, granting the new settlers tax exemptions as an incentive to settle.[111] Derbend villages were founded in a similar way and for similar purposes as a part of pious endowments as well.[112] The sixteenth century saw a rise in the number of *derbend* villages in general, and this can be observed in the tax registers discussed here as well.

Indeed, the rise of the *derbend* villages could be said to have significantly contributed to the political stabilization of Deliorman and Gerlovo as well as to the security of trade routes. All *derbend* villages found in the five tax registrations utilized for this analysis (from the mid 1480s, 1516, *c.* 1535, *c.* 1550, and 1579) are Christian or mixed, but overwhelmingly Christian (with few Muslims, mostly local converts). Some of them would have over 300 households, thus exceeding the size of some of Deliorman's towns. Yet, they would never attain urban status before the nineteenth century as they failed to develop solid Muslim communities with the related Islamic cult and educational institutions.[113] The growth of these villages cannot, in most cases, be explained by sheer natural demographic growth, but one should account for the influx of new Christian settlers from outside of the region (or occasionally, from neighboring Christian villages). The rise of *derbend* villages could thus be seen as a major factor for the expansion and consolidation of the Christian settlement network in the area.

If Deliorman, Gerlovo, and the adjacent areas featured only two *derbend* villages in the 1480s, with two more added by 1516 (all of them in Shumnu sub-province, along the slopes of the Balkan range, and of between 100 and 150 households[114]), the second quarter of

---

[110] Kiel, *Art and Society*, 93; Aleksandar Stojanovski, *Dervendžijstvoto vo Makedonija* (Skopje: Institut za Nacionalna Istorija, 1974), 34–35.

[111] Kiel, *Art and Society*, 94–101.

[112] Orhonlu, *Derbend Teşkilâtı*, 26–27.

[113] On the conditions related to a village's attainment of town status in the early modern Ottoman context (especially the presence of a Friday mosque), see the related discussion in Chapter 5.

[114] Çalık Kavak (mod. Rish, Shumen province) and Kazan Pınarı (mod. Kotel, Sliven province) c. 1485, TSMA D 167, ff. 8a, 63a.; İsmedova (mod. Smyadovo, Shumen province)

the sixteenth century saw the explosive proliferation of *derbend* villages in the region. *Circa* 1535, Deliorman, Gerlovo, and the adjacent areas had 18 *derbend* villages[115]; of these, 6 were "large" villages (between 40 and 80 households) and 7 "very large" (exceeding 80 households). *Circa* 1550, the region as a whole had 35 *derbend* villages[116] – all but four being "very large," with the largest of them being İsmedova on the northern foothills of the Balkan range, with 315 households.[117] In 1579, the area studied had 38 *derbend* villages.[118]

While the few *derbend* villages *c.* 1485 and 1516 were along the northern slopes of the Balkan range, the *c.* 1535 registration already contains *derbend* villages in Deliorman proper as well as along the Danube – a tendency that would be strengthened throughout the rest of the century. Rahova (mod. Ryahovo, Ruse province) was granted *derbend* status following an inspection by the local judge who had established that this would improve the security of shipping along the Danube between the ports of Yer Gögi (Rusçuk, mod. Ruse) and Tutrakan, in view of the frequent attacks of pirates (*haramiler*) along the river.[119] Having its new privileged status, Rahova had more than doubled its population, compared to 1516.[120] Similarly, the Christian villages of Rahoviçe and İsvalenik (mod. Svalenik, Ruse province) in Deliorman were accorded *derbend* status for being situated in dangerous places.[121]

Most of these villages had already been in existence upon receiving their new and beneficial status, some of them were newly founded by being settled with unregistered taxpayers. All in all, the 35 *derbend* villages in the *c.* 1550 registration had 2,236 *derbendci*s and a total of 4,573 Christian householders (including those without *derbendci* status), and only 80 Muslim heads of household (including those households not headed by mountain-pass guards), usually readily identifiable as

and Ayvacık (mod. Vârbitsa, Shumen province) were added in 1516; BOA TD 370, pp. 551, 549. Of these only Kazan Pınarı had (three) Muslim households in 1516.

[115] Seven in the northern sub-province of Chernovi, and 11 in the southern one of Shumnu.

[116] Fifteen in the sub-province of Chernovi, 10 in that of Hezargrad, and 10 in that of Shumnu.

[117] BOA TD 382, p. 504. İsmedova had been founded some time between the 1480s and 1516 registrations by "infidels" (*kāfirler*) from the nearby Çalık Kavak – itself a *derbend* village since the late fifteenth century – and its privileged status had been confirmed by an imperial order, see BOA TD 370, p. 551.

[118] Fifteen in the sub-province of Chernovi, 10 in that of Hezargrad, 11 in that if Shumnu, and one in the newly carved-out *nāḥiye* of Eski Cuma.

[119] BOA TD 370, p. 557; BOA TD 439, pp. 44–46, 64–65.

[120] Sixty-one and 144 households in 1516 and *c.* 1535, respectively; BOA TD 370, p. 557; BOA TD 439, pp. 44–46.

[121] BOA TD 439, pp. 102–103, 64–65.

converts. Thus, around 55 percent of the total Christian population in the area studied was concentrated in *derbend* villages in the mid-sixteenth century. This share remained stable in the second half of the century. As of 1579, the 38 *derbend* villages in area had 3,407 *derbendci*s and a total population of 5,657 Christian and 167 Muslim households; the Christian households in *derbend* villages thus accounting for almost half (48 percent) of all rural Christian households in the whole area under discussion.

The registration of *c.* 1550 also shows for the first time the appearance of large *derbend* villages as a part of a pious endowment: seven such villages in the northern sub-province of Chernovi, close to or on the southern bank of the Danube, were registered as part of the endowment of the congregational mosque in Üsküdar built by Süleyman I's daughter Mihrimah Sultan between 1544 and 1548;[122] two of these had populations well above 200 households.[123]

While the establishment and growth of *derbend* villages are usually related to the Ottoman state's efforts to improve overall security in the provinces, especially in the direction of stimulating trade and communications, the rise of the *derbend* villages in the area of this study during the sixteenth century and the institutional support that the Ottoman state lent those villages could be meaningfully viewed as a counter-measure against the influx of nomadic and semi-nomadic Turcoman settlers and the latter's being a potential source of instability and disorder. Importantly, all the *derbend* villages in Deliorman, Gerlovo, and the adjacent areas were either exclusively or overwhelmingly Christian. Not a single one of the hundreds of newly founded Turcoman villages was accorded *derbend* status in the sixteenth century. Those entrusted with the guarding of roads, mountain passes, and river fords were of local Christian origin and from established traditions of sedentary life. While the share of rural Muslims in Deliorman and Gerlovo who enjoyed some special taxation status (usually related to their semi-nomadic profile) plummeted between the 1480s and 1579, such a tendency is not to be observed among rural Christians in the area, whereby the overwhelming majority of rural Christians enjoying

---

[122] On this mosque complex in Üsküdar and Mihrimah Sultan's pious endowments, see Gülru Necipoğlu, *The Age of Sinan: Architectural Culture in the Ottoman Empire* (Princeton, NJ, and Oxford: Princeton University Press, 2005), 296–305.

[123] BOA TD 382, pp. 813–836. This is in tune with the arguments of Orhonlu, who found large *derbend* villages included in pious endowments as one of the several characteristic forms of emergence and of institutional incorporation of *derbend* villages; Orhonlu, *Derbend Teşkilâtı*, 26–27.

special taxation status and burdened with special duties were indeed *derbendci*s.[124]

Thus, many *derbend* villages developed as prosperous and privileged Christian settlements, taking advantage of both tax exemptions and the opportunity to engage in commerce. As Machiel Kiel has aptly remarked, many of the little towns that were at the forefront of the nineteenth-century Bulgarian "national revival" had gained their fame and prosperity as *derbend* villages from the fifteenth century onwards – not without the institutional support of the Ottoman state.[125] For the purposes of the present discussion, it is worth concluding that *derbend* villages played a prominent role in the growth and consolidation of the rural Christian population in the region and that the Ottoman state might have supported their foundation and growth in connection to the influx of nomadic and semi-nomadic Turcoman settlers in the first half of the sixteenth century.

---

[124] The percentage of *derbendci* householders of all rural Christian heads of household in the area studied was 9% *c.* 1485, 37% in 1516, 18% *c.* 1535, 27% *c.* 1550, and 27% in 1579. Note the incomplete nature of the *c.* 1535 tax register (BOA TD 439), with some Christian villages missing. See also Table 9.

[125] Kiel, *Art and Society*, 42–43.

5 The Development of the Urban Network in Sixteenth-Century Deliorman: The Emergence of Hezargrad and Eski Cuma, the Transformation of Shumnu into an Islamic City, and the Decline of Chernovi

5.1 Introduction: The Islamic City, the Ottoman City, and the Ottoman Balkan City

Any adequate research on Ottoman Balkan urbanism needs to be integrated into at least three broader scholarly debates: on the "Islamic city," on urban development in the Ottoman Empire at large, and on the process of the "Ottomanization" of the Balkans. The last entailed the continuous integration of patterns of socio-economic, cultural, and religious development that were new and foreign to Islamic tradition, to a greater degree than in any other part of the Empire.

Resting upon the foundation of Orientalism, early studies of "the Islamic city" differentiated sharply between "oriental" and western cultures and attributed any particular aspect of civilization in the Islamic world to the overarching influence of Islam itself.[1] Often characterized by gross generalizations based on a case study of a single city, these works presented the "Islamic city" as a "timeless" and disorderly polity that lacked social coherence and autonomous municipal institutions,[2] thus reflecting some of the features of the "oriental city" as theorized by Max Weber.[3]

---

[1] The very persistence of the terms "Islamic world," "Islamic art" as well as "Islamic (world) history" (and the frequent failure to distinguish between the latter and "the history of Islam") in Europe and North America is a testament to the longevity of these views.

[2] For an insightful analysis of the dominant early French tradition in the study of "Islamic cities," see André Raymond, "Islamic City, Arab City: Orientalist Myths and Recent Views," *British Journal of Middle Eastern Studies* 21/6 (1994), 3–18.

[3] Most notably, Weber distinguished between the "Occidental city" and its "Oriental" and "Asiatic" counterparts with respect to the lack of a coherent, self-conscious stratum (or "estate") of urbanites ("burghers") that aspired to the achievement of freedom in contrast to nearly all other known civic developments," Max Weber, *The City*, trans. and ed. D. Martindale and G. Neuwirth (Glencoe, IL: The Free Press, 1958), 91–96.

Subjecting these views to comprehensive and radical criticism, numerous scholars have worked to dismantle various elements of the traditional orientalist concept of the "Islamic city," demonstrating that first, it is hardly possible to speak of any uniform model,[4] and second, that most of the urban characteristics often postulated as typically "Islamic" (such as *hammam*s, convoluted or dead-end streets, and division into quarters according to confessional affiliation) do not owe their origins or persistence to Islamic doctrine, but could be found in pre-modern cities in various locales and relate to specific geographic, socio-economic, and cultural contexts as well as to local pre-Islamic traditions.[5] Voices calling for doing away altogether with the concept of the "Islamic city" have intensified; alternative (and problematic) typologies, such as the "oriental,"[6] or the "traditional"[7] city have been suggested. Perhaps, it might be helpful, at least to an extent, to bring back in circulation Hodgson's distinction between "Islamic" and "Islamicate"; a similar suggestion has been made by Claude Cahen, who prefers to speak of "cities in *Dar al-Islam*," rather than "Islamic cities."[8] But as André Raymond pointed out: "the ground is still far from being cleared," adding the usual caution about the need of proper contextualization in the further study of "Islamic" cities.[9]

As for the "Ottoman city," Ottomanist historiography has produced much less of a well-developed debate on the subject.[10] The available case studies on specific Ottoman urban centers have largely stayed within the realm of local or regional history rather than spurring a more systematic typological discussion of Ottoman urbanism.[11] Without doubt, being

[4] See Oleg Grabar, "Reflections on the Study of Islamic Art," *Muqarnas* 1 (1983), 8–10.
[5] A few examples of such studies are Eugen Wirth, *Die orientalische Stadt im islamischen Vorderasien und Nordafrika: städtische Bausubstanz und raumliche Ordnung,Wirtschaftsleben und soziale Organisation* (Mainz: Phillip von Zabern, 2000); Ira Lapidus, *Muslim Cities in the Later Middle Ages* (New York: Cambridge University Press, 1984) and André Raymond, *Grandes villes arabes à l'époque Ottomane* (Paris: Sindbad, 1985).
[6] Wirth, *Die orientalische Stadt*, 128–129.
[7] Raymond, "Islamic City, Arab City," 12–14.
[8] Claude Cahen, "Mouvements populaires et autonomisme urbaine dans l'Asie musulmane du moyen âge III," *Arabica* VI (1959), 258–260. This suggestion has also been followed in some recent work on urbanism in the Islamic world such as *The City in the Islamic World*, ed. Salma Jayyusi, Renata Hood, Attilio Petruccioli, and André Raymond, 2 vols. (Leiden and Boston: Brill, 2008).
[9] Raymond, "Islamic City, Arab City," 18.
[10] A relatively rare study that provides a conceptual perspective on the early modern Ottoman city is Edhem Eldem, Daniel Goffman, and Bruce Masters, *The Ottoman City between East and West: Aleppo, Izmir, and Istanbul* (Cambridge and New York: Cambridge University Press, 1999).
[11] A few examples of case studies are Heath W. Lowry, *The Islamization and Turkification of the City of Trabzon (Trebizond) 1461–1583* (Istanbul: The Isis Press, 2009), Haim Gerber, *Economy and Society in an Ottoman City: Bursa, 1600–1700* (Jerusalem: Hebrew

integrated into a single imperial polity, Ottoman cities developed some common characteristics[12] – for example, common patterns of taxation and provincial administration and a characteristic lack of city walls.[13] In addition, Ottomanist scholarship, with the partial exception of some historians specializing on the Ottoman Balkans, has steered away from the question of the "Islamic" nature of Ottoman cities, implicitly taking it for granted.

Two features of Ottoman urbanism deserve special mention: the Ottoman state's pro-active efforts aimed at transforming urban centers in accordance with its strategic (political and military) priorities, and the dynamic development of *waqf*s and the role they played in Ottoman urban growth. The Ottoman government resorted on occasion – especially during the fifteenth and the sixteenth centuries – to the forcible resettlement of people with the objective of strengthening existing urban centers or founding new ones in areas that it deemed to be of strategic importance. The state would also apply fiscal measures to stimulate the growth of specific urban centers, the most notable example being Istanbul immediately following its conquest.[14] One of the great proponents of the active role of the Ottoman state in urban planning has been Ö.L. Barkan whose work on Ottoman colonization was discussed above. He tended to rule out the "spontaneous" emergence of urban centers in the Empire and linked urban development exclusively (to the extent of overemphasizing) to state policy and the sultan's will.[15]

Ottoman cities, whether newly founded or gradually remodeled along the lines of Ottoman and Islamicate urban tradition, were perceived by the central government as centers of Ottoman administrative, legal, and military authority. The founding of new or the remodeling of

University Press, 1988), Feridun Emecen, *XVI. Asırda Manisa Kazâsı* (Ankara: Türk Tarih Kurumu, 1989), Karl Barbir, *Ottoman Rule in Damascus, 1708–1758* (Princeton, NJ: Princeton University Press, 1980), Dina Rizk Khouri, *State and Provincial Society in the Ottoman Empire: Mosul, 1540–1834* (Cambridge and New York: Cambridge University Press, 1997).

[12] Gilles Veinstein; "The Ottoman Town (Fifteenth–Eighteenth Centuries)," in *The City in the Islamic World*, vol. 1, 207.

[13] One traditional division that has been maintained is that between the Arab-speaking Ottoman provinces, where the Ottoman impact was probably the least transformative, and the Anatolian and Balkan provinces which have often been viewed as the "core" or "central" domains of the empire. Beyond the different historical patrimonies that the Ottoman empire-builders confronted in these regions, another reason for this state of affairs has been the largely different methodological approaches of the students of Arab cities (especially those of the "French School") and scholars trained as "Ottomanists."

[14] See Halil İnalcık, "The Policy of Mehmed II towards the Greek Population and the Byzantine Buildings of the City," *Dumbarton Oaks Papers* 23 (1969–70), 229–249.

[15] Ö.L. Barkan, "Quelques observations sur l'organisation économique et sociale des villes Ottomanes des XV et XVI siècles," *Recueils de la Société Jean Bodin*, tome VII, *La Ville* (Bruxelles, 1955), 291.

pre-Ottoman urban centers was an integral and eminently important aspect of the Ottoman expansion in the Balkans, and in this sense it may be compared to other expanding imperial powers in diverse geographic contexts.[16] In the context of the sixteenth century, the sense of cities as loci of authority also reflected the state's heightened sensitivity to establishing firm central control in its already far-flung provinces, a degree of control that was not ubiquitous theretofore, but was becoming imperative in the context of the Ottomans' maturing imperial vision and the intensifying rivalry with the Safavids in the East and the Habsburgs and Venetians in the West.

Importantly, while distinguishing between village residents (*ehl-i kura*) and urban residents (*şehirlüyan, şehirli cema'ati, şehirli ta'ifesi, şehir halkı, kasaba halkı*),[17] Ottoman laws did not provide for a clear-cut, formal procedure of granting town status to settlements. Ottoman administrative and legal documents (law codes, tax registers, *firman*s, charitable endowment charters [*vakfiye*s, *vakıfname*s], or Islamic court registers [*şeriye sicilleri*]) merely reflected the current status of a settlement by referring to it as a village (*karye*) or a town/city (*şehir, kasaba, nefs*) without explicitly stipulating the conditions on the basis of which a settlement would hold such a status. Of the terms associated with urban settlements, *nefs* (Ar. *nafs*) is probably the most widely used, especially in tax registers, and is equally vague regarding the urban nature of many of the settlements denoted by it, especially in the early Ottoman Balkans.[18] Ottoman tax registers from the fifteenth- and (early) sixteenth-century Balkans list as *nefs* numerous settlements which lacked the size and socio-economic structure of urban centers, some of which would later develop as what came to be "typical" Ottoman towns, others losing their status as administrative centers and becoming listed as mere villages.[19] This dynamic

---

[16] See, for example, discussions on the foundation of new or the remodeling of pre-conquest cities by the Spaniards and the English in the sixteenth- and seventeenth-century Americas; John Elliott; *Empires of the Atlantic World: Britain and Spain in America, 1492–1830* (New Haven, CT, and London: Yale University Press, 2006), 35–39, and Sabine MacCormack, *On the Wings of Time: Rome, the Incas, Spain, and Peru* (Princeton, NJ, and Oxford: Princeton University Press, 2007), 103–104.

[17] See examples in Barkan, *Kanunlar*, 3, 6, 30, 36, 42, 43, 154, 158, 181, 308, 389.

[18] Literally, *nefs* means "the very..." "...itself" – thus "nefs-i Sofya" would mean "Sofia itself" in the context of a listing of all settlements in the Sofia province, pointing to Sofia as its administrative center, but not necessarily establishing its urban status. A. Stojanovski has provided examples of settlements in Ottoman Macedonia which were alternately registered as *nefs* or *karye* in the fifteenth and sixteenth centuries, and some were referred to as both (as in "*karye-i nefs-i Tikveş*"), *Gradovite na Makedonija*, 63–64.

[19] To give a few examples of such administrative centers in the late fifteenth-century province of Niğbolu, which never developed into full-blown Ottoman cities later: Krapich, Reseleç, and others such as Mramorniçe were listed as villages (*karye*) but were yet registered as administrative centers, see NBKM OAK 45/29, TSMA D 167.

may reflect both the transitional nature of Ottoman rule in the Balkans at the time, as well as rapid demographic change.

This brings us to the question of what made a town a town according to the Ottoman authorities. Barkan identifies two major criteria: the availability of a congregational mosque (usually as a part of a *waqf* that enjoyed some measure of autonomy from the state) and a market (supervised by a state-appointed market inspector [*muhtesib*]). Barkan has been followed in this by others, most notably M. Kiel in the Ottoman Balkan context.[20] The presence of a congregational mosque (and the related institutions in a mosque complex), in turn, conditioned the existence of a fairly sizable and stable Muslim community. While in the early centuries of Ottoman rule in the Balkans, the state recognized as towns some settlements with no Muslim residents, most obviously on account of their well-established urban status upon conquest; by the sixteenth century such towns were in decline, eventually to lose their urban status and importance as administrative, commercial, or cultural centers. Concurrently, for a village to be recognized as a town by the authorities, it had to possess a congregational mosque and a functioning market; large Christian villages with no Muslim residents never made it to town status before the nineteenth century. In his seminal study on the Balkan city, Nikolai Todorov, a leading Bulgarian historian, points to the existence of 16 out of 44 Balkan urban centers in the fifteenth century that had no Muslim residents at all; by the early sixteenth century that proportion was reduced to 9 out of 84, with the number of predominantly Muslim cities steadily increasing.[21]

The growth of pious endowments, supported by Ottoman legislation, especially fiscal policies, was the other major pillar of Ottoman urban growth. *Waqf*s founded by Ottoman sultans, other members of the dynasty, Ottoman grandees, as well as people of local stature contributed greatly to the development of urban centers through the construction and upkeep of typical urban institutions in the Islamic world, such as congregational mosques and *mescid*s (smaller mosques), (religious) colleges (*medrese*s) and libraries, children schools (*mekatib-i sibyan*), soup kitchens (*imaret*s), guesthouses (*khan*s, *kervansaray*s). *Waqf*s often also provided for the upkeep of general urban facilities, such as water supply systems, roads, and bridges.[22] While being

---

[20] Barkan, "Quelques observations," 291; Machiel Kiel, "Urban Development in Bulgaria in the Turkish Period: The Place of Turkish Architecture in the Process," *IJTS* 4/2 (1989), 79–158.

[21] Todorov, *The Balkan City*, 53–56.

[22] For a brief introduction on *waqf*s and urban development, see Randi Deguilhem, "The Waqf in the City," in *The City in the Islamic World*, vol. 2, 923–952. It should be pointed out that throughout Islamic history *waqf*s were widely used by non-Muslim communities, specifically Christians and Jews as well, yet the relative importance of *waqf*s founded by non-Muslims was fairly low. See Deguilhem, 927–928.

instrumental in the transformation of cities inherited upon conquest, Ottoman *waqf*s played a formative role in the foundation and initial growth of newly created cities in the fifteenth and sixteenth centuries, such as Sarajevo – supported by the pious endowments of local governors İsa Bey and Gazi Hüsrev Bey – and, as will be shown below, Deliorman's Hezargrad, founded by grand vizier Ibrahim Pasha.[23]

In light of the transformative effect that Ottoman urbanism had on Balkan cities (in contrast to the Arab lands and, to an extent, Anatolia) and the subsequent elaboration of nationalist historiographies in the Balkan nation-states and Turkey, the historical development of the Ottoman Balkan city has become the subject of an extended and well-structured scholarly debate, albeit often marred by nationalist sentiments.[24]

Some leading Ottomanists in the region have come with sweeping, generalized models of Ottoman urbanization policies, which fit into these scholars' general approach to the broader process of Islamization and its legacy in the Balkans. The major line of division in the scholarly debate on the Ottoman Balkan city relates to the degree of transformation (along the axis of "continuity and change") and especially to Islamization, understood as conversion to Islam on the part of segments of the local population, as well as the settling of Anatolian colonists in Balkan cities and their hinterlands, especially during the fifteenth and sixteenth centuries.

Barkan has emphasized the state's central role in the revitalization or the foundation of many cities in the Balkans following the Ottoman conquest.[25] In his view, all pre-Ottoman Balkan cities that continued their existence in the Ottoman Empire (as most of them did) were de facto "re-created" by the Ottomans who furnished them with new Ottoman institutions, provided for a favorable taxation regime, regulated urban socio-economic development (e.g. through market regulations and price

---

[23] For a recent analysis of Sarajevo's early history, see York Norman, "An Islamic City? Sarajevo's Islamization and Economic Development, 1461–1604," Ph.D. diss., Georgetown University, 2005, 39–73.

[24] A testament to this statement is the existence of several edited volumes on the Balkan city under Ottoman rule, such as *La ville Balkanique, XVe–XIXe SS*, ed. Nikolai Todorov (Sofia: Editions de l'Académie Bulgare des Sciences, 1970), *Structure Sociale et développement culturel des villes sud-est Européennes et Adriatiques aux XVIIe–XVIIIe siècles* (Bucharest: AIESEE, 1975), *Gradska Kultura na Balkanu (XV–XIX vek), Zbornik Radova*, ed. Verena Han and Radovan Samardžić, 2 vols. (Belgrade: Srpska Akademija Nauka i Umetnosti, 1984–1988), as well as Nikolai Todorov's seminal monograph *The Balkan City, 1400–1900* (Seattle and London: University of Washington Press, 1983; original edition in Bulgarian, 1972).

[25] Barkan, "Quelques observations," 289–311.

controls), and encouraged and directed mass immigration of "Turkish" settlers from Anatolia, whereby the most important Ottoman Balkan cities became predominantly Muslim and Turkish, with conversion to Islam playing a minimally important role.[26]

Largely in response to Barkan's claims, and again influenced by nationalist ideology, Todorov developed his own model of Ottoman urbanization, wherein he insisted on a large degree of continuity between the pre-Ottoman and Ottoman periods, minimized the role of Turcoman colonization from Anatolia, and pointed to religious conversion, which in his mind was largely forced or at least occurred under some sort of "indirect pressure," as the main factor explaining the presence of large, and very often dominant Muslim communities in Ottoman Balkan towns.[27] This division of opinion has persisted and Barkan's and Todorov's views have been followed and advanced by a number of scholars from the Balkans and Turkey.[28]

There have been more nuanced studies on the subject, like Adem Handžić's, which takes up Bosnia as a special case, emphasizing the importance of its geographical position as a *serhad* (frontier) province with the related political, logistic, strategic, and economic factors that conditioned the development of local Ottoman towns, and the work of Behija Zlatar.[29] But by and large, the study of Ottoman Balkan urban development has long been the domain of Balkan (including Turkish) nationalist historiographies, whereby the national, ethno-religious, and political identity of the scholars involved has left indelible marks on the ongoing debate. It has been only in the past couple of decades that more detached and nuanced research on Ottoman urban centers has come into being, most notably the work of Machiel Kiel,[30] which has in many ways inspired the analysis of urban development that follows.

[26] Ibid., 290, 294.
[27] First in "Po niakoi vâprosi na balkanskiia grad prez XV–XVI vv.," *IP* 18, no. 1 (1962), 32–58, and later in *The Balkan City*, 44–60.
[28] For works supportive of Todorov's thesis, see Zdravko Pliakov, "Za demografskiia oblik na bâlgarskiia grad prez XV – sredata na XVII vek," *IP* 24, no. 5 (1968), 28–47, Traian Stoianovich, "Model and Mirror in the Pre-modern Balkan City," in *La ville Balkanique XVe–XIXe SS*, 83–110, and Strashimir Dimitrov, "Za priemstvenostta v razvitieto na balkanskite gradove prez XV–XVI vek," *Balkanistika* 2 (1987), 5–17. On Barkan's side, see M. Tayyib Gökbilgin, "Kanuni Sultan Süleyman Devri Başlarında Rumeli Eyaleti, Livaları, Şehir ve Kasabaları," *Belleten* 20 (1956), 247–285, and Kemal Karpat, "The Background of Ottoman Concept of City and Urbanity," in *Structure Sociale et développement culturel des villes sud-est Européennes et Adriatiques aux XVIIe–XVIIIe siècles* (Bucharest: AIESEE, 1975), 323–340.
[29] Adem Handžić, "O formiranju nekih gradskih naselja u Bosni u XV stoljeću," *POF* 30 (1980), 133–169, and Behija Zlatar, "Tipologija gradskih naselja na Balkanu u XVI vijeku," in *Gradska Kultura na Balkanu (XV–XIX vek), Zbornik Radova*, vol. 2, 63–73.
[30] See especially his "Urban Development."

The remainder of this chapter discusses the most important urban centers in Deliorman and the adjacent regions with special attention paid to the factors that conditioned their emergence and/or changes in their relative importance, and their evolving demographic situations, including ethno-religious composition and the processes of conversion and ethno-religious assimilation, thus testing both Barkan's and Todorov's theses.[31] Indeed, the history of the four urban centers discussed below reflects a diversity of patterns of urban transformation, suggesting that urban development in the Ottoman Balkans, even when limited to a fairly small part of the peninsula, hardly fits a single model. Yet, the Ottoman state's strategic priorities probably played the most important role in the rise and decline of urban centers in the region. Hezargrad (Herazgrad, mod. Razgrad), still dubbed "the unofficial capital of Deliorman," emerged in the first half of the sixteenth century as an essentially new urban center, the base of a *waqf* founded by the current grand vizier. The fortress of the other significant town in the region, Shumnu (mod. Shumen), to the southeast of Hezargrad, was well-established in medieval Bulgaria and was largely destroyed by the Christian armies during the Crusade of Varna (1444) and then rebuilt by the Ottomans in the late fifteenth and sixteenth centuries. The town of Chernovi (mod. village of Cherven), to the northwest of Hezargrad, is a telling example of a well-developed medieval Bulgarian town that gradually lost its importance and turned into an insignificant village by the mid-seventeenth century. Chernovi declined in parallel with the rise of Rus (later Rusçuk, mod. Ruse) on the southern bank of the Danube as the major urban center in the vicinity, a process bolstered by its strategic importance as a fortress and a growing center of commerce along the northern border of the Empire. Finally, Eski Cuma (mod. Târgovishte), to the west of Hezargrad and Shumnu, is an example of a village that grew steadily during the sixteenth century, acquiring a Friday mosque and a marketplace in the process, and was recognized as a center of a *nahiye* (district) by the late sixteenth century, attaining town status and becoming a center of a *kaza* in the first half of the seventeenth.

5.2   The Emergence of Ottoman Hezargrad

5.2.1   Ancient and Medieval Background

The present town of Hezargrad (Razgrad) and its vicinity, situated in the Ak Lom (Beli Lom) river valley, around 50km southeast of Ruse

---

[31] The process of conversion to Islam will be taken up in greater detail in Chapter 7.

(Rus, Rusçuk), has been the site of human settlement since prehistoric times.[32] According to archaeological findings, a well-structured Thracian settlement existed there in the early decades of the first century AD.[33] Upon their conquest of the region in AD 46, the Romans established a garrison camp in the vicinity, which grew into a fully fledged walled town named Abrittus (or Abritus), a few kilometers south of the present town.[34] Archaeological findings also suggest that the Roman city was swept away by Avar and Slav invasions in the fifth and sixth centuries, but by the eighth century AD a new town appeared upon the ruins of ancient Abrittus and later achieved a measure of prominence in the medieval Bulgar state (founded in 681). It is this medieval town known as Hrâzgrad (supposedly named after a boyar named Hrâz) that later gave its name to the new city founded by grand vizier Ibrahim Pasha in 1533.[35] According to archaeological excavations, like most urban centers in the northeastern Balkans, medieval Hrâzgrad ceased to exist by the mid-eleventh century as a result of continuous Pecheneg and Uze incursions.[36]

5.2.2   The Emergence of a New Ottoman Town

It is the emergence of the Ottoman town at the site in the first half of the sixteenth century that has spurred a heated debate among historians, specifically in relation to the foundation of a settlement called Yenice, which shortly thereafter attained the name of Hezargrad-i Cedid (New Hezargrad), as a part of Ibrahim Pasha's pious endowment. Most Bulgarian historians, disregarding the findings of archaeologists, prefer to see medieval Hrâzgrad as a city that continued to exist until the advent of the Ottomans in the late 1380s. Thus, Boris Nedkov identifies Hrâzgrad as the town of Agrizinus in the medieval Arab geographer al-Idrisi's famous work (completed in 1153);[37] Strashimir Lishev suggests

[32] The most exhaustive discussion of the history of the Hezargrad area in pre-historic times is to be found in A. Iavashov, *Razgrad: negovoto arkheologochesko i istorichesko minalo* (Razgrad: Razvitie, 1930), 3–30.

[33] Hristo Litsov, *Rimskiiat grad Abritus pri Razgrad* (Razgrad: Okrâzhen Naroden Muzei, Razgrad, 1959), 8.

[34] Ibid., 9–12.

[35] Ara Margos, "Kâde se e namiral srednovekovniiat Hrâsgrad?" *IP* 44, no. 12 (1988), 59.

[36] Sonia Georgieva, "Srednovekovnoto selishte nad razvalinite na antichniia grad Abritus," *IAI* 24 (1961), 21–26; later T. Ivanov suggested that the city was destroyed in the late tenth century; T. Ivanov and S. Stojanov, *Abrittus: Its History and Archaeology* (Razgrad: Cultural and Historical Heritage Directorate 1985), 72.

[37] Boris Nedkov, *Bâlgariia i sâsednite i zemi prez XII vek spored Idrisi* (bilingual edition in Arabic and Bulgarian of al-Idrisi's work's portion concerning the Bulgarian lands) (Sofia: Nauka i Izkustvo, 1960), 68–69, 82–83, 138–140.

that Hrâzgrad existed in the thirteenth and fourteenth centuries;[38] Bistra Cvetkova has posited that the thriving medieval town was "probably occupied" in the course of Çandarlı Ali Pasha's campaign in northern Bulgaria in 1388.[39] Khristo Gandev sees Hrâzgrad destroyed in the 1388 campaign and later reappearing in the sixteenth century, this time with a predominantly Turkish population.[40] However, these arguments are purely hypothetical, as there are no contemporary sources that attest to the existence of the medieval town after the mid-eleventh century. Ara Margos has argued that following Pecheneg and Uze raids, the population of the medieval town on the site of the Roman Abrittus migrated to its present location in the mid-eleventh century, but as the new site was not equipped with walls, it did not play a role in Ali Pasha's campaign of 1388 and was subsequently not mentioned by the late fifteenth-century Ottoman historian Mehmed Neşri, the premier source for that event.[41] Bulgarian scholars (especially Cvetkova and Margos) see a proof for this in the first Ottoman tax registration of the Ottoman settlement c. 1535, where it is listed as "Yenice, with another name Hezargrad-i Cedid, also known as Kayacık, pertaining to Chernovi" and apparently had a predominantly Christian population.[42]

This hypothesis that insisted on the continuity between the medieval Bulgarian town of Hrâzgrad and the Ottoman town of (New) Hezargrad, largely in tune with Todorov's model of urban development in the Ottoman Balkans, has been energetically questioned by Machiel Kiel. In a lengthy article devoted above all to the architectural history of the Ottoman town, but also paying due attention to its foundation in the 1530s and subsequent demographic and socio-economic development, Kiel rightly points out that while the settlement had both a Muslim and a (predominant) Christian population when it appeared in the first (detailed) tax registration from c. 1535, where Hezargrad was listed together with the Christian village of Kayacık,[43] later detailed Ottoman tax registers, dated c. 1550 and 1579 respectively,[44] have Hezargrad registered as a separate, wholly Muslim town, with the neighboring Christian

---

[38] Strashimir Lishev, *Bâlgarskiiat srednovekoven grad. Obshtestveno-ikonomicheski oblik* (Sofia: BAN, 1970), 82, 92, 106.

[39] Bistra Cvetkova, "Hezârghrad," *EI²*.

[40] Gandev, *Bâlgarskata narodnost prez 15-i vek*, 61, 91.

[41] Margos, "Kâde se e namiral," 60–61.

[42] NBKM OAK 217/8, f. 11a; *TIBI*, vol. 3, 441. On this *waqf* register fragment, see Chapter 4, section 4.2.5.

[43] NBKM OAK 217/8, ff. 12a-14a, *TIBI*, vol. 3, 442–445.

[44] Namely BOA TD 382 (that included both *timār* and *waqf/mülk* holdings), dated c. 1550 and TKG KK TTd 411 (including only *waqf* and *mülk* holdings), dated AH 987/ AD 1579.

village of Kayacık listed independently.[45] Kiel also correctly asserts that
no settlement named Hrâzgrad or Hezargrad is mentioned in the extant
Byzantino-Bulgarian sources, the chronicle of Mehmed Neşri, that of
Neşri's contemporary Ruhi, or in earlier Ottoman tax registers[46], and
that "only the [obviously Slavic] name suggests that there must have
been such a town."[47] Neither is such a name found in the oldest fully
preserved Ottoman tax register for the province of Niğbolu containing
demographic data from the mid-1480s.[48]

On the basis of these arguments Kiel suggested that the Ottoman
Yenice (lit. "new," "newly founded"), the standard name often given
by the Ottomans to newly founded cities or villages, also known as
Hezargrad-i Cedid, i.e. New Hezargrad, was a new Ottoman settlement
that had nothing to do with any pre-existing (pre-Ottoman) towns in the
area. Yet, he was troubled by the name "New Hezargrad," as it suggests
that an older settlement by the same name should have existed, and left
this question unanswered.

A source that may clarify substantially the issue of Ottoman
Hezargrad's foundation is the hitherto unresearched *vakfiye* (foundation charter) of grand vizier Ibrahim Pasha's pious endowment, which
provides invaluable evidence on the emergence of the new settlement.[49] Drawn by the scribe of the Imperial Council (*divan-ı hümayun*) Mehmed bin Mevlana Kara Üveys in the name of the military
judge (*kadı 'asker*) of Rumeli, Mehmed bin el-Fenari, and dated Eva'il-
i Rebi'ü'l-Evvel, AH 940 (19–29 September, 1533), it constitutes the
"birth certificate" of what would soon become known as "Hezargrad-
i Cedid," and further on simply Hezargrad. The charter gives the
boundaries of the *waqf* lands that include five villages: Yeniceköy
(New Village), the future (New) Hezargrad; Kayacık; Hasanlar, with

---

[45] Kiel, "Hrâzgrad-Hezargrad-Razgrad," 500–501, 523. As also confirmed by Hezargrad's
pious endowment charter discussed below.

[46] Namely the synoptic tax-register fragments NBKM OAK 45/29, dated 1479, and
NBKM Nk 12/9, provisionally dated from the mid-1480s, as well as in BOA TD 370 of
1530 (largely based on demographic data from the detailed BOA MAD 11 of 1516, as
discussed in the preceding chapter).

[47] Kiel, "Hrâzgrad-Hezargrad-Razgrad," 525–526.

[48] TSMA D 167, as discussed in Chapter 3.

[49] This document is preserved in the Topkapı Palace Museum Archive, registered as TSMA
E 7029. I thank the *müfti* of Razgrad, Mr. Mehmet Sali Alya for providing me with
an opportunity to make photos of a photocopy of the document, composed in Arabic,
as well as for providing me with a copy of an unpublished translation into Turkish by
Dr. Raşit Gündoğdu of the Prime Ministry's Ottoman Archive in Istanbul. As the photocopy of the original document is imperfect, I have used both versions referred to as
TSMA E 7029 (for the original version) and TSMA E 7029/Gündoğdu for the Turkish
translation, respectively.

three quarters (*mahallat*), namely Hasanlar, Sofular, and İnebeğçiler; Dobrova, with three unnamed quarters; and Duymuşlar. It is pointed out that they are close to the "aforementioned Hezargrad" and were part of the *nahiye* of Hezargrad in the *kaza* of Chernovi in the *sancak* of Niğbolu.[50] As discussed in the preceding chapter, all of them, with the exception of Hasanlar, were essentially newly founded.[51] The clear mention of a settlement named Hezargrad pre-dating the grand vizier's pious endowment in the area points to a likely reason for which the town founded by Ibrahim Pasha was known early on as New Hezargrad.

Indeed, while not mentioned in Ottoman documents prior to the *waqf* deed of 1533, a village by the name of Eski Hezargrad (lit. "Old Hezargrad") is found in the detailed tax register of *c*. 1550, where it stands as a small-to-mid-sized wholly Christian village with 17 households, or roughly 80–90 souls.[52] Close to thirty years later, in the detailed registration of 1579, Eski Hezargrad exists no more, but is listed instead as a *mezra'a* without registered residents. A note reads: "previously it was a village; as it[s population] scattered fifteen years ago, it was registered as a *mezra'a*; from the outside and the town of Herazgrad[53] some Muslims [come and] cultivate the land, they pay their '*öşr* [i.e. the canonic tithe]."[54]

In other words, the tax registrations from 1550 to 1579 show clearly that the town of "New Hezargrad/Herazgrad" was founded near enough to a pre-existing Christian settlement that Muslims from the new town founded several decades earlier could come and cultivate its land when it was abandoned. This pattern of founding a new, Muslim (or predominantly Muslim) settlement close to a pre-existing Balkan Christian settlement, or at a place where such was known to have traditionally existed, was not new to the Ottomans – the city of Saraybosna (Sarajevo) was similarly founded near the ruins of the pre-Ottoman fortress of Vrhbosna,[55]

---

[50] TSMA E 7029, 11, TSMA E 7029/Gündoğdu 7.

[51] Chapter 4, section 4.2.5. See the same section on the sixteenth-century demographics of these villages, other than Yenice/Hezargrad.

[52] BOA TD 382, p. 370.

[53] In both registers from 1579 – TKG KK TTd 411 and TKG KK TTd 151 – the name of Hezargrad (old and new) has been rendered as Herazgrad, thus being closer to the supposed medieval settlement name Hrâzgrad and the modern Razgrad. Hezargrad is likely a corruption of Hrâzgrad, as *hezâr* – meaning "one thousand" or "very many" in Persian – was a part of Ottoman vocabulary.

[54] TKG KK TTd 151, f. 134 a, "*Sābıḳa[n] ḳarye olub, on beş seneden berü perākende olmağın, mezra'a ḳayd olunub, ḥāricden ve nefs-i Herāzgrād'dan bażı Müslümanlar zirā'at idüb, 'öşrün virirler.*"

[55] Norman, "An Islamic City?" 39–42.

as was the fortress of Elbasan in central Albania in 1466, although in the latter case the element of toponymical continuity was lacking.[56]

Thus, the Ottomans were in fact reviving a settlement area that had already proven its strategic utility for military, political, and commercial purposes. The newly founded Yeniceköy, being equipped with a Friday mosque and a market, quickly became the dominant regional (and distinctly Islamic) urban center as well as the seat of a new judgeship – a sultanic edict included in a *mühimme defteri* (register of outgoing imperial edicts) dated AH 951–2/AD 1544–5 mentions explicitly the *kaza* of Hezargrad and the former judge (*ma'zul kadı*) of the city, Mevlana Ramazan.[57]

What could have been the reasons for Ibrahim Pasha's decision to found Yenice (the future Hezargrad), apart from the rise of the *waqf* institution's role in Ottoman urban development? The endowment charter (*vakfiye*) does not provide specifics.[58]

While the concurrent demographic boom in the surrounding countryside, mainly due to the influx of newcomers from Anatolia and Thrace, could in and of itself be seen as a sufficient reason for reviving this traditional urban site, centrally located on the most convenient route between Rus on the Danube and Shumnu (and further leading to Istanbul via Thrace), the broader historical context may have rendered its revivification even more expedient. As Machiel Kiel has already suggested,[59] the planting of an urban center representing the Ottoman central state and "orthodox" Sunni culture in the area could be viewed as a counterweight to the influx of "heterodox" Muslim migrants and the related regional rise of "heterodox" Islam at a time when the Empire was engaged in a grand-scale conflict with the newly founded Safavid Empire of Iran, a situation aggravated by mass rebellions in Anatolia on the part of populations perceived by the Ottoman government as pro-Safavid sympathizers – most importantly those led by Shah Kulu (1511–12), Sheykh Celal (1519), and Kalender Shah (1527). That the Ottoman suppression of these rebellions may have been the primary reason for the influx of heterodox migrants from Anatolia into the

---

[56] On the foundation of Elbasan, see Todorov, *The Balkan City*, 25, and V.L. Ménage, "Elbasan," in *EI²*.

[57] *Topkapı Sarayı Arşivi H.951–952 Tarihli ve E-12321 Numaralı Mühimme Defteri*, ed. Halil Sahillioğlu (Istanbul: İRCİCA, 2002), 195.

[58] Ibrahim Pasha's *waqf*'s foundation deed does not present concrete reasons for the establishment of the endowment and the foundation of Yenice specifically in that area at that specific time, but only broader religio-political considerations such as the grand vizier's duty to abide by the will of God and actively contribute to the maintenance of social justice and the advancement of prosperity – these will be discussed in greater detail in Chapter 6.

[59] Kiel, "Hrâzgrad-Hezargrad-Razgrad," 528.

Balkans at the time and the fact that Ibrahim Pasha led the Ottoman army that quashed the latter revolt in 1527 lend further credence to this hypothesis.[60] The (re-)foundation of Hezargrad by the almighty grand vizier may thus be viewed as a claim to the "symbolic (re-)conquest" of the region.[61] While the Balkan northeast (and Deliorman in particular) had been formally annexed by the Ottomans more than a century earlier, the degree of Ottoman central control in the region had been low in the context of the events of the preceding century and the recent influx of heterodox groups. (New) Hezargrad was an outpost not only of formal Ottoman authority but of "Ottomanness" itself – a realization of the maturing Ottoman imperial vision in a distant Balkan province.

The 1533 *vakfiye* paints a clear picture of the early development of Yeniceköy (Hezargrad-i Cedid). It provides the only known description of the original mosque as it was built in the time of Ibrahim Pasha. The present monumental mosque in the center of the city was built anew by Mahmud Pasha in 1616[62] (see Fig. 5.1) The forerunner of the present mosque around which the new settlement emerged was of much smaller stature, covered by reeds and with walls of stone, it had a fountain (*şadırvan*) in front and stood in the center of a courtyard surrounded by a wall.[63] The foundation deed stipulates that the call for the five canonical prayers (*ezan*) be performed every day, together with the call for the Friday prayer and *eid* prayers.[64] To the right side of the mosque stood a school (*dar al-ta'lim*)[65] in which local youths would be educated. Next to it was a guesthouse (*han*) with fifty rooms to host travelers and a bath-house (*hammam*).[66] The *vakfiye* further names the *mütevelli* (*waqf* superintendent), a certain Bali Bey bin Sungur, and also lists the daily stipends of the personnel that staffed the pious endowment's administration, the mosque, and the school, whereby the lieutenant *mütevelli* would receive five *dirhem*s a day, the revenue collector (*cabi*) four *dirhem*s, the scribe (*katib*) three, the imam of the mosque six, the preacher (*hatib*) six, two *müezzin*s three each, a mosque servant

---

[60] On Ibrahim Pasha's participation in the suppression of that revolt, see *Solakzade Tarihi*, 464–465, Sohrweide, "Der Sieg der Safaviden," 177–183, as well as the relevant discussion in Chapter 1.

[61] For a comparison of city foundation as an act of symbolic conquest in the context of Spanish trans-Atlantic imperial expansion, see Elliott, *Empires of the Atlantic World*, 35–39 and MacCormack, *On the Wings of Time*, 103–108.

[62] Kiel, "Hrâzgrad-Hezargrad-Razgrad," 508–515.

[63] TSMA E 7029, p. 9; TSMA E 7029/Gündoğdu, pp. 5–6.

[64] TSMA E 7029, p. 9; TSMA E 7029/Gündoğdu, p. 6.

[65] TSMA E 7029, p. 9; TSMA E 7029/Gündoğdu, p. 6.

[66] TSMA E 7029 p. 14; TSMA E 7029/Gündoğdu, p. 9.

Figure 5.1 Mosque of Ibrahim Pasha in Razgrad. Photograph by
Mariya Kiprovska.

(*kayyum*) three, the mosque cleaner (*ferraş*) one, the leading Qu'ran
memorizer/reciter (*hafız*) three, the other *hafız*es two each, the *mu'arrif*
(who would mention in thanksgiving the names of benevolent people
before the Friday prayer) two, *hafız* trainees one each, the teachers
(*mu'allim*) at the school four each, and the assistant teachers two each;
money for the clothing and books for ten needy students at the school
was also provided for.[67]

Thus, it was the Friday mosque complex supported by the pious
endowment[68] that de facto established the basic infrastructure of the new
settlement, which, while initially a village, was placed on track to soon
attain town status (and become the seat of a judgeship).

The three sixteenth–century tax registrations available for Hezargrad
– from *c.* 1535, *c.* 1550, and 1579, respectively – allow us to follow the
demographic growth and social structure, as well as the place of converts
to Islam in the newly founded Ottoman urban center.

---

[67] TSMA E 7029, pp. 16–18; TSMA E 7029/Gündoğdu, p. 10.

[68] The 1550 tax registration explicitly adds "*zāviye*" (possibly a convent that would offer a
more "orthodox" version of Sufism to the town population; however, Kiel has suggested
that "*zāviye*" in this context could stand for soup-kitchen (*imāret*)) to the mosque, as a
beneficiary of the pious endowment; BOA TD 382, p. 847.

The *c.* 1535 registration lists 83 regular Muslim households, 23 unmarried Muslim men, and 21 registered Muslims with special status in possession of *berats* (imperial diplomas that exempted them from certain taxes and assigned them the performance of certain administrative, religious, and military duties). The total population of the town must have been around 500–600 people. Unlike the 1533 *vakfiye*, which lists the newly founded settlement as a village (*karye*), the 1535 register mentions the settlement as *nefs*, which suggests that it was already considered an administrative center of sorts as well as a developing urban settlement. The settlement is not divided into quarters (*mahalle*s); all residents are listed as members of one single Muslim community.

The next tax register, that of *c.* 1550, lists the settlement with the name "Hezargrad" only; it was already officially a center of a *nahiye* (likely used interchangeably with *kaza*). The population had more than doubled, with 169 regular Muslim households, 31 households with special status (performing administrative duties or servants of the Islamic cult), as well as 60 bachelors (i.e. the total population must have been around 1,000–1,100 residents). Hezargrad already had four quarters (*mahalle*s), all named after the congregational mosque (*cami'*) or small mosque (*mescid*) they were centered around: the *mahalle* of the "noble" Friday mosque (Cami'-i Şerif) built by İbrahim Pasha, the quarter of Ahmed Bey, centered around the Ahmed Bey mosque built in 1543, as well those of the *mescid*s of Behram Bey and Iskender Bey, respectively.[69]

According to the last available sixteenth-century tax registration, that of 1579, the town did not experience notable demographic growth compared to that *c.* 1550. Still entirely Muslim, it had 204 regular households, 21 households with special status, and 40 bachelors (i.e. a total population around 1,150–1,200 souls). In addition to the existing four *mahalle*s as of *c.* 1550, a fifth one, that of the *mescid* of Mehmed Bey, had appeared.[70]

The dramatic increase in the city's population, paralleled in the case of Shumnu (and Rus), was typical of the region due to the massive influx of settlers in the first half of the sixteenth century, but also in the contemporary empire-wide context of urban (and overall) population growth.[71]

---

[69] BOA TD 382, pp. 847–849.
[70] TKG KK TTd 411, ff. 43b–44b.
[71] On the overall increase of Ottoman population and the growth of Ottoman cities in the sixteenth century, see Ö.L. Barkan, "Essai sur les données statistiques des registres de recensement dans l'Empire ottoman aux XVe et XVIe siècles," *JESHO* 1, no. 1 (Aug. 1957), 9–36, and especially 19–28. On the wider contemporary European context, see Roger Mols, "Die Bevölkerung im 16. und 17. Jahrhundert," in *Bevölkerungsgechichte Europas: Mittelalter bis Neuzeit*, ed. Carlo Cipolla and Knut Borchardt (Munich: Piper, 1971), 58–122, and especially 80–84, as well as M. Livi Bacci, *The Population of Europe*, trans. Cyntia de Nardi Ipsen and Carl Ipsen (London: Blackwell, 1999), 5–12.

Table 5.1 *The population of Hezargrad in the sixteenth century*

Neighborhood (*Mahalle*)	Households (regular) (*Hane*)	Households (other)	Households (total)	Bachelors (*mücerred*)	Total Registered
c. 1535					
A single Muslim community	83	21	104	23	127
c. 1550					
Cami'-i Şerif	50	13	63	13	76
Ahmed Bey	23	7	30	5	35
Mescid-i Behram Bey	37	6	43	11	54
İskender Bey	59	5	64	31	95
Total (1550)	**169**	**31**	**200**	**60**	**260**
1579					
Cami'-i Şerif	45	7	52	12	64
Ahmed Bey	29	1	30	4	34
Mescid-i Behram Bey	50	5	55	7	62
İskender Bey	55	2	57	9	66
Mescid-i Mehmed Bey	25	6	31	8	39
Total (1579)	**204**	**21**	**225**	**40**	**265**

5.2.3   The Socio-Economic Development of Hezargrad

The changing socio-economic and socio-cultural profile of Ottoman Hezargrad's population attests to the town's evolution during the first half century of its history, from a village that had the trappings of an urban center to a well-established, typical Ottoman Balkan town. Ottoman tax registers typically specify the occupations of all town dwellers who enjoyed some special taxation status in relation to the performance of military, administrative, or religious functions; many of them had imperial diplomas (*berats*) authorizing the performance of these functions and/ or guaranteeing them specific tax exemptions. In addition, tax registers would often specify the occupation of urban dwellers who did not have a special tax status, but had an established artisanal (or sometimes, agricultural) occupation, such as tanners, tailors, candle-makers, shepherds, etc. As artisanal occupations usually did not affect one's tax status, listing those occupations was not a rule in Ottoman bureaucratic practice.

Yet, in well-developed cities, often a large portion of the population, and sometimes the majority, would have their (non-taxation-related) artisanal occupation listed, usually replacing the patronymic following the proper personal name. This was more often the case among the Muslim community; non-Muslims' occupational designations were much rarer. The growing abundance of artisanal occupational listings within an Ottoman urban community may be viewed as a sign of the predominance of crafts and commerce in a city, at the expense of agriculture.[72]

To give a few examples, in mid-fifteenth-century Skopje (Üsküb) (1457), around half of the registered Muslim household heads and 10% of the Christian households (around 35–40% of the total city population) had occupational (mostly artisanal, but also religious) designations.[73] In 1546, slightly over 50% of Skopje's householders had a designated occupation, which also held for a bit less than 10% of the Christian households.[74] In 1478 Salonica (Selanik), 500 of 864 Muslim heads of household were identified by their respective occupational titles; in contrast, only 30 of close to 1,000 heads of Christian households were so identified.[75] In both cities, listed artisanal occupations encompassed a great range of typical pre-modern Ottoman urban trades.

An analysis of residents' occupational status in Hezargrad, which remained wholly Muslim throughout the sixteenth century, shows that the degree of specialization in crafts and commerce, at least as reflected in the three detailed tax registers for the city, increased steadily. The first tax registration of the city *c.* 1535 indicates the occupations of 18 individuals out of 127 registered adult males (106 heads of household, and 21 bachelors). The overwhelming majority of those 18 (16 to be precise) had non-artisanal occupations directly related to Ibrahim Pasha's pious endowment and the mosque and the school that were part of the endowment: 1 preacher (*hatib*), 1 prayer leader (*imam*), 1 teacher (*mu'allim*), 1 student in the school (*halife*), 2 Qur'an memorizers (*hafiz*es) and 2 assistant *hafiz*es (*şagird-hafiz*), 2 *müezzin*s, 1 *mu'arrif*, 2 preachers (*vaiz*es), 2 collectors of the *waqf* revenues (*cabi*), and 1 scribe (*katib*). Only two are

[72] Heath Lowry has argued that information about an urban taxpayer's professional occupation was "useful in identifying those who were newcomers to the city," *Islamization and Turkification*, 111. However, there is no definite proof that such references uniformly pointed to one's newcomer status or that such information would be entered in tax registers only for that reason.

[73] Eran Fraenkel, "Skopje from the Serbian to Ottoman Empires: Conditions for the Appearance of a Balkan Muslim City," Ph.D. diss., The University of Pennsylvania, 1986, 68–82, 103–106.

[74] Ö.L. Barkan, "'Tarihi Demografi' Araştırmaları ve Osmanlı Tarihi," *TM* 10 (1951-3), 25–26.

[75] Heath Lowry, "Portrait of a City: The Population and Topography of Ottoman Selanik (Thessaloniki) in the Year 1478," *Diptycha* 2 (1980–1), 280–289.

identified with typical socio-economic (and non-religious) activities: 1 camel-drover (*deveci*) and 1 tanner (*debbağ*).[76] This does not necessarily mean that none of the other registered male residents had artisanal occupations, or were agriculturalists, as is sometimes assumed when artisanal occupations are not specified. Yet, in comparison to other Ottoman cities at the time, as well as to Hezargrad's later tax registrations, the *c.* 1535 register suggests that the newly established village-cum-town was largely organized around Ibrahim Pasha's mosque complex and that its economic activity was most probably still largely agrarian. This is also confirmed by the tax-revenue breakdown. While it is not possible to analyze it precisely, as in this specific register Hezargrad was listed, by aberration, together with the neighboring Christian village of Kayacık, the tax revenues typical of an urban center – the tax (de facto rent) on small shops (*dekakin*), the market tax (*bac-ı bazar*), and the tax on the town bath (part of the pious endowment) – constituted only around 13 percent of the total tax revenue for the two settlements taken together.[77] However, the very reference to the market tax and tax rent extracted from shops does show that New Hezargrad already had a functioning marketplace (thus satisfying the second condition for attaining urban status beyond having a Friday mosque) and a nascent artisanal class.

The tax registers of *c.* 1550 and 1579 show steady progress in Hezargrad's transformation into a typical urban center. While according to the register of *c.* 1550 the number of those with professional occupations related to religio-legal and administrative duties remained stable – 16 (already including a *subaşı*, a military town superintendent, and two *kethüda*s, guild, or possibly, town wardens), the number of residents associated with artisanal occupations has increased dramatically to 21, including such jobs as butcher (*kassab*), cook (*tabbah*), tinsmith (*kalaycı*), saddler (*sarrac*), tailor (*hayyat*), cotton-fluffer (*hallac*), candle-maker (*mumcu*), town crier (*dellal*), porter (*hammal*), as well as one shepherd (*çoban*) – butchers and cooks accounting for half of those with specified artisanal occupations.[78] It should also be noted that some of these are not listed as artisans themselves, but rather as sons of such (e.g. "*Hüseyin, veled-i kassab,*" "*Kasım, veled-i hallac,*"),[79] which is ambiguous, but may suggest that the developing town was attracting members of artisanal families who possessed much-needed skills. In 1579, the number of those with listed professional occupations had risen to 56 (out of 265 registered), with 26 having administrative, military or religio-legal

[76] NBKM OAK 217/8, ff. 11a–11b, *TIBI*, vol. 3, 441–442.
[77] NBKM OAK 217/8, ff. 14a, *TIBI*, vol. 3, 445.
[78] BOA TD 382, pp. 846–849.
[79] Ibid., p. 848.

occupations, and 30 residents listed as occupied with crafts and trade. In addition to the artisanal occupations already listed in the 1550 register, the one from 1579 testifies to the presence of six tanners (*debbağ*), the most numerous artisanal group, a cobbler (*başmakçı*), a shoemaker (*pabuççu*), a sweet-maker (*helvacı*), two horse-saddle makers (*semerci*), and three soapmakers (*sabuni*), etc.[80]

The tax revenue summaries in the two registers confirm this trend. In 1550, tax revenue from typically urban economic activities, such as the market tax (*mukata'a-i ihtisab ve ihzar ve bac-ı bazar*), the rent from small shops (*mukata'a-i kira-i dekakin*), the revenue from the town bath (*mukata'a-i hammam*), and that from the *tuzhane* (a salt production or storage facility) accounted for 60 percent of the town's total tax revenue (15,737 out of 26,130 *akçe*). The revenue from market tax and the rent on artisan shops combined increased more than six times in comparison to *c.* 1535.[81] In 1579, the same taxes accounted for 69 percent of the town's total tax revenue (22,260 out of 32,476 *akçe*).[82] The two registers mention a functioning soup kitchen (*imaret*) not explicitly mentioned in the foundation charter of Ibrahim Pasha's *waqf*. In both the *c.* 1550 and 1579 tax registers, it is explicitly stipulated that the operation of the town market followed the market regulations of Shumnu.[83] This situation was clearly temporary, reflecting the fact that Hezargrad was a new and rapidly developing urban center – towns with long-lived urban traditions would normally have their own, town-specific market regulations that reflected the specificity of the town's economy and that of its hinterland. This was not yet the case with Hezargrad, and it was likely for this reason that its market was assigned to follow the regulations for Shumnu's market, located in the same geographic region and subject to similar economic and social conditions.

A version of the market regulations for Shumnu (*kanun-ı bac-ı bazar-ı Şumnu*) from this period, tentatively dated as of the last two decades of Süleyman's reign and contained in a collection of Ottoman laws compiled in the second half of the sixteenth century,[84] allows for an additional glimpse at the kind of goods that were mostly produced in urban

---

[80] TKG KK TTd 411, ff. 43b–44b.
[81] BOA TD 382, p. 850.
[82] TKG KK TTd 411, f. 44b
[83] "*Mezbūr nefs-i Hezārgrādıñ bāc-ı bāzārı kānūnu nefs-i Şumnu kānūnu üzeredir,*" BOA TD 382, p. 850, TKG KK TTd 411, f. 44b.
[84] This collection contains a number of town-specific market regulations for the northern Balkans and is preserved in Bibliothèque Nationale de France, Fond Turc No. 85, ff. 118 a-b. I have utilized the Bulgarian translation by Bistra Cvetkova published in *Turski izvori za istoriiata na pravoto v bălgarskite zemi/Fontes Turcici Historiae Iuris Bulgarici* (Sofia: BAN, 1971), vol. 2, 35–36.

centers in Deliorman and their hinterlands and traded at the local town markets. This document exactly comports with the stipulations of the 1550 and 1579 tax registers as it explicitly specifies that the marketplace law for Shumnu should be applied in the town (*kasaba*) of Hezargrad as well. While it mentions numerous agricultural commodities such as fruits and vegetables, cereals, honey and related products, it also places a distinct emphasis on the trade of sheep, milk products, and sheep hides. These stipulations, not necessarily present in the contemporary market regulations for other Balkan towns (contained in the same collection), reflect the pre-eminence of sheep breeding in the local economy, which relates to the recent influx of settlers in the countryside for whom sheep breeding was a major subsistence pattern.[85] Importantly too, the marketplace regulations stipulated dues to be levied on the sale of slaves, which suggests that the freed slaves registered in Hezargrad (and Shumnu) were not necessarily brought by their (former) owners from afar, but might have been acquired at the local market.[86]

Thus, by the late sixteenth century, Hezargrad had grown into a major regional (Sunni) Islamic urban center, with well-established religious institutions as well as trade and crafts. It already possessed a certain strategic importance and renown, sufficient that one of Sultan Mehmed III's (1595–1603) viziers, Hızır Pasha, is reported by the prominent seventeenth-century Ottoman historian Peçevi as having been sent on military campaigns to ensure the protection of "Hezargrad and the Danubian shore."[87] This must have been the vision of its founder, Ibrahim Pasha, who, by establishing his pious endowment, provided for the emergence and development of an outpost of Ottoman imperial authority as well as Sunni orthodoxy in a province undergoing a process of rapid repopulation that also entailed the influx of heterodox colonizers in the surrounding countryside.

5.3   The Growth and Transformation of Shumnu (Shumen) into an Ottoman Town

The case of Shumnu, the other main urban center in the region, differs greatly from that of Hezargrad. Situated at the foot of the Shumen plateau, 15–20km north of the Balkan range and around 40km southeast of Hezargrad, it was a well-developed medieval Bulgarian city at the time of

---

[85] Ibid., 35–36.

[86] Ibid., 36.

[87] "...*ve bir kaç def'a Hezârgrâd ṭarâfına ve Ṭūnā yalıları muḥâfaẓasına ta'yīn olunmuş idi*," Peçevi İbrahim Efendi, *Tarih-i Peçevi* (Istanbul: Enderun Kitabevi, 1982), Book Two, 286.

the Ottoman conquest. Having been settled for more than 5,000 years, the site up the plateau hosted at least six fortresses in different periods before the mid-fifteenth century, the first of them a Thracian stronghold from the fifth to the second century BC.[88] When the whole region was conquered by the Romans in the first century AD, the site was reconstructed as a Roman fortress that existed until the fourth century when it was destroyed by Gothic invasions.[89] It was in this period that the fortress acquired a lasting strategic importance as a major fortified point on the road from Byzantion (later Constantinople) to Odessos (Varna), close to the Balkan passes and controlling entry into the Roman province of Moesia Interior.[90] Restored in the late fifth/early sixth centuries as a Byzantine fortress, it was once again destroyed by Slav and Bulgar invasions in the late sixth and seventh centuries, after which it lost its importance, only to be reconstructed as a major fortress in the First Bulgarian Kingdom (681–1018) in the ninth and tenth centuries.[91] The only mention of the town under later Byzantine rule (1018–1185) comes from the mid-twelfth-century Arab geographer al-Idrisi who points to it as a populous and prosperous city under the name Myssionis.[92] It was as a part of the Second Bulgarian Kingdom (1185–1393) that it acquired the characteristics of a well-developed medieval town, with the hilltop fortress restored again and a distinct *suburbium* developing below it. Archaeological excavations have suggested the existence of a number of churches, as well as well-developed crafts, especially metallurgy and pot making.[93] An extant inscription from the reign of the last medieval ruler of central Bulgaria, John Shishman (r. 1371–93), provides the earliest mention of the town by the name of "Shumen" and specifies that the latter was a *grad* (i.e. a fortified urban center), thus confirming that the town's name indeed pre-dates the Ottomans.[94] The late fifteenth-/early sixteenth-century Ottoman chroniclers Mehmed Neşri, Ruhi Çelebi, and Idris-i Bitlisi refer to Shumnu as one of the fortresses in northern Bulgaria that surrendered without resistance to Çandarlı Ali Pasha in his 1388 campaign.[95] The fortress, reinforced by an Ottoman garrison, must have retained its importance, for it was one of the major strongholds

---

[88] Vera Antonova, *Shumen i shumenskata krepost* (Shumen: Antos, 1995), 14–16.
[89] Ibid., 16–17.
[90] Ibid., 16.
[91] Ibid., 20–28.
[92] Nedkov, *Bâlgariia i sâsednite i zemi*, 82–83.
[93] Antonova, *Shumen*, 82–116.
[94] Ibid., 10, 110–112.
[95] All three Ottoman chroniclers refer explicitly to the peaceful surrender of Shumnu, using the trope of "bringing the key to the fortress" (*Şumnu'nuŋ kilidi, Şumn kal'asınıñ kilidi, miftah-ı kal'a*) to 'Alī Pasha. Neşrî, *Cihânnümâ*, 104; *Ruhi Tarihi*, ed. Halil Erdoğan Cengiz and Yaşar Yücel, *Belleten* 14 (1989–1992), 390; İdrīs-i Bitlīsī, *Heşt Bihişt*, ed. M.

destroyed by the Christian army during the Crusade of Varna in 1444. The anonymous *Gazavat-ı Sultan Murad bin Sultan Mehmed Han* ("The Holy Wars of Sultan Murad, Son of Sultan Mehmed Khan") from the late fifteenth century devotes a separate section to the crusaders' siege of "Shumlu," and praises the fortress garrison which fought bravely against the infidels, but surrendered in the end amidst heavy cannon bombardment, whereby much of the Muslim population of the town was decimated or carried away in slavery.[96] The poem authored by the crusader Michel Beheim appears largely in tune with the *Gazavat*; it stresses that the castle of "Schemle" "lay upon a cliff and a mountain and no ordinary equipment could easily conquer it," only a "special effort" including the extensive use of cannon over several days could bring the siege to a successful end.[97]

The destruction of the fortress in 1444 must have been a veritable turning point in Shumnu's history. It lost its strategic importance as a major fortified point. As most of the fortified town's population perished in the siege, any survivors as well as new settlers would settle down below the plateau, which led to the de facto formation of a new settlement in close proximity to the former fortress. This situation had not changed much as late as the mid-seventeenth century when Evliya Çelebi described the fortress, or more precisely its ruins, as being abandoned and decaying, while the lower city was well developed and prosperous.[98] Thus, any continuity between the medieval Bulgarian urban tradition and Ottoman-era developments at the site was largely lost, save for the town's name. Shumnu would be rebuilt as an Ottoman town. It would play a role as a major fortress again only in the eighteenth century, with the emergence of the Russian threat to the Ottoman Balkans.[99]

In Ottoman administrative documents, Shumnu appears for the first time in two synoptic (*icmal*) tax register fragments from 1479 and the

---

Karataş, S. Kaya, and Y. Baş, vol. 1 (Ankara: BETAV, 2008), 377. See also Kiel, "Mevlana Neşrî and the Towns of Medieval Bulgaria," 175.

[96] *Gazavât-ı Sultân Murâd b. Mehemmed Hân: İzladi ve Varna Savaşları (1443–1444) Üzerinde Anonim Bir Gazavâtnâme*, ed. Halil İnalcık and Mevlud Oğuz (Ankara: Türk Tarih Kurumu, 1989), 52–54; English translation in Colin Imber, ed. and trans., *The Crusade of Varna, 1443–1445* (Aldershot: Ashgate, 2006), 88–89, 103.

[97] English translation by Imber, *The Crusade of Varna*, 173–174.

[98] *Evliyâ Çelebi Seyahatnâmesi*, vol. 3, 178–179; the Catholic bishop Peter Bogdan Bakšić who visited Shumnu in 1640 also noted that the city had no walls at the time, *Acta Bulgariae Ecclesiastica (ab A. 1565 usque ad a. 1799)*, ed. E. Fermendžin (Zagreb, 1887), 77.

[99] Osman Köksal, *XIX. Yüzyılda Bir Osmanlı Ordugah Kasabası Şumnu* (Ankara: Araştırma Yayınları, 2006), 54–61.

mid-1480s, respectively.[100] In the first one, it is registered as a center of a *vilayet*, a territorial-administrative unit within the province (*sancak*) of Niğbolu.[101] It is also the seat of a *ze'amet*, a revenue grant usually allotted to mid-ranking provincial military and administrative officers; in this case the *za'im* was a certain Yakub Çelebi, son of Çuhadar. The town's registered population was overwhelmingly Christian: 11 adult Muslim men, 74 adult Christian men as well as 5 Christian widows.[102] While the tax register is synoptic, providing few details about the professional occupation of Shumnu's residents or its tax structure, the entry suggests that the town's Muslims (listed as a single community/neighborhood) mostly performed military and administrative functions. It refers to five armed soldiers (*cebellü*) and another retainer (*gulam*) of the *za'im* who had to march with him on campaigns. In addition, it lists a *timar* assigned to a certain Oruçhan, son of Umur, *ser'asker* (military commander) of Shumnu, who had to participate in military campaigns with one armed retainer.[103]

The synoptic register from the mid-1480s gives a more precise picture of Shumnu's population and also demonstrates that its Muslim population had increased considerably. Again the center of a *ze'amet*, the town is registered with one imam, 7 regular Muslim households, 11 (Muslim) households of *sipahi*s (cavalrymen), *yürük*s, *güreci*s and others, together with 26 Muslim bachelors, the extraordinarily high proportion of Muslim bachelors suggesting that many of these might have been newcomers – a basis for rapid demographic growth of the Muslim population in the near future. The presence of residents of semi-nomadic origin such as *yürük*s and *güreci*s can be seen as a part of the general process of their migration into the region and gradual sedentarization. The Christian population of the town numbered 68 male heads of household, 15 bachelors, and one

---

[100] NBKM OAK 45/29, dated *ca.* 1479 and NBKM Nk 12/9, dated mid-1480s. The fully preserved synoptic TSMA D 167 of 1512, based on the register from the mid-1480s (NBKM Nk 12/9) makes it possible to verify the reliability of the data in the two late fifteenth-century fragments.

[101] As already mentioned, the Ottoman system of administrative divisions was not standardized until the mid-sixteenth century at the earliest, when the usual division of the Ottoman provinces *beylerbeyilik/eyālet, sancak, każā, nāḥiye* became customary. In fifteenth-century Ottoman bureaucratic practice, terms denoting provincial territorial units below the *sancak* level, such as *nāḥiye, każā, vilāyet*, etc. are often used vaguely and interchangeably. They are sometimes mixed up with fiscal revenue units, such as *ze'āmet*s. For a discussion of this issue based on a case study of a province in Ottoman Anatolia, see Özel, "The Transformation."

[102] NBKM OAK 45/29, f. 20a, also published in *TIBI*, vol. 2, 199. This register does not point to the marital status of registered men, so it is hard to make a reliable estimate about the total population of the town, yet it must have been around 250–450 people.

[103] NBKM OAK 45/29, f. 20a, *TIBI*, vol. 2, 201.

widow with her household.[104] For the first time, this register attests to the presence of a *kadı* (judge) in Shumnu[105] and an imam. Thus, in the mid-1480s the population of Shumnu must have comprised around 400–500 souls, of whom around 25–30 percent were Muslims, with a potential for rapid growth of the town's Muslim community. Importantly, it already had a judge (*kadı*) and a prayer leader (*imam*) to serve the rapidly growing Muslim population and very likely possessed a congregational mosque.

The development of Shumnu as a rapidly growing urban center with a quickly increasing Muslim population is further attested by the synoptic tax register from 1530, likely based on data from 1516, which lists the town as a part of the sultan's domains (*hassha-i padişah*) and the seat of a *kaza* (judgeship). The Muslim population had grown dramatically compared to the mid-1480s – up to 94 Muslim households and 41 bachelors. Shumnu's Muslim population still constituted a single neighborhood, which had its own imam, *müezzin*, and a *kayyum* (a caretaker of a mosque) which may be seen as a confirmation of the existence of a congregational mosque. Among the town's registered Muslim inhabitants there were also four sons of *sipahi*s, and seven residents of semi-nomadic Turcoman origin (*ellici*s and *güreci*s) who had settled and performed military-related duties in exchange for tax privileges. The still unitary Christian community had also expanded, to 107 households and 25 bachelors, but it was already only slightly more numerous than the Muslim citizenry. The town's population as a whole had grown to around 900 inhabitants.[106]

For the rest of the sixteenth century, we have at our disposal the detailed Ottoman tax registrations of *c.* 1535, *c.* 1550, and 1579 that shed more light on Shumnu's demographic and socio-economic development, as well as on the religious identity of its inhabitants.

In *c.* 1535, Shumnu already had 5 *mahalles*. Four of them were Muslim: Mahalle-i Cami' (the Mosque neighborhood), Mahalle-i Söğüd Pınarı (the Willow Spring neighborhood), Mahalle-i Eski Pazar (the Old Market quarter), and Mahalle-i Yolcu.[107] The non-Muslims (Orthodox

---

[104] Most of Shumnu's population in the 1480s was part of the *ze'āmet* of Shumnu, but a small portion of it – 4 Muslim households, 11 (Muslim) bachelors, and the *imām* – pertained to a separate *tīmār* held by a *sipāhī*, see NBKM Nk 12/9, f 30a, 31 a. These population figures are confirmed by the fully preserved TSMA D 167, ff. 58 a-b.

[105] Via a reference to a *tīmār*, which entitled the judge to the tax revenue of the nearby village of Ravna (or rather *Ravna-i Diğer*, "the other Ravna," as there were two villages of the same name close to one other), NBKM Nk 12/9, f. 35 b. According to the register of 1512, the judge of Shumnu had a different *tīmār* holding and was entitled to the tax revenue of the village of Çeraşoviçe and the *mezra'a* of Kaluger, with an income of 3,296 *akçe* – slightly larger than his income in the 1480s. TSMA D 167, f. 59 b.

[106] BOA TD 370, p. 549.

[107] BOA TD 439, pp. 157–160. The reading of "Yolcu" is debatable, but it is most likely a certain Yolcu Ḫıżır 'Abidīn (quite possibly a convert) registered as *pīr-i fānī* ("a saintly old man") and enjoying certain tax exemptions, who was the founder of the neighborhood, BOA TD 439, p. 159.

Table 5.2 *The population of Shumnu in the late fifteenth and early sixteenth centuries*

| Year | Muslims, a single Muslim community | | | | Non-Muslims (*Gebran*), a single Orthodox Christian community | | |
	Households (regular) (*Hane*)	Households (other)	Households (total)	Bachelors (*mücerred*)	Households (regular) (*Hane*)	Widows (*bive*)	Bachelors (*mücerred*)
1479	11	–	11	–	74	5	–
Mid-1480s	7	12	19	26	68	1	15
1516	84	9	93	41	107	–	45

Christians) resided in a single "infidel" neighborhood (Mahalle-i Gebran).[108] The tax survey of *c.* 1535 is the first one which shows Shumnu as having a majority of Muslim residents: out of 239 heads of household registered, 132 are Muslim (with 40 of those householders having some special taxation status related to performing administrative, religio-legal, or military service). The survey shows a total of 107 (Orthodox) Christian households (of whom 13 paid their taxes to Sultan Bayezid II's *waqf* in Edirne); thus, 1535 Shumnu likely had had a population of 1250–1300 souls, with a Muslim majority of around 55 percent.[109]

Like Hezargrad, by the mid-sixteenth century the town's Muslim population had nearly doubled, rising to a total of 258 households (of which 31 enjoyed tax privileges related to their special status) residing in five neighborhoods.[110] The Christian population, on the other hand, had risen only by around 50 percent (up to 152 households), a hefty increase that fits the general rapid population growth in the region, but does not match that of the town's Muslim community. Among the 152 Orthodox Christian heads of household registered in 1550, eight were denoted as *prişeleç* (i.e. strangers who have recently come from elsewhere), as compared to only two in the previous registration.[111] Remarkably, while the high percentage of Muslim bachelors persisted and intensified (reaching 33 percent of all registered Muslims), the percentage of Christian unmarried men, as compared to only 15 years earlier, sky-rocketed as well, to around 37 percent of all registered Christian taxpayers.

Such an increase can be explained by a sharp increase in the birth rates among both Muslims and Christians and/or (more likely) by an influx of residents from villages in the vicinity of Shumnu, from other regions in the Balkans (especially from Thrace), or from Anatolia. While the *c.* 1535 register explicitly mentions only two residents who originated from Anatolia, *c.* 1550 their number was seven, to which one may add two more: one registered as "İstanbullu" (i.e. coming from Istanbul) and his manumitted slave (*mu'tak-ı İstanbullu*). The high proportion of bachelors suggests that the town offered attractive opportunities to young men in the surrounding countryside (or from farther away).

Shumnu's last sixteenth-century registration (1579), confirms the already established parallel to Hezargrad in terms of general demographic growth. While the number of Muslim neighborhoods had increased from five to seven, the size of the city had increased only very slightly, with the percentage of bachelors continuing to be high

---

[108] BOA TD 439, pp. 160–161.
[109] Ibid., pp. 157–161.
[110] BOA TD 382, pp. 380–383.
[111] Ibid., pp. 383–385.

Table 5.3 *The population of Shumnu in the mid-sixteenth century*

Neighborhood (Mahalle)	Muslims					Non-Muslims (Gebran)					
	Households (regular) (Hane)	Households (other)	Households (total)	Bachelors (müicerred)	Total Registered (Muslims)	Households (regular) (Hane)	Households (other)	Households (total)	Widows (bive)	Bachelors (müicerred)	Total Registered (Non-Muslims)
C. 1535											
Cami'	13	5	18	8	26	–	–	–	–	–	–
Söğüd Pınarı	28	10	38	21	59	–	–	–	–	–	–
Eski Pazar	22	1	23	8	31	–	–	–	–	–	–
Yolcu	27	8	35	26	61	–	–	–	–	–	–
Non-Muslims	–	–	–	–	–	92	15	107	0	20	127
Total (1535)	**90**	**24**	**114**	**63**	**177**	**92**	**15**	**107**	**0**	**20**	**127**
C. 1550											
Cami'-i Şerif	55	3	58	29	87	–	–	–	–	–	–
Söğüdlü Pınarı	34	5	39	24	63	–	–	–	–	–	–
Eski Pazar	45	6	51	19	70	–	–	–	–	–	–
Yolcu	62	10	72	30	102	–	–	–	–	–	–
Veli Kadı	31	7	38	24	62	–	–	–	–	–	–
Non-Muslims	–	–	–	–	–	119	33	152	0	90	242
Total (1550)	**227**	**31**	**258**	**126**	**384**	**119**	**33**	**152**	**0**	**90**	**242**

(in both communities). An interesting development is the appearance of a small community of *Latinan* (Catholics) – most probably Ragusan merchants – a fact suggestive of the town's growing importance as a commercial center.[112]

The record of Shumnu's demographic development points to two demographic explosions which directly affected its socio-economic development and status as an urban center. The first such explosion must have happened sometime between the 1480s and 1516 and reflects above all the dramatic growth of the town's Muslim community. As discussed below, this expansion may have been the result of sizable infrastructural investment which aimed at Shumnu's further development as an Ottoman and Islamic city upon the ashes of the old medieval Bulgarian fortified city taken over by the Ottomans in the late fourteenth century and destroyed by the crusaders in 1444. The second demographic upheaval that took place in the mid-sixteenth century and correlates reasonably to similar developments in Hezargrad, could be attributed to the massive repopulation of Deliorman (and the adjacent regions) in the first half of the century and also fits well with the overall rapid demographic growth in the Empire at large (and in the Mediterranean world in general) and the even more spectacular growth of most Ottoman cities in particular. Increased migration rates from the countryside to urban centers likely played a prominent role too – this dimension, however, necessitates further research in the context of empire-wide demographic developments.

5.3.1   The Socio-Economic Development of Shumnu

Shumnu's socio-economic development from the late fifteenth through the sixteenth centuries closely reflected, and interacted in many ways with the town's demographic growth. While the synoptic nature of the extant tax registers before *c.* 1535 generally precludes a detailed analysis of the town's socio-economic development in that period, the one dated 1530 and containing information from 1516 does refer to the existence of substantial urban property as a part of Yahya Pasha's pious endowment dedicated to the upkeep of an *imaret* (soup kitchen) in Üsküb (Skopje).[113] Having been authorized by Bayezid II's *firman* in AH 911/AD 1505, Yahya Pasha – one of the great statesmen and military commanders during the reign of Bayezid II (1481–1512) – drew

---

[112] TKG KK TTd 151, ff. 165b–167b. The presence of Ragusan merchants is attested by bishops Peter Bogdan Bakšić and Philip Stanislavov several decades later when they visited Shumnu in 1640 and 1653, respectively, *Acta Bulgariae Ecclesiastica*, 77, 263.

[113] BOA TD 370, p. 555.

up the endowment's foundation charter and thus established the *waqf* in AH 912/AD 1506 for the upkeep of the mosque complex he had recently built in Skopje, that included a mosque, a soup kitchen, and a college (*medrese*).[114] What is important for the present discussion of Shumnu's urban development is that the numerous properties in the town that the donor had endowed for the said purpose, as duly listed in both documents, included a town bath (*hammam*), a nearby soap factory (*sabun-hane*), a vineyard and a garden which the pasha had recently bought from the former judge of Yenice-i Vardar (mod. Giannitsa, Greece), a certain Mevlana Sinan Çelebi.[115] The *firman* of 1505 explicitly refers to Shumnu as a *kasaba*, i.e. a small-to-mid-sized Ottoman town. The construction of the town bath and the soap factory, closely related to the requirements of Islamic ritual practice, must have happened around the turn of the sixteenth century, and may be seen as related to Shumnu's overall development as an Ottoman and Islamic urban center, which, as the two earlier tax registers (from 1479 and the mid-1480s) have shown, had started in the closing decades of the preceding century. The 1516 registration refers to 57 small artisan shops (*dekakin*), a storehouse (*başhane*), a *bozahane*, and a *kervansaray* as part of the same endowment, generating a total yearly revenue of 3,500 *akçe*.[116] The shops, not mentioned in the endowment's foundation charter, may have been constructed after 1506. The references to the properties of Yahya Pasha's pious endowment in Shumnu from 1505, 1506, and 1516, respectively, attest to substantial investment in the construction of urban property in the town and its rapid transformation into a typical Ottoman Islamic city. This case provides a pertinent example of the role which a *waqf* could play in a town's development even when the revenue generated by that property was not reserved for the upkeep of religious, educational, or social institutions in that same town (as was the case, for example, with Ibrahim Pasha's *waqf* in Hezargrad).

---

[114] Both the 1505 edict (*fermān*) and the 1506 endowment foundation charter (*vakıfnāme*) are available in heavily annotated Serbian translation in G. Elezović, ed. and trans, *Turski Spomenici* (Belgrade, Srpska Kraljevska Akademija, 1940), Vol. 1, Pt. 1; *firmān*, 384–411; *vakıfname*, 420–525, see esp. p. 430. The *fermān* is also available in facsimile, ibid., Vol. 1, Pt. 2 (Belgrade, 1952), 120–123. On Yahyā Pasha, who earned his fame as a governor of Bosnia and Bayezid II's vizier and son-in-law, see Hedda Reindl, *Männer um Bayezid: eine prosopographische Studie über die Epoche Sultan Bayezids II (1481–1512)* (Berlin: Klaus Schwarz, 1983), 336–345.

[115] Elezović, *Turski Spomenici*, Vol 1, Pt. 1, 396, 444. Yahyā Pasha's endowment included numerous urban properties in Balkan cities such as Filibe (Plovdiv), Sofya (Sofia), Niğbolu (Nikopol), and Istanbul.

[116] BOA TD 370, p. 555.

The tax registers from *c.* 1535 and *c.* 1550 do not provide further information about Yahya Pasha's *waqf*'s properties in Shumnu, but they shed some light on the town's social structure. All in all, mid-sixteenth-century Shumnu had a less pronounced "urban" profile compared to Hezargrad, with a smaller proportion of its registered taxpayers being explicitly registered as holding administrative, religio-legal, military, or artisanal occupations. *Circa* 1535, only 17 registered Muslims had occupations related to religio-legal and administrative duties, among them the mosque staff: the *imam* (listed as a *hatib* as well), a *müezzin*, and a *kayyum* (a mosque caretaker), as well as a teacher (*mu'allim*) at the *medrese* with two students (*talib-i 'ilm*). To these one should add four descendants of the Prophet (*seyyids* and *sherifs*) and one who had performed the Hajj to Mecca (*hacı*), likely seen as a part of the town elite. Among Shumnu's administrative officers one counts a *kethüda-i şehr* (city warden), two market inspectors (*muhtesib*) and two tax-collectors (*muhassıl*); the town bath (*hammam*) also had its masseur (*dellak*).[117] This situation had not changed much some fifteen years later, though one should note the appearance of a *tekye* (dervish convent), as well as the presence of deputy judge (*naib*), a pious endowment administrator (*mütevelli*) and a fortress commander (*dizdar*). The existence of the last two is somewhat difficult to account for as the available sources do not testify to the existence of pious endowments centered in the town (although there were some in villages around Shumnu), and there are also no indications that the fortress (destroyed in 1444) had been restored at the time, but the mention of a *dizdar* may refer to a military commander of a different kind.

The presence of residents explicitly associated with artisanal and trade occupations is also much less pronounced than in Hezargrad. While one observes a significant diversity of occupations, only nine residents are explicitly associated with crafts and trade *c.* 1535, and only ten *c.* 1550. Among the artisans in Shumnu at that time were carpenters (*marangoz*), tanners (*debbağ*), saddle-makers (*sarrac*), a blacksmith (*ahenger*), tailors (*hayyat*), a shoe-maker (*başmakçı*), and a felt-maker (*keçeci*). The structure of Shumnu's tax revenue in the mid-sixteenth century seems to confirm this and suggests that agriculture dominated the town's economy, with the market tax (*bac-ı bazar*) the only typical "urban" tax levied, accounting for less than one fifth of the town's revenues.[118] It should be noted, however, that the mid-sixteenth century registers discussed here do not make mention of *waqf* property in the town and the taxes levied on it.

[117] BOA TD 439, pp. 157–160.
[118] BOA TD 439, p. 161; BOA TD 382, p. 386.

5.4   The Decline of Chernovi (Cherven)

The case of Ottoman Chernovi, or Cherven, as was its original medieval Bulgarian name, represents yet another distinct model of historical development of Balkan towns during the early centuries of Ottoman rule. Situated on the Ak Lom river, roughly halfway between Hezargrad and Rus, it was one of the most important economic, political, and cultural centers in medieval Bulgaria at the time it was conquered by the Ottomans in 1388.

Like most other towns in the northeastern Balkans, Cherven is not often mentioned in medieval historical sources, but large-scale archaeological excavations in the 1960s allow a relatively reliable reconstruction of its history up to the late fourteenth century.

Archaeologists established that the site had been inhabited since antiquity and through the Middle Ages – first by the Thracians, and later, during the early medieval period, when a Byzantine citadel was built, most probably as part of Justinian I's efforts to curb barbarian invasions from the north.[119] The fortress was later utilized during the epoch of the First Bulgarian Kingdom (681–1018), although the extant narrative sources do not mention the city.[120] While it might have further developed during the years of Byzantine control (1018–1185), and some medieval Bulgarian apocryphal sources confirm its existence as of the mid-eleventh century,[121] it was during the period of the Second Bulgarian Kingdom (1185–1393) that Cherven dramatically rose in importance, most likely due to its strategic location on important roads that connected Turnovo, the capital of the restored Bulgarian state in north central Bulgaria, with the Black Sea coast and the Danubian shore,[122] and thanks to its lofty status as an archepiscopal seat, a status that it would retain till the mid-seventeenth century.[123]

---

[119] Sonia Georgieva, "Srednovekovniiat grad Cherven. Problemi i prouchvaniia," *IAI* 33 (1972), 311.

[120] Ibid., 312.

[121] Specifically in the "Vision of Prophet Isaiah," see *Khristomatiia po istoriia na Bâlgariia*, ed. P. Petrov and V. Giuzelev, vol. 1 (Sofia, 1978), 443.

[122] Georgieva, "Srednivekovniiat grad Cherven," 313 (see the reference to Škorpil on same page).

[123] A late fourteenth-century recension of "The Synodic of Tsar Boril" explicitly refers to three archbishops of Cherven, M.G. Popruzhenko, *Sinodik Tsaria Borila* (Sofia, 1928), 92. The Synodic was composed in 1211, in relation to the anti-Bogomil church council summoned by the Bulgarian Tsar Boril (r. 1207–1218); the recension published by Popruzhenko should be dated shortly after the fall of Turnovo in 1393, as its eulogy section ends with the names of a number of late fourteenth-century figures in Bulgarian political and ecclesiastic history, such as the last patriarchs of Turnovo, as well as Kera Tamara, Tsar John Alexander's daughter who was given in marriage to Murad I (who appears as "Amourat") in the late 1360s, Popruzhenko, *Sinodik*, 90–92.

Late medieval Cherven consisted of a citadel complex which included two monumental churches and housed the city's lord, most likely the archbishop himself, and a lower city, both parts surrounded by a wall.[124] It was a well-developed center of crafts in the thirteenth and fourteenth centuries, especially known for its blacksmiths.[125] Noted for its hilly and wooded surroundings, the area around Cherven was a refuge for hermits and sheltered a number of monasteries, which, together with the existence of the fortress complex, well maintained during the thirteenth and fourteenth centuries, suggests some traditions of masonry as well. One such monastery was built in the late 1210s by the future Patriarch Ioachim I of Turnovo (d. 1246), who, having received a large donation from Tsar John II Asen (r. 1218–41), hired masons from the city for the purpose.[126] Thus, Cherven was comparable to Shumnu at the time of the Ottoman conquest, each one of the most important medieval Bulgarian urban centers in the region.

One of the few fortresses in northern Bulgaria taken by force by the Ottomans during Ali Pasha's campaign of 1388, Chernovi, as it became known in Ottoman sources, seems to have lost its importance as a major fortified point in the northeastern Balkans during the first half of the fifteenth century; the fairly rich contemporary sources on the Varna Crusade (1444) make no mention of it. As the Ottoman state was overwhelmed by internal crises and foreign intervention at the time, it could hardly direct resources toward the restoration of a fortress that was likely destroyed at the time of the Ottoman conquest. However, due to its pre-Ottoman standing, Cherven retained its status as an administrative center, as the center of a *vilayet* in the late fifteenth century, and of a *kaza* or *nahiye* in the sixteenth.

The oldest available Ottoman tax registrations for the province of Niğbolu – from 1479 and the mid-1480s – list the town proper as wholly Christian, with no regular Muslim tax-paying population. In 1479, Chernovi appears as the center of a *vilayet* and a *ze'amet*, held by a certain Bali, son of Emir Gazi. The town had 107 male household heads and bachelors.[127] Things had not changed much by the mid-1480s, when

---

[124] On the citadel itself, see Sonia Georgieva and Violeta Dimova, "Zamâkât v srednovekovniia grad Cherven," *IAI* 30 (1967), 5–26.

[125] Archaeological findings suggest that medieval Cherven was a center of metallurgy and iron processing; Lishev, *Bâlgarskiiat Srednovekoven Grad*, 78–79, 81, 94.

[126] See the medieval *Vita* of Patriarch Ioachim, in Ivan Snegarov, "Neizdadeni stârobalgarski zhitiia," *Godishnik na Dukhovnata Akademiia Sv. Kliment Okhridski* 3, no. 19 (1953–1954), 163–167. As will be shown later, there were two monasteries in Cherven's vicinity according to the available Ottoman tax registers.

[127] NBKM OAK 45/29, f. 14b. As mentioned above, this register does not distinguish between heads of household and bachelors.

the town had 97 households and 13 registered bachelors, all of them Christians.[128] Importantly, both registers refer to a functioning market. The late fifteenth-century registers also make a fleeting mention of a Chernovi judge (*kadı*), in relation to his (and/or his son's) efforts to revive a decaying agricultural site nearby in exchange for a certain tax revenue accruing from revived economic activity; he failed in that effort.[129]

Yet, we have clear evidence that as of 1479, and later in the 1480s, the old fortress that stood on a hill above the town had been brought back to operation. The synoptic tax register of 1479 refers to a fortress commander (*dizdar*), a gate keeper (*bevvab*), and one regular garrison member (*merd-i kal'a*); all three were assigned revenue grants (*timars*) in lieu of a salary.[130] In addition, there were 57 *müselleman*, i.e. auxiliary military personnel, stationed in the restored fortress with the task of defending it in case of enemy attack; these troops were exempt from taxes, even if they were engaged in agriculture – most likely their main productive occupation, as they merely enjoyed tax exemptions in exchange for serving at the fortress.[131] The situation had not changed much several years later.[132]

The restoration of the fortress may be dated sometime in the last two decades of Mehmed II's reign, i.e. in the 1460s and 1470s, in the more general context of the restoration of a number of Ottoman Danubian

---

[128] NBKM N/k 12/9, f. 26b.

[129] NBKM OAK 45/29, f. 16a: "*Mezra'a-i Çervena Voda. Ḫāric ez defter olub, Çernovi ḳaḍısı Mevlānā [no name given] şenletmeğe ve bir cebellü virmeğe mültezim olub, bundan gayrü ṭālib olmadığı sebebden, üzerine ḳayd olundu. Bāḳī emr ü fermān Dergāh-ı Mu'allām'ındır.*" NBKM N/k 12/9, f. 29b: "*Mezra'a-i Çero Voda. Ḫāric ez defter olub, bundan evvel Çernovi ḳaḍısıoğlu Meḥmed şenledub, bir cebellü virmeğe mültezim olub, defter-i köhnede ḳayd itdirmiş imiş. Şimdiki ḥālde mezkūr ḳaḍızade ḥuddām olub, ma'lūl düştüğü sebebden, ḥiṣar erliğinden ma'zūl Rūm Ḫıżır oğlu Yūnus nām kimesneye āsitāne vechiyle [?] tezkire virilmiş idi. Gelüb, ḳayd itdirilmedi. Bāḳī fermān Dergāh-ı Mu'allām'ındır.*" Text in TSMA D 167, f. 56a is similar, with tax revenue amount specified as 400 *aḳçe* yearly.

[130] NBKM OAK 45/29 II, ff. 14b-15a. All these were listed as "*Mustaḥfıẓān-ı ḳal'a-yı Çernovi.*"

[131] "*Cemā'at-i müselleman ki ḳal'a-i Çernovi'de otururlar. Düşmān gelicek ḥiṣar erliğini iderler. Cem'-i 'avārıż-ı divaniyyeden mu'āf ü müsellem olagelmişlerdir, ellerinde ḥükm-i hümāyūnları vardır, 'öşr virmezler, eğer zirā'at daḥi iderlerse.*" NBKM OAK 45/29 II, f. 15a. These auxiliary forces are listed as *nefer*, i.e. individuals, without proper reference as to whether they were householders or bachelors. This convention in registering fortress garrison members is often employed in Ottoman bureaucratic practice, as from the point of view of the Ottoman fisc their marital status was inconsequential.

[132] While the NBKM N/k 12/9 fragment does not contain information about the fortress of Çernovi, TSMA D 167 which has been fully preserved and contains the same demographic information as NBKM N/k 12/9, lists a fortress commander, gate-keeper, and, just as the 1479 register fragment does, 57 *müselleman*, with a related text, which is essentially the same as in the 1479 registration, the only substantial difference being that the auxiliary forces at the fortress are listed as residing in the "town" ("*nefs-i Çernovi'de otururlar*"), which appears somewhat vague. The sixteenth-century tax registrations list them explicitly as stationed in the fortress.

fortresses after the disastrous events related to the 1444 Varna Crusade, and also in the aftermath of the Wallachian *voevode* Vlad III Ţepeş' (Dracula) ruinous invasion of the Ottoman province of Niğbolu in 1461–2 and the subsequent campaign led by Mehmed II in Wallachia, which led to Vlad's deposition.[133]

Thus, in addition to the restoration of the nearby fortress, late fifteenth-century Chernovi falls into the dwindling group of Ottoman Balkan cities that had retained their urban status above all on the basis of their importance in the pre-Ottoman period.[134] This sort of distinction was not untypical of the transitional period in the history of the Ottoman Balkans, from the conquest through the first half of the sixteenth century, when some sizable Balkan cities continued their existence without developing significant Muslim communities and the related Islamic urban institutions (in the city proper).

In that sense, Chernovi was very similar to nearby Shumnu and Rus (on the Danube), which still had negligible Muslim communities. It was in the sixteenth century, however, that the development of Ottoman administrative and Islamic urban institutions, or the lack thereof, would prove decisive to the town's stature and the preservation of its urban status.

The beginning of the sixteenth century was marked by an important change in Chernovi's development. For the first time since the earliest extant Ottoman tax registration *c.* 1479, and most probably since the Ottoman conquest more than a century earlier, Chernovi had a regular, tax-paying Muslim population within the town proper. The synoptic register of 1530 (essentially based on 1516 data) lists a small community of regular Muslim taxpayers, consisting of 5 regular households and five bachelors, in addition to the auxiliary forces stationed in the fortress.[135] The Christian community, in turn, had increased by around 50 percent as compared to the late fifteenth century (with 142 regular households, 5 widows and 62 bachelors).[136] The number of auxiliary forces (*müselleman*) stationed at the fortress remained fixed at its 1479/mid-1480s level. They enjoyed the same privileges as previously.[137]

---

[133] *Âşıkpaşazâde Tarihi*, 227–229; Neşrî, *Cihânnümâ*, 305–306. For an overview of these events, see Selâhattin Tansel, *Osmanlı Kaynaklarına Göre Fâtih Sultân Mehmed'in Siyasî ve Askerî Faaliyeti* (Ankara: Türk Tarih Kurumu, 1953), 161–168; Viorel Panaite, *The Ottoman Law of War and Peace: The Ottoman Empire and Tribute Payers* (Boulder: East European Monographs, 2000), 161–162, and the relevant discussion in Chapter 3.

[134] Todorov, *The Balkan City*, 53–55.

[135] BOA TD 370, p. 557.

[136] Ibid., p. 557.

[137] Ibid., p. 557. The text describing the *müselleman*'s duties and privileges is essentially the same as in the tax registrations of 1479 and the mid-1480s.

The three detailed tax registrations for the province of Niğbolu –
from *c.* 1535, *c.* 1550, and 1579 – furnish a lot of evidence about the
actual nature of Chernovi's socio-economic development and the ethno-
religious structure of its population. Several main trends may be outlined
with regard to the town's demographic development.

The size of the auxiliary contingent within the fortress remained stable throughout the century: 57 individuals (*neferan*) in *c.* 1535, 42 in
c. 1550, and 44 in 1579, together with several other (higher-ranking)
military personnel, such as a cannoneer (*topçu*) in *c.* 1550, and a fortress commander (*dizdar*) and a retired *sipahi* (*sipahi-i ma'zul*) in 1579.
All three registrations attest to the presence of an imam and a *müezzin*
who catered to the religious needs of the fortress personnel. There were
no converts to Islam in the fortress, save for one single exception in the
register of *c.* 1535.

On the other hand, the development of the regular, tax-paying Muslim
community that resided outside the fortress, in the town proper, was
quite uneven. While, as already seen, the 1516/1530 registration listed
ten such Muslims (five heads of household and five bachelors), there is
no trace of them in the *c.* 1535 registration. This community reappeared
c. 1550, with 13 household heads and 8 bachelors, and then dwindled to
a total of 9 (7 married men and 2 bachelors) in 1579. Importantly, the
presence of converts to Islam within this group was significant *c.* 1550,
with four converts and one identifiable son of a convert, and dominant
in 1579, when two-thirds of the Muslim residents in the town proper (6
out of 9) were converts.

The Christian population of Chernovi grew dramatically over the sixteenth century, from 142 households in 1516 and 140 *c.* 1535, to 217
c. 1550, and 272 in 1579, with a parallel steady increase in the number
of bachelors. This increase fits the general trend in dramatic population
growth in Balkan cities and in the Empire. The socio-religious cohesion
of the Christian community was reinforced by the presence of at least
two priests (one of whom may have been the town's archbishop), as well
as the existence of two monasteries in close proximity to the town (those
of Saint Michael the Archangel, and Vodine).[138]

Yet, a closer look at the socio-economic development of sixteenth-
century Chernovi, as allowed by the data contained in the three detailed
tax registers, reveals that while its Christian population grew substantially, in reality Chernovi developed the profile of a large (predominantly
Christian) rural settlement. While the respective texts formulating the

---

[138] These monasteries appear registered as *"Manâstır-ı Kilise-i İsveti Arḫangel"* and
"Manâstır-ı Kilise-i Vodine," BOA TD 382, p. 78.

Table 5.4 *The population of Chernovi*

Year	Muslims Fortress Households	Households (other)	Households (total)	Bachelors	Town Households	Bachelors	Christians Town Households	Widows	Bachelors
1479	–	–	–	–	0	0	107	4	Not listed
Mid-1480s	–	–	–	–	0	0	97	3	13
1516	57	1	58	–	5	5	142	5	62
C. 1535	57	–	–	–	Not listed	Not listed	140	0	107
C. 1550	18	3	21	24	13	8	217	0	135
1579	44	5	49	Not listed	7	2	272	0	216

duties and tax-exemption status of the auxiliary *müselleman* unit within the fortress remained similar to those in the earlier (synoptic) registrations, the data from the detailed registers from *c.* 1535, *c.* 1550, and 1579 also point out assertively that the main productive activity of its members was agriculture.[139] For the population of the town proper, that is, both the small Muslim community and the rapidly growing Christian population, the tax breakdown statistics show clearly that agriculture and related activities dominated the town's economy, with viniculture and wine-making (among the Christian community) being the single most important economic occupation.[140] Sixteenth-century Chernovi had no artisanal community of note, nor traces of a functioning market any longer. The formerly prominent, late medieval Bulgarian city was steadily losing its urban profile, it was only the historic inertia of administrative tradition and the functioning fortress nearby that allowed it to barely keep its status as a provincial center.

As Chernovi did not develop a solid and numerous Muslim community in the sixteenth century (in the way Shumnu to the south and Rus[çuk] to the north did), it never developed significant Islamic institutions. The available contemporary administrative sources do not show any existing Islamic pious endowments and related urban institutions (e.g. mosques, *medrese*s, soup kitchens, etc.) and whatever Islamic religious functionaries there were, such as an imam and a *müezzin*, they were stationed in the fortress, catering to the needs of its garrison. The small number of Muslims who lived in the city proper during the sixteenth century seemed to have been largely of local, convert origin, and the emergence of that community was most probably related to the presence of the fortress garrison nearby the town.

Following this trend, Chernovi eventually lost its importance as an urban and administrative center. A 1642–3 tax register mentions the fortress as "*nefs*," but the nearby fully Christian settlement with 79 registered adult males as a village (*karye*).[141] Around the same time (*c.* 1640) the famous Ottoman polymath Katip Çelebi would describe it as "a poor Christian village," with the ruins of the old city standing nearby,[142] while some twenty years later (1659) the Catholic archbishop of Nicopolis (Niğbolu) Filip Stanislavov still mentioned it as a city ("*Cierven civitas*"),

---

[139] As in BOA TD 382, p. 74: "*Cemā'at-i müsellemān ki kal'a-i Çernovi'de otururlar...cem'-i 'avārıż-ı dīvāniyyeden mu'āf ü müsellem olagelmişlerdir, ellerinde ḥükm-i hümāyünları vardır, ve zirā'at itdükleri 'öşrün ve bāğların rüsūmların virmezler deyü, defter-i 'atīkde mukayyed olmağın, ḥāliyā yine ber-karār-ı sabık defter-i cedīde ḳayd olundu.*"

[140] BOA TD 439, pp. 26–27; BOA TD 382, pp. 78–79; TKG KK TTd 151, ff. 29b–30a.

[141] This is an "extraordinary taxes" ('*avārıż*) register, BOA TD 771, pp. 14, 158–159.

[142] Hadschi Chalfa, *Rumeli und Bosna*, 44.

the seat of a bishopric, with two churches and a "schismatic" Bulgarian population numbering around 250 souls.[143] The settlement earned no mention in Evliya Çelebi's monumental travelogue.

Thus, Cherven/Chernovi never "made it" as an Ottoman city. As Katib Çelebi himself noted, the decline of Chernovi was paralleled by the rise of nearby Rus (Rusçuk) on the Danube. The medieval Bulgarian Cherven owed its prominence to its strategic location on major trade routes connecting the capital of the Second Bulgarian Kingdom Turnovo with the Danubian coast and the Black Sea coast (Varna), as well as to its being the seat of an archbishopric. Once medieval Bulgaria was conquered by the Ottomans, Chernovi lost much of the strategic importance it had once had, as Turnovo was no longer a capital and Orthodox Christianity was no longer the formal religion of state in the Balkans. While Rus(çuk) is outside the proper focus of this study, it is worth mentioning that it was an overwhelmingly Christian settlement in the late fifteenth century, with a negligibly small Muslim community, and thus very similar to late fifteenth-century Shumnu and Cherven. Yet, its location on the Danube led to its dramatic growth in the sixteenth century, whereby it gradually became a predominantly Muslim Ottoman city with a strategically important fortress, developed Muslim institutions, and enjoyed vigorous economic growth; all of these factors contributed to the influx of numerous new settlers into the city, both Christian and especially Muslim, with an accordingly substantial presence of converts to Islam. The decline of Chernovi and the parallel rise of Rus(çuk), then, exemplify urban transformation as influenced by the Ottoman conquest and the changes in the strategic military, political, and commercial priorities that Ottoman rule brought about.

5.5   The Rise of Eski Cuma (Cuma-i Atik, mod. Târgovishte)

A discussion on Eski Cuma could indeed be included in the preceding chapter devoted to the rural countryside, as it did not attain urban status until the first half of the seventeenth century. Yet, as it was in the sixteenth century that the settlement, initially a village, gradually attained the trappings of an urban center, it may be appropriate to place the analysis of its growth within the context of urban development in Deliorman and the adjacent regions.

---

[143] "*Episcopalis est. Habet episcopum schismaticum ritus Graeci. Domus Bulgarorum schismatorum 30 et animae 250.... Habent duas ecclesias eiusdem ritus,*" *Acta Bulgariae Ecclesiastica*, 263.

Like Hezargrad, Shumnu, and Chernovi, each of which represents a distinct model of urban development in the fifteenth- and sixteenth-century Ottoman Balkans, Eski Cuma exemplifies yet another distinct model. Hezargrad was de facto a newly established urban center that emerged as the main settlement in Ibrahim Pasha's pious endowment, and Shumnu and Chernovi had the heritage of important medieval fortified towns, one of them being transformed into a predominantly Muslim town, thus retaining its importance, and the other never developing as a true Ottoman urban center. For its part, Eski Cuma was a village established by Muslim colonists, most likely predominantly from Anatolia and Thrace, which underwent vigorous economic growth, centered around a Friday marketplace that raised its status to a center of a *nahiye* (sub-province) in the late sixteenth century and a town (*kasaba*) in the following century. In this sense, it may be viewed as a town that emerged "spontaneously," essentially without the proactive intervention of the Ottoman state (or its high-ranking representatives as in the case of Hezargrad). The connection between a thriving village Friday market which could lead to the idea of the construction of a Friday (congregational) mosque that would serve those who attended the market, thus allowing them to combine trade and worship, has already been discussed in its Ottoman Anatolian context by Suraiya Faroqhi; the existence of the two would thus satisfy the "minimum requirements" for a village's transformation into an urban center and its recognition as such by the Ottoman authorities.[144] This is just what seems to have happened in the case of Eski Cuma.

The modest beginnings of the village may be traced tentatively to the village of Çavuş,[145] which first appeared in the synoptic tax register of 1516/30 as a part of the sub-province (*nahiye*) of Shumnu.[146] The village was named so most likely because it was the part of a revenue grant

[144] Suraiya Faroqhi, *Towns and Townsmen of Ottoman Anatolia: Trade, Crafts and Food Production in an Urban Setting, 1520–1650* (Cambridge: Cambridge University Press, 1984), 57–60.

[145] As will be shown below, the village of Çavuş as of 1516/1530 appears to have had its name changed to "Cumalu, also known as Çavuş" in *c.* 1535, Cumalu in the mid-sixteenth century, and Eski Cuma in the 1570s. In the case of the *c.* 1535, *c.* 1550, and 1579 detailed registrations, it could be argued with a high degree of certainty that all of these village names referred to one and the same settlement, largely due to the presence of a village marketplace, a unique phenomenon in the area, as well as other shared demographic and socio-economic characteristics, including some tax-payers' names that were carried from one registration to the next. The identification of Çavuş as the first element of the same string in the 1516/1530 registration is somewhat less certain as this registration also contains a village named Cumalu (BOA TD 370, p. 553), but this one may be fairly safely identified with the modern village of Cherni Briag, further to the west of what later became Eski Cuma.

[146] BOA TD 370, p. 552.

(*timar*) of a *çavuş*[147] of the governor-general (*mir-i miran, beylerbeği*) of Rumeli. While this information is not contained in the 1516/1530 tax registration, due to its synoptic format, it becomes explicit in the following detailed registers dated *c.* 1535 and *c.* 1550. Çavuş, as of 1516/1530, was fully Muslim and had five households, two unmarried adult men, and one *ellici*.[148] Thus, it may be described as one of the hundreds of new Turcoman villages that appeared in the northeastern Ottoman Balkans in the early sixteenth century.

In *c.* 1535, the same village was already listed as "Cumalu, also known as Çavuş,"[149] as a part of the *timar* of a certain Osman, son of Hüseyin, *çavuş* of the provincial governor.[150] It had grown dramatically, and the structure of its population as well as its socio-economic profile betrayed a development that could lead into its gradual transformation into an urban center. Cumalu/Çavuş already had 38 Muslim households, of which 23 were regular, and 15 held some special tax status, including those of an imam (who also served as a *müezzin* and possessed an imperial diploma), a descendant of the Prophet (*şerif*), three men of *yürük* origin who performed some military service in exchange for certain tax exemptions (an *eşküncü*, an *ellici*, and a *güreci*), a head of a dervish lodge (*tekye-nişin*), as well as several householders whose tax revenue was assigned to two pious foundations: those of Ebu Eyyub el-Ansari in Istanbul and of Sultan Murad in Edirne.[151] The presence of seventeen registered unmarried Muslim men also promised rapid growth for Cumalu's Muslim community in the near future. While it is beyond doubt that the village was founded by Muslim, Turkish-speaking colonists in the early sixteenth century, and the continuing influx of such colonists is clearly visible from the presence of three residents of the village registered as *veled-i Anadolu* (a standard designation of migrants of Anatolian origin), the presence

---

[147] A lieutenant officer or agent who often performed courier functions, or served as a personal escort of high-ranking Ottoman officials, be they members of the imperial *dīvān*, or high officials at the provincial level; for a more detailed description of the duties and functions of pre-nineteenth-century Ottoman *çāvūş*es, see Pakalın, *Osmanlı Tarih Deyimleri ve Terimleri Sözlüğü*, vol. 1, 332–336, as well as Gustav Bayerle, *Pashas, Begs, and Effendis: A Historical Dictionary of Titles and Terms in the Ottoman Empire* (Istanbul: The Isis Press, 1997), 29.

[148] BOA TD 370, p. 552. As already mentioned, the *ellici*s were *yürük*-related auxiliary military personnel, usually of Turcoman origin, the term is usually used interchangeably with *yamak* (helper) in the *yürük* organization in the Ottoman Balkans.

[149] "*Cum'alu, nām-ı dīğer Çāvūş*," BOA TD 439, pp. 220–221.

[150] "*'Osmān, veled-i Hüseyin, çāvūş-ı mīr-i mīrān*," BOA TD 439, p. 219.

[151] As *re'āyā* belonging to these two *waqf*s were also spread in other villages in the region, see the appropriate discussion in Chapter 5, BOA TD 439, pp. 220–221.

of seven household heads who were registered as "son of Abdullah" (i.e. converts to Islam), suggests that the village's growth could also be attributed to its ability to attract converts, most probably from the vicinity. Together with one freed slave (a priori supposed to have been born non-Muslim), who must have been born far away, beyond the borders of the Empire, converts constituted 20 percent of the heads of household in the growing community.[152]

The fairly high percentage of converts in Cumalu may also be related to the emergence of a small Christian community in the village that did not exist in the previous registration and consisted of five Christians (whose marital status is not specified). The emergence of a Christian community in an originally wholly Muslim (and presumably Turkish-speaking) village was a very rare phenomenon, and the explanation of this development in Cumalu leads us to a discussion of its economic development which may also be seen as the key to its gradual transformation into an urban center. While there was no priest to lead the few Christians, one of them was a tailor (*hayyat*), another a miller (*değirmenci*) who settled with his son, and yet another one was mentioned plainly as *haymane*, i.e. one without a permanent registration – the category of people who often accounted for the rapid growth of Ottoman urban centers in the sixteenth century.[153] These were not the only residents of the village who held artisanal occupations. The Muslim community had at least two such recognizable craftsmen: one tanner (*debbağ*) and a soap-maker (*sabuni*), who was also a convert to Islam. The fact that the village was able to attract artisans, whether free-born Muslims, converts to Islam, or Christians, relates to the most important aspect of Cumalu's socio-economic development that set it apart from other villages in the vicinity. By *c.* 1535, the village possessed a functioning Friday market (*Cumʿa bazarı*), which also gave its new name. This weekly market's successful functioning, sanctioned by the authorities and generating a yearly tax revenue of 500 *akçe* (making it the second largest item in the village's tax revenue breakdown), was the crucial development that would facilitate its transformation into an urban center in the coming decades.[154]

---

[152] The issue of conversion to Islam will be taken up in detail in Chapter 7. Here, converts are referred to in relation to their role in the formative decades in the history of the settlement.

[153] BOA TD 439, p. 221.

[154] "*Maḥṣūl-ı bāc-ı bāzār, Cumʿaʾdan Cumʿaʾya bāzār olur, ber-mūceb-i emr: 500,*" BOA TD 439, p. 221.

Table 5.5 *The population of Eski Cuma*

Year	Muslims – a single Muslim community				Non-Muslims – a single Christian community	
	Household heads (regular)	Household heads (other)	Hoseholds (total)	Bachelors	Households	Bachelors
1516	5	1	6	2	0	0
c.1535	23	15	38	17	5[155]	0
c.1550	72	6	78	52	10	7
1579	78	7	85	43	7	9

The demographic and socio-economic data from 15 years later[156] attests to the very rapid growth of Cumalu along the lines already clearly visible around 1535. The total population of the village, which was still listed as pertaining to the *timar* of Osman Çavuş and a part of the sub-province (*nahiye*) of Shumnu, had more than doubled, with 78 Muslim households (of which 6 had one or another special tax status, including those of an imam, an armed retainer (*eşküncü*) with his son, two sons of *sipahis*, a tax-collector (*muhassıl*)), and an impressive 52 unmarried Muslim men. The Christian community had also more than doubled, with 10 heads of household and 7 unmarried men. This impressive growth parallels that of Hezargrad and Shumnu (as well as that of Rus/Rusçuk), conforming to the overall patterns of demographic development in rising urban centers in the region. It suggests the influx of residents from the outside – from Anatolia, as in the case of a certain Nasuh, *veled-i Anadolu* – but likely largely from the vicinity of the growing village, was due to the attraction of the opportunities that its rapid economic development offered. The tax revenue from market dues also attests to this boom, tripling in comparison to the previous tax registration, up to 1,500 *akçe*, which made it the largest item in the village's tax revenue breakdown (accounting for almost a quarter of the 6,614 *akçe* of total tax revenue).

The last detailed tax registration of the sixteenth century, that of 1579, is the first detailed *tapu tahrir* registration to mention the settlement by the name of Eski Cuma; it would retain this name (with certain variations, such as Eski Cuma Bazarı and Cuma-i Atik) until 1934 when its name was

---

[155] The total number of Christian adult male tax-payers is listed as one figure in the *c.* 1535 tax register, without differentiation being made between household heads and bachelors.

[156] That is, according to the detailed tax register BOA TD 382, pp. 527–529.

changed to the present-day (Slavic) Târgovishte.[157] The 1579 registration attests to a stalled demographic growth, like that experienced by all urban centers in the region, and features a correspondingly modest increase of the tax revenue generated by the marketplace (1,600 out of 7,750 *akçe* in total). The most important development in the settlement's late sixteenth-century history, however, was the change in its administrative status. While still listed as a village (*karye*), it was already the center of a newly formed sub-province (*nahiye*) with 31 other villages.[158] In the early decades of the seventeenth century, Eski Cuma would become a fully fledged (albeit still relatively small) town, having not only a functioning market, but also a congregational mosque, and would become a center of a *kaza* (judgeship).[159]

5.6   Concluding Remarks

These four case studies of urban development in Deliorman and the adjacent regions allow us to make some broader arguments about urban development in the region in particular and the nature of the Ottoman Balkan city in general. First, the four cases discussed above represent four distinct models of historical development of urban centers in the Ottoman Balkans: (1) an urban center that was de facto newly founded upon the direct intervention of a member of the Ottoman state elite and whose further development was dependent on and largely shaped by a purposive pious endowment (*waqf*) – Hezargrad; (2) an urban center that had a rich pre-Ottoman (i.e. also Christian) tradition, consisting of a fortress (*castellum*) and a lower city (*suburbium*), which largely preserved its importance and status in the first centuries of Ottoman rule, but underwent a substantive transformation, that included the emergence and growth of what became a predominant (and presumably "ortho-dox") Muslim community, together with the building of institutions of the (Islamic) cult as well as Ottoman military and administrative institutions and the personnel thereof – Shumnu; (3) an urban center that was

---

[157] TKG KK TTd, ff. 255 a-b. The very first mention of the village under the name of Eski Cuma, still pertaining to the sub-province of Shumnu, appears in a sheep-drover (*celepkeşān*) register dated AH 981/AD 1573-4 and preserved in the Ottoman archive in Sofia. See Rusi Stoykov, "Selishta i demograpfski oblik na severoiztochna Bâlgariia i iuzhna Dobrudzha prez vtorata polovina na XVI-ti vek," *Izvestiia na Varnenskoto Arkheologishecko Druzhestvo* 15 (1964): 104. The literal meaning of the modern name Târgovishte, "market-place," is a more or less close approximation of the original Turkish name.

[158] Of which 22 Muslim, 4 Christian, and 5 mixed, predominantly Christian, with small Muslim communities consisting primarily of local converts to Islam, as discussed in the preceding chapter.

[159] An explicit reference to Eski Cuma as the center of a judgeship (*ḳāḍılıḳ*) can be found in an imperial order dated AH 1037/AD 1628 in a register of outgoing orders, *83 Numaralı Mühimme Defteri 1036–1037/1626–1628* (Ankara: T.C. Başbakanlık Devlet Arşivleri

characterized by a developed pre-Ottoman urban tradition similar to that in the immediately preceding case, but which gradually declined, losing its strategic importance of the pre-Ottoman period, and never attracted Muslim residents in significant numbers (save for the fortress garrison that was on the way of losing its strategic importance around the turn of the seventeenth century), and likewise, never developed any significant Islamic urban institutions; it was gradually superceded by another town in the vicinity whose stature rose dramatically due to its location, and which acquired the related military and commercial significance under the new (Ottoman) regime – Chernovi (functionally replaced by Rus on the Danube); and (4) an urban center that developed "spontaneously," or autonomously, from a village that grew in population and gradually acquired the two institutions that constituted the minimal conditions for a settlement's "urban" status (a functioning market and a congregational mosque) – Eski Cuma.

Therefore, one cannot make an argument for a "typical" or predominant model of historical urban development that may be seen as characteristic for the whole region – unlike the development of the rural countryside that was, as discussed in the preceding chapter, quite specific to this particular part of the Balkans (i.e. Deliorman and Gerlovo, and more broadly, the northeastern Balkans). All four types of urban development discussed above largely conformed to the more general urban developmental patterns in the Ottoman Empire at large, but more specifically in the Ottoman Balkans, especially as far as pre-Ottoman cities and their transformation into Ottoman urban centers are concerned. Thus, Hezargrad's case may be compared to those of Saray Bosna (Sarajevo) and Elbasan (in Albania); Shumnu's case is broadly similar to a large number of other cities, such as Nicopolis (Niğbolu, mod. Nikopol), Tırnova (mod. Veliko Turnovo), Ohri (Ochrida, Ohrid), Sofya (Sofia), or Siroz (Serres); Chernovi could compare to Bobovac in Bosnia; and Eski Cuma compares neatly to Selvi (mod. Sevlievo), Osman Bazarı (mod. Omurtag, in the northern Balkans) and Yenice-i Çırpan (mod. Chirpan) in Thrace.[160]

While the Ottomans did not impose any strict criteria that could determine a settlement's urban status, and indeed, as discussed in the introduction to this chapter, the conferral of such a status was not formalized

---

Genel Müdürlüğü, 2001), 87. See also the very concise 1640 description of Eski Cuma by Katip Çelebi, Hadschi Chalfa, *Rumeli und Bosna*, 41, and the entry in an extraordinary levies register (*'avārıż defteri*) dated AH 1052/AD 1642–3, which attests to its further growth and refers to it as a center of a judgeship (*każā*), BOA TD 771, pp. 291–294.

[160] See also Kiel's more comprehensive typology which addresses all of Ottoman Bulgaria; Kiel, "Urban Development," 81–84.

and was not subject to an elaborate bureaucratic mechanism, an Ottoman city in the sixteenth century normally had a developed Muslim community with related institutions (most notably a congregational mosque), albeit this community did not have to be necessarily predominant demographically. This was not a condition explicitly stipulated, and in the late fourteenth and the fifteenth century there were still a number of Balkan cities that were wholly Christian. But by the second half of the sixteenth century, the age in which Ottoman society took a more recognizable and established shape and characteristics, the absence of such a community would either preclude the possible transformation of a growing village into a town, or would usually signal the decline of a city with a rich pre-Ottoman urban tradition, such as Chernovi. Similarly, the existence of a functioning market was seen as an indispensable asset of an urban center and could lead to the transformation of a village into a town, as the case of Eski Cuma demonstrates.

As for the role of the state in urban planning and development, it may be argued that the development of urban centers in Deliorman and the adjacent regions was fairly closely related to their strategic importance from the point of view of the Ottoman state, but the state's role should not be essentialized as the only important factor for the development of urban centers as Barkan has claimed. The governmental sanction for the settlement of people without permanent residence status into specific cities, such as Hezargrad and Shumnu (as well as Rus/Ruschuk) and the setting up of new military and administrative institutions in such cities at a time when the region was deemed to be in need of developing functioning urban centers is itself a testament to the attention which the central authorities attached to urban development in Deliorman. This concern was related not only to the overall population growth in the region, but also for the need of developing centers of urban orthodox Islamic culture and education in the context of the influx of numerous heterodox settlers in the surrounding rural countryside. When a certain settlement gradually developed into a nascent urban center on its own, the development of certain urban institutions, such as a Friday market, received the sanction of the central administration, as in the case of Eski Cuma. Conversely, when a developed pre-Ottoman city had lost its strategic importance in the newly developed geopolitical, religious, and economic context after the Ottoman conquest, as happened in the case of Chernovi in parallel with the rising Ruschuk on the Danube, the lack of development of Ottoman administrative institutions and encouragement or toleration of settling into a specific urban area (especially of Muslim colonists and converts to Islam) must have played a central role in the decline of the respective urban center.

Yet, it should be noted that instead of pursuing the markedly proactive stance with respect to urban development proposed by Barkan, the Ottoman state seems to have often followed an accommodationist approach, recognizing and sanctioning different aspects of urban development, tolerating certain processes (such as the movement of rural population into developing cities, etc.), rather than being the sole or invariably dominant agent of change. Among the four case studies presented above, the history of Eski Cuma (together with other similar cases in the Ottoman Balkans) shows clearly that there were indeed *formations spontanées* (to make use of Barkan's expression) in the development of the Ottoman urban network, whereby the Ottoman government sanctioned such developments as long as it did not deem them contrary to its interests.

In relation to the issue of state policies with regard to urban development, the foundation of Hezargrad holds a special place. While the act of founding the pious endowment on the part of the grand vizier Ibrahim Pasha may be seen as an individual act of charity and piety of an Ottoman grandee, it is beyond doubt that it also reflected his experiences and concerns as a statesman in the context of the Safavid-Ottoman struggle and the migration and/or forcible deportation of perceived heterodox sympathizers of the Safavid regime from Anatolia to the northeastern Balkans.

Deliorman's overall spectacular urban growth, especially in the mid-sixteenth century, both conformed to general demographic trends in the Ottoman Balkans (and in the larger Ottoman and Mediterranean contexts) and also reflected population pressure in Deliorman specifically, where the rapid economic growth of Hezargrad and Eski Cuma, as well as, to a lesser extent, that of Shumnu, attracted new residents from the vicinity as well as from Anatolia.

6 Religion, Culture, and Authority: Two Case Studies

"Padişah vekili benem."

("I am the lieutenant of the *padişah.*")

Demir Baba to Ali Pasha (Ottoman provincial governor)[1]

6.1 Introduction

The analysis of the demographic and socio-economic transformation of Ottoman Deliorman, Gerlovo, and some adjacent regions from the late fifteenth through the sixteenth centuries, largely on the basis of Ottoman tax registers, has demonstrated that during this period the area witnessed rapid demographic growth and the related spectacular development of the settlement network (both rural and urban), due mainly to the influx of mostly Turcoman newcomers from the Balkan southeast (Thrace) and Anatolia. As a result, by the second half of the sixteenth century, Deliorman and Gerlovo had become densely populated and overwhelmingly Muslim and Turkish-speaking. With neighboring Dobrudja simultaneously undergoing similar processes, the period in question very much constituted the essential, formative phase of the process of Turcoman settlement and the spread of Islam in the northeastern Balkans.

However, while Ottoman tax registers are the best source for the quantitative study of the demographic dimensions of conversion to Islam, and also allow one to study some aspects of the development of typical institutions of Islamic culture – most notably mosque complexes and dervish convents – they reveal little in the way of learning more about specific beliefs and devotional practices, as well as the role these played in the formation and development of religious identities and the "varieties of Islam" in the northeastern Balkans, and the ways all these were situated in the larger context of Ottoman religio-cultural history. This lack is especially acute in the case of the rural countryside.

[1] *DBV*, 162.

This chapter takes up the task of partially filling this gap by presenting two case studies illustrating the development of Islamic culture in
Deliorman and Gerlovo in its rural and urban contexts. First, it will discuss
the figure and the related cult of Demir Baba, the great sixteenth-century
regional (heterodox) saint in Deliorman and Gerlovo and spiritual successor to Otman Baba (via Akyazılı Baba) as *kutb* of the Abdals of Rum in the
eastern Balkans. Organized around popular oral traditions about his life
and miraculous deeds, most of which were later put to paper in his *velayetname*, and his mausoleum/convent complex, Demir Baba's cult, still very
prominent today, can very likely be seen as the most important lens through
which one may explore the religious life of heterodox Muslim communities
in early modern Deliorman and Gerlovo. The second case study focuses
on the foundation of the mosque complex of grand vizier Ibrahim Pasha
in 1533 around which the new town of Hezargrad essentially emerged and
developed, on the basis of the endowment deed (*vakfiye*) of Ibrahim Pasha's
pious endowment in Hezargrad. While the discussion of the emergence of
Hezargrad in the preceding chapter focused mainly on the demographic
and socio-economic aspects of the town's development, here an emphasis
will be placed on the religio-political considerations laid out in the *vakfiye*,
thus pointing to the ideological dimensions of Hezargrad's foundation.

6.2   Demir Baba and the Abdals of Rum of Otman Baba's Branch in Deliorman and Gerlovo

While important remarks on the memory and saintly cult of Demir
(Timur) Baba are found in travelers' accounts such as those of Evliya
Çelebi[2], and – much later – Felix Kanitz,[3] the most important and definitive written source for the saint's historical and communal role is his
little studied *velayetname* (*vita*).[4] The only extant eastern Balkan Rum

---

[2] *Evliyâ Çelebi Seyahatnâmesi*, vol. 5, 313.

[3] Felix Kanitz, *Donau Bulgarien und der Balkan: Historisch-geographisch-ethnographische
Reisestudien aus den Jahren 1860–1879*, 2. Neubearb. Auflage (Leipzig: Renger'sche
Buchhandlung, 1882), vol. 3, 329–332.

[4] The only critical edition of the work, which is used here, is *Demir Baba Velâyetnâmesi
(İnceleme-Tenkitli Metin)*, ed. Filiz Kılıç and Tuncay Bülbül (Ankara: Grafiker Yayınları,
2011), henceforth *DBV*. Other available editions are *Demir Baba Vilâyetnamesi*, ed. Bedri
Noyan (Istanbul: Can Yayınları, 1976), and *Demir Baba Velayetnamesi*, ed. Hakkı Saygı
(Istanbul: Saygı Yayınları, 1997). The last one is a summary in modern Turkish.
The only extensive and scholarly analysis of Demir Baba's *velayetname* is to be found
in Nevena Gramatikova's *Neortodoksalniiat Isliam*, 231–399, preceded by a shorter
publication by the same author, "Zhitieto na Demir Baba i sâzdavaneto na râkopisi
ot miusiulmanite ot heterodoksnite techeniia na Isliama v severoiztochna Bâlgaria,"
in *Miusiulmanskata kultura v bâlgarskite zemi. Izsledvaniia*, vol. 1, ed. R. Gradeva and
S. Ivanova (Sofia: IMIR, 1998), 400–435. For a good source-critical discussion, see also
DBV, "Introduction," 7–36.

Abdal saint's *vita* other than that of Otman Baba, it also discusses the lives of other major Balkan Rum Abdal saints such as Akyazılı Baba and Kademli Baba, and thus may be considered the major narrative source for the development of what one may term "Otman Baba's branch of the Abdals of Rum" in the sixteenth and early seventeenth centuries. Having been born in the heart of Deliorman,[5] Demir Baba is also the first (and last) major Muslim heterodox saint in the Balkans who was native to the peninsula. Thus, his story can also tell us something about the "indigenization of Islam" in the Balkans – the process by which Islamic culture became part and parcel of the regional Balkan landscape.

The *velayetname*'s content is predominantly hagiographical, dealing with the spiritual and moral qualities of the saint, most emphatically exemplified in the legendary stories about his "marvels" (*keramat*), and biohagiographical, providing information on his personal and public life as well as his interactions with the Ottoman authorities and spiritual and sectarian rivals. Unlike the *vita* of Otman Baba, Demir Baba's *velayetname*'s hagiological content, i.e. that which discusses doctrinal, theoretical, and theological points, is quite limited. However, the work clearly identifies Demir Baba doctrinally as a follower of "Otman Baba's way" as well as Otman's lineal spiritual successor as *kutb*.[6]

Also in contrast to Otman Baba's *vita*, but consonant with most early modern Ottoman hagiographical works,[7] the *velayetname* of Demir Baba was most likely composed long after the death of the saint. The anonymous author did not live in the age of his subject, rather, he composed his work in a quest to preserve the legendary stories of the life of the saint as recounted by "the storytellers and conveyors of traditions."[8] In some cases, he cites identifiable transmitters of oral tradition.[9]

The earliest year mentioned in the extant manuscript recensions can be read alternatively as AH 1029/AD 1619–20 or AH 1129/AD 1716–17.[10]

---

[5] According to the *vita*, Demir Baba was born in the village of Kovancılar (mod. Pchelina, Razgrad province). Its earliest tax registration is found in the previously discussed synoptic tax register dated 1530 but largely based on a 1516 registration, BOA TD 370, p. 558.

[6] Demir "had given a pledge of allegiance to Otman Baba" ("*Otman Baba'dan bī'at olmış*"), *DBV*, 118.

[7] See Ocak, *Menâkıbnâmeler*, 37–39, 51–65.

[8] "*...rāviyān-ı aḫbār ve nākilān-ı āṣar rivāyet iderler ki...*," usually used to introduce individual stories, *DBV*, 40, 58, 89, 96, 139.

[9] E.g. Bakacaklı Ali Dede, Mürüvvet Dede, Mehmed Abdal, Örümcek Abdal, Derviş Bali, Ali Paşa, *DBV*, 62, 142, 165, 161.

[10] The *velayetname* has reached us in three recensions – all of them originating from Deliorman. The first, dated AH 1239/AD 1824, is the most likely source for the two later copies. For a detailed discussion of the recensions, their dating, as well as the dating of the original, see *DBV*, "Introduction," 30–35, and Gramatikova, *Neortodoksalniiat Isliam*, 244–254.

While no hint is provided to its meaning, its position in the text – concluding the presentation of the saint's genealogical chain (Ar. *silsila*, Tr. *silsile*) at the beginning of the work and immediately preceding the substantive narrative exposition – likely means it refers to the assumed year of composition of the original. As the saint most probably lived from the early sixteenth to the late sixteenth/early seventeenth century and the composition of the written version of the *velayetname* appears to have followed a substantial period of gestation of oral traditions, the second reading appears more persuasive.[11] The other alternative cannot be fully excluded, though.

After the very short introduction containing references to *hadith* and urging the utmost reverence for the Prophet and his family (*ehl-i beyt*), the author traces the saint's descent over eighty-four generations from "the father of humankind" Adam (*ebu'l-beşer Adem*) via the prophets Seth, Idris, Noah, Hud, and Abraham, and then (following a number of generations) through members of the lineage and family of the Prophet: Abd Manaf, Hashim, Abd al-Muttalib, Abu Talib, the first, third and fourth imams in the Shi'i tradition – Ali, Husayn, and (Ali b. Husayn) Zayn al-Abidin – down to the saint's father, Hacı b. Turran.[12] While the inclusion of this genealogical chain has the overall aim of enhancing Demir Baba's saintly legitimacy, the references to prophetic descent (including from the Prophet Muhammad via Fatima) and descent from the first imams serves to underscore the relationship between the ages of prophesy and sainthood, which, in contrast to the *vita* of Otman Baba, is only hinted at in the introductory section of Demir Baba's *velayetname*. The claim to biological descent from Ali and his immediate descendants also highlights the belief that they are the ultimate repository and source of definitive mystical and esoteric knowledge in the age of sainthood – a foundational idea in pro-Alid (Sufi) piety.[13]

The *velayetname*'s narrative exposition consists of a string of legendary stories (*menkabe*s) centered around Demir Baba. It first discusses events

---

[11] Kılıç and Bülbül prefer the earlier dating (AH 1029), *DBV*, "Introduction," 32–33 and Gramatikova the later (AH 1129), *Neortodoksalniat Isliam*, 251–252.

[12] *DBV*, 39–40.

[13] The *velayetname* also claims for Demir Baba descent from the Prophet via his mother, *DBV*, 108. Claims to genealogical descent from the Prophet and the Holy Family are not untypical for the hagiographical accounts of heterodox Muslim saints; see Gramatikova, *Neortodoksalniiat Isliam*, 270–271. On the other hand, while descent from the Prophet is often claimed for Sunni saints too, their hagiographies usually attribute to them spiritual, and not genealogical, *silsila*s that include prominent figures in the history of the respective *tariqa* and would often lead back to the first caliph Abu Bakr and the Prophet himself, thus establishing a direct connection to the *Sunna*; see J. Spencer Trimingham, *The Sufi Orders in Islam* (New York: Oxford University Press, 1998), 10–16; Renard, *Friends of God*, 171; Karamustafa, *God's Unruly Friends*, 87–88.

that preceded and led to the birth of the saint, then traces the saint's adolescence, and provides a detailed account of his path to assuming the station of "pole of poles" under the guidance of Akyazılı Baba. Finally, it recounts his miraculous deeds following the transfer of "poleship" (*kut-biyyetlik*) from Akyazılı Baba. While the last several stories do not seem to follow a strict chronological sequence,[14] the work is characterized by a considerable degree of textual unity and abounds in cross-references to various "events" in its individual legendary stories.

Much of the account takes place in Deliorman where Demir Baba was born, grew up, and later spent the latter part of his life. As the middle part of his life was devoted to traveling, including visiting and/ or performing service at different dervish convents, mostly associated with Otman Baba's Rum Abdal branch, the narrative walks the audience through various places outside of Deliorman: the *tekye*s of Akyazılı Baba and Dursun Baba in Dobrudja, those of Kızıl Deli and Otman Baba in Thrace. The saint's travels also bring him to Gerlovo, Tanrıdağı, and the Aegean Sea coast; more distant locations such as the land of Hırvat (Croatia?) feature in his peregrinations without being very well integrated into the story line. Some of the most remarkable accounts of the saint's marvels take place far away from Deliorman – in Istanbul where he heals the Ottoman chief mufti's daughter's infertility, and in Budjak (Bucak) and Muscovy, which lands he delivers from the terror of dragons. Demir Baba is also cast as a dervish-*gazi* who actively participates in Ottoman-Habsburg wars around Budim (Buda).

6.2.1   The Abdals of Rum of Otman Baba's Branch from the Death of Otman Baba to Demir Baba's Emergence as "Pole of Poles"

One of the noteworthy features of Demir Baba's hagiographical account is that it devotes ample attention to the events that led to his birth, as he was pre-ordained to become the *kutb*. The *velayetname* then recounts Demir's spiritual "training" by Akyazılı Baba at the end of which the latter – the incumbent "pole of poles" (*kutbü'l-aktab*) from the perspective of the Abdal community– transfers the "poleship" to Demir Baba. These events which precede the tales of Demir Baba's miraculous deeds which he performed as *kutb* shed light on the nature and development of the larger Rum Abdal community in the eastern Balkans in the first three decades or so of the sixteenth century.

---

[14] See Gramatikova's discussion of the structure of the *velayetname* in *Neortodoksalniiat Isliam*, 253–254.

The developments leading up to the saint's birth are situated in the age of Sultan Süleyman, an emperor (*padişah*, *hünkar*) from the "house of Osman" (*al-i Osman*).[15] The major Abdal figures who figure in these events are Akyazılı Baba, Hacı Dede, and Kademli Baba. Akyazılı, the major saint of the age – "pole of poles" and "lord of the world" (*şah-ı 'alem*) – presides over a *tekye* on the Batova River in Dobrudja[16] and is presented as Süleyman's *kutb* (in this context, spiritual guide). Hacı Dede, Akyazılı Baba's personal Abdal servant, acts as Akyazılı's beast of burden, carrying the saint on his back "like a camel" on lengthy travels from the deserts of Baghdad to Budim (Buda).[17] Kademli Baba, the other major saintly figure of the age and Akyazılı's close associate, has a convent in upper Thrace.[18]

One day Akyazılı Baba suggests that Hacı Dede settle and have a family. Hacı Dede protests, saying that he would not leave his *pir* (spiritual guide) for a woman, whereupon the Pole of the Age discloses his most important consideration on the matter: "if you do not marry and procreate where will Black Demir (*Kara Timur*) come from?"[19] Upon the urging of his master, Hacı Dede leaves the *tekye* at Batova and travels to a convent at Gökçe Su in Deliorman to ask Turran Halife, a lieutenant of Akyazılı, for the hand of his daughter Zahide Bacu. Warmly welcomed, Hacı Dede explains the task with which he has been sent there.[20] Turran Halife pays a visit to his *pir* in Batova (i.e. Akyazılı Baba) to discuss the matter. The saint expresses his impatient desire to be the (spiritual) father of Demir. Zahide Bacu is betrothed to Hacı Dede, Turran Halife is sent back to Gökçe Su with presents, and the good news is communicated to Hacı Dede via a pigeon whereby he is instructed to await Akyazılı in his own (Hacı Dede's) village of Kovancılar in Deliorman.[21]

Described in vivid detail, the wedding festivities last for seven days and take place in Kovancılar and Gökçe Su in Deliorman, as well as in

---

[15] *DBV*, 40.
[16] Between Varna and Balchik, in the vicinity of the modern village of Obrochishte, near the Black Sea coast.
[17] *DBV*, 40.
[18] Close to modern Nova Zagora, in the vicinity of the village of Grafitovo.
[19] *DBV*, 41–42.
[20] Ibid., 43–45. It is difficult to locate Gökçe Su satisfactorily. Gramatikova suggests that it could be the modern village of Sinya Voda (old Gökçe Su, renamed in 1934), halfway between Razgrad and Târgovishte (Ott. Eski Cuma), while not excluding the possibility of another, now extinct settlement in the area, *Neortodoksalniiat Isliam*, 425. A village registered as "*İslām Fāḳih, nām-ı diğer Gökçe Su*" is found in the detailed Ottoman tax register of 1579 in the sub-province of Hezargrad, TKG KK TTd No. 151, f. 122b. It can be traced back as İslam Fakih in BOA TD 439 (*c.* 1535), p. 245, but the respective entry does not provide evidence of a extant convent.
[21] *DBV*, 45–46.

Gerlovo. Apart from the inhabitants of the settlements of the groom and
the bride, the narrator provides a detailed list of attendees including a
couple dozen individuals and groups within the Rum Abdal community.
It reads like a veritable Rum Abdal *Who's Who*, from some of Akyazılı's
closest associates in Deliorman and Gerlovo who officiate at the wedding, such as Tay Hızır, appointed as the groom's "father" (*ata*) at the
ceremony, Göçbeği, and Kız Ana, a prominent female dervish who was
appointed as the bride's best maid (*sağdıç*), to the dervishes of Kademli
Baba and Mümin Baba in Thrace, Zati Efendi and Abdi Dede, the head
of the *tekye* and the caretaker of the mausoleum (*türbedar*) of Otman
Baba, respectively, the groom's *sağdıç* Tursun (Dursun) Baba, hailing
from his *tekye* in northern Dobrudja, the famed poet Yemini Efendi as
well as representatives of various other *tekye* and village communities that
recognized Akyazılı as their supreme religious guide.[22] Thus the wedding
of the parents of the future "pole of poles" Demir Baba becomes an
occasion for a grand communal reunion, a demonstration of the strength
and unity of Otman Baba's Abdals of Rum.

While the *velayetname* is not explicit on this, two prominent contemporary Rum Abdal poets suggest that Akyazılı Baba was considered
Otman Baba's successor as the "pole of poles." In one of his poems
Muhyiddin Abdal, most probably writing in the late fifteenth century, acknowledges Otman Baba as his *pir*, but also calls for Akyazılı
to assume leadership as "commander" (*serleşker*) and "guide" (*mürşid,
rehber*).[23] More explicitly, in his massive poetic work *Fazilet-Name*, self-
dated AH 925/AD 1519, Yemini, himself mentioned in Demir Baba's
velayetname among the distinguished wedding guests, points to AH 883/
AD 1478 as the year of Otman Baba's death and AH 901/AD 1495 as
the time of Akyazılı's assumption of the poleship.[24] Thus, a line of three
Rum Abdal *kutb*s in the second half of the fifteenth and the sixteenth
centuries emerges: Otman Baba (d. 1478), Akyazılı Baba, *kutb* since
1495, and Demir Baba to whom Akyazılı would transfer the "poleship"
shortly before his death, which, as discussed below, likely happened
between 1519 and 1530.

Members of the Rum Abdal community were not the only guests
invited to the wedding. Among the attendees numbered a Chinggisid

---

[22] Ibid., 46–47.
[23] This suggests the time of writing as post-dating the death of Otman Baba, see Sadettin
Nüzhet (Ergun), *Bektaşi Şairleri* (Istanbul: Devlet Matbaası, 1930), 273–275.
[24] Dervîş Muhammed Yemînî, *Fazîlet-Nâme*, ed. Yusuf Tepeli (Ankara: Türk Dil Kurumu,
2002), vol. 1, 239; for the self-dating of the work, see vol. 1, 602; the year of Otman
Baba's death as given by Yemini also perfectly matches the respective dating in Otman
Baba's *velayetname*. See also Gramatikova, "Otman Baba," 100.

prince,[25] the governor (*sancakbeği*) of Çirmen (in Thrace), several other military commanders (*alaybeği*), a certain Karamalkoç (likely a reference to the famous Ottoman frontier lord family of Malkoçoğulları), as well as a certain Naldöken – possibly signifying the community of Naldöken *yürüks* – all of whom paid their respects to Akyazılı Baba and Kademli Baba, conferring rich wedding gifts; interestingly, the only dervish community other than the Abdals of Rum specifically mentioned as represented at the wedding are the Nakşibendis.[26]

By far, the most illustrious wedding guest outside of the Rum Abdal community is none other than the Ottoman sultan Süleyman. At one point during the festivities Kademli Baba, who serves as a "master of ceremonies," supervising the wedding preparations and the attendance of the invitees, disappears. A famous healer, he is summoned to Vize (in Thrace) to treat an Ottoman prince's favorite wife who has fallen ill. Having successfully treated the royal patient, Kademli Baba asks for permission to go back to the wedding but is brought to the presence of the Ottoman sultan who scolds Kademli and Akyazılı for not having invited him. Kademli diffuses Süleyman's dissatisfaction by pointing out that the wedding of somebody who serves as a beast of burden (i.e. Hacı Dede) would not be worthy of the attendance of "a Süleyman,"[27] whereupon the sultan gives Kademli permission to go, bestowing a wedding gift of five camels and five purses of money and communicating his greetings to "his father" (i.e. Akyazılı Baba). The story does not end here: Süleyman sends a spy to shadow Kademli to learn what the dervish would say about him at the wedding. The spy returns confirming that Kademli is loyal to the sultan and extends his prayers for his well-being (*du'acundur*).[28] In the end, Süleyman comes to the wedding in disguise to pay his respects to Akyazılı Baba and enjoy the festivities (including wrestling fights and racing contests) with only Akyazılı and Kademli aware of his true identity; the narrator reminds his audience: "in those times the [Ottoman] sultans were friends of the saints."[29]

After the wedding festivities come to an end, Akyazılı gives permission to his *halife*s and other guests to leave and, carried by the groom

[25] "*Cingiz-zāde silsilesinden ḫān-zāde*," likely meant to be a member of the Giray dynasty that ruled over the Crimea *c.* 1441–1783, including as vassals of the Ottomans from *c.* 1475 to 1774. *DBV*, 49.

[26] *DBV*, 49–52. The Nakşibendis are presented as "*gürüh-ı Nakşībendīler*."

[27] The exact usage here is "*Sen bir Süleymān'suñ*" ("You are a Süleyman" or "You are a Solomon"). In the same passage, Kademli refers to Süleyman's station/occupation as *Süleymān'lıḳ* ("Süleymanness/Süleymanship") which may also be seen as redolent of broader associations with Süleyman/Solomon in Islamic tradition. *DBV*, 49.

[28] *DBV*, 49.

[29] "*Hem ol zamān ḫünkārlar muḥibb-i evliyā idi*," *DBV*, 52.

Hacı Dede, retreats with his dervishes to his convent in Dobrudja[30] whence he sends the groom to Kovancılar in Deliorman and tells him to send news of Demir Baba's conception and appearance. Upon the future *kutb*'s birth, assisted by Kız Ana, messengers carrying the joyful news (*müjdeciler*) are sent across the land, Akyazılı and Kademli come to Kovancılar and Akyazılı gives the name Demir (Timur) to the newborn in a special ceremony (*beşik töreni*).[31]

The *velayetname* passes over Demir Baba's childhood, only pointing out that he did not leave his birthplace in Kovancılar until the age of seventeen when he was already a fine young lad (*yiğit*). At that point, Kademli Baba, nearing the end of his life, invites Akyazılı and the young Demir to visit his convent in Thrace. Many prominent figures in the Rum Abdal community, already introduced in the context of the wedding of Demir Baba's parents, come there to receive Akyazılı's blessing and to bid farewell to Kademli. On his deathbed Kademli asks Akyazılı to build a *türbe* (mausoleum) for him after a three-year wait. Akyazılı, Demir, Hacı Dede, and other important members of the Abdal community, such as the sheykh of Otman Baba's convent, Zati Efendi, and the poet Yemini Efendi, officiate at the funeral, Demir is entrusted with the most honorable task of digging Kademli's grave.[32]

Akyazılı Baba, Demir, and the latter's father Hacı Dede spend three years at the *tekye* of Kademli at the end of which period the latter's mausoleum is erected (see Fig. 6.1). This period may be seen as the first phase of Demir's "training" as a future *kutb*, as he matures under the guidance of Akyazılı Baba and has the opportunity to communicate with other important figures in the Rum Abdal community.[33] This initiation is followed by a second phase in Demir's upbringing: the three (including Hacı Dede) devote the next two years to travels in the eastern Balkans, visiting a number of *tekye*s associated with Otman Baba's Abdals of Rum. These kinds of peregrinations (*seyahat*) constitute one of the fundamentals of antinomian, non-Sharia-minded Sufism of the Babai/Kalenderi tradition – it dominated Otman Baba's career and featured prominently in Akyazılı's activities. Possibly influenced by Buddhist and Manichean tradition, *seyahat* helped maintain communal bonds, forge one's spiritual strength,[34] and could also serve as a *cursus honorum* during which a young adept would visit a number of important centers associated with the spiritual path and the respective community. In this particular context, it is both Akyazılı's farewell tour and

---

[30] *DBV*, 56–57.
[31] Ibid., 58–60. On related modern practices in Deliorman, see *Bâlgarskite Aliani*, ed. I. Georgieva, 38–41, 110–111.
[32] Ibid., 64.
[33] Gramatikova, *Neortodoksalniiat Isliiam*, 264.
[34] Ocak, *Kalenderîler*, 168–169.

Figure 6.1 Mausoleum (*türbe*) of Kademli Baba. Photograph by Mariya Kiprovska.

Demir's initiation tour which prepares the audience for the imminent transfer of the poleship from the current *kutb* to his chosen successor.

The travels of Akyazılı Baba and Demir Baba present the *velayetname*'s intended audience with an overview of the most important Rum Abdal dervish convents in the eastern Balkans. If the large gatherings of Rum Abdals on the occasions of Demir Baba's parents' wedding in Deliorman and Kademli Baba's funeral in Thrace were single-site reunions of the Rum Abdal community, this may be seen as a "reunion through *seyahat*," meant to be reimagined and mentally re-enacted by the audience and thus help it reinforce its sense of community by highlighting its most important centers and leaders and delimiting its geographical boundaries. Thus, we see Akyazılı (traveling on the back of Hacı Dede) and Demir visit a *tekye* at the Erdağı River[35] in the vicinity of Tanrıdağı (i.e. in the eastern Rhodopes and adjacent parts of Thrace), then they travel in Thrace to the convent of Otman Baba, the lodge of Mustafa Baba (where they witness the latter's death and officiate at his funeral), following that they travel again to Otman Baba's *tekye*, and end up at the convent of Kademli (Akyazılı's final visit there, as the narrator reminds his audience). This tour of convents in Tanrıdağı and Thrace is followed

[35] Possibly the modern Arda River.

Figure 6.2 Mausoleum (*türbe*) of Akyazılı Baba. Photograph by Mariya Kiprovska.

by visits to the lodges of Yolkulu Baba, Hafız Baba, Samed Baba, Dikilli Hüseyin Baba, Kız Ana, Musa Baba, and Ali Beğ Tay Hızır in Gerlovo and Deliorman. Finally, the party visits Turran Baba's *tekye* near Babadağ in northern Dobrudja, before returning to Akyazılı's convent at Batova where, after some time, Akyazılı transfers his poleship to Demir, and dies.[36] (For the mausoleum of Akyazılı Baba, see. Fig. 6.2.)

Looking at the state and nature of the Rum Abdal community in the eastern Balkans as presented to us in the first sections of the *velayetname*, two major dynamics emerge: the community's attitude toward and relationship with the Ottoman dynasty and state, and its level of socio-cultural cohesion, including the evolution of its socio-economic texture and the status of its members. Importantly, as will be elaborated below, the evidence that the *velayetname* presents regarding both dynamics finds some substantial degree of external confirmation in sixteenth-century Ottoman tax registers. In this context, it is also appropriate to briefly discuss the dating of these events.

---

[36] *DBV*, 65–66.

Regarding the first dynamic, the audience is presented with an image of the community and its leading figures as being well integrated in Ottoman society, recognizing the legitimacy and the authority of the Ottoman state and dynasty and enjoying the latter's respect and support. This harmony is in visible contrast with Otman Baba's confrontational attitude toward Mehmed II in the light of his own *velayetname* composed by Küçük Abdal in 1483. While Otman Baba emphatically rejects any gifts offered to him by Mehmed II and appears critical of and hostile to any follower of the mystical path who shows even the smallest sign of conformism vis-à-vis the Ottoman state and dynasty,[37] Akyazılı and Kademli, the two leading Rum Abdal figures between Otman Baba's death and Demir Baba's assumption of the poleship, are both presented in Demir Baba's *vita* as largely conforming to the Ottoman order. Kademli is the more extreme in this respect. In the events surrounding the wedding of Demir Baba's parents he refers to himself as the sultan's faithful servant or "your slave" (*kulunuz*), performs service for the royal family, and eagerly accepts the sultan's wedding gifts.[38] Süleyman himself is presented as "a friend of the saints" who is nevertheless prudent enough to send a spy to probe Kademli Baba's, and by association, the Rum Abdal community's attitudes toward the Ottoman dynasty and state – a test passed with flying colors by Kademli.[39]

This reciprocally amicable relationship between the Rum Abdal community of the eastern Balkans and the Ottoman state and dynasty reflected in Demir Baba's *vita* finds confirmation in an Ottoman administrative source nearly contemporary (to the events described). An entry in an Ottoman tax register dated 1530 refers to a water-mill dedicated to the pious endowment (*waqf*) of Akyazılı Baba and provides important clues to the development and standing of his dervish community at Batova from the perspective of the Ottoman state, some time shortly after his death:

The water-mill of the pass of Batova.
    The aforementioned water-mills were built by an *abdal* by the name of Üveys Derviş, the latter also dedicated them as a pious endowment in the name of the illustrious Akyazılu Baba – the mine of the mysteries of miracles and the glory of the signs of sainthood. The endowment is meant to support the dervishes who live and perform service in the area around the grave [of

---

[37] See various passages in *OBV*, 38–41, 62–63, 223–224, and 242–243.
[38] Akyazılı scolds Kademli when the latter tries to take advantage of Süleyman's benevolent attitude and attempts to solicit more gifts from the ruler at the wedding of Demir Baba's parents, *DBV*, 52.
[39] See also Gramatikova's comments in *Neortodoksalniiat Isliam*, 258–259.

Akyazılı Baba]. The mentioned community is settled on the area delimited by a judge's title-deed. They have set up a convent, a vineyard, and a garden and have been making a living there together with the petitioners (?). At present, they are ordered to pay the canonical as well as customary taxes and dues accruing from this [clearly] delimited area and the mentioned water-mill; they have been handed an edict regarding this matter and this was recorded in the register.[40]

Apart from the Ottoman state's overall supportive stance toward the community of Akyazılı Baba's convent which this entry evinces, the usage of the appellations "the mine of the mysteries of miracles and the glory of the signs of sainthood" to refer to a rural holy man of regional importance is remarkable and rare in contemporary Ottoman administrative sources. The abovementioned metaphors very much conform to the respective "titulature" used in sources emanating from heterodox communities themselves, such as the *velayetname*s of Otman Baba and Demir Baba, other saintly *vitae*, and poetic works of the epoch. Thus this administrative language very much amounts to a recognition, on the part of the Ottoman state, of Akyazılı Baba's elevated status as perceived by his own followers.

It is also relevant here to discuss the possible dating of the events described in the *velayetname*. The 1530 register entry confirms that Akyazılı Baba (who had succeeded Otman Baba as *kutb* in 1495 according to the poet Yemini) must have died not long before that registration (it is clear from the entry that this is the convent's first registration). As Yemini also suggests that Akyazılı was still alive in 1519, then, combining his reference and the 1530 tax registration, one may tentatively place Akyazılı's death in the period 1519–30.[41] Accordingly, if we follow the *velayetname*'s suggestion that Demir Baba was around twenty-two years of age at the time of Akyazılı's death, then Demir Baba's birth can

---

[40] "*Asyāb-ı derbend-i Batova. Ẕikr olan değirmenleri Üveys Dervīş nām abdāl binā' idüb, ma'den-i esrār-ı kerāmet ve şān-ı āṣar-ı velāyet Aḳyazılu Bābā ḥażretlerine vaḳf idüb, sābıḳ ḫıdmet eden derviş? mezārı üzerinde duran fuḳarāya vaḳf itmiş. Meẕkūr ṭā'ife ḥüccet-i ḳażā ile maḥdūd olan yerde mütemekkin olub, tekye ve bāğ ve bāğçe idüb, 'arż (?) ṣāḥibleri ile zindegānī iderlermiş. Şimdiki ḥālde ẕikr olan maḥdūd yerin ve asyāb-ı meẕkūreniñ resīmler ve huḳūḳ-ı şer'iyesin ve rüsūm-ı 'örfiyesin vīreler deyü emr olunub ve meẕbūr ḫuṣūṣ (?) içün ellerine ḥükm virilmeğin deftere ḳayd olunmuş,*" BOA TD 370, p. 433.

[41] A much later tax register, from the time of Selim II (1566–74), refers to "the pious endowment of the convent of the Pearl of the Ecstatics [i.e. ecstatic Sufi mystics] Akyazılu Baba" (*evḳāf-ı zāviye-i zeynü'l-meczūbīn merhūm Aḳyazılu Bābā*) on the Batova river in the district (*nāḥiye*) of Varna. This very much repeats the information in the 1530 register entry, while pointing to some later property acquisitions of the endowment, BOA TD 482, p. 186.

be tentatively placed in the first decade of the sixteenth century (more likely around 1505–10) with a wiggle room of several years.[42] On the other hand, such a dating would contradict the narrative of Demir Baba's *velayetname*, which presents the wedding of the saint's parents as happening in the reign of Sultan Süleyman (r. 1520–66). This discrepancy may possibly be explained by the fact that most of Demir's life did coincide with Süleyman's reign – as well as by the fame that Süleyman had acquired as the greatest sovereign in historical and communal memory and his reputation for courting ecstatic holy men.[43]

As for the second aspect mentioned above – the nature and level of socio-economic development and cohesion of the Rum Abdal community – Demir Baba's *velayetname* again presents us with a picture that significantly differs from Otman Baba's *vita*, and points to the extent to which the Rum Abdals had developed as a coherent community from the 1460s–1470s (Otman Baba' last years) to the 1520s (Akyazılı Baba's death). While Otman Baba is presented as a wandering antinomian mystic with a large retinue of Rum Abdal dervishes, many of them drawn from among semi-nomadic pastoralists, figures like Akyazılı and Kademli, albeit occasionally given to prolonged peregrinations, are largely settled in dervish convents, residing together with their disciples. Similarly, while the numerous dervish convents and village communities Otman Baba visits do not necessarily appear subject to his spiritual leadership (and at times he clearly faces opposition), in Demir Baba's *velayetname* we see a relatively well-organized and coherent Rum Abdal collectivity with a geographically identifiable network of village communities and dervish convents that recognize Akyazılı's spiritual leadership. This is the early, but definitive, stage of the transformation of Otman Baba's loose dervish group whose practices included mendicancy, voluntary poverty, self-isolation, and celibacy, into an increasingly institutionalized, hierarchical, and socially accepted collectivity of mostly settled groups that practiced agriculture and recognized family life as the dominant form of social organization. This process whose

---

[42] There exist alternative hypotheses regarding the dating of Demir Baba's birth. Franz Babinger refers to oral communication in the course of his terrain research in Deliorman in the early twentieth century which points to Demir Baba's year of birth some time in the mid-fifteenth century and his year of death as 1520, but Babinger expresses his doubts about the reliability of this information, "Das Bektaschi-Kloster Demir Baba," *Westasiatische Studien* 34/2 (1931): 89–90. Gramatikova suggests the year 1530 as the most probable possible year of the saint's birth, her basis for which is that this year is given in a fourteen-page summary of the *velayetname* appended to the earliest recension from Akkadınlar (Dulovo), oral traditions from Deliorman in recent decades, as well as the fact that the *velayetname* places the saint's birth in the epoch of Süleyman; Gramatikova, *Neortodoksalniiat Isliam*, 248–251.

[43] Personal communication with Cornell Fleischer.

conceptual nature has been aptly analyzed by Ahmet Karamustafa[44] will be revisited in more detail further below, following the discussion of Demir Baba's mature life in the light of his *velayetname*. For the moment, it is important to note that, once again (as in the case of the relationship between the Abdals of Rum and the Ottoman state and dynasty) we find a significant amount of corroborating evidence in contemporary Ottoman administrative sources.

A cross-examination of the *velayetname* and Ottoman tax registers from the first half of the sixteenth century reveals that the most prominent Rum Abdal convents mentioned in Demir Baba's *vita* are registered as tax-paying units, often enjoying tax exemptions and privileges accorded as a part of the state's policy of integrating such groups into the Ottoman imperial order. Apart from the *tekye*s of Akyazılı Baba near Varna and that of Otman Baba in Thrace whose earliest tax register entries have already been referred to,[45] one can point to the convents of Kız Ana, just between Gerlovo and Deliorman, as well as that of Hafızoğlu Mehmed Efendi (Dede) and the convent/community of Yolkulu Baba in Gerlovo – all of them to be found recorded (for the first time) in the earliest (preserved) detailed tax register for the province of Niğbolu, provisionally dated *c.* 1535.[46] These were larger convents that played a central role in the life of the Rum Abdal (and later, the Bektashi-Alevi) community, and some of them, such as those of Otman Baba, Akyazılı, and Kız Ana are still in existence today (the first and third still functioning). Other

[44] Karamustafa, *God's Unruly Friends*, 3–4, 85–102.
[45] For the *tekye* of Otman Baba, see Chapter 2.
[46] This is BOA TD 439, already utilized in Chapters 4 and 5. I have dated it provisionally *c.* 1535, but it could well have been compiled a bit earlier. If we accept the provisional dating of the register as *c.* 1530–5 as well as the tentative dating of the events related to the wedding of Demir Baba's parents, his birth and early life, and Akyazılı's death, as presented above, then this register would post-date the birth of Demir Baba by some 20–30 years, and was composed within (but possibly less than) 10–15 years following Akyazılı Baba's death. The convent of Kız Ana, also known in oral tradition as "Sultan Ana," is clearly identifiable in the village of Sultan Ana, BOA TD 439, p. 308. The village has five tax-paying residents, identified as dervishes, they are exempt from the basic land-tax (*çift-resmi*), but pay the canonical tithe (*'öşr*) on their agricultural produce: wheat, barley, and fodder, as well as on beehives. The first registered tax-payer is a certain Saat Dede, identified as the convent's master (*zāviye-niṣīn*), his son and three other dervishes follow, one of them, Hasan Abidin (likely a convert), is also described as *dervīṣ-i abdāl*. For later sixteenth-century registrations, see BOA TD 382, p. 369 (dated *c.* 1550), where Saat Dede is still alive, but registered as a "saintly old man" (*pīr-i fānī*) and no longer head of convent, and TKG KK TTd 151, f. 158b (dated 1579). The village is clearly traceable down to the present day, including seventeenth-century registrations as Kız Ana Tekyesi (see Andreev, *Rechnik*, 270). It was renamed Momino (a rough Bulgarian translation meaning "Maiden's Village") in 1934. The convent is still very popular with the present-day Alevi-Bektashi community in Bulgaria, especially its female members.

convents, such as that of Gökçe Su, can be only tentatively identified, and with much less certainty.[47] Similarly, Ottoman tax registers for Deliorman, Gerlovo, and the adjacent areas from the first half of the sixteenth century enable the identification of a number of important Rum Abdal figures who participated in the events surrounding Demir's birth according to his *velayetname*.

Thus, while Tay Hızır (Dayı Hızır), a close associate of Akyazılı and Kademli and a participant in Demir Baba's parents' wedding, is not readily identifiable as a taxpayer in any extant contemporary Ottoman tax register, one finds a village named Tay Hızır in the synoptic Ottoman tax register of 1530 (most likely based on an extant 1516 registration) as well as in the detailed registration of *c.* (1530–) 1535 (BOA TD 439).[48] BOA TD 439 also has an entry for the village of Tay Hızır's son

Hafızoğlu Mehmed Efendi's convent is identifiable as *Zāviye-i Ḥāfızoğlu Meḥmed Dede, nām-ı diğer Armudlu Pınarı* in Gerlovo, BOA TD 439, p. 303, later sixteenth-century registrations are: BOA TD 382, p. 404, and TKG KK TTd 151, f. 256a; in the latter two registrations it appears as *Zāviye-i Ḥāfız Dede* and *Zāviye-i Ḥāfızzāde*, respectively, with the alternate name of *Armudlu Pınarı* preserved. Ayverdi's reference to a AH 1234/AD 1818–19 Ottoman tax register, Orlin's recent valuable research on Ottoman documents related to the convent from the late eighteenth and early nineteenth centuries, and Marinov's record of local oral traditions in the 1930s suggest that the convent was close to the village of Kara Evhadlar/Ahadlar in Gerlovo (mod. Vrani Kon, Târgovishte province); the latter village's sixteenth-century registrations also suggest proximity to Hafızoğlu's convent: BOA TD 370, p. 554; BOA TD 439 p. 300; BOA TD 382, p. 556; and TKG KK TTd 151, f. 212b. See E.H Ayverdi, *Avrupa'da Osmanlı Mimari Eserleri*, vol. 4 (Istanbul: Istanbul Fetih Cemiyeti, 1982), 107, Orlin Sabev, "Bulgaristan Bektaşi Tekkelerinden Bir Örnek: Vranikon Hafız Baba Tekkesi, *TKHBVAD* 57 (2011): 175-189, and V. Marinov, *Gerlovo*, 73.

Yolkulu Baba convent's earliest extant registration (*c.* 1530–5) is found as the village of Yolkulu Dede (*Ḳarye-i Yolḳulu Dede*), with Yolkulu's son Hasan Dede registered as convent head (*tekye-nişīn*), and 11 other adult male relatives of Yolkulu enjoying tax privileges; an earlier tax registration is mentioned (but not identified, possibly the extinct 1516 registration of the region); BOA TD 439, p. 234. Later sixteenth-century registrations are: BOA TD 382, p. 475, and TKG KK TTd 151, f. 205a. Ayverdi's reference to a AH 1219/AD 1804–5 register suggests that the convent was located in the village of Veli Bey (mod. Velichka, Târgovishte province) at the time, thus signifying a possible settlement name change; Ayverdi, *Avrupa'da Osmanlı Mimari Eserleri*, vol. 4, 111. If this is the case, then the now extinct convents of Hafızoğlu Mehmed and Yolkulu Dede must have stood 5 kilometers from one another in Gerlovo, with the convent of Kız Ana/Sultan Ana some 50 kilometers to the north.

On these three convents, see also Gramatikova's thoughtful comments in *Neortodoksalniiat Isliam*, 451–456, 459–465. Her analysis has not utilized the sixteenth-century Ottoman tax registers referred to here.

[47] See footnote 20 above.
[48] BOA TD 370, p. 559, BOA TD 439, p. 80. As BOA TD 370 is a summary register, it does not provide the names of tax-payers. BOA TD 439 is detailed, but does not list a "Tay Hızır" who was most likely not among the living at the time; several sons of "Hızır" are identifiable though. For later sixteenth-century registrations, see BOA TD 382, pp. 153–154; TKG KK TTd 151, ff. 49a-b For Tay Hızır's and his convent's role in the *velayetname* of Demir Baba, see *DBV*, 47, 52, 55, 66.

Ali Baba (*karye-i Ali Baba*), whereby the latter is described as being situated in the vicinity of the village of Tay/Dayı Hızır.[49] Thus we have two villages (with convents) founded by father and son in Deliorman in the first half of the sixteenth century. As for the son Ali Baba, in Demir Baba's *velayetname* he is identifiable through his convent which Akyazılı and Demir Baba visit in their tour of the eastern Balkans shortly before the former's death.[50] The detailed tax register *c.* 1535 has "Ali Baba Tay Hızır" as the first registered taxpayer in the village, signifying that he was considered the founder and eponym of the recently established settlement. His brother Osman, son of Tay Hızır (*Osman, veled-i Tay Hızır*)[51] is registered as an *ellici*, one associated with the auxiliary military organization of the *yürüks*.[52] All of the twelve registered taxpayers in the village are described as dervishes, exempt from extraordinary taxes.[53] Just in between Ali Baba and his brother Osman in this registration, one finds a certain Göçbeği/Güçbeke, son of Salih, who may well be the Göçbeği of Demir Baba's *velayetname* – Akyazılı's disciple who delivers the new-born baby Demir into Akyazılı's hands at the naming ceremony five days after Demir's birth.[54] The registration of *c.* 1550 has

---

[49] "*Ḳarye-i ʿAlī Baba, der nezd-i ḳarye-i Ṭay Ḫıżır...*," BOA TD 439, p. 100, for later registrations, see BOA TD 382, p. 151; TKG KK TTd 151, ff. 62b-63a. The village of Tay Hızır may safely be identified with the modern village of Shumentsi, Silistra province. I identify the village of Ali Baba with modern Varnentsi, which is indeed in the vicinity (1.5 miles) of Tay Hızır/Shumentsi. Today's Varnentsi is well known for the still active *tekye* of Deniz Ali Baba. It is worth considering the possibility that Deniz Ali Baba, as he is known today, and Ali Baba, son of Tay Hızır, as identifiable in sixteenth-century Ottoman tax registers and Demir Baba's *vita*, may be one and the same person.

[50] In the first and oldest recension of the *velayetname* (the Akkadınlar/Dulovo recension), he is referred to as "Ali Beg Tay Hızır," and in the second oldest (that from Mumcular/Sveshtari) as "Ali Beg bin Tay Hızır," *DBV*, 66. While Gramatikova is of the opinion that "Ali Beg Tay Hızır" is one person, the analysis of sixteenth-century Ottoman tax registers suggests that these (Tay Hızır and Ali Beg/Baba) were a father and a son.

[51] The fact that one who is clearly identifiable as a member of the Rum Abdal community could be named Osman (Ar. *ʿUthmān*) also deserves attention. While later, down to the present, it became customary among heterodox Muslims in the region not to name their newborn sons after the first three caliphs in the Sunni tradition (Abu Bakr [Tr. Ebu Bekir], Uthman [Tr. Osman], and Umar [Tr. Ömer]), it seems like this taboo was not established in the sixteenth century. This is not the only instance in sixteenth-century tax registers where one can find such naming practices in communities which may be identified with a high degree of certainty as "heterodox." Another possibility is that this practice may have been a form of *taqiyya* (religious dissimulation), but this appears less likely.

[52] Together with four sons of "Hızır," also registered as *ellici*.

[53] "*Mezkūrlar dervīşlerdir. ʿAvārıżdan muʿāflardır. Ellerinde daḫi ḥükümleri vardır.*" BOA TD 439, p. 100.

[54] This identification is uncertain as the *velayetname* has the death of Güç Beke immediately following that of Akyazılı, which may contradict the tentative dating of BOA TD 439 by several years. It is certainly not impossible though. *DBV*, 59, 67.

Ali Baba and Osman still alive (appearing first in the entry): Ali Baba is listed as head of convent (*tekye-nişin*) and Osman does not have the privileged status of *ellici* anymore.[55]

Similarly, Hafızoğlu Mehmed Efendi, whose convent in Gerlovo hosts some of Demir Baba's parents' wedding festivities, is clearly identifiable as a taxpayer in the register of *c.* 1530–5.[56] The caretaker of Otman Baba's mausoleum, Abdi Dede, another wedding guest, can provisionally be identified in a tax register for Thrace tentatively dated from the era of Süleyman I (1520–66).[57]

This critical comparison of Demir Baba's *vita* and sixteenth-century Ottoman tax registers brings up the issue of the "historicity" of hagiographical accounts. Hagiographical accounts' utility as "historical" sources has been questioned due to their assumed "ahistorical" nature. Characteristically dominated by legends of the saints' marvelous deeds, they are often seen as fantastical products of the imagination. Nevertheless, a comparison with traditional "historical" sources may often show hagiographic works as firmly situated in "real" historical contexts and containing substantial elements of "historical narrative."[58] In addition, students of the cult of sainthood utilizing hagiographic accounts have questioned the notion that "individuals and communities are inclined to organize and remember their experience first and foremost as *history*";[59] this has been reinforced by an appeal for a more comprehensive and multilayered analysis of authorial intent that may help hagiographical accounts be "liberated from the tyranny of bland facticity."[60]

While DeWeese's insistence that "historical memory" is just one, and not necessarily the dominant aspect of communal memory, in the context of the comparison of Demir Baba's *velayetname*'s narrative

---

[55] Unlike in the preceding registration of *c.* 1530–5, nobody in the village has the status of *ellici*, which is in tune with the arguments about the gradual sedentarization of the semi-nomadic *yürük*s and their reduction to regular *re'āyā* status already developed in Chapter 5. BOA TD 382, p. 151.

[56] BOA TD 439, p. 303, with two other dervishes listed.

[57] " *'Abdī Dede, türbedār*" in the registration of the convent (*zāviye*) of Otman Baba, BOA TD 385, p. 365.

[58] Ocak, *Menâkıbnâmeler*, 38–39, 65–69. One could also remark that pre-modern historiographic works (esp. chronicles) have rarely been subjected to the level of scrutiny usually applied to hagiographic accounts in this context, see M.F. Köprülü, "Anadolu Selçukları'nın Tarihinin Yerli Kaynakları," *Belleten* 7/No. 27 (1943), 424; also quoted in Ocak, *Menâkıbnâmeler*, 66.

[59] DeWeese, *Islamization and Native Religion*, 161.

[60] Renard, *Friends of God*, 256–257.

and Ottoman administrative sources, communal memory can hardly be seen as extricated from *historical* experience. Hagiographic communities have tended to approach the legendary accounts about the lives of their patron-saints as "truths" – not necessarily *historical* "truths," but certainly *communal* ones that carry indisputable moral validity.[61] The emphasis on moral validity and the prevalence of sacrality over historicity fit especially well the communal interpretation of saints' "marvels," and this should be kept in mind in the context of the following discussion of Demir Baba's miraculous deeds.[62] However, when it comes to the more explicit biohagiographical content in the early sections of Demir Baba's *vita* (likely composed in the early eighteenth century with its earliest preserved recension dated 1824), a comparison with sixteenth-century Ottoman administrative sources which were (near-) contemporary to developments described in the *vita*, may only alert the modern reader to the tenacity of transmission of the oral traditions on the saint's life and the hagiographic community's quest to faithfully preserve the "authentic," "unadulterated" nature of those accounts. Sacrality and historicity need not be mutually exclusive.

6.2.2   The Life of Demir Baba as "Pole" in the Light of his velayetname

It was at his *tekye* at Batova that, having toured with Demir Baba the most important Rum Abdal convents, and sensing the end of his life, Akyazılı transfered the poleship to Demir.[63] As the convent's *tekye-nişin* Güçbeke (Göçbeği) also dies shortly thereafter, it appears logical that Demir Baba, the new Pole of Poles, would stay at Batova and preside at the *tekye*; however, one of the resident dervishes, a certain Sarı Yusuf, chases him away with the accusation that he is "a son of a heretic," while, equivocally, Sarı Yusuf does not deny Demir's high spiritual station as a

---

[61] See DeWeese's comments in *Islamization and Native Religion*, 160–164.
[62] Modern ethnographic and anthropological studies suggest that the factual belief in a saint's miracles can also be widespread. See for example, Valerie Hoffman, *Sufism, Mystics, and Saints in Modern Egypt* (Columbia, SC: University of South Carolina Press, 1995), 98–101.
[63] Akyazılı approaches Demir with the words: "Timur, take the poleship! Take what is your trust and belongs to you!" (*"Timur, al ḳutbiyyetlik pōstu saña ḳutlu ola. Al emānetiñ; ḥāḳ senüñdür!"*), *DBV*, 67.

saintly figure.[64] This incident is the *velayetname*'s first reference to sectarian strife and doctrinal disagreement within the Rum Abdal community.

Ousted from the Batova convent, Demir goes to the *tekye* of Dursun Baba near Babadağ in northern Dobrudja and serves there for seven years as registrar (*nakib postu*), chief baker (*Balım postu, etmekçi postu*), and keeper of the fire (*ateşçi postu*).[65] While at Dursun Baba's lodge, Demir is sent by the eponym to Otman Baba's *tekye* in Thrace. Shortly after Demir's return to Babadağ, Dursun is poisoned by a local dervish whom Demir murders in revenge.[66]

This drama is followed by many years of travels for which the text does not always provide definitive clues regarding the events' timing, sometimes moving back and forth as Demir Baba or other characters recount experiences in the distant past. Characteristically for the genre, most of the legendary stories of Demir Baba's life as *kutb* place an accent on his wonder-working feats. Already a famed miracle-worker, Demir Baba is summonned by the rulers of Özü Sahrası (Bucak) and Moskov (Muscovy) to deliver the local populations from the terror of dragons, then he travels in the lands of Hırvat (Croatia?), Kışmir (?), and Salsal (?).[67] Thereafter Demir excels as a *gazi* who employs his miraculous powers to aid the Ottoman army in and around Buda in Hungary, where he visits the *tekye* of Gül Baba in the city and encounters a high-ranking commander of the Christian king (i.e. the Habsburg emperor), a certain Marko who, having been defeated by Demir on the battlefield, accepts the saint's invitation to convert to Islam.[68]

Upon receiving a letter from his mother, Demir returns to the Balkans, visits a number of convents such as those of Otman Baba and Kızıl Deli in Thrace, and then returns to Deliorman for good after some local travels during which he works a number of miracles, he settles (*vatan edindi*) at a beautiful and secluded place known as Hotal Derbendi, abundant in water and with many water-mills around, where he spends the rest of his life.[69] While there, he is involved in conflicts with spiritual and sectarian rivals, such as the famous *abdal* (later accepted as Bektashi-Alevi) poet

---

[64] "*Eğer atañ mültehid olmasa idi, yol anuñ idi. Mültehid oğlı abdāl meger evliyā ola. Bizüm senüñ velīliğüne inkārımız yokdur. La'net ehl-i inkāra. Muṭlak veliyyu'llāhsuñ.*"; *DBV*, 67.

[65] *DBV*, 68–69. The reference to "Balım postu" here betrays Bektashi influences.

[66] Ibid., 72–73.

[67] Ibid., 79–99.

[68] Ibid., 99–108.

[69] In the same context, the *vita* mentions that soon after settling Demir Baba got his first disciple, from the (presumably nearby) village of Mumcular; *DBV*, 131. Thus the place mentioned in the *vita* is most probably the actual location of the saint's convent/mausoleum complex near the village of Mumcular (mod. Sveshtari, Razgrad province). The village's earliest registration (as "Eski Mumcular") is BOA TD 382, p. 231 (*c.* 1550), the name suggests that it had existed for some time prior. See also Gramatikova, *Neortodoksalniiat Isliam*, 507–510.

Figure 6.3 Mausoleum (*türbe*) of Demir Baba. Photograph by Mariya Kiprovska.

Virani and the leader of the local Bektashis, a certain Hüseyin Baba. He also visits Deliorman's new urban center, Hezargrad. The *velayetname* gives no account of Demir Baba's death, or the construction of his later famous mausoleum (see Fig. 6.3), but mentions several of his successors at the helm of his *tekye*.

This chronological overview of the saint's life based on his *velayet-name* appears tentative at best. Not all individual stories of Demir Baba's exploits (following his long spell at Dursun Baba's convent) necessarily follow one another chronologically. This discontinuity is especially the case with the legendary accounts toward the end of the *vita* where Demir helps Ali Pasha – an Ottoman commander and governor of Babadağ – in the Ottoman war effort at Budim, and also encounters the Bektashi leader Hüseyin Baba; the latter account follows the story of his rivalry with the poet Virani at which point Demir is mentioned to have been 120 years old.[70] While Demir Baba may have lived a very long life, this age reference is likely an exaggeration, typical of Muslim saints' *vitae*.

[70] *DBV*, 151–173.

6.2.2.1 *Debate and Contest, Marvels and Recognition: Demir Baba's Image as an Axial Saint and Communal Leader* The construction and nature of Demir Baba's image as a wonder-working saint who was an anchor of communal identity – the epitome of the community's religious, social, and moral values – follows a well-established common model developed in *vitae* dedicated to earlier saints of the heterodox Babai/Kalenderi/Abdal tradition (later assimilated into the Bektashi-Alevi tradition) as it developed in Anatolia and later in the Balkans from the thirteenth through the sixteenth centuries.[71] This model found a firm textual expression with the composition of the hagiographical accounts of Baba İlyas (*Menakıb-ı Kudsiyye*), Hacı Bektaş, Abdal Musa, Kaygusuz Abdal, Hacım Sultan, Seyyid Ali Sultan (Kızıl Deli), and Otman Baba, among others.[72] Through the hyperbolical presentation of the saint's wonder-working abilities via the utilization of a well-developed and recognizable inventory of miracle motifs and tropes, the accounts of Demir Baba's marvels present him as an ecstatic mystic (Tr. *meczub*, Ar. *majdhub*) occupying the station of sainthood (*velayet*). Having been chosen, endowed, and guided by God, he is the communal intermediary between God's divine power and mortal believers.[73] A characteristic feature of most hagiographical works of this tradition is the veneration of Ali and his acceptance as the model and epitome of sainthood.

Demir Baba's marvels span almost the entire typological gamut of miraculous tropes and motifs in Muslim hagiography.[74] His sacred power and the moral validity of the beliefs and values which he epitomizes are continuously demonstrated, tested, and confirmed in a number of encounters with various members of Ottoman society and beyond: representatives of the Ottoman authorities, sectarian rivals, members of the Rum Abdal community itself, city-dwellers, villagers, and nomads, as well as rulers and commoners (Muslim and Christian) beyond the confines of the Ottoman polity. As the saint works his wonders, those who accept his station and the beliefs and values he embodies get rewarded and those who appear hostile or have committed wrongdoing are accorded their just punishments.[75]

[71] Gramatikova, *Neortodoksalniiat Isliam*, 332; Ocak, *Menâkıbnâmeler*.

[72] Ocak, *Menâkıbnâmeler*.

[73] Gramatikova, *Neortodoksalniat Isliam*, 331.

[74] For a typological analysis of saintly marvels in Islamic hagiography, see Renard, *Friends of God*, 91–117. For a similar discussion focused specifically on the heterodox Islamic hagiographic tradition in Anatolia and the Balkans, see Ocak, *Menâkıbnâmeler*, 70–96. Due to the scope of the present study, the analysis of Demir Baba's marvels is selective; for a more detailed discussion, see Gramatikova, *Neortodoksalniiat Isliam*, 322–399.

[75] On debate and contest, see also DeWeese's discussion in *Islamization and Native Religion*, 167–179; on the religious, socio-cultural, and epistemological nature and significance of miracles and marvels, see Renard, *Friends of God*, 91–117.

The Kalenderî/Abdal hagiographic tradition can be seen as a particular constituent of the broader Islamic hagiographic tradition and the wider phenomenon of the cult of saints in Islam.[76] It also incorporates diverse pre-Islamic and non-Islamic cultural elements and influences specific to Turkic peoples and the respective socio-cultural milieux of their historical development.[77]

Doctrinally, Demir Baba's image as an axial saint as developed in his *velayetname* appears naturally closest to Otman Baba's as constructed in the latter's *vita* and very much follows the hagiological model developed there. Demir is most prevalently characterized as *kutb* and also *kutbü'l-aktab*, *kutb-i 'alem*, *kutb-i zaman*, *kutbü'd-devran*, etc. – the Pole, more fully Pole of Poles, the *Axis Mundi*, the Axis of the Age, etc.[78] The last appellation finds a confirmation in the statement that "every age has its 'sultan'"[79] and is in unison with Ibn Arabi's conceptualization of the hierarchy of the saints.[80] Closely associated with the concept of the "perfect man" (*insan al-kamil*), Demir is endowed with the Muhammadan Light, the sanctity of Ali, and the universal mission to bring justice and make this world better.[81] He is the "mine of sainthood and generosity" (*kan-ı velayet, kan-ı keramet, ma'den-i keramet*),[82] the "fountain of spiritual guidance" (*menba'-ı hidayet*),[83] "the mine of truth" (*ma'den-i hakikat*),[84] the "lord of sainthood" (*şah-ı velayet*),[85] the "lord of the world" (*şah-ı 'alem*),[86] the "fountainhead (leader) of the saints" (*ser-çeşme-i*

---

[76] See Goldziher, "The Veneration of Saints in Islam," and Renard's *Friends of God*.

[77] See Ocak, *Alevî ve Bektaşî İnançlarının İslam Öncesi Temelleri*.

[78] *Kutb* and its variations are used to characterize Demir Baba throughout the narrative.

[79] "*Her bir günüñ bir sulţānı var*," *DBV*, 102, 133. "Sultan" here is used to denote spiritual leadership and hardly contains political claims, as will be further discussed below.

[80] Whereby, according to Ibn 'Arabi's classical theory of sainthood, in every age there is one *kutb* who presides over a hierarchy of a fixed number of saints, Chodkiewicz, *Seal of the Saints*, 53–54, 89–102.

[81] In the context of Demir Baba's rivalry with the poet and mystic Virani Baba, discussed in greater detail further below, Virani admits the superior station of Demir Baba: "I realized that you are the manifestation/confirmation of the Friend of God," i.e. a "saint," but this may be understood in the more specific meaning of 'manifestation of Ali,' "You are the Muhammadan Light and the sainthood of Ali, O you, Friend of God!" ("*Bildüm tahķīķ-i veliyü'llāhsuñ, nūr-ı Muhammed, velāyet-i 'Alī'süñ yā velī*," on another occasion Demir Baba characterizes himself as a "slave/servant of Ali" ('*Alī ķulu*), *DBV*, 145, 74. Compare to similar usage for Otman Baba in his *vita*, *OBV*, 49, 83. See also Gramatikova, *Neortodoksalniiat Islam*, 287–290, 294–295.

[82] These epithets are used throughout the text, to give a few examples, *DBV*, 62, 67, 75, 86, 92, 94, 99, 107, 119, 125, 131, 141, 154, 159, and 170.

[83] Ibid., 92.

[84] Ibid., 86, 94, 96.

[85] Ibid., 92.

[86] Throughout the text, e.g. *DBV*, 82, 93, 100, 111, 123, 131, 141, 160, 172.

evliya).[87] He is compared to Ali who is referred to as "the lord of the two worlds" (*iki cihan serveri*), but not explicitly presented as such himself.[88] Demir Baba's characterization as "the seal of sainthood" (*hatm-ı velayet*)[89] should be seen as placing an emphasis on the saint's station as the ultimate proof and epitome of sainthood[90] and not necessarily as an allusion to an anticipated imminent end of the cycle of sainthood or the end of time.[91] Similarly, while Demir Baba is referred to as the *mahdi*,[92] this claim appears isolated and seems to be intended to reinforce his status as *kutb*, rather than to carry any substantive messianic overtones. However, compared to his "spiritual grandfather," Demir's claims to spiritual authority appear more muted and contained. While Otman Baba claims to be the "lieutenant of God (*Halife-i Hüda*), the "mystery of God" (*sırr-ı Hüda*), the "mystery of Muhammad" (*sırr-ı Muhammed*) as well as the reincarnation of a number of major prophets and saints, such claims are absent in Demir Baba's case (Demir is the "Light of Muhammad" and the manifestation of the sainthood of Ali, but also the latter's "slave/servant" [kul]).[93] The dialectic relationship between the ages of prophethood and sainthood in Otman Baba's *vita*, whereby Otman Baba is "the shepherd and custodian of prophethood" is reduced here to a linear and subordinate one: Demir is only "the deputy of the prophets" (*ka'im-makam-ı enbiya*).[94] This visible diminishment of claims to spiritual authority corresponds congruently to a similar reduction of claims to political authority (compared to those of both Otman Baba and Akyazılı Baba).

Demir Baba's outward mien also highlights a number of important facets of his image. The most vivid relevant clues relate to the lengthy

---

[87] *DBV*, 90.

[88] Ibid., 100–101. Compare with the use of "lord of the two worlds," *şāh-ı dü cihān*, for Otman Baba in *OBV*.

[89] Used throughout the narrative, a few examples are: *DBV*, 67, 81, 94, 105, 120, 134, 141, 154, 159.

[90] On the nature of the "seal of the saints" as expounded in Ibn 'Arabi's classical theory of sainthood, see Chodkiewicz, *Seal of the Saints*, 116–127, and esp. 122. For an earlier, and influential, discussion of the concept, which inspired Ibn 'Arabi's own writings on the issue, see al-Hakim al-Tirmidhi, *The Concept of Sainthood in Early Islamic Mysticism: Two Works by al-Hakim al-Tirmidhi*, ed. and trans. Bernd Radtke and John O'Kane (Richmond, UK: Curzon Press, 1996), 97–109.

[91] Gramatikova is of the opinion that the usage of *ḥatm-ı velāyet* in the *velayetname* signifies the chronological end of the cycle of sainthood, but the context of the narrative hardly supports this, Gramatikova, *Neortodoksalniiat Isliam*, 291.

[92] On one single occasion, *DBV*, 159.

[93] For a more detailed discussion of the epithets and appelations used to construct the image of Demir Baba as an axial saint in his *velayetname*, see Gramatikova, *Neortodoksalniiat Isliam*, 287–306.

[94] *OBV*, 235; *DBV*, 90.

peregrinations in the middle part of his life, as well as to some local travels during his later life in Deliorman. The *vita* presents Demir Baba's decision to go back to his native land and settle there largely as a response to a letter from his mother Zahide Dürdane that is brought to him while he is fighting on the Ottomans' side at Budim. The saint's mother expresses in strong terms her dissatisfaction with her son's way of life. While she thought she had given birth to a *veli* (a saint), he turned out to be a *deli* (i.e. a lunatic, mad one, but may also be a reference to an ecstatic mystic).[95] Having sent him money for a living, clothes to put on and a horse to mount, she begs him to come back to her and warns him to make no excuses, threatening that if he does not come back, she will follow him.[96] These hints about Demir Baba's ways of life are confirmed and amplified in a local dervish's description of Demir's appearance on the occasion of a visit the saint pays to the convent of Kızıl Deli in Thrace in his later life: "he wanders around chubby-faced, having completed the 'four blows.'"[97] During his peregrinations, Demir Baba normally wears a coarse felt garment.[98] His most important implements are his wooden staff – which he uses as a weapon in battle, in self-defense during his travels, or as an auxiliary instrument when working miracles[99] – a black whip,[100] a hatchet, and a begging bowl.[101] He usually walks barefoot and is sometimes scolded for wandering (semi-)naked.[102] In other words, during his travels Demir Baba emerges as the typical wandering antinomian renunciant dervish of the Kalenderi/Abdal tradition, given to voluntary poverty (*fakr*) and withdrawal from the pleasures of wordly life (*tecerrüd*) in accordance with the doctrine of complete reliance on God (*tevekkül*). This image is in unison with numerous contemporary Ottoman as well as Western observers' descriptions of renunciant dervish groups in the fifteenth and sixteenth centuries[103] and does not differ much from that of Otman Baba. However, while Otman Baba travels throughout his life and his lifestyle and appearance are emulated by most of his followers (who accompany him), Demir Baba's travels occupy only a part of his life and he usually travels alone or, occasionally, with a small suite of *Abdals*;

---

[95] "*Ben sanurdum velī doğurdum, ḥikmet-i Rabbānī meger deli doğurmışam,*" DBV, 108.
[96] "*İmdi gerekdür kim saña esvāb gönderdim, geyesüñ. At gönderdüm, süvār olasuñ. Ḥarclıḳ gönderdüm, nafaḳa idinesüñ. Ve özür bahāne eylemeyesüñ. Eğer sen gelmezseñ Deli Demir Dürdāne'yi hemān peşine bilesüñ.*" Ibid., 108.
[97] "*Ablāḳ sablāḳ çār-ı ḍarb yürür,*" ibid., 117–118.
[98] Ibid., 99.
[99] Ibid., 99–100, 106, 130, 132.
[100] Ibid., 74.
[101] One of the appelations used to describe Demir Baba in the *velayetname* is *Keşkülcü Baba*, DBV, 71.
[102] DBV, 99; some of Demir Baba's Abdals are also referred to as '*uryān* (naked), ibid. 146.
[103] Karamustafa, *God's Unruly Friends*, 13–23, 70–78; Ocak, *Kalenderîler*, 115–116.

most of his followers who accept him as *kutb* live settled in convents or in village communities.

Another major aspect of Demir Baba's outer appearance is his physical strength.[104] The epithet employed most often to convey this image is *pehlivan*, "wrestler," and more generally "hero," "champion," and "mighty man," but in a number of contexts in the *velayetname* the specific meaning of "wrestler/fighter" is evident.[105] Endowed with supernatural physical might, the saint easily overpowers his adversaries, be it infidels on the battlefield or nay-sayers who dare to question his saintly station and sacred power. The use of *pehlivan* and *pehlivanlık* (the quality of being a *pehlivan*) also connects to the overall image of Demir Baba as the Axis of the Age: he is described as the Pehlivan of the Age and the Pehlivan of the World.[106] This epithet is also employed to describe other characters in the *velayetname* – heterodox Muslim saints in the Balkans, such as Sarı Saltık and Kızıl Deli[107] as well as Christian military commanders like Pehlivan Marko and Karaca Pehlivan, Demir's battlefield adversaries in Hungary. In constructing the image of the saint, the narrator fuses physical strength with moral uprightness and sacred power, endowing bodily might with quasi-sacral qualities. While the *velayetname* is not that explicit, some oral traditions suggest a relationship between the cult of Demir Baba and wrestling contests which constitute a part and parcel of the cultural landscape of Deliorman and Gerlovo; wrestling contests are seen as prominent popular festivities, but also as a context in which one's overall personal integrity and uprightness are tested and demonstrated.[108] This can be related to the prominence of "oiled wrestling" as a popular sport, well accounted for in the modern Balkans and Anatolia, with Deliorman being one of the emblematic regions associated with it.[109]

6.2.2.2   *Demir Baba and the Community – The Saint as an Epitome of Power, Justice, and Generosity*   Demir Baba's miraculous abilities are best articulated in his dealings with followers and foes. Through the working

---

[104] Oral traditions not included in the *velayetname* also present him as tall, Gramatikova, *Neortodoksalniiat Isliam*, 285.

[105] References to Demir Baba as *pehlivān bābā*, *Timur Bābā Pehlivān*, etc., abound throughout the text of the *velayetname*, several examples are: *DBV*, 76, 79, 83, 89, 93, 95, 117,126, 134, 161, 171; in the context of his fights against the infidels at Budim, he is styled as *gāzī pehlivān*, ibid. 101; for Demir Baba's fight against wild beasts in the court of Sultan Ahmed at the end of his life, see ibid. 134–135.

[106] *Pehlivān-ı zemāne, cihān pehlivānı*," *DBV*, 99, 79.

[107] *DBV*, 99, 110.

[108] Gramatikova, *Neortodoksalniiat Isliam*, 304.

[109] While the connection to the rise of wrestling as a national sport in modern Turkey is obvious, a similar connection may be made (although not definitively proven) to the prominence of wrestling as a national sport in modern Bulgaria too.

of various miracles, the saint appears not only as the epitome of communal values, but also as the ultimate guarantor of these same values and
the community's defender against evil forces and injustice, be it during
his own lifetime or well after his death. Through his mastery of the forces
of nature and the ability to overpower evil-doers, Demir Baba emerges as
the helper of ordinary people and the deliverer of those who have fallen in
trouble – he endows people with power, blesses them with offspring and
their land with fertility, heals them from terrible diseases, defends them
against unjust and corrupt officials and notables as well as evil supernatural threats (such as dragons), and opens up water sources. Conversely,
the saint miraculously punishes those who question his sacred power, but
also those who show disrespect toward prevalent communal values, he
causes illness and death, deprives villains of offspring and good harvests,
or forces disbelievers and wrongdoers into humble submission.[110]

Demir Baba demonstrates his mastery over the forces of nature thus
when he helps his fellow dervishes at Dursun Baba's lodge in Dobrudja.
As they need to cut large trees to procure firewood for the *tekye*, the
saint causes a windstorm which fells the trees around, greatly facilitat-
ing the dervishes' task.[111] In a similar vein, Demir Baba miraculously
opens up water springs, as in the case of his encounter with a villager in
Deliorman who wishes he could satisfy his thirst, whereupon the saint
pokes the ground with his staff and a spring of splendid cold healing
water (*ayazma*) emerges. This miracle brings 2,000 people from the surrounding villages who organize festivities (*hacet bayramı*) to honor the
saint.[112] In the same story Demir Baba also plants 200 orchard trees,
an act that suggests his encouragement of agriculture.[113] Opening up a
spring could also persuade skeptics to recognize his lofty station, as in the
case of the villagers of Kara Koç who reverse their negative attitudes after
he drills a hole in a large rock to open up a spring and satisfy the water
supply needs of the village.[114] Importantly, all these "water source" marvels take place only in Deliorman – a region known for its limited and
unstable aboveground water resources, where karst springs dry up and
resume their activity unexpectedly, small creeks lose their way between
the rocks, and subterranean waters surface at various locations.[115]

One of the most characteristic motifs in the heterodox hagiographical tradition in Anatolia and the Balkans is the healing of infertility in

---

[110] Gramatikova, *Neortodoksalniiat Isliam*, 395.
[111] *DBV*, 69.
[112] Ibid., 129–130.
[113] Ibid., 130.
[114] Ibid., 127–129.
[115] Marinov, *Deli-Orman*, 28–29; Gramatikova, *Neortodoksalniiat Isliam*, 229–230.

women. In the *velayetname* this motif is situated in Istanbul where the saint, in his youth, heals ten women including the *şeyhülislam*'s daughter, so that she and the chief *müfti*'s son-in-law, Turran Efendi, can finally have a son.[116] This story is embedded as a retrospective reference within the larger account of the terrible judge of Hezargrad in the latter years of Demir Baba's life. The judge mercilessly persecutes local wandering renunciant dervishes (*ışıks*); not being content with ordering them hanged, he would go as far as to have their graves destroyed. The saint arrives in the city to help the unfortunate *ışık*s, only to find out that the judge is in fact Turran Efendi whom he had miraculously endowed with a son many years earlier. Turran Efendi welcomes the saintly man and, not having forgotten his marvellous deed, stops oppressing the dervishes.[117] Thus, the saint's marvel ultimately helps him protect members of the Abdal community from the oppression of the Ottoman authorities whose respect and support he enjoys.

By far, Demir Baba's most grandiose miracles in the service of humankind relate to his fights with dragons. Dragon fighting is a well-established *topos* in the folklore and religious traditions of most peoples of Eurasia. In Christianity, it is most emphatically integrated in the image of St. George. The dragon is the most commonly represented mythical beast in Islamic culture, and especially in Islamic architecture.[118] The slaying of dragons is also a major motif in the Anatolian-Balkan heterodox Islamic hagiographic tradition, with Sarı Saltık's being the most illustrious example. The saint's encounter with the beast – perceived as an epitome of evil, Hell, and the forces of Satan – emerges as a symbolically loaded allegorical representation of the cosmic struggle between good and evil. In the light of the intended impact in hagiographic works, the most important element of dragon-fighting legends is probably not the saint's encounter with the dragon, but the message he sends to the community (through his behavior and speech) before and in the immediate aftermath of his triumph. It is in this context that this message and the values it affirms carry the most persuasive force to the audience, as the victory over the dragon itself validates his saintly station and sacred miraculous powers in the most emphatic terms.

In the *velayetname* Demir Baba fights two dragons: one in the lands of Islam, on the plain of Özü (mod. Ochakiv in Ukraine) ruled by the

---

[116] Demir Baba is reported to have been twenty-five years of age at the time of working this miracle. *DBV*, 135–137.
[117] For the whole story, see *DBV*, 131–138.
[118] Abbas Daneshvari, "The Iconography of the Dragon in the Cult of Saints in Islam," in *Manifestations of Sainthood in Islam*, ed. Grace M. Smith and Carl W. Ernst (Istanbul: The Isis Press, 1993), 15.

lord of Bucak, a member of the Giray dynasty ("Cengiz-zade"), and the other in Muscovy. Having heard stories about Demir Baba's miracles presenting him as "the one who passes for the *kutb* of the age,"[119] the Giray khan sends an elaborate letter to the saint asking for his help. Demir Baba's response is positive, however, he states he will not fight the dragon for the sake of the khan, that "city boy" (*şehr oğlanı*), thus echoing Otman Baba's animosity toward the empowered, state-related urban classes, but for the sake of the "religion of Islam" and out of his respect for the *gazi*s who had come there.[120] After defeating the dragon using an elaborate array of arms (a German sword, a specially designed rifle, a Düldül-like horse, etc.) and observed by 80,000 people, Demir Baba performs a ritual washing of the hands, followed by a prayer.[121] "The fountainhead of the mystics and the exemplar of the munificent" declines the gift of 700 *okka*s of gold offered to him by various local communities, and instead allocates one part of it for the holy city of Medina, another part for the *tekye* of Dursun Baba in Dobrudja, and distributes the rest among the needy and his Abdals.[122]

The story of Demir Baba's exploits in Muscovy, also plagued by a dragon, is similar, the major difference being that it plays out outside the lands of Islam. The king (*kıral*) of Muscovy, having heard of Demir Baba's exploits in Bucak, suggests that he send an envoy to "the *padişah* of the Turks" (*Türk padişahına*) to summon Demir Baba, but his advisors tell him that Demir is of a special kind and that this "*pehlivan*" should be invited personally to help "for the love of Ali" (*Ali aşkına*).[123] When the king meets the saint and asks him about the *millet* (confessional community) he belongs to, Demir Baba proudly proclaims: "I am from the *millet* of Halil İbrahim."[124] After some elaborate preparations, Demir Baba defeats the dragon. The infidel king offers him a province to rule as his own, a cartload of gold, and 40,000 Muslim captives. The saint declines the first two gifts saying that he should go back to his land, but takes the captive Muslims and restores their freedom by bringing them to the lands of Islam (Özü).[125]

---

[119] "*Kutb-ı zamāne geçer,*" *DBV*, 77.
[120] "*Bak a! Canavaruñ şehr oğlanlağñ, bak a! Şaşkınuñ er nesine yarar? Anuñ içün değül dīn-i İslām ḫāṭırası içün varalum dimiş ve hem bunda gelen gāzīlerüñ ḫürmeti içün varuram inşā'allāh,*" *DBV*, 80. Importantly, no traces of similar animosity toward members of the Ottoman dynasty are found in Demir Baba's *velayetname*.
[121] Düldül was the legendary horse of Imam 'Ali. *DBV*, 81–82, 88.
[122] "*Ol erenler ser-çeşmesi ve cömerdler pişvāsı...,*" *DBV* 88.
[123] *DBV*, 89–90. In fact, the narrative suggests that the two dragons originated in Muscovy, but then one of them went to the plain of Özü, ibid., 85, 89.
[124] Ibid., 91.
[125] Ibid., 93–94.

234 Religion, Culture, and Authority: Two Case Studies

Demir Baba's mystical power is also asserted through his miraculous ability to punish those who do not accept his sainthood or wrong the community. Most typically, the saint would cast an evil look at the culprits, which would cause them to feel unwell at first, then bring about their death, usually as they try to flee, having realized that they have become the object of the Demir's wrath and giving themselves to belated repentance.[126] Thus, Abdurrahman Baba, a dervish who derides Demir's mystical powers at the convent of Dursun Baba in Dobrudja, incurs the saint's evil look and dies of fever shortly thereafter while taking refuge at a nearby convent that had remained from the "old Muslims."[127] As we shall see, the saint's avowed spiritual and sectarian rivals, the Bektashi Hüseyin Baba and the mystic Virani Baba, meet with similar fates.

Similar punishments are meted out to oppressors within the local community. The villagers of Arslan Köy[128] in Deliorman are harrassed by the arrogant Ramazan Hoca, a local *alim*, and his son; the latter would often scare the village folk by chasing them and their animal herds with his horse. The *hoca*'s son does the same to Demir Baba who is passing by with several of his dervishes. Ramazan Hoca chases away the dervishes addressing them derogatorily as "*ışık*s" and claiming that he controls the village, being in the service of the *padişah*. He fails to heed the dervishes' warnings and their seemingly odd assertion that he has an *ışık* in his own house. The moment of truth comes some time later at the wedding of the *hoca*'s son who gets killed by a falling tree branch while riding his horse recklessly. Upon learning the news, Ramazan Hoca, stricken with grief and given to repentance, admits: "Now I have become an *ışık*." Kissing Demir's hand, he exclaims, "Now I am your *abdal*, my father!"[129] Importantly here, the wrongdoer who receives his deserved punishment is cast as a representative of the Sharia-minded *ulema*.

Similarly, when Ali Pasha, governor of Babadağ, takes forty rams from Demir Baba's flock to breed them without asking for the saint's permission, his ewes fail to give birth to a single lamb, and not a single child is born in the province that same year.[130]

---

[126] On this topos in the heterodox hagiographical tradition in Anatolia and the Balkans, see Ocak, *Menâkıbnâmeler*, 91–92; for the use of similar tropes in the *vita* of Otman Baba, see *OBV*, 74–5, 150,

[127] *DBV*, 72–73. The mention of "old Muslims" may refer to pre-Ottoman Turcoman migrations.

[128] Modern Lâvino, Razgrad province. The village's first tax registration is in BOA TD 439 (*c.* 1535), p. 283, as Nebi Fakihler, and later, *c.* 1550, in TD 382, p. 292, as "Nebi Fakihler, its other name being Arslan Köy."

[129] For the whole story, see *DBV*, 157–159.

[130] *DBV*, 163–164.

6.2.2.3 Demir Baba as a gazi Following the already well-developed Anatolian-Balkan heterodox hagiographic tradition, Demir Baba's role as a *gazi*-saint is emphatically highlighted in the *velayetname*. During his peregrinations in the middle part of his life he accidentally finds himself near Budim (Buda) where he sees many people fighting and wonders what is going on. At that point the hidden prophet Hızır (Ar. *Khidr*) appears to Demir and discloses the nature of the fight, giving him a sign that the conquests are blessed by God.[131] Demir Baba runs across a fellow who shoots at him crying, "Muhammed, Muhammed!" Upon apprehending the attacker and asking him whether he is circumcised, the latter responds: "I am a Muslim."[132] Thus the saint joins the Ottoman *gaza* against the infidels. The narrative makes it clear that these events take place after the Ottoman incorporation of Buda (1541), so (if one assumes the veracity of the narrative) they relate an episode in the Ottoman-Habsburg frontier encounters some time in the late 1540s or 1550s.

Having just a single battlefield companion (the Ottoman soldier he initially meets), Demir proves his invincibility to infidel swords and bullets in several successive encounters. Entering the battle with a prayer – "In the name of God and the majesty of Muhammed Mustafa and the Lord of Sainthood Ali, the Chosen One of God"[133] – and armed with his staff, he breaks the enemy's swords into pieces, killing five or ten adversaries with a single blow; when he tells their horses to stop carrying them, the horses obey, go mad, and throw down their infidel riders.[134] Demir compares his mission to Ali's *gaza* at the Battle of Uhud[135] and inspires his single comrade, with whose help he captures 80 infidel soldiers.[136] After these successes he goes to the fortress of Buda where he is accepted with admiration by the *gazi*s, together with whom he pays a visit to the *abdals* of the convent of Gül Baba, an Ottoman warrior-saint, eventually assimilated into the Bektashi pantheon of saints, who, according to tradition, died heroically during the Ottoman annexation of Buda in 1541.[137]

---

[131] *DBV*, 99. On the prophet Hızır in Turkish Sufism, see A.Y. Ocak, *İslâm-Türk İnançlarında Hızır Yahut Hızır-İlyas Kültü* (Ankara: Ankara Üniversitesi Basımevi, 1985), 82–100, and A.J. Wensinck, "al-Khaḍir (al-Khiḍr)," *EI²*.

[132] *DBV*, 99.

[133] "*Be-nâm-ı Ḫüdâ ve devlet-i Muḥammed Muṣṭafâ, ṣâh-ı velâyet 'Aliyye'-l-murtażâ*," *DBV*, 100.

[134] *DBV*, 100.

[135] The Battle of Uhud was one of the major battles in early Islamic history, fought between the Muslims led by the Prophet Muhammad and the Quraysh Meccans north of Medina in AD 625. See C.F. Robinson, "Uḥud," *EI²*.

[136] *Demir Baba Velayenamesi*, 100–101.

[137] The earliest mention of Gül Baba's convent in Buda belongs to Georg Wernher who visited the city in 1551; the earliest related Ottoman document – a registration of repair expenses – is dated 1566; it mentions the convent's capacity to host sixty dervishes.

The saint's fame as a *gazi* spreads among the infidels. They learn that he was Akyazılı Baba's "son," the mighty *pehlivan* who had defeated dragons at Özü and Muscovy, and so many of them deem it judicious to refrain from attacking the "Turk" for at least some time.[138] The infidel king (i.e. the Habsburg emperor) thinks similarly, but his foremost commander, a champion called Marko (*Marko nam pehlivan*) is eager to defeat Demir and scolds the king for his timidity. The king accepts Marko's plan to attack the "Turk who passes for the *kutb*" in order to restore the dignity of Jesus.[139] He sends Marko on his mission with 100 select fighters. Marko finds Demir with an "Ottoman" (*Osmanlı*) contingent of seventeen *sipahis* at a nearby "Ottoman" village. Demir Baba, the "Pole of Poles" and the "Seal of Sainthood," riding a blue roan horse and fighting with his cudgel, is able to instantly floor scores of infidels.[140] He and his seventeen Ottoman *sipahi* comrades also disperse a 3,000-strong support contingent sent by the king to aid Marko in his fight against the "[semi-]naked *gazi*" (*çıplak gazi*).[141] In this last battle, the saint miraculously withstands the sword, arrows, and bullets of an infidel attacker. When Demir overpowers the infidel and invites him to the faith, the enemy soldier arrogantly declines the offer, and the "mine of miracles" and "seal of sainthood" crushes his head.[142]

In the immediate aftermath of this last battle, Demir and his comrades go back to the Budim fortress with numerous captives and rich booty. Among the captives is the fallen Marko, whose execution has been ordered by the king who has learnt of his failure. Demir invites Marko to become a Muslim and warns him not to spurn God's intercession. Marko accepts and when Demir's comrades suggest "Turran" as Marko's new Muslim name, Demir graciously allows the infidel *pehlivan* to keep his original name upon conversion to Islam.[143] When the saint urges one of Marko's captive comrades, Karaca Pehlivan, to accept Islam as well, the latter implores Demir not to force him to do so as the king would kill his children in revenge. Demir, having also asked Marko's advice in the matter, frees Karaca.[144] While these conversion motifs in Demir Baba's exploits as a *gazi* hardly suggest a substantive quest to

---

While the convent itself is extinct, the adjacent mausoleum (*türbe*) of Gül Baba is one of the most imposing extant Ottoman monuments in Buda(pest) today. See Semavi Eyice, "Gülbaba Tekkesi ve Türbesi," *TDVİA*, vol. 14, 228–230.

[138] *DBV*, 102.
[139] Ibid., 102–103.
[140] Ibid., 103–105.
[141] Ibid., 105–106.
[142] Ibid., 106.
[143] Ibid., 106–107.
[144] Ibid., 107.

spread Islam among the infidels on a mass scale,[145] they could be seen as "superiority *topoi*" highlighting the spiritual and moral supremacy of Islam over Christianity. Marko's conversion and Karaca Pehlivan's non-conversion highlight Demir's grace, generosity, and chivalry. Following all this, Demir Baba meets a group of dervishes from Akyazılı Baba's *tekye* in Batova, who have come to Budim to collect a quarter of the tax income of the Budim fortress which Sultan Süleyman had allocated as a pious endowment (*waqf*) to Akyazılı Baba's convent in Dobrudja.[146] The dervishes from Batova also bring Demir Baba a letter from his mother Zahide Dürdane who implores him to go back to his native land (as discussed above, Demir respects his mother's summons). Thus, the *gaza* episode in Demir Baba's *velayetname* casts him as a victorious warrior-saint and noble champion of the faith.[147] Like his victory over the dragon in Muscovy, this episode provides one more opportunity to stress that Demir Baba's saintly station and sacred supernatural powers were recognized and admired by and awed non-Muslims, and did so outside the Abode of Islam. However, while Demir Baba's contribution to the Ottoman war effort appears important, the Ottoman state and dynasty are recognized as the leading legitimate agents of *gaza*: the Muslim soldiers, the fortress of Budim, and the villages around are all cast as "Ottoman." The Christian infidels likewise recognize their adversaries across the Danube as "Ottoman" (as well as *Türk*), and all this happens in the age of Sultan Süleyman who has graciously endowed Akyazılı Baba's *tekye*. Compared to the late fifteenth-century *vita* of Seyyid Ali Sultan (Kızıl Deli), Demir Baba's image as a *gazi*-saint is in tune with the transformation of Ottoman *gaza* from the fourteenth to through the sixteenth centuries, whereby "war for the faith" was increasingly the preserve of the centralizing Ottoman state (and its armed forces under central state control), with the heroes of *gaza* of the early days of the Ottoman enterprise – such as individual frontier lords, Turcoman semi-nomadic adventurers, and *gazi*-dervishes – losing their leading role in the process.[148] While in Kızıl Deli's *velayetname*, Kızıl Deli, Rüstem

---

[145] On Anatolian and Balkan heterodox Sufi sheykhs' contributions to the process of conversion to Islam in the light of their *vitae*, see Ocak, "Bâzı Menâkıbnâmelere Göre."

[146] There is no documentary evidence of any Ottoman endowment in Buda supporting Akyazılı's *tekye* in Dobrudja. Rather, this claim should be read in the context of the narrative's earlier reference to Sultan Süleyman's recognition and respect for Akyazılı, as well as one more reminder of the sultan's (and by extension, the Ottoman state's) overall support for the Rum Abdals.

[147] See also Gramatikova's comments in *Neortodoksalniiat Isliam*, 306–314.

[148] On this transformation of *gaza* and its legitimization in Ottoman historiography and legal thought, see Colin Imber, "Ideals and Legitimation in Early Ottoman History," in *Süleyman the Magnificent and His Age: The Ottoman Empire in the Early Modern World*, ed. Metin Kunt and Christine Woodhead (London: Longman, 1995), 138–153.

Gazi, and their dervish-warrior companions are presented as the dominant champions of the Muslim conquest of the Balkans, and as seemingly independent saintly free-booters of sorts, with the Ottoman ruler left lingering in the background, Demir Baba's *vita* clearly casts the saint in a supporting role, firmly situated within a well-recognized and accepted Ottoman framework. All this said, one cannot fail to notice the conspicuous pro-Alid overtones in Demir's image as a *gazi*, which fits the overall spirit of the narrative.

6.2.2.4 *Demir Baba and the Ottoman Dynasty, State, and Political Order*   The discussion of the events leading to Demir Baba's assumption of the poleship and the analysis of some episodes of his life thereafter have already suggested the overall positive character of the relationship between the Abdals of Rum of Otman Baba's branch and the Ottoman dynasty, state, and authorities as presented in the *velayetname*. While readily recognizing the legitimacy of the Ottoman order, the narrative likewise stresses the Ottoman dynasty and state's positive stance toward the Rum Abdal community and its leaders. Sultan Süleyman is a "friend of the saints" who attends the wedding of Demir Baba's parents, Akyazılı Baba is his spiritual guide, Kademli Baba heals an Ottoman princess in Thrace, while Demir Baba also acts in the capacity of one of "God's friendly physicians"[149] when he heals from infertility the daughter of the Ottoman *şeyhülislam* in Istanbul, a feat that earns him the gratitude of the chief *müfti*'s son-in-law and would later help him protect some of his Abdals in Deliorman. Demir also employs his miraculous powers fighting on the Ottoman side in Hungary.

A few more episodes in Demir Baba's life as *kutb* may further amplify our understanding of the main dimensions of the relationship between the Rum Abdal collectivity and the Ottoman state. In addition to the support of the dynasty for Akyazılı Baba's *tekye* in Batova by endowing it with a part of the Budim fortress's income, the narrative's acceptance and approval of the Ottoman state's policy of supporting dervish groups' settlement and colonization in the Balkans by granting them pious endowment (*waqf*) rights and privileges is highlighted in a couple of other episodes. During Demir Baba's travels in the middle part of his life, he revives an *imaret* (soup kitchen) near the village of İnbeyleri (most likely in Dobrudja) and presides over the construction of a *tekye* and a (water-)mill, endowing the proceeds of the latter for the support of the convent.[150] Likewise, the *velayetname* tells us the family story of several *seyyid*s, distinguished by the green headgear

---

[149] In the words of John Renard, *Friends of God*, 103–104.
[150] *DBV*, 98–99.

they wear, whom Demir Baba meets in Tanrıdağı. Recognizing Demir as *kutb* and, the narrative hints, possibly his distant relatives, they tell the story of their ancestor es-Seyyid Hasan who crossed over from Anatolia into Rumeli with his three sons Ali Büzürk, Cüneyd, and Topuz. The then-*padişah* endowed (as *waqf*) es-Seyyid Hasan with land in Tanrıdağı (and possibly with some land in Gerlovo); while Ali stayed at es-Seyyid Hasan's original Rumelian abode in Tanrıdağı, Cüneyd settled and died near Dimetoka, and the youngest son, Topuz, did so in Gerlovo (the settlement he founded there must be the village of Topuzlar, mod. Topuzevo, Sliven province).[151] Thus, the narrative's (and implicitly Demir Baba's) recognition and acceptance of Ottoman policies of settlement and colonization (and the related role of the *waqf* institution) are once again in stark contrast with the *vita* of Otman Baba, whereby the latter, at least until shortly before his death, avoided settled life and frowned upon the "people of the convents" (*sahib-i tekye*) and all those who accepted any gifts or privileges from the Ottoman state.

Similarly, Demir Baba's image differs emphatically from that of his "spiritual grandfather" Otman Baba (as presented in the two respective *velayetname*s) when it comes to direct claims to political authority. As it has been shown, Otman Baba's critical and confrontational stance toward the Ottoman state and the newly emerging Ottoman order under Mehmed II is most dramatically demonstrated by his de facto non-acceptance of the political legitimacy of the Ottoman sultan. Otman Baba's *vita* presents him as meeting on several occasions with Mehmed II, where the saint repeatedly advances the claim that he, Otman, and not the Conqueror, is the true *padişah*. The Ottoman ruler is cast as kneeing before the saint and accepting the latter's claim to being the *padişah* with the words: "You are [the *padişah*], my father!" Furthermore, nowhere in Otman Baba's *velayetname* is there any mention of the "house of Osman" or even the name "Osman" itself. Instead,

---

[151] Ibid., 113–114. While the demographic analysis of Tanrıdağı and Thrace lies outside of the scope of this study, the settlement that Topuz supposedly founded in Gerlovo according to the *velayetname* may be persuasively identified with Topuzlar (i.e. "the descendants of Topuz"). The village's earliest preserved registration is in BOA TD 370, p. 551, dated 1530, likely based on 1516 data. A summary register, it does not provide much information about the villagers' identities, but in the next (detailed) registration, BOA TD 439, pp. 284–285, dated *c.* 1530–1535, one can find the village of "Topuzlar, der Gerilova" ("Topuzlar, in Gerlovo"), with 48 out of 64 registered adult male taxpayers being descendants of the Prophet (20 married *seyyid*s and 28 unmarried "sons of seyyids"). For later sixteenth-century registrations of the village, see BOA TD 382, pp. 519–521, and TKG KK TTd 151, ff. 220b–221a.

the narrative introduces a play of words implying that "Otman" may also mean "Osman."[152]

In Demir Baba's *velayetname*, together with the explicit recognition of the House of Osman (*al-i Osman*), its great representative sultan Süleyman, and repeated references to things "Ottoman" (fortresses, villages, soldiers, etc.), there is only one occasion on which the saint makes visible claims to political authority vis-à-vis the Ottoman *padişah*. This takes place in the story of the relationship between Demir Baba and Ali Pasha, the provincial governor of Babadağ, supposedly transmitted by Ali Pasha himself. In one of their meetings, Ali Pasha, taking offense at Demir's refusal to engage in a discussion of things esoteric with him, exclaims, "You are [just] an *ışık*, I am the *padişah*'s *vezir*. Why do you not obey me?" Demir Baba boldly responds, "I am the [true] representative/lieutenant of the *padişah*."[153] This, however, is a far cry from Otman Baba's claims vis-à-vis Mehmed II, such as "I am the *padişah*, you are my son" and "You are a [mere] city-dweller, I am the *padişah*." Demir Baba's claim to be the "lieutenant of the *padişah*," in competition for this honor with an Ottoman provincial executive, hints, once again, at the fateful transition which the Rum Abdal community had undergone in its attitudes toward the Ottoman state, dynasty, and order.

Thus, tracing the images of the three axial saints, Otman Baba, Akyazılı Baba, and Demir Baba, one cannot fail to notice a gradual withdrawal of claims vis-à-vis the Ottoman dynasty. In comparison with Otman Baba's grand, majestic claims challenging the legitimacy of Mehmed II as *padişah* and Akyazılı Baba's perceived status of spiritual guide to Süleyman, Demir Baba appears tamed, provincialized, and "folklorized." While the *vita* casts him as the Pole of the Age endowed by God with supernatural powers, he cannot and does not strive to question the Ottoman dynasty's legitimacy and right to worldly governance. His relationship to the dynasty is clearly subordinate, limited to his service to the Ottoman order and his claim to being the sultan's (true or legitimate) lieutenant (in the deep province) while the dynasty supports him and his community in turn.

6.2.2.5 *Demir Baba and his Spiritual and Sectarian Rivals* While rivalries and conflicts among mystics are a staple of Muslim hagiography, an analysis of this aspect in Demir Baba's *vita* further clarifies his and (his

---

[152] "*Tīz söyle ki Otman sen misiñ yoḥsa benmiyim? Tīz ḥaber vir didi. Derḥāl Sulṭān Meḥemmed ol heybetden cevāba gelüb ayıtdı kim: Otman sensiñ. Ben degülem bābācığum didi. Pes ol arada ol kān-ı velāyet Sulṭān Meḥemmed'e: Ha zinhār inān Otman benem ve sen benüm oğlumsuñ didi,*" OBV, 41.

[153] "'*Sen bir ışık olasuñ, ben pādişāhuñ bir vezīri olam. Sen beni niçün eslemezsüñ?' didüm. Pehlivān Bābā didi kim: 'Pādişāh vekīli benem...,*'" DBV, 162.

hagiographic community's) religious and sectarian identity. As already mentioned, the first such conflict occurred when Demir, already the Pole, was ousted from Akyazılı's *tekye* by a certain Sarı Yusuf for being "the son of a heretic." No mention is made of Sarı Yusuf's specific sectarian affiliation or whether he enjoyed the support of the Ottoman authorities (which is not unlikely, if the event really took place); at any rate, the episode suggests that the Abdals of Rum had active sectarian competition. A couple of decades after this expulsion may have happened, an imperial order to the *kadı* of Varna, dated 1560, ordered the inspection of Akyazılı's lodge following reports that Muslims in the area produced wine in cooperation with some *ışık*s of the *tekye*, who, while supposedly being (or rather, being expected to be) legitimate Sunni Muslims (*ehl-i sünnet ve cemaʿat*) were in effect a source of sedition and disorder.[154] This should be seen in the context of a number of similar inspections of doctrinally and socially suspect convents in the 1550s and 1560s, including the nearby lodge of Sarı Saltık and the convent of Seyyid Gazi in Anatolia (the latter being associated by sixteenth-century observers with the Abdals of Rum).[155]

Several years later, while serving at Dursun Baba's convent at Babadağ, Demir murders a certain Genc Beğ, a "hypocritical" dervish (*münafık*) suspected of having poisoned Dursun Baba.[156] This time Demir receives the backing of the authorities. When Genc Beğ's associates complain to the local Ottoman judge, he defends Demir's actions, reminding the plaintiffs that Demir was the spiritual son and successor of Akyazılı who was Sultan Süleyman's "baba."[157]

One of Demir Baba's two major rivalries, in the light of his *vita*, was with Virani Baba, one of the great (heterodox) poets of the age, who would eventually be recognized as one of the "Great Seven" among poets (*Yedi Ulu Ozan*) in what became the Bektashi (or Alevi-Bektashi) tradition from the seventeenth century onwards.[158] This conflict does

[154] *3 Numaralı Mühimme Defteri, 966–968/1558–1560* (Ankara: T.C. Başbakanlık Devlet Arşivleri Genel Müdürlüğü, 1993), order No. 1644, dated Rebiʿüʾl-Evvel AH 968/ November 20–December 19, 1560.
[155] Yürekli, *Architecture and Hagiography*, 41–45.
[156] *DBV*, 68, 75–76. Compare to the use of *münafık* (Ar. *munāfiq*) in Otman Baba's *vita* (see Chapter 2).
[157] *DBV*, 76.
[158] Virani is assumed to have lived in the second half of the sixteenth and the first quarter of the seventeenth centuries. Very little is known about his actual life. In oral tradition, he has been associated with the Bektashi order, but there is no firm evidence confirming this. As will be shown, though, the *velayetname* hints that this may have been the case. In fact, Demir Baba's *velayetname* is the only source that gives an account of Virani's death. For a selection of his poetry, see S. Nüzhet Ergun, *Bektaşi Şairleri ve Nefesleri*, vol. 1, 214–227.

not feature sectarian tensions, but is cast purely as a spiritual contest between two mystics who claimed the poleship. Virani is described as "the truth of the poets" (*hakikat-ı şu'ara*) who was from the lands where Arabic and Persian were spoken; in his ignorance, he claimed to be the *kutb* himself.[159] Virani crossed into Rumeli (the Balkans) with some of his *abdal*s and, having heard of Demir's rising fame as *kutb*, decided to prove his superiority in a direct contest with the Deliorman saint.[160] The contest between the two is cast in three "rounds." Eager to demonstrate his miraculous powers, Virani first makes some of his shepherds disappear together with their sheep and other animals and challenges Demir to account for this; the saint miraculously retrieves the shepherds and treats them with food.[161] Then Virani wishes to test Demir's "four gateways,"[162] but this quickly turns into a Qur'an contest, wherein, pointing out that he has won the respect of judges, *müftî*s, and *medrese* professors, thus emphasizing his self-identification with "high" Islamic culture, Virani pityingly comments on Demir's ignorance.[163] Having offered to be tested on a *sura* of Virani's choice, Demir recites Virani's chosen verses impeccably and provides a commentary (*tefsir*). The dumbfounded poet is forced (once again) to recognize Demir's superiority and saintly station.[164] The final round is a running contest – several pairs of followers of Demir and Virani, respectively, try to outrun one another. In the final leg, Demir and Virani face one another. Despite being much older than Virani (he is presented as 120 years old while Virani's age is given as 30 years), Demir runs "like a horse" and seals the win for his "team."[165] In the end, he urges Virani to recognize his superiority and lets him go.

The prominent Hurufi aspects and influences in his work have been noted by Fatih Usluer, *Hurufî Metinleri 1* (Ankara: Birleşik Yayınları, 2014), 94–129 (commentary), 130–232 (texts). A.Y. Ocak has argued forcefully for the need to consider the development of heterodox mystic poetry in Anatolia and the Balkans in its proper historical context. Thus, he warns against the characterization of many prominent heterodox poets as "Bektashi" and reminds that it was only from the seventeenth century onwards that they came to be seen as Bektashi, but in their proper historical context they should be seen as Kalenderi poets; this is in tune with Ocak's more general argument that Bektashism emerged from the broader "Kalenderi" heterodox movement, *Kalenderîler*, 209–210.

[159] *DBV*, 139.
[160] Ibid., 139–140.
[161] Ibid., 142–144.
[162] This phrase refers to a major Bektashi concept. Also, one of Virani's disciples is named Telli Bektaşi. While these can be read as hints to Virani's possible Bektashi identity they should not be necessarily seen as a "proof" that Virani was a "Bektashi." Modern scholarship highlights his Hurufi leanings and would not place him doctrinally far away from the Abdals of Rum, see Usluer, *Hurufî Metinleri 1*, 94–129. The conflict between Demir and the Bektashis is discussed below.
[163] *DBV*, 144–145.
[164] Ibid., 145.
[165] Ibid., 147–149.

Having left, Virani realizes he has been struck by Demir's "sword of esoteric knowledge," and decides to visit Otman Baba's convent to pay his
respects (as previously advised by Demir). However, he dies on his way
at Hafızzade's *tekye* in Gerlovo.[166]

As in the *vita* of Otman Baba, the single clearly identified rival sectarian dervish collectivity – which proves to be Demir's arch-rivals – is
the followers of Hacı Bektaş. The first related reference appears during
Demir Baba's travels to some major (heterodox) convents in Thrace in
the later part of his life. A story embedded in a conversation among the
already mentioned *seyyids*, descendants of es-Seyyid Hasan Baba, whom
Demir meets on his way between the convents of Kızıl Deli and Otman
Baba, tells us that the saint was treated with animosity at Kızıl Deli's
lodge. The *torlak*s there who were wearing the Bektashi headgear (*Bektaşi
tac*, i.e. the distinctive 12-gored cap characteristic of the Bektashi order)
conspired to kill Demir, for "his fault was that he was not a Bektashi, as
he had sworn loyalty to Otman Baba."[167] Thus, from the perspective of
Demir Baba's *vita*, Kızıl Deli's convent was associated with the Bektashi
order of dervishes, whose members were markedly hostile to the Rum
Abdal saint and those who followed Otman Baba's way. As already mentioned, by the mid-sixteenth century the *tekye* of Kızıl Deli must have
become a part of the Bektashi network of convents. Balım Sultan, who is
credited with the (re-)organization of the Bektashi collectivity as a hierarchical Sufi brotherhood, spent his early dervish career at and eventually served as a superintendent of that same lodge, before heading the
convent of Hacı Bektaş in central Anatolia at the turn of the sixteenth
century.[168] In what eventually crystallized as the Bektashi "pantheon of
saints," Kızıl Deli would occupy the second rank (after Hacı Bektaş himself), and Balım Sultan, the third.[169]

Another, more extensive episode in the later life of Demir Baba further
amplifies this picture of hostility between Demir and the Bektashis. The
leader of the local Bektashis (presumably in Deliorman, in the vicinity of
Demir's residence), a certain Hüseyin Baba, having heard of Virani's fate
and being concerned about Demir's rising fame, decides to challenge the

---

[166] The same convent in which some of Demir Baba's parents' wedding festivities took
place. *DBV*, 150.
[167] "*Ammā Kızıl Delü'nün torlaklarınun Timur Baba'ya eyü himmeti yok. Helākine ḳasd iderler
imiş… Pehlivānuñ şuçı bu kim Bektaşi değül. Otman Bābā Sultan'dan bī'at olmuş ve daḫi
emīrzāde.*" *DBV*, 118. Demir's "pledge of allegiance" to Otman Baba should be understood in the sense that he followed Otman Baba's "way." Demir was born after Otman
Baba's death.
[168] Birge, *The Bektashi Order of Dervishes*, 56–57; Yürekli, *Architecture and Hagiography*, 32–36.
[169] Yürekli, *Architecture and Hagiography*, 38; Köprülü, "Bektaş. Hacı Bektaş Veli," *İA*,
vol. 2, 461.

saint. He sends some of his dervishes (*bir alay Bektaşi*) to steal sheep from Demir Baba's shepherds.[170] When Demir learns of the Bektashis' misdeed, he summons the perpetrators and interrogates them. Upon learning that it was Hüseyin Baba who sent them to collect "what is due to Hacı Bektaş Veli," he beats them with his staff.[171] Demir is reminded by one of his disciples that Hüseyin Baba's dervishes have long insulted and harassed some of his (Demir's) adepts. Demir decides to go to Hüseyin Baba's convent to settle accounts. As the Bektashi Hüseyin realizes that he will not be able to stop him, he tells his dervishes not to resist.[172] In what is meant to be a ritual humiliation and the symbolic closing of Hüseyin Baba's convent, Demir Baba extinguishes the *tekye*'s lamp (*çırağ*) and takes with him a number of children (orphans sheltered at the convent) and animals.[173] He also casts a spell so that Hüseyin would not see light anymore. When Hüseyin Baba's dervishes come back they see their now-blind leader and urge him to meet Demir and ask for forgiveness in hope of getting his eyesight back.[174] When Hüseyin does that, Demir tells him that he cannot restore Hüseyin's eyesight as this is in the powers of the "*mehdi-i sahib-i zaman* (?)."[175] He urges Hüseyin to "accept the faith" (*imana gelsün*) and to go pay his respects at the *tekye* of Otman Baba. Going back, Hüseyin repents, but does not follow the rest of Demir's suggestions. Demir pays one last visit to Hüseyin Baba, only to see the latter dying. The saint digs the Bektashi's grave, buries him with his own hands, and says a prayer, calling upon the Three, the Seven, and the Forty.[176]

6.2.2.6 *Positioning the Abdals of Rum (of Otman Baba's Branch) in the Ottoman Sectarian and Socio-Cultural Spectrum* Where could one place the Abdals of Rum in Deliorman and Gerlovo in the Ottoman sectarian and socio-cultural spectrum? While an exhaustive and definitive answer is outside of the scope of this study, a few tentative remarks may be offered. In the light of the *velayetname*s of Otman Baba and Demir Baba, one can define the Abdals of Rum of Otman Baba's branch as a "heterodox" collectivity whose beliefs and practices had several broadly defined characteristic features. First, they have a *kutb*-based mystical conceptualization of Islam and the cosmic order, upheld by a hierarchy of saints, with the Pole occupying the apex of the hierarchy. Second, Rum Abdal beliefs

---

[170] *DBV*, 151.
[171] Ibid., 151–152.
[172] Ibid., 154.
[173] Ibid., 154.
[174] Ibid., 155–156.
[175] Ibid., 156.
[176] Ibid., 156. This is a reference to the hierarchy of saints more extensively discussed in Otman Baba's *vita*.

entailed a strong pro-Alid coloration and reverence for the Holy Family, Ali himself being the epitome of sainthood, and with Otman Baba and Demir Baba considered descendants of the Prophet (and Ali). Third, both *vitae* prominently feature antinomian practices and beliefs characteristic of Babai/Kalenderi/Abdal collectivities: voluntary poverty and withdrawal from worldly pleasures, mendicancy, celibacy, the peculiar practice of *chahar darb* as well as some beliefs typically attributed to these "heterodox" groups, such as the belief in re-incarnation and the transmigration of souls.

However, a critical comparison of the two *velayetname*s reveals several major aspects of the evolution which the Rum Abdal community underwent from the late fifteenth to the late sixteenth centuries: a visible recession of the *kutb*'s claims to spiritual and political authority and the abandonment of most of the clearly antinomian practices and beliefs, at least by the greater part of the collectivity. If voluntary poverty, itinerancy, mendicancy, and celibacy were "mainstream" in the case of Otman Baba and his disciples, in Demir's *vita* they are restricted to Demir Baba and select disciples, and observed only in specific periods of their lives. Most of Demir Baba's followers are settled, married,[177] and engaged in productive activities, most notably agriculture, as also confirmed by contemporary Ottoman tax registers. Demir Baba's *vita* likewise suggests that the Rum Abdal community was also developing a nascent hierarchical organization with a network of convents and *halife*s that recognized Demir as their *kutb* whereby Otman Baba's convent in Thrace seems to have been considered the main locus of religious legitimacy of the Rum Abdals.[178]

All this confirms the argument that in the late fifteenth and the sixteenth centuries the Abdals of Rum (of Otman Baba's branch) were in the process of transition from a loose collectivity of deviant, renunciant, and itinerant dervishes, to an increasingly hierarchical, institutionalized, sedentary, and "conformist" (vis-à-vis the Ottoman imperial order) Sufi collectivity in line with the mainstream *tarikat* tradition of "institutional Sufism."[179]

---

[177] With the exception of some celibate dervishes in convents. However, Demir is presented as urging some of his prominent celibate disciples – like Batovalı Ali Abdal, Demir's *ḫalīfe* who would succeed him as his Deliorman convent's *tekye-nişīn* – to marry (which Batovalı Ali does). *DBV*, 139.

[178] This is suggested by Demir's numerous visits there where he is accepted by the dervishes, personally selected by Akyazılı, as *kutb* and Akyazılı's "son" ("Dedemzāde"), *DBV*, 165. Otman Baba's convent is also the one which Demir's major rivals – the Bektashi Hüseyin and Virani Baba – are urged to visit and repent, and thus accept Otman Baba's "way."

[179] This is further reinforced by the use of phrases such as *ḳavl-ı tarīḳatda* ("in the parlance of *tarikat*s") employed, for example, when Güçbeke/Göçbeği Dede explains his connection to Akyazılı and Demir. *DBV*, 59.

It is noteworthy that while pro-Alid motifs are central to the construction of the image of both Otman Baba and Demir Baba, the two *vitae*
provide little evidence to suggest that the Rum Abdals of Otman Baba's
branch were adherents of Shi'ism. The presence of elements of belief
broadly associated with as "Shi'ism" – the cult of Ali, Hasan, Husayn,
and the Holy Family – is not sufficient, in and by itself, to define groups
espousing such beliefs as Shi'i.[180] Neither *velayetname* contains a significant mention or elaboration of the concept of the imamate (*imama/
imamet*) or significant hints equating the *kutb* with the Imam, or specifically the Twelfth Imam; the Twelve Imams (or any other number of
imams) are not mentioned once in either *vita*.[181] This silence implicitly
but clearly contradicts Vahidi's account of 1522 in which he paints the
Abdals of Rum as fervent Twelver Shi'is.[182] As argued in Chapter 2, on
the basis of Otman Baba's *vita*, the cult of Ali most probably entered his
(and his followers') beliefs via Hurufism (and not through the missionary work of the Safavid revolutionary movement). As Hamid Algar has
asserted, "Hurufism must be regarded as a decadent and fantastic offshoot of Sufism, not of Shi'ism."[183]

In this context, it is worth recapitulating the connection between
the Abdals of Rum of Otman Baba's branch and the Bektashi order.
In Otman Baba's *vita* we have seen the followers of Hacı Bektaş as a
nascent dervish collectivity, emerging around the growing cult of the
saint. As mentioned, from the sixteenth century onwards, starting with
Balım Sultan's efforts, the Bektashis underwent a process of transformation into an institutionalized (and increasingly hierarchical and centralized) *tarikat*. During this almost certainly protracted process, the
Bektashis strengthened their relations with the dynasty, capitalizing on

---

[180] Mélikoff, *Hadji Bektach*, 47–50.
[181] On Shi'i conceptualizations equating the *kutb* with the Imam, see P. Kunitzsch and
F. De Jong, "al-Ḳuṭb," *EI²*. Indeed, the use of "imam" as a title is quite limited in the
two *vitae*. While the gamut of appelations employed to refer to 'Alī b. Abī Ṭālib in both
works is very rich, he is not referred to as "Imām 'Alī" a single time in Otman Baba's
velayetname, and only three times (out of numerous mentions) in the Demir Baba's *vita*.
In the first instance, "İmam Ali" is mentioned as the origin/last element of the genealogy of Hacı Bektaş ("...bin İmām 'Alī"); however, in Otman Baba's genealogy immediately following, the origin/last element is just "Ali." "İmam Ali" is also mentioned as
a part of the purported words of a (Bektashi) adversary of Demir Baba at the *tekye* of
Kızıl Deli, and once in reference to the son of an *'âlim*, DBV, 118, 122, 157. Hasan
and Husayn are mentioned as "imams" only a couple of times in a single paragraph in
Otman Baba's *vita*, and only as part of saintly genealogies in the *vita* of Demir Baba.
OBV, 8–9; DBV, 118.
[182] *Vāhidī's Menākıb-i Hvoca-i Cihān*, ff. 41a–47a; Karamustafa, *God's Unruly Friends*, 70–72.
[183] Hamid Algar, "The Hurufi Influence on Bektaşism," in *Bektachiyya: Études sur l'ordre
mystique des Bektachis et les groupes relevant de Hadji Bektach*, ed. Alexandre Popovic and
Gilles Veinstein (Istanbul: Les Éditions Isis, 1995), 52.

their association with the Janissary Corps. The Bektashi order acted as a "melting pot," gradually assimilating other groups of the Kalenderi/ Abdal variety as well as Kızılbaş groups which the Ottoman state was happy to wean off the influence of the Safavid Empire of Iran.[184] The "centralization" of authority within the order and the related implied tendency and ability to assimilate other "heterodox" collectivities with their convents (and "saints") finds further affirmation in the fact that at the latest by the turn of the seventeenth century the sheykhs at the central convent of Hacı Bektaş had the right to control the appointment of sheykhs in other Bektashi convents, which right was affirmed by the Ottoman state.[185] In the second half of the seventeenth century, the famous Ottoman traveler Evliya Çelebi would show the tendency to associate many, if not most "heterodox" convents in Anatolia and the Balkans, with the Bektashi order (including the major Balkan (originally) Rum Abdal saints – Otman Baba, Akyazılı Baba, Kademli Baba, and Demir Baba – and their *tekye*s).[186] Inventories of Bektashi convents as of 1826 (the year of the dissolution of the order) drawn up by the Ottoman fisc would place an official stamp on this "fact" of assimilation (from the perspective of the Ottoman state), which Evliya Çelebi had suggested a century and a half earlier.[187]

The *vitae* of Otman Baba and Demir Baba largely confirm this picture, but add important insights into the nature of the processes referred to above and betray a largely hostile, albeit somewhat ambiguous relationship between the Bektashis and the Rum Abdals. The growth of the Bektashis as an organized collectivity can be traced by comparing the two accounts: in Otman Baba's *vita* they are referred to as "the dervishes of Hacı Bektaş" or as individual sheykhs who travel to pay homage to Haci Bektaş's convent in Anatolia; in Demir Baba's account they are stably and explicitly identified as "Bektashis" (*Bektaşi, Bektaşiler*).

Importantly, Hacı Bektaş is a revered figure in both *velayetname*s. In Otman Baba's *vita* he is mentioned as the *kutb* of his age in Anatolia, and in Demir's *velayetname* his genealogy (going back to "İmam Ali") is given

[184] Karamustafa, "Kalenders, Abdals, Hayderis," 128; Suraiya Faroqhi, "Conflict, Accomodation, and Long-term Survival: The Bektaşi Order and the Ottoman State (Sixteenth–Seventeenth Centuries)," in *Bektachiyya*, 171–184, and esp. 177–184; ibid., *Der Bektaschi-Orden*, 46–47, 129–131; Köprülü, "Abdal," 36–38.
[185] Faroqhi, "Conflict, Accomodation, and Long-term Survival," 178–180.
[186] *Evliyâ Çelebi Seyahatnâmesi*, vol. 3, 197, 213; vol. 5, 313; vol. 8, 341–344. See Faroqhi's critique of Evliya Çelebi's tendency to characterize some heterodox convents as "Bektashi" when contemporary (or later) sources do not provide corroborating evidence or present evidence to the contrary, *Der Bektaschi-Orden*, 17–21.
[187] The 1826 inventories of Bektashi convents studied by Faroqhi include at least the convents of Demir Baba and Kademli Baba, see Faroqhi, "Agricultural Activities," 92–96.

together with those of Demir and Otman Baba. One of Akyazılı's disciples calls his master "the Bektashi truth"[188] (the only occasion on which the term is used in this sense, in all other cases it signifies belonging (or not belonging) to a collectivity).

Nevertheless, in both *vitae* the followers of Hacı Bektaş are the single dervish collectivity with which the Rum Abdals are engaged in open hostilities. However, in Otman Baba's case they are simply seen as "conformists" upon whom Otman frowns (among others); Otman's major opponent is Mehmed II himself (representing the new imperial order and seen as Otman's direct rival). Conversely, in Demir Baba's account, while the legitimacy of the Ottoman order is categorically recognized, it is the Bektashis who are cast as the great enemy – they want to kill Demir (at Kızıl Deli's *tekye*), and he causes the death of the local Bektashi leader in Deliorman and buries him with his own hands.

This difference suggests the possible motivations for which the two *vitae* were composed in their respective historical contexts. Both works were penned in perceived moments of urgency. Otman Baba's *vita* was composed at a time when the "centrifugal forces" in fifteenth-century Ottoman society (one of whose prominent representatives was Otman Baba) were in the process of losing the battle vis-à-vis the centralizing state of Mehmed II and Bayezid II, and Demir Baba's *velayetname* was composed in the period of the Bektashi order's ascendancy that threatened the gradual assimilation of other "heterodox" collectivities in the Balkans and Anatolia. Demir Baba's *velayetname*'s claim that the Ottoman state (especially in the person of Sultan Süleyman) was supportive of the Rum Abdals could be seen as a weapon to safeguard their "right" to maintain their sectarian identity and socio-political autonomy vis-à-vis both the Bektashis and the pressures of the state, especially in the context of the Ottoman quest for "orthodoxy" from the sixteenth century onwards.

One last issue to be briefly touched upon is the Rum Abdals' connection to followers of Sheykh Bedreddin and the (pro-Safavid) Kızılbaş, respectively. While there are important contemporary references to the presence of followers of Sheykh Bedreddin in Deliorman (and Dobrudja) in the first half of the sixteenth century,[189] and while their beliefs and

---

[188] "*Yā kān-ı kerem sen Ḥaḳ āşināsı bir velisüñ, ḥaḳ(-ı) Bektāşīsüñ, ṣāḥib-i mürüvvetsüñ, ḥaḳ senüñdür*" ("O mine of mercy, you are a saint who knows the Truth [i.e. God], you are the Bektashi truth, you are the munificent one, you have the say"). *DBV*, 63. While this claim is certainly hard to interpret, it may be tentatively argued that the assertion that Akyazılı was "the Bektashi truth" could be understood in the sense of his quality of being the epitome of the values and beliefs associated with Hacı Bektaş.

[189] Most importantly Neşrî's chronicle, *Cihânnümâ*, 232, and the report of the Judge of Sofia, Bali Efendi, Tietze, "Sheykh Bali Efendi's Report."

practices must have been relatively close to, or compatible with Kalenderi/
Rum Abdal "heterodoxy" (in fact, it has been argued that Bedreddin's
revolt played a formative role in the development of that heterodoxy),
Sheykh Bedreddin is never mentioned in the *vitae* of Otman Baba and
Demir Baba. Most likely, as Michel Balivet has argued, many of the followers of Sheykh Bedreddin were sheltered (or assimilated) by other heterodox groups, such as the Rum Abdals and the Bektashis.[190] It may be
argued that, from the perspective of authorial intent in the case of both
vitae, there does not seem to be a reason for which Bedreddin would be
included, while other important figures of medieval heterodoxy (Mansur
al-Hallaj, Sarı Saltık, Hacı Bektaş) do constitute an integral part of Rum
Abdal memory. The question of the extent to which Sheykh Bedreddin,
and his teachings and followers were related to or integrated into other
"heterodox" groups in early modern Ottoman history remains open. It
is a fact though, that in modern times, Bedreddini communities do have
their place on the map of heterodox Islam in the eastern Balkans.[191]

As for the Kızılbaş, the situation is somewhat similar. The appellation
is not mentioned in either *vita*, and again, one may surmise that Kızılbaş
migrants from Anatolia who most probably came to Deliorman and
Gerlovo in the first half of the sixteenth century did find refuge within
the Rum Abdal community as well as within the growing Bektashi collectivity, although little of this potential process transpires in the sources.
It should be noted, though, that what eventually became known as "the
Kızılbaş of (Ottoman) Anatolia" were historically very much a part and
parcel of the Kalenderi/Rum Abdal heterodox tradition who developed
sympathies for the Safavid cause and accepted some of the Shi'i-oriented
beliefs spread by Safavid propaganda.[192] The appellation "Kızılbaş"
itself developed more as a political designation to signify a relation to
the Safavid revolutionary movement and state. In this case, the possible fusion of Rum Abdals in Deliorman and Gerlovo who most probably originated from Thrace and Tanrıdağı and Kızılbaş migrants from
Anatolia into the Balkans in the first half of the sixteenth century could
be seen as a reunion of sorts of different groups of the Babai/Kalenderi/
Rum Abdal variety, whereby those migrating from Anatolia into the
Balkans in the sixteenth century would have had an intense exposure to
Safavid propaganda. Such a hypothesis finds a tentative confirmation in

[190] Balivet, *Islam mystique*, 98, 108–111.
[191] Especially in Deliorman and Thrace, Zarcone, "Nouvelles perspectives," 4–6; Fr. De
Jong, "Problems," 205; Irène Mélikoff, "Le problème Bektachi-Alevi: quelques dernières considérations," in *Au banquet des Quarantes: exploration au coeur du Bektachisme-
Alevisme* (Istanbul: Les Editions Isis, 2001), 72.
[192] Ocak, "Babaîler İsyanından Kızılbaşlığa," 150–151.

the presence of a relatively long poem (*nefes*) by *Hatayi* (Shah Ismail's *nom de plume*) embedded in the *velayetname* of Demir Baba.[193]

What we know for sure is that numerous sources from the nineteenth century onwards do refer to Kızılbaş in Deliorman and Gerlovo and that this is the dominant self-identification[194] of the heterodox Muslim population of the two regions today. Heterodoxy remained fragmented, however, and the process of Bektashi assimilation of other similar groups was never complete. Recent field studies point to two major heterodox groups in Deliorman: the "Babais" (who could be seen as rooted in the Rum Abdal tradition, though in fact, the term "Babai" is historically older), consisting of two branches – those who recognize the authority of the head of Otman Baba's *tekye* (*Otman Babalılar*), and those who consider the *tekye* of Demir Baba as their primary shrine (*Demir Babalılar*); and the Bektashis, also adhering to two branches – the Çelebis (following the perceived biological descendants of Hacı Bektaş), and the Babagan (celibate) branch, very much the legacy of Balım Sultan.[195] The heterodox community in Gerlovo considers itself autonomous Bektashi, following the authority of its own *dede* residing in the village of Yablanovo (Alvanlar).[196]

6.3   The Foundation of Hezargrad as an Assertion of the Ottoman Imperial Order

While Chapter 5 provided a detailed discussion of the demographic and socio-economic aspects of the emergence and early development of Hezargrad, the new urban center of Deliorman founded in 1533, this section will pay some attention to the political and ideological dimensions of the city's foundation, especially as a counterpoint to the development of

[193] *DBV*, 43–44. The same poem (with minor variations) is easily identifiable in Hatayi's *divan*, see S. Nüzhet Ergun, *Hatayî Divanı. Şah İsmail Safevi. Edebi Hayatı ve Nefesleri* (Istanbul: Istanbul Maarif Kitaphanesi, 1956), 2nd edn., 112–113. It is also worth noting the presence of the *ene'l hak* claim and the explicit connection to Mansur al-Hallaj in Hatayi's poetry, *Hatayî Divanı*, 59.
[194] Together with "Aliani," which is the Bulgarian version of the Turkish "Alevi."
[195] De Jong, "Problems," 204–205; Zarcone calls Otman Baba "The Hacı Bektaş" of a great part of the Alevis (i.e. Kızılbaş) in Bulgaria today, "Nouvelles perspectives," 7; Mélikoff, "Le problème Bektachi-Alevi," 67, Mélikoff also reports, on the basis of her terrain research in Deliorman (mainly among Babais in the 1970s and 1980s) that Hacı Bektaş was not particularly revered by the local Kızılbaş, who directed their devotion to other saints, especially Demir Baba, the explanation provided being that Janissaries who settled in the region (presumably in the seventeenth and eighteenth centuries) left bad memories, ibid., 67, 74. This reminds one of the stance of Otman Baba's and Demir Baba's *vitae* – again, the "problem" is not Hacı Bektaş himself, but the people perceived to be his followers (i.e. the "Bektashis").
[196] De Jong, "Problems," 205.

heterodox Islamic culture in Deliorman's countryside as discussed in the light of the analysis of Demir Baba's *velayetname*.

As it was already pointed out in Chapter 5, Hezargrad was (re-) founded as a purely Islamic city by the grand vizier Ibrahim Pasha. As Machiel Kiel has already argued, the foundation of the town whose centerpiece was Ibrahim Pasha's mosque complex (including a *medrese*) was probably meant as the centralizing Ottoman state's response to the repopulation of the region by heterodox groups, both "indigenous" Balkan communities of the Babai/Kalenderi/Rum Abdal variety which had their origins in the late fourteenth- and fifteenth-century south-eastern Balkans[197] (most notably Thrace and Tanrıdağı) and migrants from Anatolia of similar confessional orientation (forcibly deported or migrating on their own will).[198] This hypothesis is supported by the fact that Ibrahim Pasha himself had participated in the suppression of one of the large-scale anti-Ottoman (and pro-Safavid, as perceived by the Ottoman state) rebellions in Anatolia, that of Kalender Shah in 1527. Thus, acutely aware of the threat that heterodox populations (and potential sympathizers of the Safavid cause) could pose to the legitimacy of the Ottoman imperial order, the grand vizier most probably took the decision to found the city in the years immediately following his participation in putting down Kalender Shah's revolt.[199] Situated on the southern edge of the Wild Forest and enjoying adequate water supply in the Ak Lom river valley, the new settlement had potential to develop and serve as a point of Ottoman imperial presence in the region, also helping revive the old road between the rising city of Rus (Rusçuk) on the Danube and Shumnu to the south (and leading to Istanbul over the Balkan mountain passes).

In this context, a look at the opening section of Ibrahim Pasha's pious endowment charter – in essence the birth certificate of the new Ottoman town – will facilitate a better understanding of the Ottoman dynasty and state's vision for the imperial order they strove to build and uphold as well as, more implicitly, the place that the newly founded provincial town occupied in this vision.

The *vakfiye*'s opening section presents a description of the terrestrial order created by God and upheld by his vicar, the Ottoman sultan, and his servants. This vision is in harmony with numerous Ottoman historiographic works, starting with Tursun Beğ's *Tarih-i Ebü'l-Feth* (*History of*

---

[197] And, specifically in the case of Deliorman, possibly even earlier groups, such as the descendants of the Turcomans led by Sarı Saltık who migrated to the northeastern Balkans in the mid-thirteenth century, as discussed in Chapter 3.
[198] Kiel, "Hrâzgrad-Hezargrad-Razgrad," 528.
[199] Ibid., 528.

the Conqueror, composed *c.* 1490) and continuing with force in the sixteenth century.[200] The foundation charter starts with a profuse praise of God, Creator of heaven and earth, who adorned the earth with mountains (rocks) and trees and provided for places (*tekye*s and mosques) for people to worship him as his Prophet had brought the light of the true faith and the rightful *şeriat*.[201]

When God wants a domain to prosper, he needs a discerning and vigilant lieutenant, a sultan, to whom he would grant this domain to manage its resources, guard its constituent parts and protect its subjects, prevent oppression, and eliminate improprieties.[202] This just sultan, being a generous ruler and "the shadow of God on earth" (*zill Allah ta'ala fi'l-ard*), possesses the power to regulate the affairs of society and serves as a point of recourse and refuge for the wronged and oppressed.[203] He, who had the authority to award and punish people according to their deeds, is God's deputy (*khalifa*) and came from the dynasty of Osman and thus stood highest among the sultans of the age; at present, this is the sultan, son of a sultan, son of a sultan, Sultan Süleyman Shah Khan, the son of Sultan Selim Shah Khan, the son of Sultan Bayezid Khan, the son of Sultan Mehmed Khan.[204]

The sultan is in turn aided by those who occupy high ranks in his exalted state: viziers and governors who guarantee justice, treat people of high and low station alike with grace and virtue, and regulate their affairs.[205] The loftiest station in the sultan's hierarchy of servants is occupied by the grand vizier Ibrahim Pasha b. Yunus Beğ – the most generous among them, the one who best uses the pen and the sword, who can best discern good from evil and thus best direct the affairs of the community; he is the state's representative in regulating its relations with other states, the deputy (*ka'im-makam*) of the sultanate, the commander of the soldiers of Islam who strive in the way of *gaza*, the

---

[200] See Tursun Bey, *Târîh-i Ebü'l-Feth*, ed. Mertol Tulum (Istanbul: Baha Matbaası, 1977). Most notably, in the context of this discussion, Tursun Beğ opens up his history with a discussion of "why (the common) people need the noble presence of an emperor, the shadow of God on earth" (*"güftär der zikr-i ihtiyâc-ı halk be-vücüd-ı şerif-i pâdişâh-ı zillu'llâh"*). Tursun Beğ's opening exposition could thus be considered a manifesto of Mehmed II's Ottoman centralism, and the author, who served for decades at the highest levels of Ottoman administration, including as finance minister under the Conqueror, was certainly an appropriate figure to pen it, see ibid. 10–30. For a good discussion of sixteenth-century Ottoman historiography and its main ideological points, see Fleischer, *Bureaucrat and Intellectual*, 235–252, 273–292.

[201] TSMA E 7029, p. 1; TSMA E 7029/Gündoğdu, p. 1.
[202] TSMA E 7029, pp. 2–3; TSMA E 7029/Gündoğdu, pp. 1–2.
[203] TSMA E 7029, p. 3; TSMA E 7029/Gündoğdu, p. 2.
[204] TSMA E 7029, p. 3; TSMA E 7029/Gündoğdu, p. 2.
[205] TSMA E 7029, pp. 3–4; TSMA E 7029/Gündoğdu, p. 2

refuge of the believers, the advisor (*müsteşar*) of the sultan's commanders and governors, the one who educates the people of knowledge and
supports the destitute and weak.[206] This disposition is how (in the context of this order of things) the people came to be a community that
obeys the state.[207] Compared to the *velayetname* of Otman Baba (and less so to that
of Demir Baba), this clearly represents an alternative and competing
conceptualization of the cosmic and terrestrial order. While in the two
saints' *vitae* (less emphatically so in Demir Baba's *velayetname*) it was
the *kutb*, chosen and endowed by God, who presided over a hierarchy of saints that upheld the order of the world; in the context of the
new Ottoman imperial vision, it is the sultan, endowed by God with
a domain to govern, and his viziers and commanders who uphold the
terrestrial order.

The remainder of the *vakfiye* (discussed in Chapter 5) reflects the
practical realization of this imperial vision at the Ottoman provincial
level. By providing for the construction and maintenance of a mosque
complex (that also included a *medrese*, a primary school, and a cara-
vanserai) which would serve as the nucleus of a new urban center
with a clear potential for development, the grand vizier (and thus the
Ottoman state) essentially established a stronghold of the evolving
Ottoman imperial order, as well as Sunni orthodoxy, in the deep province of Deliorman, and, as already mentioned, this effort was most
probably meant to serve as a counterweight to the rise of heterodox
movements in the surrounding countryside. Commenting on the current state of affairs in the city and its surroundings (based on his personal observations in the 1970s and 1980s), and pointing out that "the
villages of the Deli Orman still abound of Kızılbaş/Alevi sectarians,"
Machiel Kiel concluded: "The foundation of a bulwark of orthodox
Islam in the form of the mighty mosque and schools of Ibrahim Pasha,
to which the town of Razgrad owed its very existence, and centuries of
anti-propaganda and suppression of these groups by the instruments
of the State, have been in vain."[208] One may disagree with such a statement. It is doubtful that Ibrahim Pasha, and the Ottoman state at
large, envisioned the definitive uprooting of heterodox sectarians in the
region. Rather, in the light of the pragmatic Ottoman imperial tradition of managing and accommodating dissent, the state would remain
content with keeping potentially insubordinate and rebellious groups

---

[206] TSMA E 7029, pp. 4–5; TSMA E 7029/Gündoğdu, pp. 2–3.
[207] TSMA E 7029, p. 6; TSMA E 7029/Gündoğdu, p. 3.
[208] Kiel, "Hrâzgrad-Hezargrad-Razgrad," 562.

at bay and (if possible) under control. The newly founded Hezargrad that grew out of Ibrahim Pasha's pious endowment as an outpost of Ottoman imperial authority and culture in distant Deliorman, and thus presented an alternative and an instrument of containment vis-à-vis the rise of religio-political heterodoxy in the region, certainly came to serve this purpose well. The categorical acceptance of Ottoman dynastic legitimacy as reflected in Demir Baba's *velayetname* (in stark contrast to Otman Baba's *vita*'s confrontational attitudes) is a strong, even if only implicit, testament to this.

7 Issues in Religion, Culture, and Authority: Conversion to Islam and Confessionalization

7.1 Conversion to Islam in Deliorman and Gerlovo

Beyond the initial, "formal" inclusion of a certain territory within the Dar al-Islam, which represented the most basic level of "Islamization" of a certain area, conversion to Islam is one of the two major aspects of "Islamization" as defined in this study, the other being "Islamization of space/territories," that is, the effective integration of areas, usually recently incorporated into the "Abode of Islam," within the Islamic world's socio-cultural and religio-political landscape.[1]

How may one understand the basic meaning of the act of conversion to Islam and its immediate as well as long-term consequences? To begin with, western, and especially Weberian conceptualizations informed by (Judeo-) Christian contexts that relate the act of conversion to a "change of heart," i.e. a matter of belief and spiritual transformation, fit neither Islamic legal theory nor actual practice. Islamic theology and law have formulated a multi-layered understanding of conversion (to Islam) whereby they distinguish between conviction of the heart, confession with the tongue, and action with the limbs (i.e. ritual practices such as prayer, ablution, etc.).[2] In this context, classical Muslim theologians have emphasized "the sacred power of the external to affect the internal, of the form to shape the spirit, and of religious ritual and "ritualized" and sacralized social interaction to serve as a channel for divine grace ... wherein the adoption of the *name* and basic ritual forms are the crucial first steps," which "open the way" for the Islamization of hearts.[3] Thus,

---

[1] Islamization of space and territories was thus the result of the establishment of Muslim administrative and religio-cultural presence through the functioning of Islamic administrative, military, and cultic institutions, the construction of architectural edifices specifically reflecting the presence of Islam (i.e. mosques, *madrasas*, Sufi convents, etc.) as well as through the influx, at least initially, of human agents of Islam, i.e. Muslims from elsewhere – military and administrative personnel, sedentary or (semi-)nomadic, urban or rural colonizers. Beyond this, one may also speak of "Islamization" of practices, concepts, or ideas. See the introduction to Chapter 4.

[2] See L. Gardet, "Īmān," *EI²*.

[3] De Weese, *Islamization and Native Religion*, 56.

conversion to Islam is not (necessarily) meant to be a spiritual watershed event, but only the beginning of a journey. The formal requirements for conversion were the same, regardless of gender, social status, or age: a standard form of the act of conversion was lifting one's right index finger and pronouncing the *shahada* in the presence of two sound male Muslim witnesses.[4] However, even putting on "Muslim" clothes could be deemed sufficient.[5]

The act of conversion entailed the immediate change of name,[6] clothes (especially men's headgear), legal and taxation

---

[4] Krstić, *Contested Conversions*, 22.

[5] See for example, a *fatwa* by the great sixteenth-century Ottoman jurist and *şeyhülislâm* Ebū's-Sü'ūd Efendi, which stipulated that if an infidel changed his clothes (i.e. started wearing "Muslim" clothes) and, upon being asked "Are you a Muslim or an infidel?" answered out of fear "I am a Muslim," said infidel was to be considered to have legally converted to Islam; M. Ertuğrul Düzdağ, *Şeyhülislâm Ebussuûd Efendi Fetvaları Işığında 16. Asır Türk Hayatı* (Istanbul: Enderun Kitabevi, 1983), 89 (No. 362). Two *fatwa*s of the seventeenth-century Ottoman *şeyhülislam* Çatalcalı 'Alī Efendi (d. 1692) stipulate that if non-Muslims join Muslims in prayer (in a congregational mosque) or if a non-Muslim declares "I became a Muslim," these actions would be sufficient to view the respective non-Muslims as having legally converted to Islam. However, as these come from a later period, it cannot be proven that such legal interpretations were widely accepted in the sixteenth century. See *Fetāvā-i 'Alī Efendi* (Istanbul: Maṭba'a-i Āmire, AH 1311/AD 1893–4), 176–177.

[6] Upon conversion, "new Muslims" would take "Muslim" personal names that, in the Ottoman context, could cover a wide gamut of Arab, Persian, and Turkic names. Choice of one's new Muslim name would be very much influenced by the convert's immediate environment. Thus, urban converts would likely take "classical" Arab names, such as Mustafa and Mehmed (Muhammad) (e.g. BOA TD 439, p. 159). In rural areas, especially in Deliorman and Gerlovo's context, where the main human agents of Islam in the late fifteenth and sixteenth centuries were of semi-nomadic Turcoman origin, Turkic and Persian names could often be the preferred choice for a convert's new name; for example, Turkic names such as Kulfal, Durmuş, Alagöz, or Sevindik (e.g. BOA TD 439, pp. 22, 85, 201, 221) as well as Persian ones such as Şirmerd and Pervane (e.g. TD BOA 439, pp. 95, 162) All such names could be found in both rural and urban contexts, however. Upon conversion, male converts would also adopt a patronymic, which in most cases was "son of Abdullah" (also "son of Abidin"). While both (especially Abdullah) could be given names, the incidence of the two as given names in Ottoman Balkan tax registers is extremely rare, the two names were thus "reserved" for use as converts' patronymics in the Ottoman Balkans. This also seems to have been the case in areas in Anatolia (like cities) where conversion to Islam played a prominent role; see Lowry, *Islamization and Turkification*, 150. In some Ottoman Balkan contexts, converts would preserve their original, non-Muslim patronymics, which would be duly entered in Ottoman tax registers; in the western Rhodopes (*kazā* of Nevrekob/Nevrokop) one may observe converts' names such as "Saruca, son of Petko" and "Hamza, son of Dimo" (BOA TD 7, dated 1478–1479, pp. 352, 369); on this phenomenon see also Radushev, *Pomatsite*, vol. 1, 193. On women converts' naming practices we know much less, especially in the rural context, as Muslim women are virtually absent from Ottoman tax registers and their presence in other Ottoman administrative documents is relatively limited. See also V.L. Ménage, "The Patronymics of Converts," an appendix to his article "Seven Ottoman Documents from the Reign of Mehemmed II," in *Documents from Islamic Chanceries*, ed. S.M. Stern (Oxford: Cassirer, 1966), 112–118.

status,[7] and, usually, a change of one's community (though close contacts between converts and their former coreligionists were far from unusual). Personal "motivations" and the "factors" that conditioned the process of conversion have been a "classic" concern among scholars.[8] The usual array of "factors" includes fiscal benefits (lower tax burden), opportunities for social advancement, "religio-cultural" factors (such as similarities between Islam and other religions, especially Christianity, on the popular level), personal motives (e.g. romantic involvement and marriage), communal pressure (especially in urban contexts),[9] or, in relatively rare cases, outright coercion. However, the sources that we possess, especially those that relate meaningfully to the present study, rarely allow us to make an informed judgement about "motives" on a case-by-case basis.[10]

Western students of conversion to Islam have tended to give preference to "material" or "worldly" factors (i.e. financial benefits and opportunities for social advancement), most notably, the exemption from *cizye* (the poll-tax for non-Muslims), usually levied during the period under discussion at the rate of 1 gold piece (or around 60–70 *akçe* in the mid-sixteenth century).[11] This exemption should also be seen in combination

---

[7] The most basic way in which the Ottoman state "recognized" the new status of a recent (adult male) convert was to move him (under his new name) from the "Infidels" to the "Muslims" section in a settlement's tax registration entry.

[8] For an overview of these "factors," see Minkov, *Conversion to Islam in the Balkans*, 64–109; Bulliet, *Conversion to Islam*, 33–42; and Speros Vryonis, *The Decline of Medieval Hellenism in Asia Minor and the Process of Islamization from the Eleventh to the Fifteenth Century* (Berkeley, Los Angeles, and London: University of California Press, 1971), 351–402.

[9] Apart from lower-key, usually unrecorded, forms of communal pressure, the famous traveler Evliya Çelebi tells us of cases such as "the nice custom" practiced in Vodine (Edessa) and Karaferye (Veria), whereby on the "days of the red eggs" (i.e. Easter), local Muslims would go out and seek Christians whom they would force to convert to Islam; the new converts would be paraded before the local Muslims and awarded with presents; *Evliyâ Çelebi Seyahatnâmesi*, vol. 8, 82–83.

[10] One rarely hears the voices of converts, especially as far as their motivation to convert to Islam is concerned. Conversion self-narratives are quite rare in the Ottoman context and usually come from high-profile converts; see Krstić, *Contested Conversions*, 98–120. This likely reflects the fact that the act of conversion itself was not necessarily expected to signify a true "change of heart" or a "spiritual transformation." Minkov's *Conversion to Islam in the Ottoman Balkans* discusses a specific type of source, petitions for the conferral of new clothes on converts (in fact, usually the monetary equivalent thereof) that were composed by Ottoman scribes of the central administration and addressed to the Empire's central financial administration. While these petitions, mostly from the late seventeenth and early eighteenth century, do highlight some salient aspects of conversion to Islam, they concern a very small portion of actual converts (only covering some of the most proactive and those especially interested in material benefits), and their formulaic language provides limited insight on the more complex motivations that most "new Muslims" had in making the decision to convert.

[11] Kiel, "Razprostranenie na Isliama," 74; Radushev, *Pomatsite*, vol. 1, 80–84, H. İnalcık, et al., "Djizya," *EI²*.

with the related exemption, upon conversion, from the substantial ecclesiastic taxes that Christians had to pay: these amounted to around 12–30
akçes annually (paid to the local archbishop), as well as the fees for various services charged by the local priests.[12] At the same time, the salaries
of Muslim servants of the cult were usually paid by Muslim pious endowments.[13] While Islamic law requires the payment of zakat (the canonical
Islamic alms-tax), its collection was less organized and concerned only
members of the Muslim community that met certain substantial standards of material well-being; overall zakat rates were lower as well.[14]

However, such "material" factors could hardly act in isolation. As
Mircea Eliade has convincingly argued, even those who have consciously
made their choice of a profane life never succeed in doing away with
religious behavior; "even the most desacralized existence still preserves
traces of a religious valorization of the world."[15] Conversion was an act
conditioned by a complex and variable matrix of factors and influences
of diverse nature that were in continuous interaction with one another,
heavily influenced by one's socio-cultural environment. The continuously
growing presence of Islam in its various doctrinal and socio-cultural
manifestations in a certain area led to its increasing social acceptance
(including the acceptance of conversion to Islam itself).[16]

The remainder of the present discussion will highlight some important aspects of conversion to Islam in sixteenth-century Deliorman and
Gerlovo with a focus on conversion's demographic, socio-economic, and
socio-cultural dimensions (as the available sources shed little light on the

[12] Josef Kabrda, Le Système fiscal de l'église orthodoxe dans l'empire Ottoman (d'après les documents turcs) (Brno: Universita J.E. Purkyne, 1969), 65–67; Olga Todorova, Pravoslavnata
tsârkva i bâlgarite: XV-XVIII vek (Sofia: Akademichno Izdatelstvo "Marin Drinov,"
1997), 108–111.
[13] Radushev, Pomatsite, vol. 1, 205–206.
[14] This comment on zakāt should be seen as tentative as little is known about its collection in the Ottoman Empire. On the assessment and collection of zakāt in Islamic law
see Joseph Schacht, "Zakāt," in EI¹, as well as "Zekat," in M.Z. Pakalın, Osmanlı Tarih
Deyimleri ve Terimleri Sözlüğü, vol. 3 (Istanbul: Maarif Basımevi, 1954), 650–651.
[15] The Sacred and the Profane: The Nature of Religion, (New York: Harper and Row,
1961), 23–24.
[16] Richard Bulliet has utilized the concept of "innovation diffusion" to explain the historical dynamics of conversion to Islam in the pre-modern Islamic world. In his interpretation, the earliest converts to Islam were "innovators" who emerged as the pioneers in
the process of conversion. As more information about Islam spread (including via the
increasing number of converts), the intensity of the process increased over the centuries, reaching a peak and then subsiding as the pool of potential converts decreased. The
process over time thus could be graphically expressed through a standard bell-shaped
curve; Bulliet, Conversion to Islam, 23, 27–32. To this one should add the importance of
the concomitantly increasing social acceptance of Islam and conversion to Islam, as well
as the "indigenization" and acculturation of Islam in areas gradually integrated into the
Islamic world.

purely "religious" aspects of the phenomenon). Still, an attempt will be made, to the extent it is possible, to connect the socio-cultural aspects to religio-cultural ones. While a distinction will be drawn between "rural" and "urban" conversion, some important connections between urban centers and their hinterlands will be highlighted.

7.1.1   Conversion to Islam in the Countryside: General Remarks

As shown in Chapter 4, the number of rural Christians in Deliorman and Gerlovo and adjacent areas (i.e. from the northern slopes of the Balkan range to the Danube) increased from 2,107 households (as compared to 615 Muslim households) in *c.* 1485 to 11,621 households (as compared to 13,629 Muslim households) in 1579. Throughout the period of this study, the majority of rural Christians remained concentrated mostly in large villages right along the Danube just to the north of Deliorman and to the south of Deliorman along the northern slopes and foothills of the Balkan range (including Gerlovo proper, but also some adjacent areas). In Deliorman itself, Christian villages were less numerous, especially compared to the hundreds of newly founded Muslim settlements. As also argued in Chapter 4, this remarkable shift in the balance between Muslims and Christians in the countryside was due above all to the influx of Turcoman migrants and not to conversion to Islam, as happened to be the case in the central-western Balkans (e.g. the western Rhodopes, Albania, and Bosnia).

While the earliest, synoptic tax registers utilized in this study – whose data pertains to the mid-1480s and 1516 – do not yield data on converts to Islam, later, detailed registers, such as those from *c.* 1550 and 1579, show the percentages of new converts (of all registered Muslim heads of household) in the area's countryside to be 10.9 percent as of *c.* 1550 and 8.1 percent in 1579, respectively – mostly of seemingly local/regional origin, but also including some manumitted slaves who must have been brought from far away.[17] While significantly lower than in cities[18] and in

---

[17] These convert percentages have been calculated on the basis of the numbers of all male heads of household with the patronymic "*'Abdullāh*" (and in fewer cases "*'Abidīn*") in rural settlements for the sub-provinces of Chernovi, Hezargrad, and Shumnu in the detailed tax register of *c.* 1550 (BOA TD 382) and the sub-provinces of Chernovi, Hezargrad, Shumnu, and Eski Cuma in the two detailed registers (*tīmār* and *evḳāf*) dated 1579 (TKG KK TTd 151 and 411). Convert bachelors have not been included in the calculation nor have residents in urban centers who will be discussed in the following section.

[18] In the early modern Balkans in general, but in Deliorman in particular as well, with the percentage of converts in Hezargrad, for example, hovering between 20 percent and 30 percent, see the following section.

rural areas in the western Balkans where conversion to Islam was the dominant process in the formation of Muslim communities,[19] these percentages attest to the still-significant role that conversion to Islam played in the area under discussion, especially when one takes into account the accumulation of converts and their descendants over the generations.

While the number of mixed villages (having both Christians and Muslims, the latter being almost invariably local converts) grew from the late fifteenth to the late sixteenth centuries and while this overall increase in mixed villages may be seen as a sign of the gradual establishment of Islam as an integral part of the socio-cultural and religious landscape in the area under discussion, the overwhelming majority of sixteenth-century rural converts appears in Muslim villages newly founded by Turcoman colonists. This fact is again in contrast to areas in the central and western Balkans, especially those such as the western Rhodopes that neither developed sizable urban centers nor experienced significant Turcoman colonization. Thus, in the western Rhodopes (which came to be predominantly populated by *pomak*s), one observes a long-drawn process of rural conversion from the late fifteenth to the early eighteenth century, with the result being the gradual transformation of most villages from being wholly Christian to being wholly (or predominantly) Muslim.[20] The process was well advanced by the mid-sixteenth century.[21]

The great majority of mixed villages in the area did not develop sizable Muslim communities. In some cases, such as the village of Taban (mod. Sandrovo, Ruse province), close to the Danube, converts appeared in the first half of the sixteenth century, as of *c*. 1535 (a head of household and his bachelor son), but by the next tax registration, as of *c*. 1550, they had disappeared.[22] In most mixed villages the number of converts constituted a stable, small share of the overall village population.[23] The main reason

---

[19] For example, in the 1569 tax registration of the *ḳażā* of Nevrekob in the western Rhodopes, the percentage of converts among all registered rural Muslim heads of household is 24.4 percent, Radushev, *Pomatsite*, vol. 1, 194. The western Rhodopes host the great majority of Bulgarian *pomak*s (Bulgarian Slavophone Muslims).

[20] For a discussion of this phenomenon, see Radushev, *Pomatsite*, vol. 1, 258–402, and Kiel, "Razprostranenie na Isliama," 56–79.

[21] On the basis of his research on Ottoman tax registers for the *ḳażā* of Nevrekob, Radushev argues that the "turn of the tide" with respect to conversion to Islam in the area took place in the 1530s, when the social environment had changed enough to tolerate and accommodate apostates (from Christianity) in the rural countryside, *Pomatsite*, vol. 1, 195. Kiel's research on the district of Chepino, again in the western Rhodopes, largely confirms Radushev's observations, "Razprostranenie na Isliama," 60–62.

[22] BOA TD 439, p. 126; BOA TD 382, pp. 43–45.

[23] These observations are based on sixteenth-century tax registers. While the tax-register source base for the seventeenth century is quite sparse, preliminary observations on BOA TD 771, an "extraordinary taxes" register (*'avāriż defteri*), dated 1643–1644, suggests that conversion to Islam did gain momentum in a number of mixed (originally Christian) villages, but still remained limited, especially as compared to areas in the

for such a development was that converts in overwhelmingly Christian rural environments would often feel socially isolated and very likely ostracized.[24] In the western Rhodopes, such converts hardly had anywhere else to go and thus were forced by circumstance to endure the initial communal pressure and ostracism of their Christian neighbors until their existence as converts became increasingly acceptable and Muslim communities grew. By contrast, in Deliorman, Gerlovo, and adjacent areas, such converts in Christian villages, and not less importantly, those who contemplated converting to Islam but would not dare to do so in their original Christian settlements, had ready outlets. The hundreds of newly founded Muslim villages in the area provided them with an opportunity to settle and avoid such social strains. As of *c.* 1535, only 68 of 270 rural Muslim settlements (including settled *mezra'*as) did not have at least one convert, and *c.* 1550 only 91 of 466. Those local converts integrated into nearby Muslim Turcoman villages would in all probability also undergo a process of gradual linguistic assimilation. Such villages were not the only such outlet. The rapidly growing urban centers in the area – especially the newly founded Hezargrad which remained wholly Muslim until the seventeenth century, as well as Shumnu – provided even better opportunities for the integration of local converts.[25]

Yet there were originally wholly Christian villages in which Muslim communities took root and seemed to grow over time. One example is the village of Razboyna (in mod. Târgovishte province) to the west of Shumnu. A mid-sized, wholly Christian village in the 1480s with 37 households and seven bachelors, in 1516 it already had one Muslim household (most likely headed by a local convert) together with 46 Christian households and 26 bachelors. *Circa* 1535, we see Razboyna with a still-growing Christian community: 65 heads of household and 28 bachelors, but also with an already sizable group of Muslim residents: one head of household bearing the patronymic "Abdullah" ("Ali, son of Abdullah"),

Balkans where conversion to Islam dominated the process of formation of Muslim communities.

[24] Radushev, *Pomatsite*, vol. 1, 191–195; Bulliet, *Conversion to Islam*, 41. In this context, it is worth considering a *fatwa* by Ebu's-Sü'ud, which determines that if two Muslims lived in an (otherwise) "infidel" village, they could prohibit, with the affirmative opinion of a judge, the local Christians from beating a wooden plank (in lieu of a church bell) in their churches. It is likely that this ruling addressed the situation of recent converts who found themselves isolated among their former coreligionists. If this is the case, the ruling essentially aimed at alleviating the discomfort such recent village converts to Islam could experience in a predominantly Christian milieu. Obviously, it also affirms such newly-converted Muslims' superior social standing. Düzdağ, *Şeyhülislâm Ebussuûd Efendi Fetvaları, fatwa* no. 407.

[25] As well as Rus (Rusçuk) on the Danube where the converts from Taban most probably relocated.

three bachelors – two of whom were likewise "sons of Abdullah" and the third a son of the oldest convert (Cafer, son of Ali), and one butter maker (*yağcı*), also "son of Abdullah." Thus, of the five registered Muslims in the village, four were first-generation Muslims, and the fifth, second-generation.[26] Around fifteen years later (*c.* 1550), the Muslim community in the village had grown to nine heads of household and four bachelors, of whom four heads of household bore the patronymic "Abdullah," with four of their sons – one head of household and three bachelors – identifiable as second-generation converts. The only second-generation convert from the previous registration, Cafer, son of Ali, is already present as a head of household and has one registered bachelor son, and one notes two more sons of Ali, most probably brothers of Cafer who had come of age and already had families. Thus, of 13 registered Muslims in the village, 12 were clearly identifiable as first- or second-generation converts to Islam, while the village's Christian community had grown to 92 heads of household and 75 bachelors.[27] In 1579, the village had 11 Muslim heads of household and three Muslim bachelors, most of whom were again readily identifiable as first or second-generation converts, while the Christian community numbered 70 households and 116 bachelors (!).[28] The process of conversion must have continued, as in 1720 we see a villager from Razboyna, together with his wife and two children, traveling to the sultan's court to convert, receive money for new clothes, and ask for an appointment as a *sipahi*.[29]

The tax registers do not give many clues to the possible motives for conversion to Islam of the local rural population. Factors such as fiscal pressure and the quest for social advancement certainly played a considerable role in the process. E. Radushev has calculated that the tax burden of Muslims levied by the Ottoman state could be half that of non-Muslims, taking into account the significantly lower land tax paid by Muslim bachelors (12 *akçe* per year as compared to 25 *akçe* for non-Muslim bachelors), together with the exemptions from the *cizye* and ecclesiastical taxes.[30]

It should not be forgotten that the gradual indigenization of Islam in the Balkans (i.e. the process by which it became to be viewed as a "local" phenomenon that also integrated elements of pre-Islamic Balkan

---

[26] BOA TD 439, p. 312.

[27] BOA TD 382, pp. 499–500.

[28] TKG KK TTd 151, ff. 250a–250b.

[29] NBKM f. 1A, No. 57254; the document is also available in Bulgarian translation and facsimile in *Osmanski izvori za isliamizatsionnite protsesi na Balkanite (XVI–XIX v.)*, ed. and trans. M Kalitsin, A. Velkov, and E. Radushev (Sofia: BAN, 1990), 172–173.

[30] Radushev, *Pomatsite*, vol. 1, 214–230.

religious and socio-cultural traditions) probably had the greatest influence on the process of religious conversion. One factor that contributed to this process was the relative fluidity and adaptability of religious
beliefs, especially on the level of "popular religion" on both the Christian
and Muslim sides.

7.1.2 "Colonizing Heterodox Dervishes" and Conversion to Islam

At this point it is appropriate to consider the role of "colonizing dervishes"
in conversion to Islam in the countryside. As early as in the 1920s, F.W.
Hasluck linked conversion to Islam in the Ottoman domains to proselytizing "heterodox" Sufi dervishes,[31] in tune with then-popular theses on Islam
as a "missionary religion"[32] and Christian conceptualizations of proselytiza-
tion as the work of dedicated preacher-missionaries.

However, the available sources do not yield much evidence supporting
such a hypothesis in the early modern Ottoman context. The most obvious place to look for traces of such a purported proselytizing ethos on the
part of Sufi mystics, and conquering/colonizing dervishes in particular,
would be saintly *vitae*, whose authors (or compilers) would hardly have
had a reason to conceal or edit out stories about saints' missionary activities aimed at converting non-Muslims. Yet, while conversion episodes do
have their place in the Ottoman hagiographic tradition that developed
in the fifteenth and sixteenth centuries, such stories usually function as
"superiority *topoi*" aimed at establishing Islam's primacy over other religions (especially Christianity). Conversion episodes appear in two major
contexts: first, in relation to *gaza* and conquest, whereby infidels, be they
holders of political and military power (e.g. high-ranking commanders),
representatives of the cult (most often Christian priests), or common
folk, accept Islam as a sign of submission in defeat, thus furnishing tes-
timony to the political (and moral) superiority of Islam as the "true religion" favored by God, and secondly in peaceful contexts, whereby it
is usually Christian priests or monks who, won over by the charisma
and spiritual power of Sufi mystics, accept Islam, thus providing proof
for Islam's superiority coming from Christianity's foremost representatives.[33] One exception related to "mass conversion" appears in the *vita*

---

[31] Hasluck, *Christianity and Islam*, vol. 1, 340.
[32] In his influential study *The Preaching of Islam: A History of the Propagation of the Muslim Faith* (Westminister: Archibald Constable & Co., 1896), Sir Thomas Arnold defines Islam as a "missionary religion." Ibid., 1–7.
[33] For examples drawn from early modern Ottoman, Sunni as well as "heterodox," hagio-graphic works, see Ocak, "Bâzı Menâkıbnâmelere Göre"; Vryonis insists on the "desire of the dervishes to convert the Christians" and refers to similar examples from the same pool of saintly *vitae*, but he does not fail to emphasize the Sufis' missionary activities

of Hacı Bektaş in which the saint girds Sarı Saltık and his associates with swords (just as he does to Kızıl Deli in the latter's *vita*) and sends them to Georgia where Sarı Saltık converts the local ruler to Islam; later the common people follow their ruler's example, but in the end all renege on Islam and turn to their old religion! Sarı Saltık also converts the people of Kaligra (Kaliakra, in Dobrudja), having ridden them of the terror of a dragon.[34]

In the three *velayetname*s of heterodox Muslim saints who gained fame in the fifteenth- and sixteenth-century Ottoman Balkans – Kızıl Deli (Seyyid Ali Sultan), Otman Baba, and Demir Baba – conversion stories take place, if at all, exclusively in the context of holy war and conquest. Thus, Kızıl Deli and associates convert local Christians upon the conquest of fortresses in Thrace (such as Gelibolu, Kavak, and Dimetoka) as well as Christian captives and their relatives; a local Christian hero who loses a fight with Kızıl Deli's fellow warrior-dervish Tahir also converts to Islam.[35] Demir Baba, in his manifestation of a warrior-saint near Budim, invites to the faith the defeated Christian commander Pehlivan Marko who obliges, but grants Marko's valiant fellow Christian fighter Karaca Pehlivan's respectful wish to remain Christian; however, Demir kills a defeated infidel who arrogantly turns down the saint's invitation to convert.[36] In the *vita* of Otman Baba, who spent all of his long life traversing Anatolia and the Balkans, conversion stories are virtually absent (as is any contact with non-Muslims, for that matter).

Ottoman administrative sources related specifically to Deliorman and Gerlovo do not offer much evidence of dervishes' missionary activities among Christians either. Tax-register material does not provide any

---

among Turcomans too, *The Decline of Medieval Hellenism*, 358, 363–396; see also Ahmet Karamustafa's insightful discussion on Sarı Saltık, "Islamization through the Lens of the *Saltuk-name*," in *Islam and Christianity in Medieval Anatolia*, ed. A.C.S. Peacock, Bruno DeNicola, and Sara Nur Yıldız (Farnham, UK, and Burlington, VT: Ashgate, 2015), 349–364.

[34] *Vilâyet-name. Manâkıb-ı Hünkâr Hacı Bektâş-ı Velî*, 45–47; see also Ocak, "Bazı Menkıbnamelere Göre," 39.

[35] *VSAS*, 165/195, 168/202, 171/207–208, 172/211. Richard Eaton has noted the use of the motif of conquering Sufi dervishes who converted local populations to Islam in the context of late medieval Bengal. However, he asserts that these tropes were later interpolations in sixteenth-century hagiographic texts devoted to those legendary "*gazi-dervishes*" and argues that there is little reliable evidence confirming that there ever were Sufi "holy warriors" in the Bengali context; ibid., *The Rise of Islam and the Bengal Frontier*, 71–77. This differs from late medieval and early modern Anatolia and the Balkans where dervishes often acted in association with semi-nomadic Turcoman warriors.

[36] *DBV*, 106–107.

substantive clues of Sufis attempting to settle in Christian villages (or mixed villages in which Muslims were usually of convert origin).

Nevertheless, the role that "colonizing dervishes" played in the "Islamization of space" and the economic utilization of the countryside, including the organization of agricultural production (and in some cases, animal husbandry) centered in their convents, could relate meaningfully to the process of rural conversion to Islam. Rural dervish convents could be seen as a point of attraction by some local Christians, whereby Muslim ("heterodox") saintly figures' religious and spiritual charisma could draw the interest of potential converts. No less importantly, dervish convents could provide attractive employment coupled with lower tax burdens. Settling in a dervish convent could thus provide an appealing alternative to local rural non-Muslims, both on account of the spiritual support and communal ambience, and the competitive economic conditions that such an alternative offered. Conversion to Islam would be a "natural" part of a non-Muslim's integration into his new *tekye* environment, albeit one may still speculate about the specific motivations of such converts.[37]

This set of factors could possibly explain the high number of converts among the resident dervishes in Otman Baba's *tekye* in Thrace in the early sixteenth century. To give a few relevant examples in the specific context of Deliorman, Gerlovo, and the adjacent areas: *c.* 1535 in the convent of Bali Bey, son of Yahya Pasha in the village of Gürgen Pınarı (Sadine) in Deliorman, one of four servants of the *tekye* was a convert (a certain "Pervane, son of Abdullah").[38] In the same year, among the five registered (male) dervishes of the convent of Sultan Ana (i.e. Kız Ana – the best maid at the wedding of Demir Baba's parents) one sees "Hasan, [son of] Abdullah" recorded also as "*derviş-i abdal.*"[39] In the dervish village of Ali Baba, son of Tay Hızır – another prominent figure in Demir Baba's *velayetname* – two out of twelve dervishes, all of them exempt from extraordinary taxes (*avarız*), appear to be converts too.[40] In *c.* 1550, in the convent of Burhan Dede near Hezargrad, one sees, in addition to the eponymous Burhan Dede and his three sons, two other convent residents (registered as *gulam-ı tekye*, "men/youths of the *tekye*") named Bayezid and Ahmed, both "sons of Abdullah."[41]

[37] See also Barkan's related comments in "Vakıflar ve Temlikler," 303–304.
[38] BOA TD 439, p. 93.
[39] Ibid., p. 308.
[40] Ibid., p. 100.
[41] BOA TD 382, p. 350.

7.1.3   Conversion and Converts to Islam in the Urban Centers: The Cases of Hezargrad and Shumnu

While in the countryside, conversion to Islam had a pronounced regional coloration, in urban contexts it had a more uniform nature, largely typical of all the early modern Ottoman Balkans. Regardless of the surrounding countryside, by the mid-sixteenth century the overwhelming majority of Ottoman cities had sizable Muslim communities, and in most of them Muslims were in the majority.[42] Avenues of upward social mobility, Balkan urban milieux were characterized by high proportions of converts and their descendants. Cities attracted numerous converts from without – mostly from their hinterlands – as they offered recent converts or conversion-minded non-Muslims from the nearby countryside far better opportunities for social integration within large (if not dominant) Muslim communities. The pronounced presence of converts in cities itself made conversion a widely accepted socio-cultural and religious choice (as compared to the ostracism these converts could face in their native, predominantly Christian villages). In addition, a visible portion of first-generation converts could be manumitted slaves with origins far away from their newly adopted city of residence. Cities also attracted converts from the inside in the case of "mixed cities" (such as Shumnu), as it was in an urban context that the contrast in social stature and the discrimination of non-Muslims would be most palpable, due to everyday direct contact between Muslims and non-Muslims. In the same context, though, urban non-Muslims had the opportunity to acquire firsthand knowledge about Islam and Muslims' "ways of living," which could entail contact with recent converts from their own community and thus shape their decision to convert as well.

The motivational matrix that conditioned the appearance of these new urban Muslims must have been complex enough to include factors of financial, social, religious, and psychological nature. Apart from the exemptions from *cizye* and ecclesiastic taxes which would result from conversion to Islam, be it in the countryside or in a city, the new urban convert became exempt from one more basic Ottoman tax – the *ispençe* – levied on adult non-Muslim men at the uniform rate of 25 *akçes*,

---

[42] Speros Vryonis, "Religious Changes and Patterns in the Balkans, 14th–16th Centuries," in *Aspects of the Balkans: Continuity and Change*, ed. Henrik Birnbaum and Speros Vryonis (The Hague and Paris: Mouton: 1972), 162–164. Marc Gaborieau has remarked that while reliable statistics are not available, Muslims played a leading role in urban life in contemporary Mughal India and were more urbanized as compared to Hindus, ibid. "Indian Cities," in *The City in the Islamic World*, ed. Salma Jayyusi, Leiden & Boston: Brill, 2008), vol. 1, 185–187.

regardless of marital status, land ownership, or residence.[43] The *ispençe* is sometimes seen as the non-Muslim equivalent of the *çift resmi* – the standard land tax for all Muslim landed and married villagers levied at the rate of 22 *akçe*s, with Muslim bachelors paying 12 *akçe*s.[44] Thus, if a new convert to Islam lived in the countryside, he would have to start paying the *çift resmi* instead of *ispençe*, which would be especially beneficial for bachelors, but not that much for heads of household. Muslim urban residents, however, usually did not pay the *çift resmi* (even if they engaged in agriculture, they paid tax only on the agricultural produce, but not on land), and thus an urban convert would be completely exempt from paying the *ispençe* without having to pay any similar tax levied on Muslims.[45]

Summed up, the fiscal advantage for an urban convert would be around 120–130 *akçe*s a year, which would mean cutting the tax burden by up to half. As it is known from a number of salary lists from construction projects compiled by the Ottoman administration, an urban construction worker, be he a carpenter or a mason, earned 7–8 *akçe*s a day, which gives a rough estimate of what conversion to Islam could save in terms of daily wage labor.[46]

However, the convert was not just a "calculating subject," his or her choice was not only supposedly "rational" but also broadly "social." The sixteenth century may generally be characterized as the zenith of the (Muslim) Ottoman Empire. Ottoman expansion and prosperity also entailed the development of Islamic urban institutions that offered attractive educational and employment opportunities. All this must have had a distinct psychological effect on the Ottomans' Christian subjects. Combined with the modest formal requirements associated with conversion, the broader attraction of socio-economic advancement and belonging to a prosperous and successful community must be seen beyond the confines of fiscal considerations.

7.1.3.1 *Conversion and Converts in Sixteenth-Century Hezargrad* The three detailed sixteenth-century tax registrations for Hezargrad attest to the pronounced presence of converts, usually denoted by the patronymic

---

[43] Thus, in effect, the *ispençe* functioned as a second poll tax on non-Muslims, in addition to the *cizye*. There were some groups that were sometimes partially or fully exempt from it in the fifteenth and sixteenth centuries, usually non-Muslim *re'āyā* performing some "special services" to the Ottoman state, such as *derbendcis*, *voynuks*, mine workers (*ma'denciler*), falconers (*doğancılar*), etc. On the origins and nature of *ispençe*, see Halil İnalcık, "Osmanlılar'da Raiyyet Rüsumu," *Belleten* 23 (1959): 602–608.

[44] The *çift-resmi* gradually became the monetary equivalent of seven services that peasants had to provide for their respective *tīmār*-holder. See İnalcık, "Osmanlılar'da Raiyyet Rüsumu," 577–600.

[45] Milan Vasić, "Socijalna struktura jugoslovenskih zemalja pod osmanskom vlašću do kraja XVII vijeka," *Godišnjak Društva Istoričara Bosne i Hercegovine* 37 (1986), 69–70.

[46] Kiel, "Razprostranenie na Isliama," 74–75.

Abdullah for former Ottoman *dhimmi*s, or, in the case of manumitted slaves, by the term *mu'tak* (lit. "manumitted"), with reference to their former owner who freed them (e.g. "Kasım, *mu'tak* of Mehmed").

Looking at the numbers of convert heads of household the following picture of Hezargrad's dynamics of conversion appears.[47] The 19 converts as of *c.* 1535 (all "sons of Abdullah") comprised 18% of all registered heads of household; the 41 *c.* 1550 (32 sons of Abdullah and 9 manumitted slaves) 20.5% of all registered; and the 76 (75 "sons of Abdullah" and 1 manumitted slave) in 1579 accounted for 34% of all registered heads of household. As the progeny of converts cannot be identified as such unless they have already reached adulthood and are listed immediately after the converted father (e.g. "Mustafa, son of Abdullah; Hasan, son of Mustafa"), the small number of identifiable sons of converts (4 *c.* 1535, 3 *c.* 1550, and 10 in 1579), must represent only a small part of all "second-generation converts."

This brings us back to the issue of the origins of Hezargrad's population. Machiel Kiel has tried to downplay the role of conversion to Islam in sixteenth-century Hezargrad, emphasizing instead the "real Turkish element" of the town's population by pointing to five heads of household in the *c.* 1550 registration described as "sons of the Anatolian" (*veled-i Anadolu*), as well as one registered as "son of the Karamanian" (*veled-i Karamanlu*), also denoting Anatolian origin.[48] In the 1579 registration, only two men (both married) were designated as being of Anatolian origin. Listing one's geographic origin in tax registers was not strictly practiced, however; there might have been more residents in the newly established town who had migrated directly from Anatolia, yet there is no proof for that. Quite likely, many of the residents were native Turkish speakers from Hezargrad's hinterland or from other parts of the Balkans (e.g. Thrace), thus being more distant descendants of Anatolian migrants to the Balkans. As for converts, their registration as such must have been comprehensive, as conversion signified a change of tax status. As high percentages of new Muslims persisted during the sixteenth century, the

---

[47] In tune with the overall approach to demographic analysis in this study, a preference has been accorded to the use of numbers for married men (i.e. heads of household), especially in calculating growth, relative demographic strength of different population groups, etc., the reason being that the registration of unmarried men has traditionally been not as reliable and consistent as that of heads of household and that bachelors were in fact household members (and not the heads thereof) who had just reached maturity. See related discussion in Cook, *Population Pressure in Rural Anatolia*, 64–66, and Lowry, *Islamization and Turkification*, 177–180.

[48] Kiel, "Hrâzgrad-Hezargrad-Razgrad," 539–540. Kiel was writing in 1991 and thus was responding to the anti-Turkish claims of Bulgarian nationalist historians (especially in the context to the so-called "Revival Process" in the 1980s).

Table 7.1 *Converts to Islam in Hezargrad (numbers and percentages)*

Neighborhood (mahalle)	Married converts (regular – non-slave origin)	Manumitted slaves (all married)	Married converts (total)	Percentage of converts (of all married men)	Bachelors
C. 1535					
A single Muslim community	**19**	**0**	**19**	**18% (19/104)**	**0**
C. 1550					
Cami'-i Şerif	7	5	12	19% (12/63)	0
Ahmed Bey	12	1	13	43% (13/30)	0
Mescid-i Behram Bey	9	1	10	23% (10/43)	1
İskender Bey	4	2	6	9% (6/64)	2
Total (c. 1550)	**32**	**9**	**41**	**20.5% (41/200)**	**3**
1579					
Cami'-i Şerif	19	0	19	37% (19/52)	2
Ahmed Bey	16	0	16	53% (16/30)	0
Mescid-i Behram Bey	14	0	14	25% (14/55)	2
İskender Bey	17	1	18	32% (18/57)	1
Mescid-i Mehmed Bey	9	0	9	29% (9/31)	0
Total (1579)	**75**	**1**	**76**	**34% (76/225)**	**5**

cumulative effect must have been such that by the end of the century the majority of Hezargrad's population were either converts themselves or had at least one convert among their parents or grandparents.[49] As in other Ottoman cities,[50] there were neighborhoods with persistently high percentages of convert residents, like that of Ahmed Bey, or ones, such as that of İskender Bey, where the share of converts increased dramatically from mid- to late sixteenth century – thus offering converts a welcoming social milieu.

As the city was founded in 1533 as a purely Muslim urban center, the initial core of Hezargrad's population (including Ibrahim Pasha's *waqf* and mosque complex personnel as well as the city's military-administrative officers) must have been Turkish speaking. As the city would remain wholly Muslim throughout the sixteenth century, converts could only come "from the outside," most probably from the neighboring villages, such as the nearby large, fully Christian Kayacık; some could have been without permanent registration (*haymane*) theretofore, and yet others, being of servile origin, must have hailed from more distant lands. All these would mix with the Turkish-speaking "core" (chiefly through inter-marriage), and thus would likely undergo a natural process of "ethno-linguistic assimilation," becoming in time a part and parcel of that same Turkish-speaking and Muslim "core." A rare Western traveler's account – that of Jacques Bongars (alias Jacobus Bongarsius) who passed through Hezargrad in July 1585 – described the town as "*Crasgrada, beau bourg orné de belle mosquées, habité de Turcs.*"[51]

---

[49] A very rough calculation of this measure shows that in 1550 around 34% of the registered married adult men were either first- or second-generation converts (along the paternal line only), and in 1579 around 56% were first-, second-, or third-generation converts (i.e. they were either converts themselves, or had a father or a grandfather who must have been a convert). To give an idea how I have made the calculation: for 1550, I have extracted the number of convert heads of household and those designated as originating from Anatolia from the 1550 number of all heads of household (200-41-6=153). If we assume that the two registers (from 1535 and c. 1550) represent roughly two different generations, and this seems to be the case, as the percentage of overlapping names is very low), then of these 153 households c. 1550 that should be the natural progeny of the generation represented in the previous register, around 18% (the percentage of converts in c. 1535) should be descendants of converts (i.e. 27 heads of household). To these I have added the first-generation converts in 1550 (41 heads of household) and obtained a total of 68 first- or second-generation converts, for a total of 34% of all married men in 1550. A similar procedure has been followed for calculating the figure for 1579. In making these calculations, I have largely followed the example of Lowry, *Islamization and Turkification*, 161–162.

[50] See, for example, the case of sixteenth-century Trabzon, Lowry, *Islamization and Turkification*, 162–163.

[51] J. Bongars' short description of his travel from Vienna to Constantinople in 1585 has been published (in the original French) under the title "J. Bongars' Tagebuch seiner Reise von Wien nach Konstantinopel im Jahr 1585" as an appendix in Hermann Hagen's *Jacobus Bongarsius. Ein Beitrag zur Geschichte der gelehrten Studien des 16.–17. Jahrhunderts*

A newly established (Muslim) city, such as Hezargrad, offered a recent convert an abundance of opportunities for socio-economic advancement, indubitably in excess of what a Muslim village could provide. Some converts integrated quickly into the urban class of administrative officials and servants of the cult who enjoyed special tax exemptions and other socio-economic privileges, even if usually at a lower level. Thus, as of c. 1550, the *sheykh* of the *zaviye* (dervish convent) was a certain "Mahmud, son of Abdullah,"[52] the town crier (*dellal*) was a convert too.[53] Among Hezargrad's converts in 1579 were two servants in the soup kitchen (*ferraş-ı imaret*) in the Cami'-i Şerif quarter, and one more such servant appears in the ward of the *mescid* of Behram Bey, which was also the home of other well-placed converts who possessed *berat*s, such as a caretaker of a mosque (*kayyum*) and a cook in the soup kitchen (*tabbah-ı imaret*). The newly founded neighborhood of the *mescid* of Mehmed Bey also had a convert *kayyum*.[54]

7.1.3.2 *Conversion to Islam in Shumnu* The issue of conversion to Islam in Shumnu differs substantially from the case of Hezargrad. While the latter had been (re-)founded as a new, exclusively Muslim town with Ibrahim Pasha's richly endowed pious foundation as its basis, Shumnu carried on its existence as an urban center from under the medieval Bulgarian state through the Ottoman conquest. Despite its destruction in 1444, it remained an administrative district center during the second half of the turbulent fifteenth century, still overwhelmingly populated by Slavic-speaking (Bulgarian) Orthodox Christians. Only during the sixteenth century did Shumnu gradually and definitively become a "typical" Ottoman city, with a predominantly Muslim population but retaining a strong Orthodox Christian community as well.

While the pre-1535 synoptic tax registers reflect only the significant increase in the town's population, with the proportion of Muslims gradually rising, the detailed registers of c. 1535 and c. 1550 reveal percentages of converts to Islam which were substantial, albeit slightly lower than those in Hezargrad. In c. 1535, 26 out of a total of 114 registered married Muslims in Shumnu, or 23 percent, were identifiable converts to Islam, all of *dhimmi* origin. In addition, there were ten identifiable

(Bern: A. Fischer, 1874), 62–72. His very short, but important reference to Hezargrad is on page 72; Bongars seems to make a clear distinction with respect to the different languages spoken on his way (he clearly distinguishes between Bulgarian and Turkish as spoken languages), so it might be assumed that he meant that Hezargrad was populated largely by Turkish-speaking Muslims, and not just Muslims ("Turk" being often used interchangeably with "Muslim" in early modern Europe).

[52] BOA TD 382, p. 847.
[53] Ibid., p. 848.
[54] TKG KK TTd 411, ff. 43b–44b.

(adult) sons and grandsons of converts. Most likely these converts came largely from the town's Christian quarter (*mahalle-i gebran*) or its rural hinterland. Unlike the case of Hezargrad, none of Shumnu's converts in *c.* 1535 had a religio-legal, administrative, or military occupation, but there was at least one *hacı*[55] who had performed the pilgrimage to Mecca – a testament to his affluence and (likely) a desire to enhance his socio-cultural status within the local Muslim community.

As of *c.* 1550, the percentage of converts had decreased markedly, to 17 percent (45 out of 258 registered Muslims), but this time a signifi- cant portion (12 out of 45) were manumitted slaves. Three of those were registered as convent servants (*hıdmetkar-ı tekye*) at Selim Dede's newly established dervish convent (of unspecified but presumably "Sunni" orientation) constituting the majority (three out of five) of the convent residents.[56] Another of Shumnu's manumitted slaves was most probably brought by his former owner who came from Istanbul.[57]

As in Hezargrad and other Ottoman cities (e.g. Trabzon), the distribu- tion of converts by quarter (*mahalle*) was highly uneven: the percentage of registered converts in the Old Market quarter (*mahalle-i Eski Pazar*) was three times higher than that in the Willow Spring quarter (*mahalle-i Söğüd Pınarı*) in *c.* 1535.[58] The quarter of Yolcu must have been named after its founder, listed *c.* 1535 as a "son of Abdullah."[59] Muslim neigh- borhoods which developed a strong core of converts tended to serve as a magnet for newly coming converts from within the town's Christian neighborhood, its rural hinterland, or farther away.

As of 1579, one observes a further decline in the overall percentage of converts in Shumnu, down to 12 percent. Yet, if one takes into account the fact that in 1579 there were no converts of servile origin (as opposed to the twelve as of *c.* 1550), the percentage of converts of *dhimmi* origin is not much lower than in the mid-sixteenth century. Yet, converts' share of Shumnu's Muslims in 1579 was around three times lower than that of nearby Hezargrad.

It is hard to definitively explain Shumnu's visibly lower percentages of converts as compared to nearby Hezargrad. Unlike the latter, Shumnu was an originally Christian (Bulgarian) city and the presence of a still very strong, tightly-knit orthodox Christian community (40 percent of the city residents in 1579) concentrated in one neighborhood and headed

---

[55] "*Hācī Ḥamza, veled-i 'Abdullāh*," BOA TD 439, p. 159.
[56] BOA TD 382, p. 383.
[57] Ibid., p. 382.
[58] BOA TD 439, pp. 158–159. On the case of Trabzon, see Lowry, *Islamization and Turkification*, 152–170.
[59] "*Yolcu Ḥıżır, veled-i 'Abdullāh*," BOA TD 439, p. 159.

Table 7.2 *Converts' numbers in Shumnu by neighborhood (*c. *1535 and* c. *1550)*

Neighborhood (*mahalle*)	Married converts (regular – non-slave origin)	Manumitted slaves (all married)	Married converts (total)	Percentage of converts (of all married Muslim men)	Bachelors
C. 1535					
Camiʿ	4	0	4	22% (4/18)	0
Söğüt Pınarı	4	0	4	11% (4/38)	1
Eski Pazar	8	0	8	35% (8/23)	0
Yolcu	10	0	10	28% (10/35)	0
Total (1535)	**26**	**0**	**26**	**23% (26/114)**	**1**
C. 1550					
Camiʿ	10	2	12	21% (12/58)	2
Söğüt Pınarı	4	2	6	15% (6/39)	1
Eski Pazar	9	4	13	25% (13/51)	0
Yolcu	8	0	8	11% (8/72)	1
Veli Kadı	2	4	6	16% (6/38)	1
Total (1550)	**33**	**12**	**45**	**17% (45/258)**	**5**

Table 7.3 *Converts in Shumnu by neighborhood in 1579*

Neighborhood (*mahalle*)	Married converts (*dhimmi* origin)	Manumitted slaves (all married)	Married converts (total)	Percentage of converts (of all married Muslim men)	Bachelors
Camiʿ-i Atik, Yolcu, and Solak Sinan	14	0	14	20% (14/69)	0
Söğüt Pınarı	2	0	2	5% (2/38)	1
Camiʿ-i Cedid and Eski Pazar	12	0	12	12% (12/103)	6
Veli Kadı	0	0	0	0%	0
Total (1579)	**28**	**0**	**28**	**12% (28/231)**	**7**

by its priest (*pop*, *papaz*),[60] could have been a deterrent to conversion, at least among the Christians in the city. The Orthodox church in the Balkans had developed various instruments to prevent its parishioners from converting to Islam: anti-Islamic rhetoric and propaganda, punitive measures on those who socialized with Muslim neighbors (including excommunication in extreme cases), as well as nurturing the images of neo-martyrs, presented as ones who lost their lives for resisting conversion, and thus serving as role models for the rank-and-file parishioners in a socio-political milieu seen as generally hostile to the Christian faith and community.[61]

However, the presence of a strong urban Christian community cannot itself explain the fairly low percentage of converts in late sixteenth-century Shumnu. Rus (Rusçuk) on the Danube (to the northwest of both Shumnu and Hezargrad) may serve as an instructive counterexample. While the ratio between Muslim and Christian inhabitants there followed a pattern very similar to that in Shumnu from the late fifteenth through the sixteenth centuries, the percentages of converts to Islam very much echoed Hezargrad's pattern: around 24 percent c. 1550, and up to 30 percent in 1579.[62] One tentative explanation of this apparent discrepancy may be sought in Rusçuk's rise as a major strategic military and commercial center on the Danube and its concomitant socio-economic prosperity; Shumnu's economic development was not that vigorous and thus may have attracted fewer newcomers (and converts in particular).

7.2. Confessionalization and Confession Building: Insights from Deliorman and Gerlovo

The concept of "confessionalization" was introduced in early modern European historiography in the late 1970s and 1980s to denote a socio-historical phenomenon that allegedly had a profound and far-reaching impact on the development of early modern European states and societies.[63] Growing out from the quest to implement the principle of *cuius*

---

[60] For Shumnu's priests, see BOA TD 439, p. 160; BOA TD 382, p. 384; TKG KK TTd 151, f. 166b.
[61] Todorova, *Pravoslavnata tsârkva i bâlgarite*, 224–237; on Orthodox Christian neo-martyrdom in the early modern Ottoman domains, see Krstić, *Contested Conversions*, 121–142. In fact, Balkan Christian neo-martyrs lost their lives almost invariably due to apostasy from Islam, not resistance to conversion.
[62] BOA TD 382, pp. 51–59; TKG KK TTd 151, ff. 12a–18a.
[63] Most notably in the work of Wolfgang Reinhard and Heinz Schilling; see, for example, Reinhard, "Gegenreformation als Modernisierung? Prolegomena zu einer Theorie des konfessionellen Zeitalters," *Archiv für Reformationsgeschichte* 68 (1977): 226–252; "Konfession und Konfessionalisierung in Europa," in *Bekenntnis und Geschichte: Die Confessio Augustana im Historischen Zusammenhang*, ed. Wolfgang Reinhard (Munich:

regio, eius religio ("whose the realm, his the religion"), as agreed upon in the Peace of Augsburg of 1555, "confessionalization" has been viewed as a process that aimed at confessional homogenization leading to more clearly defined confessional identities and boundaries, entailing a measure of "social disciplining," and providing an impetus to early modern state formation and the crystallization of cultural and political identities through a strengthened relationship between states and confessional churches.[64]

Among the methods of "confessionalization" most readily identified by Wolfgang Reinhard were the establishment of "pure doctrine" and its formulation in a confession of faith, the propagation and enforcement of this "pure doctrine" and the norms it articulated, placing personnel embracing this "new orthodoxy" in key positions and marginalizing "dissidents," propaganda and censorship (especially regarding printed materials) as well as the internalization of new norms through education (including elementary education), visitations, and the imposition of church discipline enforcing the "correct" performance of rites and, in more extreme cases, the expulsion of confessional minorities to strengthen confessional homogeneity.[65]

Europeanist advocates of the concept of "confessionalization" as a valid paradigm of social history have argued that it deeply affected both public and private life and stress its modernizing impetus.[66] While the use of the concept has drawn considerable criticism, especially on account of the unevenness of the nature of confessionalization in various European societies (particularly beyond the Germanic lands), the alleged overestimation of the "pressure for confessionalization" and the connections between "confessionalization" on the one hand, and state formation and modernization on the other, the "confessionalization"

Vögel, 1981), 165–189; "Zwang zur Konfessionailisierung? Prolegomena zu einer Theorie des konfessionellen Zeitalters," *Zeitschrift für historische Forschung* 10 (1983): 253–273, "Reformation, Counter-Reformation, and the Early Modern State: a Reassessment," *The Catholic Historical Review* 75 (1989): 383–404, and Schilling, "Die Konfessionalisierung im Reich: Religiöser und gesellschaftlicher Wandel in Deutschland zwischen 1555 und 1620," *Historische Zeitschrift* 246 (1988): 1–45.

[64] Ute Lotz-Heumann, "Confessionalization," in *Reformation and Early Modern Europe: A Guide to Research*, ed. David Whitford (Kirksville, MO: Truman State University Press, 2008), 136–157, esp. 138–141. This chapter by Lotz-Heumann provides an excellent general overview of "confessionalization" as a historical paradigm, its history, use, and critique; of similar utility are Chapters 5 and 6, "Konfessionalisierung als wissenschaftliches Paradigma" and "Der Epochencharakter des konfessionellen Zeitalter," in Stefan Ehrenpreis and Ute Lotz-Heumann, *Reformation und Konfessionelles Zeitalter* (Darmstadt: Wissenschafliche Buchgesellschaft, 2002), 17–29.

[65] See Reinhard's works already referred to above as well as Lotz-Heumann, "Confessionalization," 140–141.

[66] Lotz-Heumann, "Confessionalization," 139.

paradigm has stimulated a meaningful debate as well as numerous new studies, which have brought about some relevant modifications of the paradigm's initial formulation.

The concept of "confessionalization" entered Ottomanist historiography only recently. Evaluating its usefulness in early modern Ottoman history, Tijana Krstić has argued that "the Ottomans experienced analogous developments and even implemented policies leading to integration of politico-religious spheres similar to those taking place throughout the Habsburg and other contemporary European domains."[67] Krstić points out that the emergence of the (officially Twelver Shiʻi) Safavid Empire of Iran (1501–1722) which posed a direct threat to "Ottoman dynastic legitimacy and claim to leadership in religion," led to the intensification of the "Sunni-Shiʻa" polarization that entailed Sunnitization in the Ottoman domains and conversion to Twelver Shiʻism in the Safavid realm.[68] In her view, the apparent chronological parallelism between West European and Islamic world "confessionalizations" is not a coincidence; rather, "the process of formation of distinct confessional territorial blocks and forging of "religious orthodoxies" unfolded simultaneously in both Muslim and Christian empires in the sixteenth century as a consequence of imperial competition between the Ottomans and Habsburgs on the one hand and the Ottomans and Safavids on the other."[69]

Kaya Şahin has offered a more nuanced interpretation of "confessionalization" in the Ottoman and Safavid contexts, acknowledging its usefulness for the productive problematization of a number of issues, such as "the new symbiotic relationship between religion and politics in both empires, the organization of religious establishments in light of the empires' ideological necessities, the growth of external and internal propaganda that reasserted religious principles and moral norms, a new emphasis on ritual and the political supervision of the individual subjects' compliance, and, finally, the territorial demarcation of respective beliefs."[70] Şahin, however, points out that the Ottoman state lacked the resources, and possibly the vision, to pursue the imposition of confessional homogeneity at the level at which this was carried out in western Christendom.[71] Exploring the development of Sufi orders in "the age of state-building and confessionalization," Derin Terzioğlu highlights the limits of the sixteenth-century Ottoman state's capacity to "dictate right belief" and emphasizes its assertive but accommodationist approach

---

[67] Krstić, *Contested Conversions*, 13.
[68] Ibid., 12.
[69] Ibid., 14.
[70] Şahin, *Empire and Power*, 208.
[71] Ibid., 209.

aimed at the "institutionalization and domestication" of Sufi orders (especially those whose beliefs and practices could raise "red flags").[72] The process of articulation of a religious "orthodoxy" of sorts had visibly begun by the second half of the fifteenth century. Prior to the emergence of the Safavid threat, the Ottomans' main religious "other" was the Christian infidels to the west. The emerging imperial vision under Mehmed II and Bayezid II (prior to the rise of the Safavid threat) necessitated a further articulation of religious identity, stemming from the organic relationship between imperial claims to authority and "right belief" (and the related rise of the *medrese*-trained *ulema* as a prop and agent of the new imperial project), at least at the ideological level.[73] The emergence of the Safavid challenge undoubtedly gave a huge boost to this process, adding much political urgency and expediency, also furnishing the Ottomans with the ultimate "confessional other" *within* the Dar al-Islam, thus significantly stimulating the articulation of Ottoman "Sunni orthodoxy" as well as of the Ottoman state's legitimacy as a defender of "true Islam." Sixteenth-century Ottoman *ulema* produced numerous *fatwas*[74] and treatises[75] which elaborated "right belief" and provided a religio-legal justification of the mass persecutions of the Kızılbaş and the enforcement of "correct" socio-religious behavior.[76]

---

[72] Terzioğlu, "Sufis," 86–99.

[73] While the socio-religious order of the Anatolian and Balkan frontier zones prior to the early-to-mid-fifteenth century was characterized by the fluidity and negotiability of religious identities (aptly captured by Cemal Kafadar's use of the term "metadoxy"), the emerging imperial vision under Mehmed II and Bayezid II could not afford to remain "indifferent" or "latitudinarian" on matters of "right belief," at least in principle; the connection between imperial vision and the state's embracement of a "high," "scriptural" conceptualization of religion is also evident. As it has been shown in Chapter 2, this new stance of the Ottoman state manifested itself not only "in principle," but also in action, as demonstrated by Bayezid II's persecutions of antinomian dervishes who were seen as a challenge to the Ottoman state's centralizing drive, and even earlier, as in the case of the suppression of Ḥurūfīs in Edirne in 1444; İnalcık, *Fatih Devri*, 37.

[74] On the *fatwa* of the noted jurist Nūreddīn Ḥamza Ṣaru Görez that accused the Safavids and their supporters in Anatolia of *küfr* (blasphemy) and *irtidād* (apostasy) and authorized Selim I's fight against the Safavids as well as the persecution and execution of Safavid supporters on Ottoman soil, see Şehabeddin Tekindağ, "Yeni Kaynak ve Vesîkaların Işığı Altında Yavuz Sultan Selim'in İran Seferi," *TD* 17, no. 22 (March 1967): 54–55. On the anti-Safavid/Kızılbaş *fatwas* of *şeyhülislam* İbn-i Kemāl (d. 1536), see Elke Eberhard, *Osmanische Polemik gegen die Safawiden im 16. Jahrhundert nach arabischen Handschriften* (Freiburg im Breisgau: Klaus Schwartz, 1970), 164–165. For a selection of *şeyhülislam* Ebū's-Sü'ūd Efendi's anti-Kızılbaş *fatwas* (under the heading of "apostasy"), see *fatwas* Nos. 479–489 in Düzdağ, *Şeyhülislâm Ebussuûd Efendi Fetvaları*, 109–112.

[75] For example, İbn-i Kemāl's "*Fī takfir al-rawāfiḍ*" (On the Condemnation of the Heretics), Tekindağ, "Yeni Kaynak," 55–56; an excerpt from the Arabic original is reproduced by Tekindağ on pages 77–78. Eberhard's *Osmanische Polemik* provides an excellent overview of sixteenth-century Ottoman anti-Safavid propaganda.

[76] Beyond the Safavids/Kızılbaş, see Ebū's-Sü'ūd's *fatwas* on questionable behavior of Sufis and ordinary Muslims that could evoke accusations of heresy, unbelief, apostasy, or

Not only the *ulema*'s legal rulings and polemical treatises, but also, importantly, Ottoman administrative language (especially as manifested in *mühimme defterleri*) reflects an evolving "search for confessional vocabulary" in the quest for articulating religio-political identity, both vis-à-vis the Safavids and all those Muslims in the Ottoman domains whose behavior could bring about suspicions of heresy (*ilhad, rafz, rafizilik*). This included not only accusations of *bid'at* (unlawful "innovation") against perceived Safavid sympathizers, Sufis, and other Ottoman Muslims, but also the introduction in Ottoman bureaucratic parlance of concepts such as *ehl-i sünnet ve cema'at* (the people of the Prophetic Tradition (the Sunna) and the Community, i.e. the true "Sunnis"),[77] and the redefinition of traditional notions like *ehl-i Islam* ("the people of Islam"), *memalik-i Islam* ("the domains of Islam"),[78] and notably, *mezheb* (Ar. *madhhab*) – in the sense of "confessional community."[79]

What then could be made of the apparent silence of the sources regarding any large-scale persecutions of groups like the Rum Abdals in Deliorman and Gerlovo's countryside in the sixteenth century? We know that a major Rum Abdal convent, that of Akyazılı Baba in Dobrudja, was inspected on accusations of questionable practices (the production

---

"incorrect" ritual and practice, Düzdağ, *Şeyhülislâm Ebussuûd Efendi Fetvaları*, 83–88, 112–118 (Nos. 338–356, 490–530).

[77] "*Topkapı Sarayı Arşivi H. 951–952 Tarihli ve E-12321 Numaralı Mühimme Defteri*, 32 (order No. 451). The concept of *ahl al-sunna wa'l-jamā'a* (Ar.) was prominent in the formative centuries of Islamic history and sought to delineate the followers of "true" Prophetic Tradition as opposed to those who "strayed" from it, including early adherents of (proto-) Shi'ism; see G.H.A. Juynboll, "Sunna," *EI²*.

[78] While prior to the emergence of the Safavid state *ehl-i İslâm* and *memālik-i İslâm* were mainly employed to highlight the opposition between the Ottomans and their Christian adversaries, entries in mid-sixteenth-century Ottoman registers of outgoing imperial orders (*mühimme defterleri*) demonstrate that such notions were already used as a delinator between the Ottomans and the "lowly Kızılbaş" (*Kızılbaş-ı evbāş*) and their domains as well. Ottoman ("Sunni") Muslims and the Ottoman domains were referred to as *ehl-i İslâm* and *memālik-i İslam*, respectively, while the same did not hold for the Safavids and their domains; see *Topkapı Sarayı Arşivi H. 951–952 Tarihli ve E-12321 Numaralı Mühimme Defteri*, 327–329 (orders Nos. 451 and 453).

[79] *6 Numaralı Mühimme Defteri 972/1564–1565* (Ankara: T.C. Başbakanlık Devlet Arşivleri Genel Müdürlüğü, 1995), order No. 897. This order to the judge of Taşköprü in Anatolia addresses a certain İsmā'īl's vigorous heretical propaganda and the issue of his "expulsion" (*iḫrāc*) from *mezheb-i ehl-i sünnet ve cemā'at*, i.e. the *madhhab* of those who follow Prophetic Tradition (the "Sunnis"). The judge is instructed to apprehend and dispatch İsmā'īl to the capital. While *madhhab* had the traditional meaning of a school of legal thought (such as the four established Sunni "schools," the Ḥanafī, Mālikī, Shāfi'ī, and Ḥanbalī), here it is used as a designation of a "confessional community" or a "religious denomination," which meaning would gain popularity in later Ottoman Turkish, and remains the most prominent connotation of the word in modern Turkish (as in "Sunni and Shi'i," "Catholics and Protestants").

and consumption of alcohol),[80] just as was the nearby *tekye* of Sarı Saltık on suspicion of blasphemy reportedly uttered by one of the resident dervishes, whereby the judge of Varna was instructed to investigate the matter, inspect all the resident dervishes, and determine whether they belonged to *ehl-i sünnet* (the people of the Sunna) or *ehl-i bid'at* (the people of "unlawful innovation").[81] In Demir Baba's *velayetname*, a dervish at Akyazılı Baba's *tekye* expels the young Demir on the count of the latter's being "the son of a heretic" (*mültehidoğlu*).[82]

Yet, "heterodox" groups in Deliorman and Gerlovo (which, as suggested in Chapters 4 and 6, must have absorbed Kızılbaş migrants and deportees from Anatolia in the sixteenth century) apparently came to be integrated reasonably well into the provincial Ottoman political-administrative order. Tax-register data reflect a dramatic demographic growth and favorable socio-economic development in the countryside, including in rural settlements that may clearly be identified as adhering to "heterodox" (especially Rum Abdal) Islam. Demir Baba's *vita* certainly does not betray signs of state-sponsored persecutions or intense political pressure. To the contrary, Sultan Süleyman is cast as "a friend of the saints" and Demir features notably as a *gazi*-saint fighting on the Ottoman side at Budim. If the *velayetname* singles out a confessional adversary to the Rum Abdals, it is the Bektashis who appear to pose a threat to the preservation of Rum Abdal identity, not the "Sunnitizing" Ottoman state.

All this, together with other Ottoman policies, such as the toleration of Shi'ites in Ottoman Lebanon,[83] and the Ottoman state's support of the Shi'i-leaning Bektashi order,[84] raises again the question of the applicability of the concept of "confessionalization"[85] – at least as formulated in early modern Europeanist historiographic debates – to the Ottoman context. While "confessionalization" may prove useful in problematizing a number of facets of Ottoman religious policy within the context of the developing Ottoman imperial project, it may also stimulate a critical comparison between Western Christendom and the Ottoman (as well

[80] *3 Numaralı Mühimme Defteri 966–968/1558–1560*, order No. 1644, dated Rebi'ü'l-Evvel AH 968/November 20–December 19, 1560.
[81] *3 Numaralı Mühimme Defteri 966–968/1558–1560*, order No. 418, dated 10 Safer 967/ November 11, 1559.
[82] *DBV*, 67.
[83] See Stefan Winter, *The Shiites of Lebanon under Ottoman Rule, 1516–1788* (Cambridge and New York: Cambridge University Press, 2010).
[84] Saim Savaş, *XVI. Asırda Anadolu'da Alevilik* (Ankara: Türk Tarih Kurumu, 2013), 113–116.
[85] See also M. D. Baer's review of Krstić's *Contested Conversions*, *Journal of Islamic Studies* 23/3 (2012), 391–394.

as the Safavid) domains regarding the nature and definition of "confession building" and the latter's connections to state formation and socio-cultural identities. While the sixteenth century saw the intense articulation of Ottoman "Sunni orthodoxy" in the quest for establishing the Ottoman dynasty as the indisputable champion of "true Islam," we know little of the actual implementation of policies that could have sought to establish a degree of confessional homogeneity and "social discipline" in the wider Ottoman society even vaguely reminiscent of Western Christendom's experience. For example, in the 1530s, Ebu's-Sü'ud issued a *fatwa* that obliged Muslim villagers to build mosques (if they did not previously exist) and regularly attend communal prayers – an injunction clearly connected to Ottoman accusations of neglect of prayer levied against suspected Safavid supporters in Ottoman Anatolia, but also aimed at the general strengthening of "orthodox" religious identity among the Muslim population of the empire.[86] But to what extent were such legal rulings implemented, especially in low-key provincial contexts?

Not only did the Ottoman state not necessarily have the resources to impose confessional homogeneity (there was no "Ottoman church" or a well-organized and unified system of elementary education), "confessionalization" in the Ottoman case, at least from the perspective of the state and the dynasty, seems to have related primarily to the rough demarcation of confessional boundaries and the establishment of the political primacy of "true Islam" (as defined by the Ottoman *ulema*) and the Ottoman state and dynasty as its upholders. Mass persecutions of alleged sympathizers of the Safavid cause took place in the first half of the sixteenth century, at the height of the Ottoman-Safavid conflict, and in Anatolia – in close proximity to a Safavid state that posed a very palpable religio-political and military threat to Ottoman sovereignty and legitimacy. Once the conflict had subsided, in the second half of the sixteenth century Ottoman authorities would be on the lookout for suspected pro-Safavid activities in Anatolia and Iraq (and would thus make their vigilante presence known), but would generally refrain from mass persecutions.[87] Apart from that, and especially in the Balkans – far away from the politically sensitive zones of the Sunni-Shi'i contest – Ottoman authorities would be concerned with the endorsement of "right belief" (and practice) primarily in highly

---

[86] Savaş, *XVI. Asırda*, 116–117; this *fatwa*, dated 1533–4, is from a manuscript recension of Ebû's-Sü'ûd's *Ma'rûżât*.

[87] Colin Imber, "The Persecutions of Ottoman Shi'ites According to the Mühimme Defterleri, 1565–1585," *Der Islam* 56 (1979): 245–273.

visible social and spatial contexts (such as public urban spaces and popular Sufi convents).[88]

In this relation, it is worth revisiting one more of Ebu's-Sü'ud's *fatwas* – on the Kızılbaş on Ottoman soil and what is due to them given their heretical behavior. The great jurist offers a standard treatment: those (Kızılbaş) who make light of (*istihfaf*) the Qur'an, the Sharia, and the "religion of Islam," curse the caliphs Abu Bakr and Umar, disrespect the *ulema* and their religious knowledge, etc., are to be considered apostates and deserve execution.[89] But Ebu's-Sü'ud then makes a twist, not explicitly called for in the original question posed: those (among the suspected Kızılbaş) in the cities and villages who appeared to have "corrected" themselves (apparently on their own initiative) and did not openly follow beliefs and practices that could bring their "uprightness" into question, should be left in peace.[90] This ruling may be viewed as implicitly reflecting the Ottoman state's conceptualization of its "confessional" policies. As long as the political loyalty (and "docility") of its subjects was maintained and they refrained from open demonstration of "dissident" religio-political beliefs and practices, the state did not seem to have wholeheartedly and energetically pursued the definitive and mass eradication of such ("non-Sunni") beliefs and practices.[91] To return to Deliorman, the examples of the prominent Rum Abdal Ali Baba's *tekye* as well as that of Şüca Dede – the administration of which was ordered transferred to "the respected *ulema* and notables of the area" after the namesake dervishes' scions perished (as discussed in Chapter 4) – suggest that if "Sunnitization" was on the Ottoman state's agenda, it appears to have been a long-term, low-intensity project – more a policy of containment (and slow marginalization and/or assimilation) – rather than an energetic quest for confessional homogenization that targeted quick and visible results. In the context of Deliorman and Gerlovo, provincial centers such as Hezargrad and Shumnu – through which the state projected its authority and hegemonic religio-political perspective – evidently played an important role in this "policy of containment" as well.

---

[88] See examples derived from *mühimme defterleri* (other than the ones already cited above) in Ahmet Refik, *On Altıncı Asırda Rafizilik ve Bektaşilik* (Istanbul: Muallim Ahmet Halit Kitaphanesi, 1932).

[89] Düzdağ, *Şeyhülislâm Ebussuûd Efendi Fetvaları*, 110–111 (No. 481).

[90] "*Ammâ şehirlerde ve köylerde kendü hâlinde salâh üzerine olub, bunların sıfatlarından ve ef'allerinden tenezzühü olub, zâhir hâlleri dahi sıdklarına delâlet eyleyen kimselerin kizbleri zâhir olmayınca, üzerlerine bunların ahkâmı ve 'ukûbâtı icrâ olunmaz*," Düzdağ, *Şeyhülislâm Ebussuûd Efendi Fetvaları*, 111 (No. 481).

[91] Compare to the toleration of Sunnis in Safavid Iran in the reign of Shah Tahmasp, even if limited to the upper strata, whereby "as long as Sunnites refrained from an open display of their religious affiliation, they were mostly unharmed." Rula Jurdi Abisaab, *Converting Persia: Religion and Power in the Safavid Empire* (London: I.B. Tauris, 2004), 26.

Conclusion

The present study has discussed the demographic, ethno-religious, and religio-cultural transformation that the regions of Deliorman and Gerlovo in the northeastern Ottoman Balkans (together with some adjacent areas) underwent from the second half of the fifteenth century through the sixteenth century. This transformation may be said to have had two major aspects: the repopulation of that theretofore largely underpopulated area that entailed the formation of a demographically dominant Muslim community – due to both the influx of Muslims from outside the region and conversion to Islam of parts of the local population, and the gradual incorporation of Deliorman and Gerlovo into the Ottoman political and administrative-territorial framework, whereby the latter was itself evolving and maturing as a part of the consolidation of the Ottoman imperial bureaucratic regime. In line with the "connected histories" approach advanced by Sanjay Subrahmanyam, the history of Deliorman and Gerlovo in the late fifteenth and sixteenth centuries allows for opportunities to link contingent local and regional events and processes to macroscopic themes such as the expansion of the Islamic world and empire building in early modern Eurasia.[1]

The analysis of Ottoman tax registers for the eastern portion of the province (*sancak*) of Niğbolu for the late fifteenth and the first half of the sixteenth centuries has demonstrated that the essential repopulation of the area under study and the definitive formation of the Muslim community in Deliorman and Gerlovo started in the late fifteenth century, mostly at the southern end of the area studied (i.e. Gerlovo and the vicinity) and progressed rapidly in the first half of the sixteenth century, thus contradicting the relatively widespread view that by the late fifteenth century Deliorman and the adjacent areas were densely populated and already possessed a well-shaped and dominant Muslim population.

The formation of the Muslim community in Deliorman and Gerlovo's countryside appears to be largely the result of two main migration

---

[1] Subrahmanyam, "Connected Histories," see also Fletcher's related "Integrative History."

currents – "heterodox" groups "native" to the Balkans – from Thrace (and possibly from the eastern Rhodopes), most importantly Abdals of Rum of Otman Baba's branch and semi-nomadic Turcoman associates whose forefathers had migrated as conquerors and colonizers into Ottoman Rumeli in the second half of the fourteenth and the first half of the fifteenth centuries, and (again, mostly semi-nomadic Turcoman) migrants from Anatolia who crossed into the Balkans in the first half of the sixteenth century in the context of the Ottoman-Safavid conflict, whereby many of those may have been perceived as sympathizers of the Savavid cause in Ottoman Anatolia. While there is some evidence that some of these Turcoman migrants could have been deportees directed by the Ottoman state from Anatolia to the Balkans (as the case of a large groups of deportees [*sürgünan*] in Pravadi in the 1510s suggests), whereby deportees originally directed to other parts of the Balkans (esp. Dobrudja) may have spilled over to Deliorman, the Ottoman state was not fully in control of and did not play a dominant proactive role in the repopulation of Deliorman and Gerlovo.

Deliorman and Gerlovo were ecologically attractive to Turcoman semi-nomadic migrants, they may have also appeared attractive for "heterodox" groups (including non-Sharia-minded dervishes) as the area already had an established place in the memory of "heterodox"-minded Muslim communities (more specifically in relation to the legacy of Sheykh Bedreddin, but also within the context of the growth of the Abdals of Rum of Otman Baba's branch, as well as possibly other heterodox collectivities, most notably the Bektashis). The sparsely populated Deliorman and Gerlovo (and likely Dobrudja as well) emerged as a safe haven of sorts for Turcoman migrants, whether from other parts of the Balkans (most notably Thrace) or from Anatolia.

The confluence of these two migration currents – from the southeastern Balkans and Anatolia – is reflected in the fact that while "Kızılbaş" eventually came to be the dominant (self-)identification for most of the "heterodox" population in Deliorman and Gerlovo,(originally) Rum Abdal saints such as Otman Baba and Demir Baba (the latter being native to Deliorman) developed as the main regional/local saintly cults in the area (as well as in the wider eastern Balkans). In many ways the formation of rural Muslim communities in the northeastern Balkans (including the still much under-researched Dobrudja) may be seen as an outgrowth of the same process in Thrace as well as in Anatolia.[2] The dominant role of Turcoman migration and colonization in the eastern Balkans, in the context of the nature of the Ottoman conquest of the Balkans as well as the

---

[2] See Vryonis, *The Decline of Medieval Hellenism.*

proximity of Anatolia which made further migrations from there feasible, conditioned the Turkish linguistic identity of these Muslim communities, in contradistinction to the western Balkans (e.g. Bosnia and Albania) and other areas in the frontier zones of the Islamic world (e.g. Bengal) where local languages predating "Islamization" were preserved within newly formed Muslim communities.[3]

However, the role of conversion to Islam in the formation and growth of the Muslim community in Deliorman and Gerlovo should not be underestimated. The present study has demonstrated that during the sixteenth century converts to Islam played a very prominent role in the growth of urban Muslim communities in the area studied, and that the role of conversion in the rural countryside was not insignificant either. While further research on the seventeenth and eighteenth centuries is necessary (though, unfortunately, such research is hard to conduct in view of the rather thin source base for this period), preliminary analysis of the only two extant fairly comprehensive Ottoman tax registers for the seventeenth and eighteenth centuries (both of them of the *avarız*, or "extraordinary taxes" variety),[4] as well as an overview of the much more reliable demographic data for the nineteenth[5] and twentieth centuries, suggests that conversion to Islam played a role in the development and growth of the Muslim community in Deliorman and Gerlovo in the seventeenth and eighteenth (and possibly the nineteenth) centuries that was likely greater than in the sixteenth century, when the essential (Turkish-speaking) core of the Muslim community in the area formed. This augmentation of Deliorman and Gerlovo's Muslim community – to the extent preliminary research suggests – could be seen as a natural outgrowth of the stage of essential formation in the late fifteenth and sixteenth centuries. Intense "Islamization of space" – i.e. the effective integration of the area within the Ottoman territorial-administrative and, more broadly speaking, Pax Islamica's socio-cultural and religio-political landscape through the development of Ottoman-Islamic administrative, social, educational, and religious institutions as well as through the related increased presence of human agents of Islam from the outside (administrative, military, and religious personnel, artisans and traders in the urban centers as well as semi-nomadic Turcomans and dervishes in the countryside) – led to the gradual "indigenization" of Islamic culture, in its various manifestations, and thus rendered "Islamization of people"

[3] See Eaton, *The Rise of Islam and the Bengal Frontier.*
[4] These are BOA TD 771, dated AH 1052/AD 1642–3 and BOA KK 2915, dated AH 1165/AD 1751.
[5] For the nineteenth century, see Halime Doğru, *1844 Nüfus Sayımına Göre Deliorman ve Dobruca'nın Demografik, Sosyal ve Ekonomik Durumu* (Ankara: Türk Tarih Kurumu, 2011).

(i.e. conversion to Islam) an increasingly socially acceptable choice.[6] The
dominant role of Turcoman colonization in the essential formation of
the Muslim community in Deliorman and Gerlovo through the sixteeth
century created conditions for the gradual ethno-linguistic assimilation
of converts (largely of local origin) as part of their integration into their
new religious community.

The history of Deliorman and Gerlovo in the late fifteenth and sixteenth centuries also presents an instructive example of the "imperiali-
zation" of the Ottoman polity in a regional setting, far away from the
imperial center. The early modern Ottoman state partook in a more general, pan-Eurasian, process of state centralization of authority and "the
growth of coercive state apparatuses" which entailed the articulation of
institutional, ideological, and technological bases of empire building,
including the development of bureaucracy and record keeping on paper
at both the central and regional levels, the expansion of paid armed units
directly answerable to the imperial center, the construction of elaborate
political ideologies that legitimized centralized dynastic rule, as well as
the utilization of gunpowder technology and changes in military strategy
and tactics in the context of the "military revolution."[7]

The incorporation of Deliorman, Gerlovo, and adjacent areas into
the evolving Ottoman imperial framework was a gradual process that
included the rise of regional cities as strongholds of imperial authority
(as well as "imperial" culture that entailed the endorsement of Ottoman
"Sunni orthodoxy"), the gradual marginalization and assimilation of
groups that had made formative contributions to the rise of the Ottoman
frontier principality, but whose traditional subsistence patterns and
religio-political ethos would not fit with the overarching prerogatives of
the developing Ottoman imperial regime, as well as the astute and pragmatic use of incidentally available local and regional resources to manage
and accommodate dissent. If for the Turcomans and non-Sharia-minded
dervishes who migrated to Deliorman and Gerlovo in the late fifteenth
and the first half of the sixteenth centuries the area likely was, at least
initially, a "safe haven" of sorts, for the centralizing Ottoman imperial

[6] Compare to early modern Bengal (as well as frontier areas in the western Balkans such
as Bosnia) where "Islamization of space and territories" was characterized by the intensive development of Islamic administrative, social, religious, and educational institutions
within the context of of the integration of these areas into Islamic polities, but the influx
of Muslim settlers from elsewhere, especially in the countryside, was limited and did not
have a pronounced impact on demographic development.
[7] Subrahmanyam, "Connected Histories," 738, 744. On the elaboration of imperial
ideologies and the related "imperial cultures," specifically in the context of early modern Islamic empire building, see Stephen F. Dale, *The Muslim Empires of the Ottomans,
Safavids, and Mughals* (New York: Cambridge University Press, 2010), 77–105, 135–176,
and 208–246.

state it may have been a "safety valve" that could accommodate dissenting and potentially rebellious groups, keeping them away from sensitive areas of acute political and military conflict and tension and/or diminishing economic resources (due to population pressure, for example). While the sixteenth-century Ottoman imperial regime was hardly "all powerful" in a distant Balkan province as some statist-minded historians may like to see it, it proved, over time, essentially successful in setting and developing the broad macropolitical mechanisms of consolidation of state authority.[8] The increasingly successful efforts of the Ottoman state to adapt to demographic and socio-economic changes that occurred as a result of population movements it could not always fully control fit with observations about the increasing degree of centralization within the Empire during the reigns of Selim I and especially Süleyman I made in different contexts.[9] Of crucial importance in this context is the fact that while the focus area of this study proved attractive to incoming Turcoman semi-nomads as it offered favorable conditions for animal husbandry, Deliorman and Gerlovo also possessed potential for the development of agriculture, which would be, indeed, increasingly realized from the sixteenth century onwards. The accommodationist approach that the Ottoman government pursued with regard to taxation policies induced the gradual settlement and agrarianization of Turcoman newcomers to the area (and their descendants). Within this context, the Ottoman authorities entrusted local Christian villagers with guarding mountain passes and river fords to enhance the security of the area and also facilitate trade and stimulate economic growth.

In a similar vein, the history of sixteenth-century Deliorman and Gerlovo allow for some additional insights into Ottoman confessional policies as an integral facet of early modern Ottoman empire building, especially with regard to the Ottoman imperial regime's approach to religio-political dissidents. The integration of Muslim "heterodox" groups within the fabric of provincial society in the northeastern Balkans without recourse to persecution and violence, but with an eye toward their gradual accommodation (and assimilation over the long term, to the

---

[8] While the scope of this study extends only to the late sixteenth century, the early modern Ottoman imperial regime would keep up with its pragmatic and accommodationist approach to managing dissent beyond that point in time; see Karen Barkey, *Bandits and Bureaucrats: The Ottoman Route to State Centralization* (Ithaca, NY, and London: Cornell University Press, 1994) and *Empire of Difference: The Ottomans in Comparative Perspective* (New York: Cambridge University Press, 2008), as well as Tezcan, *The Second Ottoman Empire.*

[9] Kafadar, *Between Two Worlds*, 138–154; Lindner, *Nomads and Ottomans*, 75–103; Şahin, *Empire and Power in the Reign of Süleyman*, 214–242; Fleischer, "On Gender and Servitide."

extent possible) is consonant with observations made in other contexts within the Empire. As Stefan Winter has argued in his study on the history of Shi'ite communities in early modern Ottoman Lebanon, "[I]f the Empire, having formally espoused Sunni Islam, could not explicitly tolerate religious dissidence, the pragmatism sometimes shown in accommodating and indeed integrating deviant groups and individuals is no less a defining feature of its history."[10] In the context of the Ottoman state's limitations, in terms of both resources and vision, to pursue confessional homogeneity at a level comparable to that observed in western Christendom, further research on Ottoman, as well as Safavid, confessional policies would help for a more nuanced understanding of the particularities of the Islamic world's (Sunni/Shi'i) and Western Christendom's (Catholic/Protestant) experiences.[11] It would thus also facilitate understanding "confessionalization" in the Ottoman/Safavid context on its own, Islamic world terms in light of the recently initiated debate on the usefulness of the concept in early modern Islamic historiography.

[10] Winter, *The Shiites of Lebanon under Ottoman Rule*, 8.
[11] Şahin, *Empire and Power in the Age of Süleyman*, 208.

Select Bibliography

ARCHIVAL AND MANUSCRIPT SOURCES

Başbakanlık Osmanlı Arşivi.
BOA TD Nos. 7, 50, 65, 309, 370, 382, 385, 439, 482, 581, 771.
BOA MAD 11.
BOA KK 2915.
BOA MD Nos. 3, 22, 35, 40, 42, 83.
Topkapı Sarayı Müzesi Arşivi.
E 5566, E 7029, D 167.
Topkapı Sarayı Müzesi Kütüphanesi.
Yazıcızade Ali, *Tevarih-i Al-i Selcuk*, Revan No. 1390.
Tapu ve Kadastro Genel Müdürlüğü.
TKG KK TTd Nos 150, 151, 411.
Natsionalna Biblioteka "Sv. Sv. Kiril and Methodii," Orientalski Otdel.
OAK 45/29, OAK 217/8, OAK 12/9, Or 73.

PUBLISHED ARCHIVAL AND LITERARY SOURCES

3 Numaralı Mühimme Defteri, 966–968/1558–1560. Ankara: T.C. Başbakanlık
    Devlet Arşivleri Genel Müdürlüğü, 1993.
6 Numaralı Mühimme Defteri 972/1564–1565. Ankara: T.C. Başbakanlık Devlet
    Arşivleri Genel Müdürlüğü, 1995.
83 Numaralı Mühimme Defteri 1036–1037/1626–1628. Ankara: T.C. Başbakanlık
    Devlet Arşivleri Genel Müdürlüğü, 2001.
370 Numaralı Muhâsebe-i Vilâyet-i Rûm-ili Defteri (937/1530). Ankara: T.C.
    Başbakanlık Devlet Arşivleri Genel Müdürlüğü, 2002.
Akgündüz, Ahmed. *Osmanlı Kanunnâmeleri ve Hukukî Tahlilleri.* 9 volumes.
    Istanbul: Fey Vakfı Yayınları, 1990–.
Ali Efendi. *Fetava-yı Ali Efendi.* Istanbul: Matba'a-i Amire, 1311/1893–4.
Anonim Tevârîh-i Âl-i Osman. F. Giese neşri. Edited by Nihat Azamat.
    Istanbul: Edebiyat Fakültesi Basımevi, 1992.
Aşıkpaşazade. *Âşıkpaşazâde Tarihi [Osmanlı Tarihi (1285–1502)].* Edited by
    Necdet Öztürk. Istanbul: Bilge Kültür Sanat, 2013.

Aşıkpaşazade. *Aşıkpaşazade Tarihi*. Edited by Ali Bey. Istanbul: Matba'a-i Amire, 1332/1914.

Aytaş, Gıyasettin, Ali Sinan Bilgili, and Selahattin Tozlu, eds. *Osmanlı Arşiv Belegelerinde Kızıldeli (Seyyid Ali Sultan) Zaviyesi (1401–1852)*. Ankara: Gazi Üniversitesi Türk Kültürü ve Hacı Bektaş Veli Araştırma Merkezi, 2010.

Barkan, Ömer Lütfi, ed. *XV ve XVI-ıncı Asırlarda Osmanlı İmparatorluğunda Zirai Ekonominin Hukuki ve Mali Esasları. Birinci Cilt: Kanunlar.* Istanbul: Burhaneddin Matbaası, 1945.

Comnena, Anna. *The Alexiad of the Princess Anna Comnena*. Translated by Elizabeth A.S. Dawes. New York: Barnes and Noble, 1967.

Demir Baba Vilâyetnamesi. Edited by Bedri Noyan. Istanbul: Can Yayınları, 1976. Edited by Hakkı Saygı. Istanbul: Saygı Yayınları, 1997. *(İnceleme-Tenkitli Metin)*. Edited by Filiz Kılıç and Tuncay Bülbül. Ankara: Grafiker, 2011.

Doukas. *Decline and Fall of Byzantium to the Ottoman Turks*. Translated and edited by Harry Magoulias. Detroit, MI: Wayne State University Press, 1975.

Düzdağ, M. Ertuğrul, ed. *Şeyhülislâm Ebussuûd Efendi Fetvaları Işığında 16. Asır Türk Hayatı*. Istanbul: Enderun Kitabevi, 1983.

Edirne Salnamesi: 1310 Sene-i Hicriyesine Mahsus. Edirne: Matba'a-i Vilayet, 1310/1893.

Elezović, Gliša, ed. and trans. *Turski Spomenici*, vol. 1, Part 1. Belgrade: Srpska Kraljevska Akademija, 1940.

Elvan Çelebi, *Menâkıbu'l-Kudsiyye fî Menâsıbi'l-Ünsiyye (Baba İlyas-ı Horasani ve Sülâlesinin Menkabevî Tarihi)*. Edited by İsmail Erünsal and Ahmet Yaşar Ocak. Istanbul: İstanbul Üniversitesi Edebiyat Fakültesi Matbaası, 1984.

Nüzhet (Ergun), Sadettin. *Bektaşi Şairleri*. Istanbul: Devlet Matbaası, 1930. *Bektaşi Şairleri ve Nefesleri*. 3 volumes. Istanbul: İstanbul Maarif Kitaphanesi, 1955.

Evliya Çelebi, *Evliyâ Çelebi Seyahatnâmesi*. Edited by Seyit Ali Kahraman, Robert Dankoff, Zekeriya Kurşun, and İbrahim Sezgin. Istanbul: Yapı Kredi Yayınları, 2011, 10 books in 2 vols.

Fermendžin, E. *Acta Bulgariae Ecclesiastica (ab A. 1565 usque ad a. 1799)*. Zagreb: Ex officina Societatis Typographicae, 1887.

Giese, Friedrich, ed. *Die altosmanische anonymen Chroniken=Tavarih-i Al-i 'Usman*. 2 volumes. Breslau: n.p., 1922–5.

Hadschi Chalfa, Mustafa Ben Abdalla [Katip Çelebi]. *Rumeli und Bosna, geographisch beschrieben*. Translated by Joseph von Hammer. Vienna: Verlag des Kunst- und Industrie-Comptoirs, 1812.

Hagen, Hermann. *Jacobus Bongarsius. Ein Beitrag zur Geschichte der gelehrten Studien des 16.-17. Jahrhunderts*. Bern: A. Fischer, 1874.

Halil bin Ismail bin Şeyh Bedrüddin Mahmud. *Sımavna Kadısıoglu Şeyh Bedreddin Manâkıbı*. Edited by Abdülbaki Gölpinarlı and İsmet Sungurbey. Istanbul: Eti Yayınevi, 1967.

Hoca Sadeddin. *Tacü't-Tevarih*. 2 volumes. Istanbul: Tabhane-i Amire, 1862–3.

İbn-i Kemal (Kemalpaşazade). *Tevârih-i Âl-i Osman. I. Defter*. Edited by Şerafettin Turan. Ankara: Türk Tarih Kurumu, 1970. *Tevârih-i Âl-i Osman. IV. Defter*. Edited by Koji İmazawa. Ankara: Türk Tarih Kurumu, 2000.

İdris-i Bitlisi, *Heşt Bihişt*. Edited by M. Karataş, S. Kaya, and Y. Baş, vol. 1. Ankara: BETAV, 2008.

Imber, Colin, ed. and trans. *The Crusade of Varna, 1443–45*. Aldershot and Burlington, VT: Ashgate, 2006.

İnalcık, Halil, ed. *Hicrî 835 Tarihli Sûret-i Defter-i Sancak-ı Arvanid*. Ankara: Türk Tarih Kurumu, 1954.

İnalcık, Halil and Mevlud Oğuz, eds. *Gazavât-ı Sultân Murâd b. Mehemmed Hân: İzladi ve Varna Savaşları (1443–1444) Üzerinde Anonim Gazavâtnâme*. Ankara: Türk Tarih Kurumu, 1989.

Iorga, Nicolae, ed. *La campagne des croisés sur le Danube (1445)*. Paris: Librarie Universitaire J. Gamber, 1927.

İz, Fahir, ed. *Saltuk-name: The Legend of Sarı Saltuk Collected from Oral Tradition by Ebu'l Hayr Rumi (Text in Facsimile with a Critical and Stylistic Analysis and Index by Fahir İz)*, 7 vols. Cambridge, MA: Harvard University Department of Near Eastern Languages and Civilizations, 1974–84.

Jagić, Vratislav. "Konstantin Filosof i njegov Život Stefana Lazarevića Despota Srpskoga." *Glasnik SUD* 42 (1875): 223–377.

Kalitsin, Mariia, Velkov, Asparuh, and Evgeni Radushev, ed. and trans. *Osmanski izvori za isliamizatsionnite protsesi na Balkanite (XVI-XIX v.)*. Sofia: BAN, 1990.

Kanitz, Felix. *Donau Bulgarien und der Balkan: Historish-geographisch-ethnographische Reise Studien aus den Jahren 1860–1879*, 2. neubearb. Auflage. 3 volumes. Leipzig: Renger'sche Buchhandlung, 1882.

Kaygusuz Abdal (Alâeddin Gaybî) Menâkıbnâmesi. Edited by Abdurrahman Güzel. Ankara: Türk Tarih Kurumu, 1999.

Kovachev, Rumen, ed. and trans. *Opis na nikopolskiia sandzhak ot 80-te godini na XV vek*. Sofia: NBKM, 1997.

[Küçük Abdal.] *Otman Baba Velâyetnâmesi (Tenkitli Metin)*. Edited by Filiz Kılıç, Mustafa Arslan, and Tuncay Bülbül. Ankara: Grafiker, 2007.

Minorsky, Vladimir. *Persia in A.D. 1478–1490: An Abridged Translation of Fadlallah b. Ruzbihan Khunji's Tarikh-i 'Alam-Ara-yi Amini*. London: Luzac and Co., 1957.

Nachev, V., and N. Fermandzhiev, eds. *Pisahme da se znae*. Sofia: Izdatelstvo na Otechestveniia Front, 1984.

Nedkov, Boris, ed. and trans. *Bâlgariia i sasednite i zemi prez XII vek spored Idrisi*. Sofia: Nauka i Izkustvo, 1960.

Neşrî, Mevlânâ Mehmed. *Cihânnümâ [Osmanlı Tarihi (1288–1485]*. Edited by Necdet Öztürk. Istanbul: Bilge Kültür Sanat, 2013.

Oruç Beğ. *Oruç Beğ Tarihi [Osmanlı Tarihi (1288–1502)]*. Edited by Necdet Öztürk. Istanbul: Bilge Kültür Sanat, 2014.

Peçevi İbrahim Efendi. *Tarih-i Peçevi*. Book Two. Istanbul: Enderun Kitabevi, 1982.

Petrov, P. and V. Giuzelev, eds. *Khristomatiia po istoriia na Bâlgariia*, vol. 1. Sofia: Dârzhavna Pechatnitsa, 1928.

Popruzhenko, M. G., ed. *Sinodik Tsaria Borila*. Sofia: Dârzhavna Pechatnitsa, 1928.

Refik, Ahmet. *Anadolu'da Türk Aşiretleri, 966–1200*. Istanbul: Devlet Matbaası, 1930.

Ross, E. Denison. "The Early Years of Shah Ismail, Founder of the Safavi Dynasty." *Journal of the Royal Asiatic Society* 28 (1896): 249–340.

Ruhi. *Ruhi Tarihi*. Edited by Halil Erdoğan Cengiz and Yaşar Yücel. *Belleten* 14 (1989–1992): 359–472.

Şahin, İlhan, and Feridun Emecen, eds. *II. Bayezid Dönemine Ait 906/1501 Tarihli Ahkâm Defteri*. Istanbul: Türk Dünyası Araştırmaları Vakfı, 1994.

Şah Ismail I Safavi (Hatayi). *Il canzoniere di Şah Ismail Hatai*. Edited by Tourkhan Gandjei. Naples: Instituto Universitari Orientale, 1959.

Hatayî Divanı. Şah İsmail Safevi. Edebi Hayatı ve Nefesleri, 2nd. Edited by S. Nüzhet Ergun. Istanbul: Istanbul Maarif Kitaphanesi, 1956.

Sahillioğlu, Halil, ed. *Topkapı Sarayı Arşivi H.951–952 Tarihli ve E-12321 Numaralı Mühimme Defteri*. Istanbul: İRCİCA, 2002.

Snegarov, Ivan, ed. "Neizdadeni starobalgarski zhitiia." *Godishnik na Dukhovnata Akademiia Sv. Kliment Okhridski* 3, no. 19 (1953–1954): 151–174.

Solakzade, Mehmed Hendemi Çelebi, *Solakzade Tarihi*. Istanbul: Mahmud Bey Matbaası, 1298/1880–1.

Spandounes, Theodore. *On the Origins of the Ottoman Emperors*. Translated by Donald Nicol. Cambridge: Cambridge University Press, 1997.

TIBI, vol 2. Edited by Nikolai Todorov and Boris Nedkov. Sofia: BAN, 1966. vol. 3 (2 pts.). Edited by Bistra Cvetkova and Asen Razboinikov. Sofia: BAN, 1972.

al-Tirmidhi, al-Hakim. *The Concept of Sainthood in Early Islamic Mysticism: Two Works by al-Hakim al-Tirmidhi*. Edited and translated by Bernd Radtke and John O'Kane. Richmond, Surrey: Curzon Press, 1996.

Turski izvori za istoriiata na pravoto v bâllgarskite zemi/Fontes Turcici Historiae Iuris Bulgarici. 2 volumes. Edited and translated by Bistra Cvetkova. Sofia: BAN, 1971.

Tursun Bey. *Târîh-i Ebü'l-Feth*. Edited by Mertol Tulum. Istanbul: Baha Matbaası, 1977.

Usluer, Fatih, ed. *Hurufi Metinleri 1*. Ankara: Birleşik Yayınları, 2014.

Vahidi. *Vāhidī's Menākıb-i Hvoca-i Cihān ve Netīce-i Cān*. Edited by Ahmet Karamustafa. Cambridge, MA: Department of Near Eastern Languages and Civilizations, Harvard University, 1993.

Velâyetnâme. Hacı Bektaş-ı Veli. Edited by Hamiye Duran, 2nd edn. Ankara: Türkiye Diyanet Vakfı, 2014.

Vilâyet-nâme: Manâkıb-ı Hünkâr Hacı Bektâş-ı Veli. Edited by Abdülbaki Gölpınarlı. Istanbul: İnkılâp Kitabevi, 1958.

Yazıcızâde Ali. *Tevârîh-i Âl-i Selçuk (Selçuklu Tarihi)*. Edited by Abdullah Bakır. Istanbul: Çamlıca, 2009

Yemînî, Dervîş Muhammed. *Fazîlet-Nâme (Giriş-İnceleme-Metin)*. 2 volumes. Edited by Yusuf Tepeli. Ankara: Türk Dil Kurumu: 2002.

Zeno, Caterino. "Travels in Persia." In *A Narrative of Italian Travels in Persia in the Fifteenth and Sixteenth Centuries*, translated and edited by Charles Grey, *Works Issued by the Hakluyt Society*, vol. 159, 1–65. New York: Burt Franklin, 1878.

STUDIES

Abisaab, Rula Jurdi. *Converting Persia: Religion and Power in the Safavid Empire*. London: I.B. Tauris, 2004.

Alexandrescu-Dersca, Marie-Mathilde. *La campagne de Timur en Anatolie, 1402,* 2nd edn. London: Variorum Reprints, 1977.

Algar, Hamid. "The Hurufi Influence on Bektaşism." In *Bektachiyya: Études sur l'ordre mystique des Bektachis et les groupes relevant de Hadji Bektach,* edited by Alexandre Popovic and Gilles Veinstein, 39–53. Istanbul: Les Éditions Isis, 1995.

Allouche, Adel. *The Origins and Development of the Ottoman-Safavid Conflict (906–962/1500–1555).* Berlin: Klaus Schwartz Verlag, 1983.

Antonova, Vera. *Shumen i shumenskata krepost.* Shumen: Antos, 1995.

Antov, Nikolay. "The Ottoman State and Semi-Nomadic Groups along the Ottoman Danubian *Serhad* (Frontier Zone) in the Late 15th and the First Half of the 16th Centuries: Challenges and Policies." *Hungarian Studies* 27, no. 2 (2013): 219–235.

"Emergence and Historical Development of Muslim Communities in the Ottoman Balkans: Historical and Historiographical Remarks." In *Beyond Mosque, Church and State: Alternative Narratives of the Nation in the Balkans,* edited by Theodora Dragostinova and Yana Hashamova, 31–56. Budapest and New York: Central European University Press, 2016.

Arjomand, Said Amir. *The Shadow of God and the Hidden Imam: Religion, Political Order, and Societal Change in Shi'ite Iran from the Beginning to 1890.* Chicago and London: The University of Chicago Press, 1984.

Arnakis, George. "The Role of Religion in the Development of Balkan Nationalism." In *The Balkans in Transition: Essays on the Development of Balkan Life and Politics since the Eighteenth Century,* edited by Charles and Barbara Jelavich, 115–144. Berkeley, CA: University of California Press, 1963.

Arnold, Thomas. *The Preaching of Islam: A History of the Propagation of the Muslim Faith.* Westminister, UK: Archibald Constable and Co., 1896.

Arslan, Hüseyin. *Osmanlı'da Nüfus Hareketleri (XVI. Yüzyıl): Yönetim, Nüfüs, Göçler, İskanlar, Sürgünler.* Istanbul: Kaknüs Yayınları, 2001.

Atanasov, Georgi. "Etno-demografski promeni v Dobrudzha (X-XI v.)." *IP* 47, no. 2 (1991): 75–84.

Ayverdi, Ekrem Hakkı. *Avrupa'da Osmanlı Mimari Eserleri.* 6 books in 4 vols. 2nd. edn. Istanbul: Istanbul Fethi Cemiyeti, 1978–82.

Babinger, Franz. "Der Islam in Kleinasien." *ZDMG* 76 (1922): 122–156.

"Marino Sanuto's Tagebücher als Qwelle zur Geschichte der Safawijja," in *A Volume of Oriental Studies presented to Edward G. Browne,* edited by Thomas Arnold and Reynold A. Nicholson, 28–50. Cambridge: Cambridge University Press, 1922.

"Das Bektaschi Kloster Demir Baba." *Westasiatische Studien* 34 (1931): 8–93.

Balivet, Michel. "Deux Partisans de la fusion religieuse des chrétiens et des musulmans au XVIe siècle: Le turc Bedreddin de Simavna et le grec Georges de Trebizond." *Byzantina* 10 (1980): 363–396.

Islam mystique et révolution armée dans les Balkans Ottomans: vie de Cheikh Bedreddin le «Hallaj des Turcs» (1358/59–1416). Istanbul: The Isis Press, 1995.

Barbir, Karl. *Ottoman Rule in Damascus, 1708–1758.* Princeton, NJ: Princeton University Press, 1980.

Barkan, Ömer Lütfi. "XV. ve XVI. Asırlarda Osmanlı İmparatorluğunda Toprak İşçiliğinin Organizasyonu Şekilleri." *İÜİFM* 1, no. 1 (1939): 29–74, no. 2 (1939): 198–245, and no. 4 (1940): 397–477.

"Osmanlı İmparatorluğunda bir İskân ve Kolonizasyon Metodu Olarak Vakıflar ve Temlikler." *VD* 2 (1942): 279–386.

"Osmanlı İmparatorluğunda bir İskân ve Kolonizasyon Metodu Olarak Sürgünler," *İÜİFM* 11 (1949–50): 524–569; 13 (1951–2): 56–78; and 17 (1953–4): 209–237.

"'Tarihi Demografi' Araştırmaları ve Osmanlı Tarihi," *TM* 10 (1951–3): 1–26.

"Quelques observations sur l'organisation économique et sociale des villes Ottomanes des XVI et XVI siècles." *Recueils de la Société Jean Bodin*, vol. 7, *La Ville* (Bruxelles, 1955), 289–311.

"Essai sur les données statistiques des registres de recensement dans l'Empire ottoman aux XVe et XVIe siècles." *JESHO* 1, no. 1 (Aug. 1957): 9–36.

Bashir, Shazad. *Fazlallah Astarabadi and the Hurufis.* Oxford: Oneworld, 2005.

Beldiceanu-Steinherr, Irène. "La conquête d'Adrianople par les Turcs; la pénétration turque en Thrace et la valeur de chroniques Ottomanes." *Travaux et Memoires 1* (1965): 439–461.

"La vita de Seyyid 'Ali Sultan et la conquête de la Thrace par les Turcs." In *Proceedings of the 27th International Congress of Orientalists ... 1967*, edited by D. Sinor, 275–276. Wiesbaden: Otto Harrasowitz, 1971.

"Seyyid 'Ali Sultan d'après les registres ottomans: L'installation de l'Islam hétérodoxe en Thrace." In *The Via Egnatia under Ottoman Rule (1380–1699)*, edited by Elizabeth Zachariadou, 45–66. Rethymnon: Crete Univesity Press, 1996.

Bentley, Jerry H. "Early Modern Europe and the Early Modern World." In *Between the Middle Ages and Modernity: Individual and Community in the Early Modern World*, edited by Charles H. Parker and Jerry H. Bentley, 13–31. Lanham, MD: Rowman and Littlefield, 2007.

Bilgili, Ali Sinan. "Osmanlı Arşiv Belgelerine Göre Kızıldeli (Seyyid Ali Sultan) Zaviyesi (1401–1826)." *TKHBVAD* 53 (2010): 89–114.

Binswanger, Karl *Untersuchungen zum Status der Nichtmuslime im Osmanischen Reich des 16. Jahrhunderts: mit einer Neudefinition des Begriffes "Dhimma."* Munich: R. Trofenik, 1977.

Birge, John K. *The Bektashi Order of Dervishes.* London: Luzac & Co., 1937.

Biserova, Sofiia. "Etnografski materiali za selo Bisertsi." In *Bâlgarskite aliani: sbornik etnografski materiali*, edited by Ivanichka Georgieva, 34–104. Sofia: Universitetsko Izdatelstvo "Sv. Kliment Ohridski," 1991.

Bobchev, Stefan. "Za deliormanskite turtsi i za kâzâlbashite." *Sbornik na BAN* 24 (1929): 1–16.

Brown, Peter. *The Cult of Saints: Its Rise and Function in Latin Christianity.* Enlarged edition. Chicago, IL, and London: The University of Chicago Press, 2015.

Bulliet, Richard W. *Conversion to Islam in the Medieval Period: An Essay in Quantitative History.* Cambridge, MA: Harvard University Press, 1979.

Cahen, Claude. "Mouvements populaires et autonomisme urbaine dans l'Asie musulmane du moyen âge III." *Arabica* 6 (1959): 258–260.

Chatterjee, Partha. *The Nation and Its Fragments: Colonial and Postcolonial Histories.* Princeton, NJ: Princeton University Press, 1993.

Chodkiewicz, Michel. *Seal of the Saints: Prophethood and Sainthood in the Doctrine of Ibn 'Arabi.* Translated by Liadain Sherrard. Cambridge: The Islamic Texts Society, 1993.

Çıpa, H. Erdem. *The Making of Selim: Succession, Legitimacy, and Memory in the Early Modern Ottoman World.* Bloomington, IN: Indiana University Press, 2017.

Cook, Michael. *Population Pressure in Rural Anatolia.* London and New York: Cambridge University Press, 1972.

Cvetkova, Bistra. *Geroichnata sâprotiva na bâlgarite protiv turskoto nashestvie.* Sofia: Narodna Prosveta, 1960.

"Hezargrad." *EI2.*

Daneshvari, Abbas. "The Iconography of the Dragon in the Cult of Saints in Islam." In *Manifestations of Sainthood in Islam,* edited by Grace M. Smith and Carl W. Ernst, 15–25. Istanbul: The Isis Press, 1993.

De Jong, Frederick. "Problems Concerning the Origins of the Qızılbaş in Bulgaria: remnants of the Safaviyya?" In *Convegno sul tema: la Shī'a nell'Impero Ottomano,* 203–15. Rome: Accademia Nazionale Dei Linzei, 1993.

Dennis, George T. "The Byzantine-Turkish Treaty of 1403." *Orientalia Christiana Periodica* 33 (1967): 72–88.

De Weese, Devin. *Islamization and Native Religion in the Golden Horde: Baba Tükles and Conversion to Islam in Historical and Epic Tradition.* University Park, PA: The Pennsylvania State University Press, 1994.

"Foreword." In Köprülü, *Early Mystics in Turkish Literature,* viii–xxvii.

Diaconu, Petre. "The Petchenegs on the Lower Danube." In *Relations Between the Autochthonous Population and the Migratory Populations on the Territory of Romania,* edited by Miron Constantinescu, Ştefan Pascu, and Petre Diaconu, 235–40. Bucharest: Editura Academiei RSR, 1975.

Dimitrov, Strashimir. "Za datirovkata na niakoi osmanski registri ot XV vek." *IBID* 25 (1968): 241–247.

"Za yurushkata organizatsiia i rolyata i v etnoasimilatsionnite protsesi." *Vekove* 1–2 (1982): 33–43.

"Za priemstvenostta v razvitieto na balkanskite gradove prez XV-XVI vek." *Balkanistika* 2 (1987): 5–17.

"Novi danni za demografskite otnosheniia v iuzhna Dobrudzha prez pârvata polovina na XVI v." *Dobrudzha* 14–16 (1997–9): 278–333.

Dimitrov, Strashimir, N. Zhechev, and V. Tonev, *Istoriia na Dobrudzha,* vol. 3. Sofia: BAN, 1988.

Drinov, Marin. "Istorichesko osvetlenie vârhu statistikata na narodnostite v iztochnata chast na bâlgarskoto kniazhestvo." *Periodichesko Spisanie* 7 (1884): 1–24, and 8 (1884): 68–75.

Džaja, Srećko. *Konfessionalität und Nationalität Bosniens und der Herzegovina. Vorempanzipatorische Phase, 1463–1804.* Munich: Oldenborg, 1984.

"Bosnian Historical Reality and Its Reflection in Myth." In *Myths and Boundaries in South-Eastern Europe,* edited by Pål Kolstø, 106–129. London: Hurst and Company, 2005.

Eberhard, Elke. *Osmanische Polemik gegen die Safawiden im 16. Jahrhundert nach arabischen Handschriften.* Freiburg im Breisgau: Klaus Schwartz, 1970.
Eaton, Richard. *The Rise of Islam and the Bengal Frontier, 1204–1760.* Berkeley, CA: University of California Press, 1993.
Ehrenpreis, Stefan, and Ute Lotz-Heumann. *Reformation und Konfessionelles Zeitalter.* Darmstadt: Wissenschafliche Buchgesellschaft, 2002.
Eldem, Edhem, Daniel Goffman, and Bruce Masters. *The Ottoman City between East and West: Aleppo, Izmir, and Istanbul.* Cambridge and New York: Cambridge University Press, 1999.
Eliade, Mircea. *The Sacred and the Profane: The Nature of Religion.* New York: Harper and Row, 1961.
Emecen, Feridun. *XVI. Asırda Manisa Kazâsı.* Ankara: Türk Tarih Kurumu, 1989.
İlk Osmanlılar ve Batı Anadolu Beylikler Dünyası. Istanbul: Kitabevi, 2001.
"Yaya ve Müsellem." *TDVİA.*
Emecen, Feridun, Yusuf Halaçoğlu, and İlhan Şahin. "Turkish Settlements in Rumelia (Bulgaria) in the 15th and 16th Centuries: Town and Village Population." *IJTS* 4 (1990): 23–40.
Ersal, Mehmet. "Şücaeddin Veli Ocağı: Balkan Aleviliğindeki Yeri, Rolü ve Önemi." *TKHBVAD* 63 (2012): 207–230.
Faroqhi, Suraiya. "Agricultural Activities in a Bektaşi Center: The Tekke of Kızıl Deli, 1750–1830." *Südost-Forschungen* 35 (1976): 69–96.
"Population Rise and Fall in Anatolia, 1550–1620." *Middle Eastern Studies* 15 (1979), 422–445.
Der Bektaschi-Orden in Anatolien (vom späten fünfzehnten Jahrhundert bis 1826). Vienna: Verlag des Instituts für Orientalistik der Universität Wien, 1981.
Towns and Townsmen of Ottoman Anatolia: Trade, Crafts and Food Production in an Urban Setting, 1520–1650. Cambridge: Cambridge University Press, 1984.
"Conflict, Accomodation, and Long-term Survival: The Bektaşi Order and the Ottoman State (Sixteenth-Seventeenth Centuries)." In Popovic and Veinstein, *Bektachiyya,* 171–84.
Filipović, Nedim. *Princ Musa i Šejh Bedreddin.* Sarajevo: Svjetlost, 1971.
Fleischer, Cornell. *Bureaucrat and Intellectual in the Ottoman Empire: The Historian Mustafa Ali (1541–1600).* Princeton, NJ: Princeton University Press, 1986.
"The Lawgiver as Messiah: The Making of the Imperial Image in the Reign of Süleyman." In *Soliman le Magnifique et son temps,* edited by Gilles Veinstein, 159–177. Paris: Documentation Française, 1992.
Fletcher, Joseph. "Integrative History: Parallels and Interconnections in the Early Modern Period." In *Studies on Chinese and Islamic Inner Asia,* article no. X, edited by Beatrice Forbes Manz (Aldershot: Ashgate Variorum, 1995).
Fraenkel, Eran. "Skopje from the Serbian to Ottoman Empires: Conditions for the Appearance of a Balkan Muslim City." Ph.D. diss., The University of Pennsylvania, 1986.
Friedmann, Yohanan. *Tolerance and Coercion in Islam: Interfaith Relations in the Muslim Tradition.* Cambridge: Cambridge University Press, 2003.
Gandev, Khristo. *Bâlgarskata narodnost prez 15-ti Vek,* 2nd edn. Sofia: Nauka i Izkustvo, 1989.

Gellner, Ernest. "Tribalism and State in the Middle East." In *Tribes and State Formation in the Middle East*, edited by Philip S. Khoury and Joseph Kostiner, 109–126. Berkeley, Los Angeles, and London: University of California Press, 1990.

Georgieva, Ivanichka, ed. *Bâlgarskite aliani: sbornik etnografski materiali.* Sofia: St. Kliment Ohridski University Press, 1991.

Georgieva, Sonia. "Srednovekovnoto selishte nad razvalinite na antichniia grad Abrittus." *IAI* 24 (1961): 9–36.

"Srednovekovniiat grad Cherven. Problemi i prouchvaniia," *IAI* 33 (1972): 305–14.

Georgieva, Tsvetana. *Prostranstvo i prostranstva na bâlgarite, XV-XVI vek.* Sofia: IMIR, 1999.

Gerber, Haim. *Economy and Society in an Ottoman City: Bursa, 1600–1700.* Jerusalem: Hebrew University Press, 1988.

Gökbilgin, M. Tayyib. *XV-XVI Asırlarda Edirne ve Paşa Livası: Vakıflar-Mülkler-Mukataalar.* Istanbul: Üçler Basımevi, 1952.

Gökyay, Orhan Şaik. "Şeyh Bedreddin'in Babası Kadı Mı İdi?." *Tarih ve Toplum* 1, no. 2 (1984): 96–98.

Rumeli'de Yürükler, Tatarlar ve Evlâd-ı Fâtihan. Istanbul: Istanbul Üniversitesi Edebiyat Fakültesi Yayınları, 1957.

Golden, Peter. *An Introduction to the History of the Turkic Peoples.* Wiesbaden: Harrassowitz, 1992.

Goldziher, Ignaz. "The Veneration of Saints in Islam." In Goldziher, *Muslim Studies*, edited by S.M. Stern, translated by C.R. Barber and S.M. Stern, vol. 2, 255–342. London: George Allen and Unwin, 1971.

Gramatikova, Nevena. "Zhitieto na Demir Baba i sâzdavaneto na râkopisi ot miusiulmanite ot heterodoksnite techeniia na Isliama v severoiztochna Bâlgaria." In *Miusiulmanskata kultura v bâlgarskite zemi. Izsledvaniia,* vol. 1, edited by R. Gradeva and S. Ivanova, 400–35. Sofia: IMIR, 1998.

"Otman Baba – One of the Spiritual Patrons of Islamic Heterodoxy in Bulgarian Lands." *Études Balkaniques* 3 (2002): 71–102.

Neortodoksalniiat Isliam v bâlgarskite zemi. Minalo i sâvremennost. Sofia: Gutenberg, 2011.

Hadžijahić, Muhamed. "Sinkretistički elementi u islamu u Bosni i Hercegovini," *POF* 28–29 (1978-9): 301–329.

Han, Verena, and Radovan Samardžić, eds. *Gradska Kultura na Balkanu (XV-XIX vek), Zbornik Radova.* 2 volumes. Belgrade: Srpske Akademije Nauka i Umetnosti, 1984-8.

Handžić, Adem. "O islamizaciji u sjeveroistočnoj Bosni u XV i XVI vijeku." *POF* 16–17 (1966-7): 5–48.

Hasluck, Frederick W. *Christianity and Islam under the Sultans.* 2 volumes. Oxford: Oxford University Press, 1929.

Imber, Colin. "The Persecutions of Ottoman Shi'ites According to the Mühimme Defterleri, 1565–1585." *Der Islam* 56 (1979): 245–273.

The Ottoman Empire: 1300–1481. Istanbul: The Isis Press, 1990.

"Ideals and Legitimation in Early Ottoman History." In *Süleyman the Magnificent and His Age: The Ottoman Empire in the Early Modern World,* edited by Metin Kunt and Christine Woodhead, 138–153. London: Longman, 1995.

İnalcık, Halil. *Fatih Devri Üzerinde Tetkikler ve Vesikalar.* Ankara: Türk Tarih Kurumu, 1954.

"Ottoman Methods of Conquest." *Studia Islamica* 2 (1954): 103–129.

"Osmanlılar'da Raiyyet Rüsumu." *Belleten* 23 (1959): 575–610.

"The Policy of Mehmed II towards the Greek Population and the Byzantine Buildings of the City." *Dumbarton Oaks Papers* 23 (1969–70): 229–249.

The Ottoman Empire: The Classical Age, 1300–1600. London: Weidenfeld and Nicolson, 1973.

"The Emergence of the Ottomans" and "The Rise of the Ottoman Empire." In *The Cambridge History of Islam,* edited by P.M. Holt, K.S. Lambton, and Bernard Lewis, vol. 1, 263–291, and 195–323. Cambridge: Cambridge University Press, 1970.

"Dervish and Sultan: An Analysis of *Otman Baba Vilayetnamesi.*" In ibid., *The Middle East and the Balkans under the Ottoman Empire: Essays on Economy and Society,* 19–36. Bloomington, IN: Indiana University Press, 1993.

"The Ottoman Succession and Its Relation to the Turkish Concept of Sovereignty." In ibid., *The Middle East and the Balkans Under the Ottoman Empire,* 37–69.

"Osmanlı Sultanlarının Unvanları (Titülatür) ve Egemenlik Kavramı." In ibid., *Doğu Batı. Makaleler II,* 187–192. Ankara: Doğu Batı Yayınları, 2008.

İnalcık, Halil, and Donald Quataert, eds. *An Economic and Social History of the Ottoman Empire, 1300–1914.* Cambridge: Cambridge University Press, 1994.

Jayyusi, Salma, Renata Holod, Attilio Petruccioli, and André Raymond, eds. *The City in the Islamic World.* 2 volumes. Leiden and Boston: Brill, 2008.

Kabrda, Josef. *Le Système fiscal de l'église orthodoxe dans l'empire Ottoman (d'après les documents turcs).* Brno: Universita J.E. Purkyne, 1969.

Kafadar, Cemal. *Between Two Worlds: The Construction of the Ottoman State.* Berkeley, Los Angeles, and London: University of California Press, 1995.

Karamustafa, Ahmet. "Kalenderis, Abdals, Hayderis: The Formation of the Bektaşiye in the Sixteenth Century." In *Süleyman the Second and His Time,* edited by Halil İnalcık and Cemal Kafadar, 121–129. Istanbul: The Isis Press, 1993.

God's Unruly Friends: Dervish Groups in the Islamic Middle Period, 1200–1550. Salt Lake City, UT: University of Utah Press, 1994.

"Yesevilik, Melametilik, Kalenderilik, Vefa'ilik ve Anadolu Tasavvufunun Kökenleri Sorunu." In *Osmanlı Toplumunda Tasavvuf ve Sufiler,* edited by Ahmet Yaşar Ocak, 61–88. Ankara: Türk Tarih Kurumu, 2006.

Sufism: The Formative Period. Berkeley, CA: University of California Press, 2007.

"Islamization through the Lens of the *Saltuk-name.*" In *Islam and Christianity in Medieval Anatolia,* edited by A.C.S. Peacock, Bruno DeNicola, and Sara Nur Yıldız, 349–364. Farnham, UK, and Burlington, VT: Ashgate, 2015).

Karpat, Kemal. "The Background of Ottoman Concept of City and Urbanity." In *Structure Sociale et développement culturel des villes sud-est Européennes et Adriatiques aux XVIIe-XVIIIe siècles,* 323–340. Bucharest: AIESEE, 1975.

"Dobruca," *TDVİA.*

Kastritsis, Dimitris. *The Sons of Bayezid: Empire Buildidng and Representation in the Ottoman Civil War of 1402–1413* Leiden and Boston: Brill, 2007.

Khazanov, Anatoly. *Nomads and the Outside World*, 2nd edn. Madison, WI: University of Wisconsin Press, 1994.

Khoury, Philip, and Joseph Kostiner, "Introduction: Tribes and the Complexities of State Formation in the Middle East." In *Tribes and State Formation in the Middle East*, edited by Khoury and Kostiner, 1–22. Berkeley: University of California Press, 1990.

Kiel, Machiel. *Art and Society in Bulgaria in the Turkish Period*. Assen: Van Gorcum, 1985.

"A Monument of Early Ottoman Architecture in Bulgaria: The Bektaşi Tekke of Kıdemli Baba Sultan at Kalugerovo – Nova Zagora." *Belleten* 25 (1971): 53–60.

"Sarı Saltık ve Erken Bektaşilik Üzerine Notlar." *Türk Dünyası Araştırmaları Dergisi*, 2, no. 9 (1980): 25–36.

"Urban Development in Bulgaria in the Turkish Period: The Place of Turkish Architecture in the Process." *IJTS* 4, no. 2 (1989): 79–158.

"Anatolia Transplanted? Patterns of Demographic, Ethnic and Religious Changes in the District of Tozluk (N.E. Bulgaria), 1479–1873." *Anatolica* 17 (1991): 1–29.

"Hrâzgrad–Hezargrad–Razgrad. The Vicissitudes of a Turkish Town in Bulgaria," *Turcica* 21–23 (1991): 495–569.

"Mevlana Neşri and the Towns of Medieval Bulgaria: Historical and Topographical Notes." In *Studies in Ottoman History in Honour of Professor V.L. Ménage*, edited by Colin Heywood and Colin Imber, 165–187. Istanbul: The Isis Press, 1994.

"Razprostranenie na Isliama v balgarskoto selo prez osmanskata epokha(15‑18 V.): kolonizatsiia i isliamizatsiia." In Gradeva and Ivanova, *Miusiulumanskata kultura po bâlgarskite zemi*, vol. 1, 56–126.

"The Ottoman Imperial Registers: Central Greece and Northern Bulgaria in 15th-19th Century: The Demographic Development of the Two Areas Compared." In *Reconstructing Past Population Trends in Mediterranean Europe (3000 B.C.-A.D. 1800)*, edited by John Bintliff and Kostas Sbonias, 195–218. Oxford: Oxbow, 1999.

"Sarı Saltık: Pionier des Islam auf dem Balkan im 13. Jahrhundert." In *Aleviler/Alewiten: Kimlik ve Tarih/Identität und Geschichte*, edited by Ismail Engin and Erhard Franz, vol. 1, 253–86. Hamburg: Deutsches Orient-Institut, 2000.

Kılıç, Remzi. *Kanuni Devri Osmanlı-İran Münasebetleri (1520–1566)*. Istanbul: IQ Kültür Sanat Yayıncılık, 2006.

Kılıç, Rüya. *Osmanlıda Seyyidler ve Şerifler*. Istanbul: Kitap Yayınevi, 2005.

Kiprovska, Mariya. "The Military Organization of the Akıncıs in Ottoman Rumelia." M.A. thesis, Bilkent University, 2004.

"The Mihaloğlu Family: Gazi Warriors and Patrons of Dervish Hospices." *OA* 32 (2008): 193–222.

Kolstø, Pål. "Introduction: Assessing the Role of Historical Myths in Modern Society." In *Myths and Boundaries in South-Eastern Europe*, edited by Pål Kolstø, 1–34. London: Hurst & Company, 2005.

Köprülü, M. Fuat. *Türk Edebiyatında İlk Mutasavvıflar*. Istanbul: Matba'a-i Amire, 1918.

Les Origines de l'Empire Ottoman. Paris: Boccard, 1935.

"Abdal," *Türk Halk Edebiyatı Ansiklopedisi,* fsc. 1, 23–56. Istanbul: Türkiyat Enstitüsü, 1935.

"Anadolu Selçukları'nın Tarihinin Yerli Kaynakları," *Belleten* 7, no. 27 (1943): 379–522.

The Origins of the Ottoman Empire. Translated and edited by Gary Leiser. Albany, NY: SUNY Press, 1992.

Early Mystics in Turkish Literature. Translated and edited by Gary Leiser and Robert Dankoff. London and New York: Routledge, 2006.

Kowalski, T., J. Reychmann, and A. Zajaczkowski. "Deli-Orman," *EI2.*

Krstić, Tijana. *Contested Conversions to Islam: Narratives of Religious Change in the Early Modern Ottoman Empire.* Stanford, CA: Stanford University Press, 2011.

Lapidus, Ira. *Muslim Cities in the Later Middle Ages.* New York: Cambridge University Press, 1984.

"Tribes and State Formation in Islamic History." In Khoury and Kostiner, *Tribes and State Formation in the Middle East,* 25–47.

Lemerle, Paul. *L'émirat d'Aydin, Byzance et l'Occident.* Paris: Presses Universitaires de France, 1957.

Levend, Agah Sırrı. *Gazavāt-Nāmeler ve Mihaloğlu Ali Bey'in Gazavāt-Nāmesi.* Ankara: Türk Tarih Kurumu, 1956.

Lindner, Rudi Paul. *Nomads and Ottomans in Medieval Anatolia.* Bloomington: Indiana University Press, 1983.

Livi Bacci, Massimo. *The Population of Europe.* Translated by Cyntia de Nardi Ipsen and Carl Ipsen. London: Blackwell, 1999.

Lotz-Heumann, Ute. "Confessionalization." In *Reformation and Early Modern Europe: A Guide to Research,* edited by David Whitford, 136–157. Kirksville, MO: Truman State University Press, 2008.

Lowry, Heath W. "Portrait of a City: The Population and Topography of Ottoman Selanik (Thessaloniki) in the Year 1478." *Diptycha* 2 (1980–1): 254–293.

"The Ottoman *Liva Kanunname*s contained in the *Defter-i Hakani.*" *OA* 2 (1981): 43–74.

The Nature of the Early Ottoman State. Albany, NY: SUNY Press, 2003.

The Shaping of the Ottoman Balkans, 1350–1550: The Conquest, Settlement and Infrastructural Development of Northern Greece. Istanbul: Bahçeşehir University Publications, 2008.

The Islamization and Turkification of the City of Trabzon (Trebizond) 1461–1583. Istanbul: The Isis Press, 2009.

In the Footsteps of the Ottomans: A Search for Sacred Spaces and Architectural Monuments in Northern Greece. Istanbul: Bahçeşehir University Press, 2009.

Lowry, Heath W., and İsmail Erünsal. *The Evrenos Dynasty of Yenice-i Vardar: Notes and Documents.* Istanbul: Bahçeşehir University Publications, 2010.

Manz, Beatrice Forbes. *The Rise and Rule of Tamerlane.* Cambridge and New York: Cambridge University Press, 1989.

Marinov, Vasil. *Gerlovo: oblastno geografsko izuchvane.* Sofia: n.p., 1936.

Deli-Orman (iuzhna chast): oblastno geografsko izuchvane. Sofia: n.p., 1941.

Matschke, Klaus-Peter. *Die Schlacht bei Ankara und das Schicksal von Byzanz.* Weimar: Herman Böhlaus Nachfolger, 1981.

Mazzaoui, Michel. *The Origins of the Safawids: Šī'ism, Sūfism, and the Gulat.* Wiesbaden: Franz Steiner, 1972.

Mélikoff, Irène. "La communauté Kızılbaş du Deli Orman en Bulgarie." In ibid., *Sur les traces du soufisme turc: Reserches sur l'Islam populaire en Anatolie*, 105–13. Istanbul: The Isis Press, 1992.

——— *Hadji Bektach: un mythe et ses avatars.* Leiden, Boston, and Köln: Brill, 1998.

——— "Les voies de pénétration de l'hétérodoxie islamique en Thrace et dans les Balkans aux XIVe-XVe siècles." In Zachariadou, *The Via Egnatia Under Ottoman Rule*, 159–70.

——— "Le problème Bektachi-Alevi: quelques dernières considérations." In *Au banquet des Quarantes: exploration au coeur du Bektachisme-Alevisme*, 65–86. Istanbul: Les Editions Isis, 2001.

Ménage, V.L. "The Patronymics of Converts." Appendix to ibid., "Seven Ottoman Documents from the Reign of Mehemmed II." In *Documents from Islamic Chanceries*, edited by S.M. Stern, 112–18. Oxford: Cassirer, 1966.

Minkov, Anton. *Conversion to Islam in the Balkans: Kisve Bahası Petitions and Ottoman Social Life, 1670–1730.* Leiden: Brill, 2004.

Minorsky, Vladimir. "The Poetry of Shah Ismail I." *BSOAS* 10 (1942): 1006a–1053a.

——— "Shaykh Bali Efendi on the Safavids." *BSOAS* 20 (1957): 437–451.

Mottahedeh, Roy. *Loyalty and Leadership in an Early Islamic Society.* Princeton, NJ: Princeton University Press, 1980.

Moutafchieva, Vera. *Agrarian Relations in the Ottoman Empire in the 15th and 16th Centuries.* Boulder, CO: East European Monographs, 1988.

Mutafciev, Petâr. "Die angebliche Einwanderung von Seldschuk-Türken in die Dobrudscha im 13. Jahrhundert." *Spisanie ne Bâlgarskata Akademiia na Naukite (Klon Istoriko-Filologichen)* 56 (1943): 1–130.

Nicol, Donald. *The Last Centuries of Byzantium, 1261–1453*, 2nd edn. Cambridge: Cambridge University Press, 1993.

Nock, Arthur D. *Conversion: The Old and New in Religion from Alexander the Great to Augustine of Hippo.* Oxford: Oxford University Press, 1933.

Norman, York. "An Islamic City? Sarajevo's Islamization and Economic Development, 1461–1604." Ph.D. diss., Georgetown University, 2005.

Ocak, Ahmet Yaşar. "Bâzı Menâkıbnâmelere Göre XIII.-XIV. Yüzyıllardaki İhtidâlarda Hederodoks Şeyh ve Dervişlerin Rolü." *OA* 2 (1981): 31–42.

——— *Osmanlı İmparatorluğunda Marjinal Sûfilik: Kalenderîler (XIV.-XVII. Yüzyıllar).* Ankara: Türk Tarih Kurumu, 1992.

——— *Kültür Tarihi Kaynağı Olarak Menâkıbnâmeler: Metodolojik Bir Yaklaşım.* Ankara: Türk Tarih Kurumu, 1992.

——— *Babaîler İsyanı: Aleviliğin Tarihsel Altyapısı Yahut Anadolu'da İslam-Türk Heterodoksisinin Teşekkülü*, 2nd rev. and enl. edn. Istanbul: Dergah Yayınları, 1996.

——— *Alevî ve Bektaşî İnançlarının İslâm Öncesi Temelleri.* Istanbul: İletişim Yayınları, 2000.

"Babaîler İsyanından Kızılbaşlığa: Anadolu'da İslâm Heterodoksisinin Doğuş ve Gelişim Tarihine Kısa Bir Bakış," *Belleten* 64, no. 239 (2000): 129–159.

Sarı Saltık: Popüler İslâm'ın Balkanlar'daki Destanî Öncüsü. Ankara: Türk Tarih Kurumu, 2002.

"Syncrétisme et esprit messianique: le concept de *qotb* et les chefs des mouvements messianiques aux époques seldjoukide et ottomane (XIIIe-XVIIe siècle)." In *Syncrétismes et hérésies dans l'Orient seldjoukide et ottoman (XIV-e-XVIIIe siècle)*, edited by Gilles Veinstein, 249–257. Paris, Dudley, MA: Peeters, 2005.

Osmanlı Toplumunda Zındıklar ve Mülhidler (15.-17. Yüzyıllar), 4th edn. Istanbul: Tarih Vakfı, 2013.

Ortaçağ Anadolu'sunda İki Büyük Yerleşimci/Kolonizatör Derviş: Dede Garkın ve Emîrci Sultan, Vefâiyye ve Yeseviyye Gerçeği. Istanbul: Dergah Yayınları, 2014.

Orhonlu, Cengiz. *Osmanlı İmparatorluğunda Aşiretleri İskân Teşebbüsü (1691–1696)*. Istanbul: İstanbul Üniversitesi Edebiyat Fakültesi Basımevi, 1963.

Osmanlı İmparatorluğunda Derbend Teşkilâtı. Istanbul: Istanbul Üniversitesi Edebiyat Fakültesi Yayınları, 1967.

Özel, Oktay. "Limits of the Almighty: Mehmed II's 'Land Reform' Revisited," *JESHO* 42, no. 2 (1999): 226–246.

Panaite, Viorel. *The Ottoman Law of War and Peace: The Ottoman Empire and Tribute Payers*. Boulder, CO: East European Monographs, 2000.

Parker, Charles H. *Global Interactions in the Early Modern Age, 1400–1800*. Cambridge: Cambridge University Press, 2010.

Petrov, Petâr. "Vâstanieto na Konstantin i Fruzhin." *Izvestiia na Instituta po Istoriia* 9 (1960): 187–214.

"Antituretskaiia koalitsiia balkanskih stran v nachale XV veka." In *Trudy 25-go Mezhdunarodnogo Kongresa Vostokovedov*, 501–504. Moscow, 1962.

Radushev, Evgeni. *Pomatsite: Khristianstvo i Isliam v zapadnite Rodopi s dolinata na reka Mesta, XV – 30-te godini na XVIII-ti vek*. 2 volumes. Sofia: NBKM, 2005.

Raymond, André. *Grandes villes arabes à l'époque Ottomane*. Paris: Sindbad, 1985.

"Islamic City, Arab City: Orientalist Myths and Recent Views." *British Journal of Middle Eastern Studies* 21, no. 6 (1994): 3–18.

Refik, Ahmet. *On Altıncı Asırda Rafizilik ve Bektaşilik*. Istanbul: Muallim Ahmet Halit Kitaphanesi, 1932.

Reindl, Hedda. *Männer um Bayezid: eine prosopograpshische Studie über die Epoche Sultan Bayezids II (1481–1512)*. Berlin: Klaus Schwarz Verlag, 1983.

Reinhard, Wolfgang. "Zwang zur Konfessionailisierung? Prolegomena zu einer Theorie des konfessionellen Zeitalters." *Zeitschrift für historische Forschung* 10 (1983): 253–273.

"Reformation, Counter-Reformation, and the Early Modern State: A Reassessment," *The Catholic Historical Review* 75 (1989): 383–404.

Renard, John. *Friends of God: Islamic Images of Piety, Commitment, and Sainthood*. Berkeley, Los Angeles, and London: University of California Press, 2008.

Şahin, Kaya. *Empire and Power in the Reign of Süleyman: Narrating the Sixteenth-Century Ottoman World*. New York: Cambridge University Press, 2013.

Savaş, Saim. *XVI. Asırda Anadolu'da Alevilik*. Ankara: Türk Tarih Kurumu, 2013.

Sohrweide, Hanna. "Der Sieg der Safaviden in Persien und seine Rückwirkungen auf die Schiiten Anatoliens im 16. Jahrhundert." *Der Islam* 41 (1965): 95–223.

Sözer, Hande. *Managing Invisibility: Dissimulation and Identity Maintenance among Alevi Bulgarian Turks.* Leiden: Brill, 2014.

Stoianovich, Traian. "Model and Mirror in the Pre-modern Balkan City." In *La ville Balkanique XVe-XIXe SS*, edited by Nikolai Todorov, 83–110. Sofia: Editions de l'Académie Bulgare des Sciences.

Stojanovski, Aleksandar. *Dervendžijstvoto vo Makedonija.* Skopje: Institut za Nacionalna Istorija, 1974.

Gradovite na Makedonija od krajot na XIV do XVII vek: Demografski Proučuvanja. Skopje: Zavod za Unapreduvanje na Stopanstvoto vo SRM "Samoupravna Praktika," 1981.

Structure Sociale et développement culturel des villes sud-est Européennes et Adriatiques aux XVIIe-XVIIIe siècles. Bucharest: AIESEE, 1975.

Stubenrauch, Wolfgang. *Kulturgeographie des Deli-Orman (Nordostbulgarien).* Berlin: Komissionsverlag von J. Engelhorns Nachf. Stuttgart, 1933.

Subrahmanyam, Sanjay. "Connected Histories: Notes towards a Reconfiguration of Early Modern Eurasia." *Modern Asian Studies* 31, no. 3 (1997): 735–762.

Tansel, Selâhattin. *Osmanlı Kaynaklarına Göre Fâtih Sultân Mehmed'in Siyasî ve Askerî Faaliyeti.* Ankara: Türk Tarih Kurumu, 1953.

Tekindağ, M. C. Şehabeddin. "Yeni Kaynak ve Vesîkaların Işığı Altında Yavuz Sultan Selim'in İran Seferi." *TD* 17, no. 22 (March 1967): 49–78.

Terzioğlu, Derin. "Sufis in the Age of State-Building and Confessionalization," in *The Ottoman World*, edited by Christine Woodhead, 86–99. London and New York: Routledge, 2011.

Tezcan, Baki. *The Second Ottoman Empire: Political and Social Transformation in the Early Modern World.* New York: Cambridge University Press, 2010.

Tietze, Andreas. "Sheykh Bali Efendi's Report on the Followers of Sheykh Bedreddin." *OA* 7–8 (1988): 115–122.

Todorov, Iliia. "Letopisniiat razkaz na Pop Metodi Draginov." *Starobâlgarska Literatura* 16 (1984): 62–75.

Todorov, Nikolai. "Za demografskoto sâstoyanie na balkanskiia poluostrov prez XVI-XVI vek." *Godishnik na Sofiiskiia Universitet – Filosofsko-istoricheski Fakultet*, 52 (1959): 193–225.

ed. *La ville Balkanique, XVe-XIXe SS.* Sofia: Editions de l'Académie Bulgare des Sciences, 1970.

The Balkan City: Socio-Economic and Demographic Development, 1400–1900. Translated by Peter Sugar. Seattle, WA: University of Washington Press, 1983.

Todorova, Maria. "Identity (Trans)Formation among Bulgarian Muslims." In *The Myth of "Ethnic Conflict": Politics, Economics, and "Cultural" Violence*, edited by B. Crawford and R. Lipschutz, 471–510. Berkeley, CA: University of California at Berkeley, International and Area Studies, 1998.

"Conversion to Islam as a Trope in Bulgarian Historiography, Fiction and Film." In *Balkan Identities: Nation and Memory*, edited by Maria Todorova, 129–57. New York: New York University Press, 2004.

Todorova, Olga. *Pravoslavnata tsârkva i bâlgarite: XV-XVIII vek.* Sofia: Akademichno Izdatelstvo "Marin Drinov," 1997.

Trimingham, J. Spencer. *The Sufi Orders in Islam.* New York: Oxford University Press, 1998.

Usluer, Fatih. *Hurufilik: İlk Elden Kaynaklarla Doğuşundan İtibaren.* Istanbul: Kabalcı Yayınevi, 2009.

Vasić, Milan. "Socijalna struktura jugoslovenskih zemalja pod osmanskom vlašću do kraja XVII vijeka." *Godišnjak Društva Istoričara Bosne i Hercegovine* 37 (1986), 65–82.

Verlinden, Charles. *The Beginnings of Modern Colonization: Eleven Essays with an Introduction.* Translated by Yvonne Freccero. Ithaca, NY: Cornell University Press, 1970.

Vryonis, Speros. *The Decline of Medieval Hellenism in Asia Minor and the Process of Islamization from the Eleventh to the Fifteenth Century.* Berkeley, Los Angeles, and London: University of California Press, 1971.

——— "Religious Changes and Patterns in the Balkans, 14th–16th Centuries," In *Aspects of the Balkans: Continuity and Change,* edited by Henrik Birnbaum and Speros Vryonis, 151–76. The Hague and Paris: Mouton, 1972.

Weber, Max. *The City.* Translated and edited by D. Martindale and G. Neuwirth. Glencoe, IL: The Free Press, 1958.

Werner, Ernst. *Die Geburt einer Großmacht – Die Osmanen, (1300–1481),* 4th edn. Weimar: Hermann Böhlaus Nachfolger, 1985.

Winter, Stefan. *The Shiites of Lebanon under Ottoman Rule, 1516–1788.* Cambridge and New York: Cambridge University Press, 2010.

Wirth, Eugen. *Die orientalische Stadt im islamischen Vorderasien und Nordafrika: städtische Bausubstanz und raumliche Ordnung, Wirtschaftsleben und soziale Organisation.* Mainz: Phillip von Zabern, 2000.

Wittek, Paul. *The Rise of the Ottoman Empire.* London: The Royal Asiatic Society, 1938.

——— "Les Gagaouzes = Les gens de Kaykaus." *Rocznik Orientalistyczny* 17 (1951–2): 12–24.

——— "Yazijioghlu Ali on the Christian Turks of the Dobruja." *BSOAS* 14 (1952): 639–68.

Woods, John E. *The Aqquyunlu: Clan, Confederation, Empire: A Study in 15th/9th Century Turco-Iranian Politics.* Minneapolis, MN: Bibliotheca Islamica, 1976.

Yıldırım, Rıza. *Seyyid Ali Sultan (Kızıl Deli) ve Velâyetnâmesi.* Ankara: Türk Tarih Kurumu, 2007.

——— "Turkomans Between Two Empires: The Origins of the Qizilbash Identity in Anatolia (1447–1514)." Ph.D. diss., Bilkent University, 2008.

Yürekli, Zeynep. *Architecture and Hagiography in the Ottoman Empire: The Politics of Bektashi Shrines in the Classical Age.* Surrey, UK, and Burlington, VT: Ashgate, 2012.

Zarcone, Thierry. "Nouvelles perspectives dans les recherches sur les Kızılbaş-Alévis et les Bektachis de la Dobroudja, de Deliorman et de la Thrace orientale." *Anatolia Moderna* 4 (1992): 1–11.

Zhelyazkova, Antonina. "Islamization in the Balkans as an Historiographical Problem: The Southeast-European Perspective." In *The Ottomans and the Balkans: A Discussion of Historiography*, edited by Fikret Adanir and Suraiya Faroqhi, 223–266. Leiden, Boston, and Köln: Brill, 2002.

Zlatar, Behija. "Tipologija gradskih naselja na Balkanu u XVI vijeku." In Han and Samardžić, *Gradska Kultura na Balkanu (XV-XIX vek)*, *Zbornik Radova*, vol. 2, 63–73.

Index

Niğbolu (province) (cont.)
  invasion of, 94, 106, 192
  law-codes for, 123
  lowlands of, 133–34
  tax registers from, 107–09
  western zone of, 109n. 60
  non-Muslims
    discrimination of, 32, 35–36
    in tax registers, 10
    and waqfs, 37, 162n. 22
    see also Christian village/communities;
      Christians
northeastern Balkans
  in general, 94
  anti-Ottoman rebellions in, 94
  and Crusade of Varna, 104–06
  incursions into
    in general, 94
    by Pontic Turcomans, 95, 113, 167
    by Vlad III Țepeș, 106
  migration to, 119
  Muslim communities in
    origins of
      and followers of Bedreddin, 8, 113–14
      and Ottoman-Safavid conflict, 114
  oral traditions of, 119
  Ottoman rule in, 94–95
  population of, 115
  power struggles in, 99–101
  see also Balkans
Novasel, 152

Ocak, Ahmet Yaşar, 54, 88, 97, 102n. 33,
    104n. 44, 113, 242n. 159
occupations
  in Eski Cuma (city), 199
  in Hezargrad (city), 175–77
  in Salonica, 175
  in Shumnu (city), 181, 188
  in Skopje, 175
  in tax registers, 174–75
Oghuz Turcomans, 50–51
Orhan I, 28, 58, 63, 64
Orhonlu, Cengiz, 138
Orientalism, 158
Orthodox Church, 105
Oruç Beğ Tarihi (Oruç Bey), 88
Oruç Bey, 88n. 213
Oruçhan b. Umur, 181
Osman b. Hüseyin, 198
Osman b. Tay Hızır, 221
Osman I, 56–57, 58
Osman Pazarı, 127n. 36
  see also Ala Kilise (sub-province)
Otman Baba
  in general, 93

convent of
  registration of, 89–92
  waqf status of, 91, 92
  mention of, 214
  death of, 211
  followers/disciples of, 88, 91–92
  influences on
    of cult of seven, 76–77
    of Hurufism, 76
  mausoleum complex of, 77, 89, **90f. 2.1**
  as "pole of poles," 74, 75
  vita of, 71–92
    Abdals of Rum in, 72, 73
    Abdals of Rum in Anatolia in, 79–80
    antinomian practices in, 245
    change of direction in, 86–87
    conversion stories in, absence of, 264
    dating of, 61n. 89
    differences between vita of Kızıl Deli
      and, 71–72
    followers in, 73
    Hacı Bektaş Veli in, 247–48
    historical context of, 248
    Holy Family in, 75–76
    identified as Abdal of Rum in, 72
    incarnationist claims in, 75, 82, 83–
      84, 86, 98, 228
    and institutionalized Sufism, 80–81
    messianism in, 75
    Mihaloğlu Ali Bey in, 78–79
    millenarianism in, 75
    mission among yürüks in, 77–78
    peregrinations in, 72–73, 118, 229
    period covered by, 62
    relationships in
      with Bayezid Baba, 81
      with Bektashis, 83, 248
      with Mahmud Çelebi, 81–82
      with Mehmed II, 74, 84–86,
        216, 239–40
      with Mümin Derviş, 81
      with ulema, 84–85
    stay in Istanbul in, 73, 81, 84–85, 86
    theory of sainthood in, 73–74
    as wandering mystic in, 218
  mention of, 9, 55, 148, 206
  see also Abdals of Rum
Ottoman chronicles, 47
Ottoman conquest, see expansion
Ottoman Empire
  administrative language used in
    and confessional vocabulary, 278
    for districts, 109n. 60
    for saints, 217
  and boundaries of conquered polities,
    107n. 56

Lightning Source UK Ltd.
Milton Keynes UK
UKHW020647060622
403983UK00006B/773

9 781316 633748